AF576731

BACKGROUND TO
THE LONG SEARCH

NINIAN SMART

Some books by the same author

Reasons and Faiths

World Religions: a Dialogue

Document and Argument in Indian Philosophy

Philosophers and Religious Truth

The Yogi and the Devotee

The Philosophy of Religion

The Religious Experience of Mankind

The Concept of Worship

The Phenomenon of Religion

Mao

The Science of Religion and the Sociology of Knowledge

BACKGROUND TO
THE LONG SEARCH

BRITISH BROADCASTING CORPORATION

Published by the
British Broadcasting Corporation
35 Marylebone High Street
London W1M 4AA

ISBN 0 563 12779 1

First published 1977

Designed by Peter Campbell
Picture research by Diana Souhami

Printed in England
by Jolly & Barber Limited
Rugby, Warwickshire

CONTENTS

FOR LIBUSHKA

PREFACE

I have written this book in conjunction with the television series *The Long Search*. I owe much to the stimulus of the team in executing that series, especially to Peter Montagnon and Ronald Eyre, but also to Jonathan Stedall, Mischa Scorer, Malcolm Feuerstein and Caroline Mackersey.

Also I am grateful to Oliver Hunkin, who helped to initiate the series, and to Barbara Cannell and Vanessa Hardwicke, whose cheerfulness kept so much going.

I am very conscious of my debt to Peter Campbell, of BBC Publications, a brilliant adviser and good friend: much of any merit in the book belongs to his work on it.

Ms Deirdre Grant and Mrs Margaret Lambert typed up the manuscript with kind aplomb and cheering speed. My wife, Libushka, gave me advice on what would and what would not interest an international public. Partly because of all these excellent friends I enjoyed writing the book.

Lancaster
18 October 1976

NINIAN SMART

The mandala, as it appears in its various forms, opposite and through the book, contains some major symbols of the world religions.

INTRODUCTION

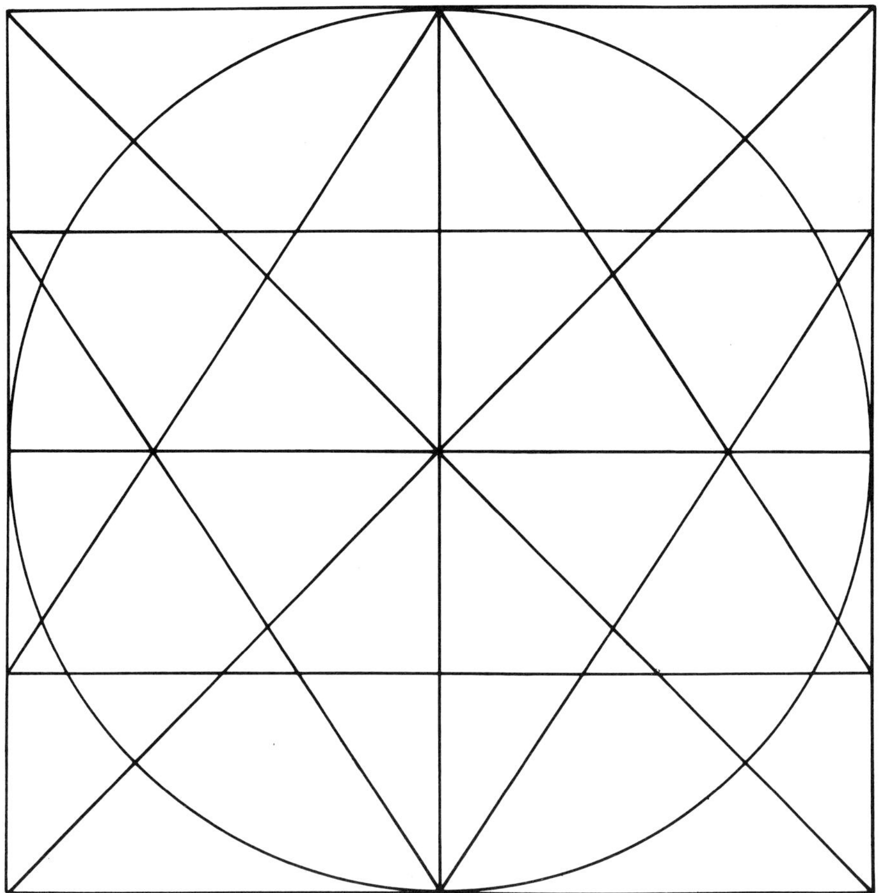

The nature of the Search. *If all men believed the same things, our planet would lose half its excitement, as well as many of its problems. Men's pictures of the world impel some to sanctity; others to hatred. They supply many with a special sense of belonging. If we wish to understand humanity, we need to explore this gallery of pictures. For much of history and hope is formed by the ways men perceive themselves and their world.*

Furthermore the explorer of beliefs may come to clarify his own values. He may find one or other of the pictures bewitching, or he may be inspired to paint his own. Perspectives on truth and goodness can be viewed in the many stories and systems through which men have tried to organise their attitudes to living. Thus the search for understanding occurs at two levels. One level is to do with our finding out how men see the world, and how they respond to what they see. The other level is to do with finding out the truth, so far as we can. One level is about men; the other is about the truth of what men have believed.

There are atheists and rationalists who see nothing but folly in religions, and they can too easily be led into thinking therefore that the exploration of religion is unimportant. This is an absurdity, since what moves men, whether it be foolish or wise, justified or unjustified, good or evil, must vitally concern us if we wish to understand men's various responses to life.

Seeing the world as others see it

Indeed, if we are to search properly we must be able to put aside our own presuppositions and our own judgments about truth and value. We must try to enter into the lives of others, and see the world from their point of view. No historian can fail to neglect the standpoint of the actor; we need to see what Caesar saw as he was poised to cross the Rubicon, and what Stalin had in mind when he made his fateful treaty with Hitler. In religion, we need to be able to think and feel what it is like to be a Muslim on his way to Mecca or a Buddhist as he sits in meditation. It is not much good measuring the responses of the Muslim or the Buddhist by the feelings of a Christian or an agnostic. This is the challenge and glory of the study of humanity – the task always of trying to look through other eyes. But it is not easy, and some have even doubted whether it is at all possible. It is sometimes argued that faith is something so intense and personal that it can only be experienced from the inside. To know what it is like to be a Jew you have to be a Jew; to know what it is like to be a Hindu you have to be a Hindu.

Such criticism of the very idea of exploring other men's faiths has some truth, but only some, and it can be a dangerous attitude. The truth of it is that a person may have lived through his faith in a way that no outsider can match. But it does not follow that the outsider cannot have a better understanding because of trying to enter into that person's experience. Moreover, the outsider may see the context of that person's faith more clearly because he is just a bit detached. I remember how once in the space of a few days two scholars came to lecture to my students about Hinduism. One was a Hindu, and very firm in his interpretation of the faith. The other was a noted Indian Christian, who gave a broad and sympathetic picture of Hinduism in its variety. The latter brought about more understanding than did the Hindu, as it happened. Further, we are all men and share certain kinds of feelings, so that the attitude of others is never totally alien to us. In any event, even if we cannot hope for perfect understanding, we can hope for deeper knowledge than we now have. It is one of the noblest aspects of human life that we can strive to look at the world not just through our own eyes, but from the standpoint of others. We ought to be passionately committed to this kind of dispassion. It is one of the most important things in education (and by that I do not just mean formal schooling, but all those processes through which we help one another to fulfil our talents) to foster empathy, standing in the shoes of others.

Empathy

I use the word 'empathy' here, perhaps not the most graceful expression in the English tongue, because we do not always agree with those we understand. We are not always in sympathy with the views of others. So the term 'empathy' avoids the suggestion of agreement. In any event, the world would be dull indeed if the only folk we understood were those with whom we were in agreement. It would be the death of creative argument, and ultimately the death of learning from others.

But much of what we discover about religions has to do with other facts – the place and date of the birth of the Buddha or of Muhammad, the geographical spread of a faith, the items of belief listed in a creed or formula, the kind of building used and so forth. But even such outer information is worth having, for without the outer forms a religion could have no inner spirit. But we do here raise a question about assumptions – a question which runs through much of the enterprise of the comparative study of religion, or the history of religions as the study is sometimes also called. In explaining a religion or some item of symbolism or belief, there is the question: To whom is this explanation directed? If a person such as me is to serve as an interpreter, into what language should I be interpreting?

The listeners

I make the assumption that it is to Westerners that I interpret. I hope that this does not mean that others may not learn something from what is written here. But because of the assumption, I have varied my approach in different of the essays. Thus in treating Eastern religions and cultures I have tended to stick more closely to a conventional order of presentation, though I have had necessarily to be highly selective in the facts and motifs I have tried to bring out. But a special problem arises in relation to Christianity, Judaism and Islam. Thus because Westerners have lived with the Christian and Jewish heritages over the centuries, they often assume that they know more about them than they really do. Sometimes too the Westerner is alienated from the faith of his tradition. It is too easy to identify Christianity with what is taught in Sunday school or heard on the radio. How many folk have heard of the monk of war, or have any notion about Romanian Christianity, or understand anything of Augustine of Aquinas, or about the St Thomas Christians in India, or about the varieties of Anabaptism or about the origins of Congregationalism – all the facets and varieties of Christianity which make the tradition so fascinating, baffling and complex? And so in treating of Christianity I have not followed a conventional historical path, but tried to show anew the older meanings of Christendom in its heyday as well as some of the new manifestations of the faith in post-Reformation and modern times.

In regard to Judaism and Islam I have also adopted somewhat special measures. For most Westerners, whether Jewish or not, the terrible events of the twentieth century must be in the fore of their consciousness in any thinking about the meaning of that suffering yet resilient faith; and with that question I have started, preparing a later time for visiting the life of Moses. Regarding Islam, the West is so full of errant images, bequeathed by Crusade and warfare, mutual hostilities and a certain incomprehension born of the very closeness of the historic relationship between the Christian and Muslim religions. I have thus been keener here to try to bring out the delights of Islam, to counteract the images which are currently reinforced by the misfortunes too of modern politics.

Since religion cannot be divorced from those forces which challenge its traditional expression, it is necessary too to have a perspective on modern sciences, together with such unruly offspring of Western faith as Marxism and humanism. For they too represent living options and can supply insights even for those whose eyes are fixed firmly upon the spiritual aspects of existence; indeed in a vital sense they represent spiritual ideas, but of a non-transcendental kind. They are themselves pictures in that gallery to which I earlier referred. In dealing with science I relate it to a place, to the new frontier, rich in Nobel Prizewinners and the counter-culture, California.

What is left out

If the essays in this book are a way of introducing and explaining the religious and other living movements in the world, they perforce leave much out – many of those dead religions like those of the Aztecs and the Incas, flickering onwards only in the disguise of Catholic saints, latter-day substitutes for the old gods, or the religions of Greece and Rome, dead save in so far as they have entered the Christian and European heritage. Nor is it feasible to deal adequately with those multitudinous cultures which find their expression in small-scale societies, from the Amazon to Papua and from the far north to Africa. All we can do there is to sample their condition in the contemporary world. But the message coming out of such selections is that we should never fail to remember those whom we do not know. The human realities of those whose cultures we do not even begin to contemplate are still as glorious and agonising as any other human realities.

Methods of exploration

Shortly I shall trace a fuller geography of the human spirit, both in time and in space, and so give some perspective upon these aspects of religion which we can, and cannot, explore here on the printed page. But before that, let us look briefly to methods in the exploration. For I trust that this book is an occasion and a stimulus for going on. The world of religion can hardly be explored properly in a few chapters, but the methods of navigation can be important as well as the charts the chapters provide. What then are these methods? I have begun to sketch them out in writing about empathy. Let me try to outline useful ideas on how to pursue the exploration of religion in a number of suggestions (but the main unwritten rule is to remember how inadequate and subject to revision the rules are).

First, the best way to learn about a faith is to live among those who practise it. You do not need to believe to join activities – among anthropologists they call this joining in 'participant observation'. So, consider: if you want to find out about Catholics, attend Mass. It is true that sometimes religious groups are sensitive to unheralded outsiders: can you wander easily, as a Gentile, into an Orthodox synagogue or go to a Passover meal? Here you need friends, tact and a little instruction in the rules of the sacred. But you may also feel: it is hardly easy for me to be a participant observer in a Buddhist or Muslim society. Again, I assume you live in the West. And this brings us to the second, and connected, rule: why not make the best of what you have got?

We have great opportunities in the modern world. One finds Taoists in Colorado, Buddhists in Scotland, Hindus in Germany, Muslims in France, Jews in Morocco, Zen masters in California, Africans in London, Catholics in Iceland, Lutherans in India – and so forth, for we are a mingled world. There are all around us opportunities in the guise of friendships for making, culturally, journeys beyond the dreams of airways.

Third, it is vital to remember that the adherent of a faith or culture is only one man or woman. He is not a spokesman as such, though he will probably try to be one. He is scarcely an expert. He is what he is, an adherent. Imagine a New Jersey Catholic telling an Indian about Catholic Christianity or a Scottish Presbyterian expounding the faith to a Chinese. How far is it likely they would give a rounded or plural perspective on the variety and riches of the Christian tradition? So treat the adherent sincerely, but with more than a grain of salt.

Fourth, remember that the questions you ask may not fit – may be foreign to the faith or cultural system you are trying to explore. It is not much use asking a Buddhist or a Jain as to how he thinks about God's providence, for he does not believe in God (as the Westerner understands that idea). So one should shut off as many assumptions from one's enquiries as possible, and feel your way into the other man's system of ideas.

Fifth, do not imagine that religion is more important in people's lives than it is. It may have deep doctrines, but men also live in a world of everyday concerns. Saints are somewhat infrequent. And very often religion's place in the 'ordinary' world will lead to a just appreciation of its influence, which may turn out to be surprising after all.

Sixth, it is no bad idea to look to religious art, and that at two levels. One level is the great art, seen in galleries and lavish books. This can penetrate to essences of faith, though it can also fail to be in tune with real concerns, for art can obtrude on spirituality. Another level is popular imagery – the cheap prints from India or Rome. They tell you a lot about what appeals to humbler folk and in doing so may convey something of the basic symbols. Again, in the modern world both modes of art are not too difficult to come by.

Seventh, many get accosted by religious folk collecting money in the streets, selling or giving away pamphlets, gospels, whatever, ringing the doorbell, canvassing in one way or another. You need to watch out if you are not to be tiresomely buttonholed, for why should men so roughly intrude upon your life? But much can be learned from questioning such people – they often have in their grasp a nugget of wisdom and truth, even if they may express it in a harsh or insecure way. Thus I have some constructive talks with the Witnesses, Mormons and devotees of Krishna.

Eighth, it is useful to pursue religions through histories, encyclopedias and autobiographies. One must be discriminating about all of these, of course, as much rubbish is written in the name of religion, and scholarship on the subject is not as wide as it might be. But beyond this book, or any book, there are many others.

Ninth, it is always vital to distinguish at all times the preacher from the describer, the one who expounds his faith from the one who depicts it. The distinction cannot be absolute, but should be kept in the mind. Much confusion and misrepresentation can thereby be avoided.

Tenth, it is worth bearing in mind that religions are organic – the various parts or aspects are interrelated. Thus doctrines are not just statements about reality but also ways of expressing experience and the ritual dimension of religion. For instance, talk of God occurs in the context of the awe which God inspires in the believer and of the worship which ritually expresses the believer's response. So the more connections you can make, the better.

Eleventh, though it is always good to break down attitudes that stand in the way of empathy, it is a fact that people explore best what they think they may love. Thus I personally have long felt affinities for Buddhism, even despite – in fact perhaps because of – its great difference from the Episcopalianism which forms my background. Thus I have found pleasure and profit in exploring the message of the Buddha and the lives of Buddhists. So it is always well worth while consulting one's instincts in the process of exploration. Those who are genuinely concerned with understanding a religious tradition other than their own will feel some of this concern already in their bones before they set out on their particular quest.

Finally, it is useful to remember that the study of religion cannot promise a solution to problems of the truth and of what are the higher insights of faith, but it can promise greater knowledge of mankind and a vision of new perspectives, which may indeed generate wisdom about the ultimate. It is just that no promises of the latter can be made.

You will see from these rules and suggestions that there is no finality in the long search, and certainly it is not to be found here in this book, which is merely (but I hope illuminatingly) a stage along the way.

The geography of the search

It is doubtless useful now to scan a chart of the spiritual and religious movements which have moulded world history. I shall shortly say something briefly about the deep origins of religions buried in the prehistoric past, but first let us contemplate the religions which are visible in human history.

First, there are some major religions which have proved powerful in mission and cultural influence: notably Christianity, Islam and Buddhism. Each of these divides into halves. Thus Christendom drifted into two halves, the Orthodox and the Catholics, based respectively in Byzantium and in Rome. With the expansion of Europe into the New World, Latin America became largely Catholic, while the North, because of its pattern of colonisation, became predominantly, as did Northern Europe, Protestant. In the late colonial age, Christianity was carried into Asia and Africa, and made a decisive mark on the latter continent.

Islam, exploding out of Arabia in the seventh century, overran the hitherto largely Christian Middle East, and made its way across the southern shores of the Mediterranean into Spain and over through Central Asia into India, and eventually took a grip upon Malaya and Indonesia. Again: a division between the Sunni tradition in the West and the Shia, stretching East from Iraq. Latterly too Islam has made progress in black Africa south of the Sahara, and even has made some inroads into black culture in the United States.

Buddhism, much earlier than Christianity, embarked in its peaceful spread through India and up into Central Asia, whence it was carried along the silk route into China. Thence it spread to China's neighbours – Korea, Japan, Vietnam, while out of India the Lesser Vehicle was carried into Sri Lanka, Burma, Thailand and most of the rest of South-East Asia. In later centuries, at the end of the first millennium AD it dwindled in India, but was successful in penetrating Tibet and the Mongolias. So hardly a country of Asia has been unaffected by Buddhism. If the Mahayana has been dominant in the Far East, and its offshoot the Vajrayana (the Diamond Vehicle) in Tibet and beyond, in southern and South-East Asia the Theravada has flourished.

However, though Christianity has succeeded in maintaining a presence in those countries dominated by Marxism, the state of Buddhism in Communist countries is altogether more doubtful. This is partly because Buddhism depends quite heavily on monastic organisation, which is both suspect and easily dispersed in a modern totalitarian society. Thus Buddhism no longer retains its old vitality in China, North Korea, Tibet, the Mongolias, or Cambodia; and is under pressure in Laos and Vietnam. All of which must remind us that in addition to the three older religions which have had broad missionary spread, the new faith of Marxism (again divided into Eastern and Western varieties) has had notable modern success, in the area of the Soviet Union and Eastern Europe, in China and South-East Asia, and in Cuba, Angola and elsewhere. Thus in the modern world, the four most potent universal belief systems are Buddhism, Islam, Christianity and Marxism. Buddhism though weakened in much of the East is resilient in Japan and penetrating into Western culture, where it probably has a modest but significant future.

Two other religions, sometimes seen as world religions because of their wide influence, are important but not so mission-minded as the big four just alluded to – namely Hinduism and Judaism. Of course, both attract some proselytes; but on the whole you need to be born a Hindu to be truly a Hindu and likewise with Judaism. The spread of Hinduism is wider than at first appears, for we tend to identify it primarily with the religion (or religions – Hinduism is more like a confederation of cults than a single system) of the Indian subcontinent. But the teachings and customs spread into South-East Asia; and in the modern era migrant Indians have taken it to Guyana and elsewhere in the Caribbean, to Fiji, East Africa and even England.

Judaism, early accustomed to dispersal and adaptation to a variety of cultures within whose fabric it survived, has in the last two centuries seen both a colossal expansion and a terrible contraction. The expansion came through migration to the United States, now the dominant citadel of Jewishness. This was partly a consequence of the release of Jews in Europe from the confines of the ghetto, following upon the Napoleonic reforms and conquests. The contraction came through Hitler's holocaust which effectively destroyed Jewry in middle and eastern Europe (save for one or two countries like Romania). The establishment of the Jewish state of Israel after World War II has given Judaism a political base, even though to a large extent the Israelis are secularised. In between traditional Orthodoxy and secularism lies the vigorous Reform type of Judaism, especially vital in the dynamic milieu of the United States.

Within the fabric of Indian culture three significant, but numerically not so powerful, religions continue with a fair amount of vigour – namely the religions of the Parsees, survivors from a great Zoroastrian past, of the Jains, ancient contemporaries and predecessors of the Buddha, and of the Sikhs, born of a medieval synthesis between Islam and Hinduism. For differing reasons none of the three functions as a missionary faith, though each claims to have a world view of general validity.

Buddhism in China and Japan has lived in a creative way in relationship to other, indigenous traditions. Thus it was useful to look upon Buddhism, Confucianism and Taoism as the three religions of China: yet in certain ways they were less rivals than different aspects of one complex religious and social system. In Japan Shintoism, the native 'way of the gods', to some extent coalesced with Buddhism, though in the modern period its militant phase as State Shintoism, up till 1949, set it apart from its pacific partner. It is worth noting that before and especially after World War II, a number of lively new religions, some with a Buddhist background, have sprung up in Japan, of which the Soka Gakkai is the most dynamic and mission-minded.

Three centres of religion

To sum up so far: three great centres of religious culture have dominated the northern hemisphere – the Middle East, cradle of the three great Semitic monotheisms of Judaism, Christianity and Islam; India, birthplace of Buddhism, Jainism, Hinduism and Sikhism, and host to the Parsees; China and Japan, which have given birth to Confucianism, Taoism and Shinto. Europe has given rise to a major ideology, rival to the old missionary religions, namely Marxism, also wearing Chinese garb through the policies and writings of Mao.

Ancestries

However, it is important to notice that the great religions have tended to take up into themselves certain motifs from the cultures they have penetrated or replaced. Thus while the Parsees are the explicit inheritors of Zoroaster's religion, there are elements of that ancient Persian religion in Judaism, Christianity and Islam – there is for example the picture of the end of history and the last judgment in which the hopes, fears and imagery of the Semitic religions were given some Zoroastrian content. Indeed Persia acted as a bridge between India and the Mediterranean. For out of the matrix of its ancient religion came patterns injected into Buddhist and Hindu myth; while westwards in the Roman Empire came the cult of Mithras, an influential mystery religion among the legionaries.

Indeed the Romano-Greek world into which Christianity moved through the missionary endeavours of Peter and Paul and their successors was highly complex. Early Christianity seemed at one level a rival to the so-called mystery religions – the cults of Isis, Demeter at Eleusis, Mithras (as we have seen) and others. Such religions offered a kind of sacramental transformation of the individual who underwent the appropriate rites. But on the whole such religions did not have a systematic philosophy, and neither did the older and official worship of the gods, such as

Jupiter and Neptune and (later) the Emperors. On the other hand, there were philosophies which to some extent took the place of religions, but without much in the way of priestly or ritual organisation. Thus there was austere and pantheistic Stoicism, strong in courage and in self-control. There was Epicureanism, more worldly but stressing moderation and indifference to the gods (thought to be indifferent to us). There was Neo-Platonism, a mystical and contemplative, possibly part Indian-influenced, development of the thought of Plato himself. Christianity, as it grew a philosophical mind, could use ideas from these sources, in the name of a new synthesis. Perhaps the only comparable force in the Mediterranean world was Manichaeanism, founded by the Persian Mani, and bringing together elements from both Buddhist and Mediterranean sources. Its defeat was ultimately completed with the stamping out of the early medieval form of the religion, known as the Albigensian heresy.

In northern Europe, Christianity came to displace the old Nordic and Celtic religions, which were to survive largely as folklore and also perhaps in some aspects of the spirit of northern Christianity.

Although the religions of the ancient Near East, ranging from Egypt through Babylon to Sumer, near the Persian Gulf, were largely buried by Zoroastrian state religion and by Christianity, already some elements from their thinking and symbolism had entered into the Biblical heritage, albeit transformed – such as the creation myth and the story of the Flood. And Egyptian spirituality had a late renaissance in the formation of the Christian monastic tradition from St John Cassian onwards. The Middle East has thus seen many layers of religion: the old city cults of men's early civilisations; Zoroastrianism; Hellenic culture; Judaism and its Christian offshoot; and then Islam. The deserts are littered with the bones of many faiths and the stones of many temples. Further to the East, in the Indus Valley and down into Western India, was a related culture, whose religion however remains obscure, though possibly containing features later to emerge in Indian yoga. It was a culture probably destroyed by the invading Aryans, upon whose rites and hymns was based the ancient lore of the Brahmins. Two other, quite independent groups of city cultures should be mentioned, buried however by the Conquistadors in the New World – the pre-Columbian cultures of Central America and of the Incas. If Catholicism built up an imposing edifice in their place, perhaps it never fully replaced the older cults, designed to ensure the stability and prosperity of empires with high technical ability.

Africa and the White Frontier

Meanwhile, the past of other continents is more difficult to unravel, until the modern period. In black Africa a mosaic of small-scale religions predominated, though imposing kingdoms such as Benin in the West and the culture based in Zimbabwe in southern Africa were also to be found. However, the coming of the European had various traumatic effects upon the continent. The Cape was colonised by the Dutch and became a country of white settlers. The West coast was the main scene of action by the slavers, who destined millions of blacks for the plantations of Brazil, the Caribbean and the American south – a migration without parallel in human history, and the cause of new black cultures in the Western world, giving birth to the religion of the spiritual, and the complexities of Voodoo and other adaptive cults. But the main tide of religion flooding into Africa was Christian. Catholic missions, chiefly in areas controlled by France, Belgium and Portugal, and Protestant ones elsewhere gave Africa a strong Christian stamp. It is perhaps the most Christian of the continents today, although it is also in process of generating a whole flock of indigenous variants on mainstream Christianity through which black Africa synthesises older values and the newly arrived and modernising religion.

The process of colonisation and conquest had similar effects elsewhere. The Spanish Philippines were won over to Catholicism. Christianity made headway, despite Islam, in Indonesia. In the Pacific Islands and in New Zealand, Polynesian religion was overwhelmed by Protestant Christianity, while that great western outpost of the sturdy Polynesian navigators, Madagascar, acquired both types of Western Christianity.

Yet still, scattered across the world, there remain great numbers of men who live in small societies with each its distinctive gallery of gods and spirits, and in that world there are important kinds of spirituality which should not be ignored in an age too often influenced by the big battalions and universal belief-systems. These cultures are, however, much under pressure and have difficulty fighting off material and mental invasions, destructive of the old fabric of life, which pour across their frontier with the white empires and technology – a frontier which can be called for convenience the White Frontier, a boundary in the mind, between radically different ways of life. Indeed, one of the major areas of enquiry for the historian of modern religion and for our current search and exploration is to be found in the changes occurring beyond that White Frontier. New religious systems are born there, to cope with social and spiritual changes.

Thus the Ghost Dance and Peyote cults of the Plains Indians, the Ratana Church among the Maoris, the cargo cults of Papua and New Guinea, the Voodoo in Haiti, and the Rastafari in Jamaica are all instances. And even in large-scale societies similar movements have sometimes brought responses to outside invasion and social disruption, such as the Taipings of mid-nineteenth-century China (who nearly overthrew the Manchu dynasty, and in fact captured the old southern capital Nanking); or the Cao Dai sect in Vietnam, synthesising French, Chinese, Buddhist and Catholic culture. So there is much action along what I have called the White Frontier, as we shall see in more detail later on in this book.

Science, democracy and religion

But also in the modern world, within the bosom of European and American civilisation, other disturbances have been encountered. These partly had to do with the rise of science. The scientific revolution sparked by the Renaissance has led to some division in the European and Western worldview. The successes of science even against tendencies to a literal interpretation of doctrines have led to an uneasy relationship between scientific enterprise and religious experience, between new forms of knowledge and old forms of authority. True, there may be a later convergence between the way of the spirit and the Tao of science. But it is an evident fact of the nineteenth and twentieth centuries that the split has had deep psychological and intellectual effects for Western man. So science has been disturbing for many religious people, and poses new questions about man's place in nature.

These problems have, as it happened, lived side by side with another but related explosion of new feeling and thinking – democratic liberty as seen in the aspirations of English, American, French and other ideals of democracy, dedicated to a certain pluralism.

The modern Western state is a legacy of these developments. Typically, it provides toleration of different religions, with no one religion as the state religion, or if there is one its establishment and power are largely symbolic, as with the Church of England. Thus Christianity in such states becomes in effect a set of denominations. Even in those countries such as Italy and Ireland where Catholicism has an historic grip upon the majority of the population, other denominations can carry on freely. This pluralism in modern democratic societies means the final demise of the idea that an ideology or belief system is a necessary element in the stability of society – an idea that goes back to the *pax deorum* ('peace of the gods') of the Roman empire, when proper reverence paid to the right gods was a condition of peace and prosperity.

However, the plural character of society is also significantly relevant to the ongoing development of science, which depends upon the critical appraisal of ideas and the fashioning of new concepts and theories. These possibilities are enhanced in free societies. It may be that through this openness the older clashes between religion and science will become obsolete and that, as I suggested earlier, a new convergence will come to pass.

Meanwhile the nineteenth and twentieth centuries have also seen the emergence of some new religions apart from those I have discussed already in relation to the events along the White Frontier. America, for instance, has been mother to some remarkable new movements. There was the Mormon faith of the Church of Jesus Christ of the Latter Day Saints, having its origins in the visionary experience of Joseph Smith II, in upper New York State. There arose too the wide-ranging and remarkably persevering Jehovah's Witnesses, making significant headway in the Third World. There was the new synthesis of Christian Science, taught by a woman. The mid-nineteenth century saw the novel and enlightened faith of Bahai, coming from an Islamic background but dedicated to modern reforms and world government. In India, the Ramakrishna movement gave Hindu ideas new relevance and meaning, especially for the West, which it has reached through its missions. In this century Sri Aurobindo's evolutionary and mystical theology has attracted many adherents to the movement's headquarters in Pondicherry. So we might go on, for the modern epoch is rich in spiritual creativity.

Beginnings

But I have still left unanswered the question: And how did religion begin? The pious might wish to say that however much men may have distorted faith, originally it came through a primeval revelation from God. Interestingly enough such a notion has been backed by anthropological evidence in the writings of Father Wilhelm Schmidt, a Catholic anthropologist. But such evidence is at best doubtful for it rests on drawing conclusions about primeval men from 'primitives' (i.e. men living in small-scale societies with a primitive technology) observed in the contemporary world. But they too have cultures which must have changed over the centuries. Further, the precursors of homo sapiens have been pushed farther and farther back in time through the East African discoveries by paleontologists, so now we reckon man as having developed millions of years ago, not a hundred thousand or so. If we know a little about such creatures, we yet can scarcely expect to find artifacts telling us anything about their beliefs. Even where we do have good archaeological remains but no decipherable records, as with the Indus Valley civilisation, we continue to be much in the dark about the belief-system, social structure and so forth of the inhabitants of those wonderful dead cities. The fact is that any theory of the beginnings of religion must rest upon speculation.

Can we then try to probe those origins by using ideas drawn from psychoanalysis, sociology and so on? If religion always is seen to fulfil some psychological or social need, then presumably that was so even in the earliest days. Unfortunately, it is hard for psychologists to agree on the matter, and some influential theories, such as that of Freud, rest upon shaky empirical evidence regarding the history of religions. Thus Freud thought of God as a projected Father-figure; but it is hard to understand the application of this idea to Taoism or to the Buddha in Sri Lanka. Furthermore, though there is much which is suggestive in psychoanalytic accounts of religion, religion itself tends to be multiple in its relevance: it not only fulfils psychological needs but has many other functions as well. It gives a picture of man's place in the cosmos. It underpins social values. It provides rituals to cope with living. It symbolises men's deeper feelings in the face of death and suffering. It expresses numinous awe, and spiritual peace. For such reasons, no one theory of religion is likely to work as an overall account. However, our exploration of the many varieties and meanings of religion is still relatively in its infancy, for we are only near the beginning of a long search. Yet, perhaps disappointingly, it is necessary to say that at this time we cannot do more than guess at the distant origins of religion in the earliest man's consciousness. In the last chapter of this book I attempt to sketch such an imagined religious awareness, as men first began to be aware of themselves as different from the rest of animals and nature.

The patterns of religion

But in any case we can say something about patterns of religion, and in particular about those types of experience that appear in the story of religions and which are central for those who wish to understand religion. For surely those who look on religion as something simply derived from forces and feelings in human society and psychology are wrong – for they neglect the specific religious source of some central experience crucial in the history of the human spirit.

Consider the history of Israel, how Moses encountered God mysteriously in the burning bush, how Isaiah had a vision in the Temple, how Jeremiah received his call, how Job was confronted by the shattering message of God, and so on. Perhaps not all these experiences are historical. But there is little doubt that prophetic visions were central in the ongoing interplay between Yahweh and his chosen people. Consider too the early days of Christianity. It is of course hard to discern the nature of the mysterious appearance of the risen Lord which transformed the lives and hopes of the Apostles. But we have a detailed account of the conversion of Paul, which was as it turned out quite seminal for the success of the Christian mission. Again it was a series of overwhelming visions which injected Allah's message into the consciousness of the Prophet Muhammad and so set off the astonishing career of Islam. In other religions both small-scale and great we can see the recurrence of prophetic vision, in which the divine erupts numinously, awe-inspiringly, into men's minds. It is hard to see these events simply as psychological crises, though they may occasion them or be occasioned by them (as it seems with Paul). They rather are instances of men's perception of what Rudolf Otto, the German philosopher and historian of religion, called the *mysterium tremendum et fascinans*, 'the mystery which causes awe and which fascinates'. To such an experience he gave the label 'numinous', from the Latin *numen*, meaning a spirit. There is no doubt that this is one of the main types of specifically religious experience which has been vital in the ongoing history of religions.

But there is another kind of spiritual experience almost as crucial as the numinous. Consider the history of early Buddhism. We can see both from the accounts of the Buddha's life and from autobiographical sketches of the lives and conversions of early monks and nuns that inner enlightenment, often accruing upon the practice of meditation or (to use the chief Indian word) yoga, was central in the attainment of liberation. It was indeed the ultimate source, through the teaching of the Buddha and the monks who maintained the preaching of the Dharma (Law), of the power of Buddhism. Indeed, a similar type of contemplative, interior vision is vital in many forms of Hindu spirituality, especially in the highly influential Non-Dualistic Vedanta of the great Śankara, Hinduism's most renowned medieval philosopher and theologian. Further we find similar motifs in early Taoism, and in Zen, in Islamic Sufism and Christian mysticism – however differently these various movements may have interpreted their inner experiences doctrinally. I conclude therefore that alongside the numinous we must place the mystical: alongside the prophet, the contemplative (though of course a person might combine both styles of spirituality).

Thus I believe that much in the history of religions can be understood by a sort of chemistry in which in differing ways the two major motifs of religious experience can be combined. Early Islam emphasises overwhelmingly the numinous and the response of worship; later the mystical was absorbed within Islamic piety, though not without tensions, as we shall see when we come to explore the Sufi movement which expressed and encouraged the contemplative life.

By contrast early Buddhism dealt centrally with the mystical and the numinous gods were banished to the sidelines – though later awesome celestial Buddhas, like great divinities, animated the worship of the Mahayana and the rituals of Tibetan Buddhism. Again, Orthodox and Catholic Christianity have traditionally stressed both the numinous, in the worship of God, and the mystical, in the interior life. The chemistry, then, of the relative balance between these two ingredients runs through the great religions.

But naturally the vehicles through which experience is expressed are culturally determined. The symbol of Vishnu's various ornaments, weapons and attributes is typically Indian, yet they convey the *mysterium tremendum* in the pages of the *Bhagavadgita* and elsewhere; by contrast God in the book of Job is pictured through the imagery of the Hebrew mind, but again the awesomeness shines frighteningly through as Job confronts his Maker. And also we have to take account of ways in which radically new and creative symbols are injected into religious history, through the inspiration of the major prophets and mystics.

Nor must we forget the effects of social change. Very often deep challenges to the existence or integrity of a nation or group will throw on the scene a new prophet, a new faith, as a means of dealing with the crisis. Thus the trauma of exile in Babylon caused the Israelites to reinterpret their relationship to God. In modern times, the crises of the White Frontier have generated, as we have already noted, a host of new spiritual movements aiming partly at reform and the realignment of social forces. Only by reaching to heaven it seems can groups solve their difficulties on earth. It is not of course surprising that religion should perform this healing function in ages of crisis – for one of its major roles is to illuminate the anguishes and limits of life: it deals in the interplay with eternity and death and between the transcendent world and turbulent human relationships in this world.

We should never neglect the social dimension of religion, nor should we forget the ways in which it has shaped societies, yet there should always be recognition of the spiritual forces shaping faiths. I do not mean by this that we should necessarily accept a theory of revelation by God or a theory of the existence of the Ultimate, such as Brahman in Hinduism or the Truth-body of the Buddha in Buddhism – for we must not be hasty in assumptions in our exploration, and we do not need to begin from some fixed view of reality. But whatever sceptics may say about God or the Tao, there is no denying the actual effect of spiritual forces; be they real or imaginary, they enter dynamically into men's lives, and have at crucial points altered the directions of history. Whatever we think of Christ's resurrection, the experience of Paul and other apostles launched a new framework for western civilisation; just as the messages of Allah transformed the Middle East, and the enlightenment of the Buddha virtually all Asia. So it is vital not to write off the deliverances of the Spirit, and this is what our search is essentially about.

I have, then, sketched something of the methods, aims and background for the exploration of world religions and ideologies. The essays now following are, as I have said, a chart for the exploration which I hope will extend well beyond the written page.

The Long Search

Since this book has been written in conjunction with the television series, The Long Search, and so serves as its companion, I shall conclude this introduction with a mention of the geographical overlap between book and films. For the book itself serves to help those wanting to continue explorations excited by the images and speech on the screen. In brief, the films were made in northern Bihar (north India), in Sri Lanka or Ceylon, in Japan, in Taiwan, in the Toraja country in Celebes, Indonesia, in Cairo and elsewhere in Egypt, in Israel and New York and London (in relation to Judaism), in Indianapolis and elsewhere, relative to Protestantism, in Romania and in Rome, Leeds and Spain (regarding the Catholics), in southern Africa, and in California, where new religions and sciences abound. The films are irreduceably selective: they need to be. The book is a map to show the areas surrounding the wonderful and mysterious places where the films were made.

HINDUISM 1

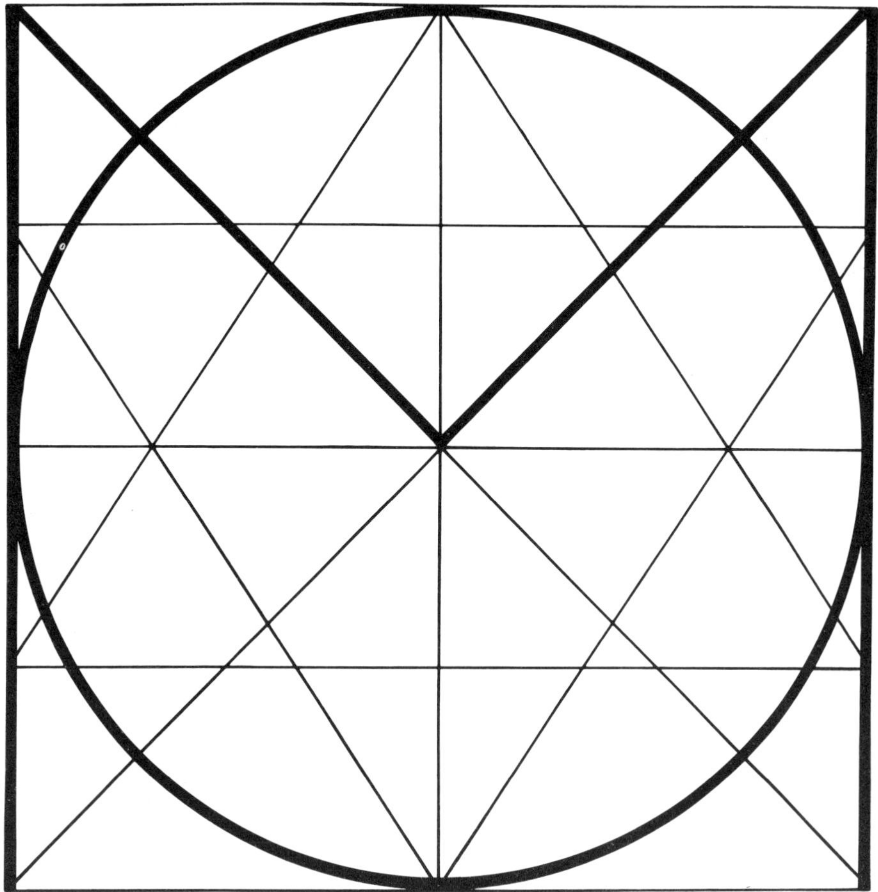

Hinduism is the name we have come to give to the loosely-knit cults and beliefs of the majority of people in the Indian subcontinent. In a way it is like a federation of religions. However, it is held together by certain general features. It operates within the structure of a caste system under the religious dominance of the Brahmins, whose sacred language, Sanskrit, is the vehicle of scriptures and other sacred writings. Some of these, the Vedic hymns, date back into the second millennium BC *and express something of the culture of the Aryans who invaded India from the north-west up to and around 1500* BC. *Later the famous and mysterious works known as the Upanishads were composed (8th to 4th centuries* BC*). The Song of the Lord or* Bhagavadgita, *the most influential devotional work in Hinduism, was composed about four centuries later. This was the period when Hinduism established its classical form – the proliferation of temples, the worship of the*

great gods Vishnu and Shiva, seen as alternative ways of picturing the Supreme Being, the elaboration of the caste hierarchy and the acceptance of belief in rebirth or re-incarnation.

Since the establishment of the British Raj in the nineteenth century Hinduism was challenged by Western values and Christian missions. Its response was to absorb Western educational ideas and to shape a modern Hindu ideology in which the genius of Hinduism is seen not only in its methods of contemplation but also in its ability to weave together different forms of religion and spirituality. This theme of diversity in unity is offered as a way of approaching world religions. Do they not all ultimately point to the same Truth? So modern Hinduism sees itself as a model of toleration. In various forms its higher theology or Vedanta is spreading too into Western countries, for instance through the work of the Ramakrishna mission. Hinduism also has provided a framework for Indian democracy, and entered deeply into the work of the architect of national independence, Mahatma Gandhi.

India, however, is undergoing great changes. Can Hinduism adapt its somewhat other-worldly ideals to the new ways of scientific thinking helping to reshape Indian industry and agriculture? How seriously can the educated Indian take belief in re-incarnation, so vital in the fabric of Hindu attitudes to the world? No doubt in its great richness and devotional power, Hinduism will continue to generate new forms of faith, relevant to the late twentieth century.

India: The matrix of Hinduisms

Geological speculation now maintains that the Indian subcontinent once adhered to Africa. As the continents drifted it slid into the underbelly of north Asia and, in a slow-motion crash, threw up the Himalaya range. The name means the 'snow store'. The Himalayas feed the mighty Indus and the sacred Ganges, and men have often looked to them as a source of holiness, as a divine mediation between heaven and earth, between the waters of the celestial realm and the rivers here on earth. They also made a physical barrier.

There were only two ways of invading India: from the north-west, whence came the ancient Aryans, and later the Muslims who were to create the Mughal empire; and from the sea, whence, ultimately, came the British. There was also the east: the Japanese in World War II tried this tricky route and were bloodily stopped at Kohima and Imphal. And it was by the north-west or the sea that India exported her culture. Buddhism surged into Central Asia and hence along silk routes to China and beyond; it also rode the waves to Ceylon, South-East Asia and Canton.

Relative physical isolation has allowed India to absorb such imports as came its way and put its own stamp on them: we cannot understand Indian civilisation without looking both for the unity it fashioned and the diversity, whether of race, language, custom or religion, which is the basis of its extraordinary vitality.

Language

The Aryans who dominated northern India from about 1500 BC onwards spoke a tongue related to Greek and Latin. This evolved into the classical and sacred language Sanskrit. Later north Indian languages developed into a variety of tongues such as Hindi, Bengali, Punjabi, and Gujerati, just as Latin gave rise to the various languages of Mediterranean Europe. But southerners were never fully dominated by the north, and at the lower end of India's bent triangle are the quite different Dravidian languages such as Tamil, Telugu, and Kanarese. So linguistically India is even more diverse than Europe. But unifying it was a Brahmin-controlled culture, which used Sanskrit as its sacred medium. And scattered through India like plums in a pudding are smaller tribal groups, Nagas, Todas, and so on, who have never quite been assimilated. Diversity extends to dress, food, shape of temples, appearance and styles of living as well as language. It is no surprise then to find that Hinduism is really a sort of federation of Hinduisms.

The Indus flows through the westerly plain. What is now the Punjab, west of Delhi, was the first great settlement area for the invading Aryans. They were responsible for the collapse of the cities and culture of the Indus civilisation: the peoples no doubt intermingled, but the Aryan culture dominated, and spread down the eastern plain along the Ganges, where round Patna a flourishing way of life developed that saw the rise of the Jains and the Buddhists, as well as the extension of orthodox Brahmin religion. Gradually, from this northern base, characteristic Hinduism spread into South India, till by the latter part of the first millennium AD the most vital Hinduism was to be found in the South. Here too the most complex and awesome temples were built. At the same time came the first signs of the Muslim incursions which were to alter the life of the old centres of Hinduism in the north-west and north. The Mughals ultimately spread their power far into the south, but the Dravidian culture was never quite so permeated as was the northern.

Geography dictated that the British domination of the fully formed Hindu religion and society proceeded in the opposite direction; it was the north-west which was subdued last.

The characteristics of Hindu religion

Though the ancient Vedas or sacred scriptures of the Aryans, and the later holy books such as the Upanishads, are important, and their acceptance a sign of orthodoxy, they were composed before some of the main features of Hinduism developed. India is the land of temples; but the ancient Aryans didn't have them – even now Vedic ceremonies are often performed in a temporary shelter or sanctified space in the open air. The temples of India house images, often very elaborate ones – but the use of images was later than the fifth century BC, when some of the main Upanishads were composed. It was only later that temples and images became two main items of Hinduism.

What else? There is the rough division in Hindu imagination and devotional practice between the worship of Vishnu and of Shiva, the two great gods, or manifestations of deity. Vishnu's incarnations include the playful and loving Krishna, deity of the great *Bhagavadgita*; Shiva is the awesome yogi whose lingam symbolises creation, and whose spouse, Kali, symbolises the destructive powers of the godhead. But even these great gods, regarded by most Hindus as alternative ways of picturing the Supreme, had not emerged fully into their colossal influence at the time of the Upanishads. So far then, the marks of Hinduism are: temples, images and the Vishnu-Shiva alliance.

Equally important is Hinduism as a social arrangement – seen above all in the caste system. Again, it is a late invention which did not exist in its modern form at the time of the Buddha and the Upanishads. What *did* exist then was a system of classes known as the *varnas*. This was a development of a structure which the Aryans brought into India and shared to some extent with other Indo-European speaking cultures (such as the Greeks and Celts). The structure was originally threefold: warriors, priests and servitors (artisans, traders and agriculturalists). The conquered peoples became a fourth class at the bottom; in settled times the priests became the highest class, both socially and sacredly. The top three classes then were the Brahmins (priests), kshatriyas (warriors) and vaishyas (servitors). These are the pukka people, the so-called twiceborn, for they are born a second time, into upper Aryan society, at the initiation ceremony when a boy is invested with the sacred thread, a kind of string worn round his torso and over his shoulder. Below them are the ex-conquered folk, the shudras, or labourers. As time went on an even lower class was formed, the 'fifth', now referred to as the untouchables or, more charitably, by the name Gandhi conferred on them, Harijans or sons of God. The main structure of Hindu society follows this fivefold division.

The caste system implies more than all this, but before we come to it, let us just reflect on what the class structure outlined above involves. First and most obviously it means a division of labour – though most Brahmins no longer perform the priestly function, and follow a whole range of occupations: clerks, cooks, or even soldiers. Second, the class system was hereditary. Normally it did not permit marriage between classes: it was, therefore, endogamous as to classes. Third, the system meant that it became unusual or prohibited for members of different classes, and later castes, to eat together. It involved what has been called *commensality*.

What then is caste proper, and how did it emerge? Caste or *jāti* is a set of rules which preclude intermarriage, the sharing of food, and other intimate contacts. These subgroups grew up for a variety of reasons – different sorts of artisans formed guilds which imposed a ban on marrying out for instance. Regional differences multiplied groups: a Brahmin from Bengal may not intermarry with a Brahmin from South India. The Bengali may eat fish, the southerner may not. As tribes were assimilated they too became subgroups within the wider framework. Religious differences could also play a part (one group might be followers of Vishnu, another of Shiva, and so on). For all these and other reasons a complex caste system was evolved and given religious sanction. Caste makes the rich human mosaic of India hierarchical.

I was once talking to a young Christian in Mangalore on the west coast. We were in the mission compound which contained a church, a school, and houses for many of the faithful. I asked whether only Christian families lived in the compound. He replied unselfconsciously, 'No, some other castes live here as well'. Christians do not accept the system, but if no one will intermarry with you, you can't intermarry with them, and you become willy-nilly another piece in the mosaic.

The Gods and the One

Who are the gods? Some come down from the ancient times, from a Vedic culture we see in the mysterious ancient hymns: gods like Agni, animating fire, Indra, thunderous and warlike, and Brahmā, the somewhat distant creator-deity and god of the Brahmins. (Already in the ancient hymns there are suggestions that all the gods are but different names for the one reality). Then there are the mighty gods, surging upwards in popular cults as Hinduism developed beyond the old wisdom. There is Shiva, perhaps foreshadowed in the Indus civilisation, and his variously depicted consort – his creative energy, for in India creative power is ascribed more to the female than the male principle – the dynamic Durga, and the dark Kali. There is Vishnu, more serene and garlanded than Shiva, manifesting himself in a variety of incarnations or *avatars*, such as the worthy and noble Rama, and Krishna, dark blue and amorous; and due to return to earth in a future time as Kalki. But Vishnu can show terrifying power – nothing is more awesome than Krishna revealing his godhead in the *Bhagavadgita*. Arjuna who sees his majestic outpouring, brighter than the light of a thousand suns, like a personalised H-bomb explosion, pleads that his hair stands on end in sheer terror. For the gods are both powerful – frightening even – and loving. Then there are some gods associated with Vishnu and Shiva, such as the cheerful Ganesh, good for business, with an auspicious elephant's head, and the goddess Sarasvati, good for learning and worshipped by schoolchildren and students. There is Lakshmi, lucky, and a whole variegated crowd of lesser and local deities. Even Queen Victoria attracted a brief cult. And below the gods are the tree spirits, the holy snakes, the sacred cows, the monkeys, reminders of the tricky and delightful monkey-god Hanuman and Shiva's sacred bull Nandi; even a husband has a godlike stance to the pious Hindu wife. So the range of spirits and deities is immense.

The gods and ritual

Often a god will be tended from dawn to dusk by priests, his image roused in the morning, bathed, given food as if for breakfast and so on through the day. The food of the gods may be given sacramentally to the worshippers. Images may be paraded through the streets and fields at festivals. The lingam of Shiva may be anointed with ghee and garlanded. Rituals, fervours and visits to the temples and shrines and pilgrimages to famous gods are seemingly never-ending, in a teemingly pious land – there are thirty-three crores (ten millions) of gods it is sometimes said (the Vedic gods originally were thirty-three; but India always multiplies stunningly, whether it be men or gods).

People think, of course, that the gods can help them. They may ward off smallpox or help with examinations or bring a man-child or help the crops grow. Men's anxieties are directed towards them, for does not religion cater for our dreads and sorrows and keenest hopes? But beyond these concerns the gods have a spiritual power, and attract intense devotion partly for that reason. The devotion is often called *bhakti*, an attitude in which the believer casts himself upon the mercy and love of god. For the god may bring him to liberation from the dreads and worries of the world, and beyond that a liberation which is blissful and a joyous communion with the Highest.

In South India there was long dispute, in the middle ages, between the cat and monkey schools. The cat school thought that the relation between the individual and God is like that of a kitten to its mother: the mother transports the little one from A to B by the scruff of the neck – so God takes the individual from here to eternity: liberation is by God's grace alone. But the mother monkey carries her little one on her hip: the little one has to do something, to cling to the mother's waist. Grace and works: faith and deeds – here is an Eastern echo of a problem found in the West. At any rate, one of the marked attitudes to the gods in Hinduism is *bhakti*. Overwhelmingly Hinduism is a devotional religion, and the images are the condensation of the presence of God. Is this a singular God?

Modern Hindus themselves have tried to show the West that all religions, all cults, all spiritual ideas, really point at the same truth. Our human reactions to the divine and our human attempts to express these in ideas and images are, it is said by some of the leading figures of modern Hinduism, like fingers pointing at the moon. Do not look at the fingers, but use them to gaze at the one moon. Are the millions of deities and spirits one after all, then? And if so who or what is that One? A good question, to which Hindus have (you will not be surprised) given different answers. But let us select two of these, which represent, in my opinion, the main choices in the splendid history of Hinduisms.

Shankara

The first answer is expressed in the Upanishads and later set forth most systematically and radically by the great philosopher and spiritual leader, Shankara (ninth century AD). Much of the Upanishads are sacred musings upon the meaning of religion, and, above all, the meaning of the rites and sacrifices administered with increasing elaboration by the Brahmin priesthood. That these rites served the well-being of men and the universe was not doubted, but what was their real and secret power? It is like the question of nuclear power – we know how to manipulate it, but are increasingly worried as to whether we fully understand the inner constitution of the atoms which are split to cause the power to flow. So, what was the inward significance of the horse-sacrifice, the sprinklings of ghee, and the various chants used with such solemn power? The answer in the Upanishads is as follows.

The inner power, called Brahman, which animates both the priesthood itself and the ritual actions is, indeed, that which pervades and animates the whole universe. What is here on earth is also the secret of the stars and the whole world around us. So Brahman is to be thought of as the divine basis of everything. It is the Godhead.

But men had long been experimenting with yoga and bodily austerities, with a view to gaining spiritual power and to penetrating to the secret of consciousness. According to the Upanishads the soul within us which such meditation can reveal is the Ātman or self. The bold equation in the Upanishads is that, just as the yogi and the priest can come together, so likewise can the powers they explore and represent. Or to put it more plainly, Brahman is Ātman. The Godhead animating the world is to be found within, smaller than a grain of mustard-seed, in the Self. So one answer to the question, What is the One? is: Brahman/Ātman. It is the Holy Power behind all things and in our own consciousness, in the Self.

Continued on page 38

HOLY PLACES

Many religions are anchored in places regarded as holy and thus as points of intersection between the divine and human worlds. Temples and churches function as such: but more important are those special places which focus the geographical mind of the believer. Rome, Banaras, Mecca, Lourdes – such places acquire a kind of sanctity through the pressure of much devotion and pilgrimage. Since men live in space and time it is not surprising that men's religions select special times and places to symbolise and make real the eruption of the divine into the earthly sphere. Even secular ideologies have their own sense of sacred places.

This picture is eloquent of devotion, but the object is no traditional saint. These folk are queueing in Red Square, Moscow to see the embalmed body of Lenin, founder of the new Russia and successor of both tsars and holy men.

Holy places speak to human anxieties, sorrows and joys. Here (right) the faithful are at Lourdes, in the Pyrenees in southern France – a great centre of the cult of the Virgin and focus of hope for the sick in mind and spirit. The Virgin appeared to a girl in a grotto in 1858, and gradually the fame of the place grew. It is perhaps no coincidence that the area is noted for ancient prehistoric caves used for sacred purposes. The cave is often seen as holy and a good site for sacraments, partly because it represents some kind of enclosure within the living earth.

Likewise, below, in Kashmir pilgrims come to visit a sacred cave. The rich are conveyed in palanquins.

Of all holy places perhaps Mecca is the most potent. Every Muslim, if his resources and circumstances reasonably permit, should make the pilgrimage (hajj) *to the city which saw the revelatory mission of Muhammad. The requirements are fairly complex, and involve visiting sacred spots in a state of holiness (wearing pilgrim dress, abstaining from sex, and so forth). One central spot is the Ka'aba, here seen surrounded by a throng of pilgrims. It is a stone structure containing a black stone, dating to pre-Islamic times (the Arabs venerated sacred rocks).*

Here (right) pilgrims from West Africa are on their way to Mecca. Note that the men are bareheaded and the women (mainly inside the bus) are veiled. The picture illustrates the pilgrim dress necessary for a visit to Mecca.

٢٣٩٩
ركاب ٥٥

PIYAL

Hasidic Jews are here by the Wailing Wall in Jerusalem. Devotion is expressed through praying by the wall, which reminds Jews of the old Temple, destroyed in AD *70. The capture of this holy spot in the 1967 war between Israel and the Arabs caused great emotion. The place is a poignant focus of sorrow for the sufferings of the Jews and for the renewal of commitment to faithfulness to God's law, despite all the tribulations.*

One of the main places of pilgrimage in Ceylon (Sri Lanka) is Adam's Peak (left), where there is a footprint of the Buddha, a trace of his mythic visit to the sacred island. The mountain figures in non-Buddhist traditions. According to Islamic lore Adam and Eve met at the mountain called Arafat, by Mecca, after being cast out of Eden, and then met again, it is said, at Adam's Peak. Mountains are frequently thought of as divine because they mediate between heaven and earth.

Shankara took this idea further. If the equation is correct we are already divine. The trouble is that we do not realise it (and it is not enough to nod when told about all this, for realising it means feeling it in the depths of our being). We are kept from this liberating knowledge by ignorance. Because we are ignorant we assume that there is much else besides Brahman. We look on the world about us and our own selves as independent realities, instead of seeing them as being in essence nothing but God. Thus for us the world becomes an illusion, *māyā*. In this world of illusion it is no doubt useful to worship the gods; even Vishnu and Shiva, however, seen from the vale of ignorance, are a kind of illusion. We must go beyond everyday religion to a realisation of our own divinity. How can we worship ourselves, after all? Shankara's ideas form the main basis for modern Hindu responses to the challenge posed by Western, and more particularly Christian, influence, and we will return to them later.

But Shankara, though dynamic and authoritative, was not without his critics. There were those who thought his claim that even the great gods are caught in the grand illusion implied that traditional religion itself – the whole network of the Brahmins' rituals and the basis of their superiority – is illusory. Because of this he was sometimes accused of being a crypto-Buddhist: Buddhism had vigorously criticised Brahmanical orthodoxy, repudiated sacrifice, and implicitly rejected the caste system. Moreover in not recognising the authority of the Veda or the power of the great Hindu gods the Buddhists had become rivals to the Hindus. However, while Shankara may have been criticised by his contemporaries, the more important critique came from the twelfth-century Rāmānuja, another South Indian, who represents the other great Hindu viewpoint.

Rāmānuja

For Rāmānuja the chief trouble with Shankara was that his doctrines ultimately destroyed the meaning of that fervent devotion, *bhakti*, which is the glory of the Hindu response to God. If Vishnu (and Rāmānuja was a Vaishnava or follower of Vishnu) is less than the highest reality and if the religion of worship belongs to the sphere of ignorance, then devotion or *bhakti* has little meaning. So Rāmānuja rejected the story of the grand illusion. For him, both common sense and religion point to a real world, and revelation declares that behind it all there is a real God who can bring salvation. That God liberates men and brings them into communion with him in heaven. The universe is created by him, as it unfolds itself and goes again after vast ages to sleep and starts all over again, in a long pulsating rhythm, like cosmic Atlantic rollers of time. Behind all this vastness, and within it all, is Vishnu the creator. Indeed, Rāmānuja uses the analogy of body and soul to illustrate the divine operation. My soul controls my body, but imperfectly. I can raise my arm at will, but cannot always control the secretions of my liver, my heartbeat or my hiccups. The universe is God's body, but over it he has perfect control. He is the soul controlling the body – its ruler and its inner core.

This system of ideas expressed well men's sense of dependence on God, and the way in which our salvation is entirely due to his love. In short it expressed well the religion of *bhakti*. As for the gods, they are but the many offshoots and representations of the one Divine Being. In him all spiritual forces have their focus.

Through him, men's karma and destiny are controlled. From him there issues forth intense love of creatures.

So whether one treads the path of Shankara (a path usually called Advaita or Non-Dualism) or the path of Rāmānuja (referred to as Qualified Non-Dualism), the gods turn out in their different ways to be reflections of the One. This idea is not only found among the intellectuals; it reaches down far into the consciousness of ordinary people and deep back into India's spiritual history.

Rebirth and karma

A pervasive belief among Hindus (a belief shared in principle with, among others, the Jains and Buddhists) is rebirth or reincarnation. According to this all living beings are in a continuing flux of births, passing from one life to another. An animal which dies is reborn in another form and may even become a man, just as a man may take another form, whether as animal or spirit, after his death. The only way of terminating this otherwise endless series of lives is by attaining liberation. Indeed liberation in the Indian tradition means above all the individual's escaping the round of rebirth, and so attaining a transcendent bliss – beyond the material world and the vicissitudes of *samsāra* or the cyclical life in which we are normally implicated.

Reincarnation provides a fabulous framework for understanding men's moral, material and spiritual conditions. The murderer will suffer in a gruesome purgatory, or later, in another human life, through his sufferings and poverty. The ant will rise to be the god Indra. The rajah's bloody hands will bring him suffering through thousands of ghostly and animal lives. The sick man may have erred before he was born. Miseries may cluster towards a whole people, a concentration of retribution (I have heard a sad Buddhist from Vietnam say this).

Rebirth is also a whole series of threads binding together the levels of life. The Hindu sees man as merely one level in a hierarchy of life, from the lowest spirits and insects right through to the gods and beyond.

The moral law which dictates the never ceasing rises and falls in life is called *karma* – literally 'action', for it is through our deeds that our futures are formed. Sometimes karma is looked on as an automatic law, something like gravity, that is part of the deep structure of the universe. Sometimes it is seen, as by Rāmānuja, as the expression of God's will for living beings, and the way in which he brings them through tribulations to ultimate salvation and heavenly bliss.

Knowledge and holy men

When one's life is ripe for it one may wish to withdraw from ordinary cares to pursue the higher spiritual life and to attain a kind of living liberation – in the world still, but not of it. This emphasis upon withdrawn meditation and the quest for high knowledge is something relevant to Shankara. For did he not postulate that it is by *knowing* one's own true divine nature that ignorance and illusion is dispelled? If Rāmānuja stressed *bhakti* then Shankara stressed knowledge.

The real meaning of such knowledge can be seen reflected in the lives of India's holy men. As often elsewhere in the world's religious traditions it is thought that for the higher knowledge the guidance of a guru is needed. He is the Indian version of the Zen master or the Catholic spiritual director, though in the Indian case the guru tends to be, as it were, a freelance: very often they are individuals who attract attention for their holiness. They tend not to be organised. But since there are so many holy men, so many recluses and monks, so many leaders and miracle-workings in the Indian kaleidoscope, the picture I shall here present is a stylised, rather simplified one.

First, let us note that the Hindus have long had a theory about the stages of life which indicates a regular way of 'leaving the world' to become a holy man. The stages are four. First, a child or young person is in the condition of being a student, during which time he learns the ancient lore from a Brahmin teacher; thereafter he marries and becomes a father and householder. When his eldest son is grown up and capable of taking over the household cares, he begins to withdraw – he is a 'forest dweller', to translate the term literally, for in older days he would make himself a hermitage near the village in the jungle. Young people might come to him finally for instruction. Then, at the last, *sannyāsi*, stage, he becomes a wandering holy man.

His wandering has two sides to it. First, it symbolises his utter homelessness. He no longer has family or geographical ties: he is sometimes figured in Indian literature as a migratory bird, leaving no tracks in the air. Second, his wandering is a kind of pilgrimage: he will find his way to such holy places as Hardwar and Banaras where his holy withdrawnness and spiritual wisdom may act as a magnet and an example to the mass of pilgrims. Of course many Hindus do not follow the four stages, but they represent an ideal. I remember talking to an economist at Delhi University who, glancing round a little shyly at his colleagues, told me that it was his desire to leave the world in search of spiritual truth. He was leaving the technical but unsatisfying world of economic theory behind him.

Another kind of holy man in India is the one who joins an order of monks, such as that founded by Shankara which is especially strong in South India. In modern times the best-known order has been that of the Ramakrishna Mission, an organisation dedicated to good works and education as well as to meditation, and expressing the world-view of Ramakrishna and his famous disciple Vivekananda. They have adapted older Indian ideas to modern conditions and have borrowed techniques from Western missionaries.

But holy men and gurus appear in all sorts of ways. A man may begin to acquire a reputation for insight and holiness, and round him there may gather a group of disciples who form his ashram. Thus Gandhi established an ashram in Ahmedabad, and there are ashrams of different kinds scattered through the length and breadth of India. There are even Christian ashrams where men live in the Hindu way, though owing their allegiance to Christ.

Commonly men go to seek a good guru, but are often disappointed. How does one indeed tell a genuine holy man from a fraud? This may be an acute issue in these latter days, when so many holy men from the East are making their homes (and sometimes riches) in the West. You have to use your judgment, but here are some tips. If a guru becomes rich, beware. He may say that the faithful wish to heap good things upon him as symbol of the divine, just as gold is used to adorn churches and images. But still beware. Again, a guru should display psychological insight. If he understands you, then he is likely to be genuine. Third, his teachings should be practical and not a lot of metaphysical smoke. Fourth, if he talks in platitudes, beware. He should be deep, not a bore. But apart from that the two of you have to click. One man's guru may be another man's tyrant.

That said, I have found much of interest in the gurus I have met. Perhaps the most interesting was one in Bombay who ran a statistics advisory service as a kind of business. He had mathematical disciples working for him in an office complete with meditation room overlooking the Brabourne cricket stadium. He wanted to modernise Hinduism, to act in the world. He looked to have become properous but, when I was sitting at his feet, we gained a little rapport. He said something about Western materialism, a favourite and not altogether absurd theme in modern India (though some Indians obviously grasp at Western goodies). I asked deferentially if a record of Beethoven's choral symphony was material and he chuckled, simpatico. Still, I wasn't there to sit at his feet for ever.

Authority in the mind

In India there is a long tradition that the power of the holy man comes from his inner experience. To train himself towards attaining the inner vision which will spill over through serenity of face and life and power into other men's minds the *sannyāsin* has sometimes tried great austerities, like sitting in the noon sun surrounded by four fires, to generate scorching heat. Indeed the old word for austerity was heat. There is a relic of this in the sauna, for it originated in the heat-ordeal of shamans (or prophets) in north Asia – a practice maybe connected with the Indian methods. The group that perhaps represents austerity most clearly and surprisingly in India is the community of Jains, about whom I write in Chapter 6. But Jains are not alone in *tapas* or 'heat', the heat of self-repression. Sometimes the power this *tapas* was supposed to bring frightened even the gods, and some of Shiva's awesome power flows from being the Mahayogin or Great Yogi. For austerity after all conduced to a sense of vision or release, and this meant a new knowledge. Knowledge is power. And thus we come again to the idea of authority in the mind. In general it is through various techniques of training that the holy man gains that knowledge-power which can shine through to others and in particular to his disciples. Thus there has long been a fascination with the various kinds of yoga.

Yogas and Yoga

The general word for these techniques of mind and body training is yoga. But we can easily get confused for there is also one particular school of Indian philosophy called the Yoga School. This has some features which would not be agreed with by all practitioners of yoga. Thus it is convenient to think of the Yoga School as having a capital Y, and yoga in general as having a small y. Briefly, the teachings of the Yoga School are these. First, there are many souls, indeed innumerable souls, embedded in the universe, attached, as it were, to bodies of all kinds, whether humans or hogs or ants or gods or tortured spirits, and whether in this world or in some higher or lower world. The souls suffer, by their entanglement in the jungle of life, which is full of disappointment, disease, troubles, death, amputations, and what you see in the miseries of men. So release from the round or rebirth must be achieved, and the way is through yoga and in particular Yoga. The particular path envisaged does not primarily mean calling on God, nor even aiming at unity with the divine. Rather it means purifying consciousness in such a way that the individual comes to see the true nature of his own soul, and, in seeing that, sees that it is different from the natural world in which it is entangled. And so it attains liberation and after the yogi's death exists in deathless isolation, no longer subject to rebirth and the sufferings of the world. The Yoga School does not deny God's existence, but he is seen simply as an ideal – as a soul never subject to suffering and rebirth.

But some go in for yoga for different reasons, for instance to attain direct knowledge of and identity with the divine. Buddhist yoga is built on different presuppositions again – for them there is neither soul nor God, but only the possibility of nirvana (and what this is we shall see in Chapter 2). And there are others who have looked on yoga mainly as a physical activity – practising what is called *hatha yoga*, which is a development of the idea that certain postures – the lotus position and so on – and certain techniques of breathing bring a kind of physical and mental wellbeing. It is this type of yoga which has in the 1960s and 1970s made such a hit in the West, and there is no doubt that it can bring surprising results. But in India the chief aim in all this has been the attempt to gain higher states of consciousness, and so we get back to the idea of authority in the mind. These higher states culminate in the emptying of the mind of all usual thoughts and images, and this blankness, so hard to attain, sets the scene for a higher kind of perception of the truth.

Here we meet a central problem: are all mystical experiences the same? Does the Christian mystic see the same 'blank' as the Buddhist or the adherent of the Yoga School? Does the Muslim Sufi see the same 'blank' as the seer of the Upanishads or the Gita? Those who think that all religions point to the same truth say 'Yes'. I believe that in a way they are right, but in another way wrong – that it is what faiths *make* of mysticism which may be important.

So, the authority in the mind flows from self-discipline, which by shutting out the world brings forth an inner vision from the 'blank'. It is a kind of enlightenment often characterised as coming from the beyond. The yogi or the guru who has seen what lies Beyond has authority and power; in some degree he is like a god.

The Mystical and the Numinous

The famous writer on religions, Rudolf Otto, whose *The Idea of the Holy* made a large impact in the period immediately after World War II, coined the term *numinous* to express the awe-inspiring and powerful, even frightening, aspect of the Holy, or divine. We have seen a traumatic type of vision in the *Bhagavadgita*, when Arjuna's hair stood on end. So it is with all the gods – they are mysterious and give rise to awe. And so it is too, often, with holy men: a theme in India is that of the mystic who, losing himself in his vision, finds the Beyond within himself, and can perform all sorts of wondrous tasks. He is mystical within, but magical seen from the outside. So too, perhaps, with the nature of God.

Yet the awe-inspiring gods also bring succour and relief to the faithful, and attract the fervent *bhakti* and joyous celebrations that punctuate Indian religious life. How can one reconcile the quiet of the inner 'blank', the motionlessness of the Jain saint, the withdrawn life of the *sannyāsi*, with this amazing ebullience – the jostle and bellringing and offerings which are such a part of Indian devotion? How does yoga blend with the festivities of Diwali, when Indian streets are bright with lights?

Is it perhaps like stained glass in a church window? If you are inside the church the window glows with splendid colours: Christ and God are there in glory and the saints work their loving magic upon the faithful who gaze upwards at them. But go outside into the quiet of the churchyard and the mysterious lights are not there – the windows look unsatisfying. The holy man is one who has worshipped within the temple, but come outside. He has seen the many-splendoured pantheon of the gods, but he has gone beyond them. They are vehicles for raising men to the Beyond, but that Beyond is beyond them. That indeed is how many Hindus think, and it is a theme which has been of great influence and importance in the modern period.

When the land was taken over by the British Raj and Christianity came to challenge many traditional values Hindus looked at their own faith anew. They modernised it, while keeping the age-old spiritual values and the gaiety of their celebrations and temple-life. In these and other ways Indians adjusted to new circumstances. Muslims incidentally were slower, perhaps because they lived in their own, post-imperial dream; they, after all, ruled from Delhi before the British came.

India goes West

The coming of the West by sea ended with the British in power. The Portuguese, Dutch and French successively succumbed to British seamanship and gunnery in the Indian Ocean. It was all about trade, it was said, and the first British landpower in India was the East India Company, known popularly as John Company.

The East India Company was there to trade. It was strong in Bombay, had life in Madras, and flourished in Bengal. Soldiers could help trade, but could not be too much relied on. John Company was not an army, but a band of merchant adventurers, incorporated in a different country. Fast profits were expected, so missionaries were, till late on, kept out. Christian propaganda against a fairly pliable Hinduism and a rather stunned Islam might upset the natives. But in due course all this was to change. The missionaries were admitted at the end of the first quarter of Hinduism's crucial century; and the Company was transformed into the Empire after the Mutiny, some quarter of a century later. All this meant administrative, ideological and Christian challenges to the existing order.

Widows should not be burnt. Thugs (who were highway robbers dedicated to the worship of the goddess Kali) were exorcised. New kinds of education crept in, and then grew as universities and colleges were established. Caste was condemned. Hinduism was seen by the invaders as polytheism. Macaulay thought that if you taught Hindus Christianity and Western science, the Hindu way of life would be seen to be absurd. The opposite happened: the infusion of new forces released new energies and helped to revivify the Hindu tradition. There was a resurgence: in a sense it was the invention of the very idea of Hinduism. The Western and Christian challenge forced the educated Hindu, almost for the first time, to ask what it *meant* to be a Hindu. Thus in the latter half of the nineteenth century, the Hindu was put on a new path, one summed up by the work of Ramakrishna and his disciple Vivekananda, but implicit in many other ideas and thinkers of the time.

Ramakrishna

Ramakrishna was a Bengali, without Western education, and not all that well equipped educationally in traditional Indian terms. But he was a spiritual genius. He had early visions and proved to be an excellent guru, with a burning sense of the unity of men and a rich sense of how to teach through symbols, parables and stories. The book enshrining all this, called in Western style *The Gospel of Sri Ramakrishna*, is full of truth seen in an earthy and amazingly parable-rich way. His great disciple Swami Vivekananda was a kind of Paul to Ramakrishna's Christ. By the early part of the twentieth century the Ramakrishna Mission was established. It did good works. It still runs hospitals in India, and is active in education inside India and outside, in centres for the propagation of understanding about the felicities and depths of the Hindu tradition. It operates admirably, and is well directed towards new preaching. The message is characteristic of what may be called the modern Hindu ideology.

What is that teaching? Before expounding the new essence of Hinduism, let us see what the questions were, and the challenges, which needed to be answered.

The intrusion of the British and, more generally, the West into the perfumed and sometimes unjust jungle of the Hindu world posed certain questions. The most radical was: Why Hinduism? Christianity seemed to make the chaos of India ridiculous. Here was a relatively clear faith invading the fabric of a religiously plural society. The new missionaries might come to see Christ as the crown of Hinduism; but they would not become part of it in the style of the great but unsuccessful Roberto de Nobili, who, in the older days, had lived at Madurai in South India, to outward appearance a Brahmin and not an upper-class Italian. Most of the new missionaries through the British connection (de Nobili, though Italian, had come through the Portuguese connection) were Protestants, and often Evangelical at that. They misunderstood the lingam and Indian ideas of heaven and much else besides. Although some became great scholars of the Hindu world (men like J. N. Farquhar), the thrust was mainly towards reforming and maybe destroying Hindu culture. It was, up to a point, effective, for while India did not choose Christ en masse, it did respond to Christian ideas in ways which set the scene for the new Hinduism. And the social impact of the West was great: Christianity questioned the gods – was this not polytheism? – while the new rule questioned the caste system, and the Western ethos questioned the traditions of Indian knowledge – was not modern science Western? The railways and the colleges brought the Indian intelligentsia into a new world. Above all, the Hindus felt the Christian challenge as a disparagement of their own cultural traditions.

The modern Hindu ideology

The answer to these challenges was partly given by nationalism, partly too by the religious tradition. Polytheism was not a problem, all gods were known to be one ultimately – not Hindu gods but all the world's gods – Christ, Yahweh, Allah, the Tao, Vishnu, Shiva, African deities – these were all the same. So Christian exclusiveness, enshrined in the white spires of churches in the cantonments (where the whites tended to live) and the missionary ethos of conversion were met by the stupendous claim that the Hindu accepted the Christian precisely because Hindus looked to a more universal goal. Hinduism is tolerant, insouciant, plural in its world outlook and therefore basically in opposition to evangelical Christianity. It could be all things to all men – and that without failing to see the one Reality. Thus argued, and felt, Ramakrishna and Vivekananda, and later the President of India, Radhakrishnan. The ideology implied a kind of tolerance, and thus supported the hypertolerant moral attitudes through which Gandhi sought peace and unity. Though they were not typical of the people. Gandhi as a travelling saint and Vivekananda as a gifted man with an unadorned golden tongue echoed a wide sentiment.

The modern Hindu ideology latched on to those ideas of levels of truth and perception foreshadowed by Shankara and before him, according to an influential series of interpretations, by the Upanishads. The idea of levels of truth could be used to see the relationship between religions. Some beliefs might be lower than others in their value and truth. An incarnation, such as the *avatar* of Vishnu, Krishna, is below Vishnu, who in turn is below the secret manifestation of the divine Reality who is beyond the world and yet through the Creator energetic. Why not then see other faiths in this way, as different expressions of the one Truth?

This ideology of 'anything you can feel we can feel deeper' lent a dignity to the Indian nationalist movement and a certain special flavour to the democracy that India was to establish on independence. To some extent it fitted well with the pragmatism of the dying Raj. It still sways the thinking of many Hindus. But is it true that all religions point to the same truth? Yes and no. First, the yes.

The mystic and the devotee

The theme of the unity of all religions is popular with those who emphasise the inner quest, the mystical. It was taken up, for instance, by Aldous Huxley. What he called the perennial philosophy saw religion from the inner, mystical or contemplative point of view. And it does emerge, from such investigations as have been sensitively done, that similar visions accrue from the 'blank' of the contemplative life in very varied religions. Naturally interpretations differ. The Christian sees God in the cloud of unknowing, the Hindu sees Brahman in the depths of his yoga, the Chinese speak of the Tao, the Way and so on. And of course the presuppositions and sentiments the mystic brings to bear will give his quest a distinctive flavour. The Muslim Sufi sees his mysticism in the context of a new quest for Allah while the Buddhist sees it as the eightfold path. But despite the external and mental differences it does seem plausible to look on all mystics as gaining a similar 'blankness' and inner light.

So if you see the mystical as being at the heart of religion, belief in the unity of religions looks good. Nor is this all. For after all the *bhakti* and devotion of different faiths are similar. Many have remarked on the likeness of sentiment in the Gita and in Paul. Muslim piety is fervent and resembles aspects of Catholicism. In the Buddhism of the Pure Land movement devotion to the Buddha Amitabha is strangely reminiscent of devotion to the heavenly Christ. So worship and *bhakti* are similar in a variety of faiths. These resemblances in mysticism and devotion have led some to see the same awesome but merciful God everywhere.

But not all religions centre on God – Jainism and the Buddhism of South and South-East Asia, for example, do not. And the monotheistic religions in particular are alas (or perhaps alas, for feelings differ here), though united in piety, deeply divided as to the nature of God and the society he envisages. The Jew thinks that God forbids pork and that Jewish obedience to the Law is of the essence of religion. The Muslim has a different law. The Christian worships Christ – to the Jew incredible, to the Muslim blasphemous. I recently chaired a discussion between a Christian Arab, a Muslim Palestinian and a Jewish American on the problem of Israel. It became so bitter, though all three were trying to expound only the religious meaning of their differing positions, that a colleague of mine was moved to remark: 'These damned monotheists have too many gods'. And though bitterness is in large part political here it does reflect a certain divisiveness in the devotions which the faithful pour out to their divine ideal.

And many religious people do not accept the dominance of the mystical, preferring to rely upon the uniqueness of their own religious faith. The logic of Christianity or of Islam for instance ultimately rules out the doctrine of the fundamental unity of all religions as depicted by the Hindu. They specify a unitary goal – not surprisingly people do not, perhaps cannot, agree on what this goal should be. So though recurrences of the mystical and the devotional can be pointed to by those who believe in the unity of religions, the notion of unity seems unworkable as a total belief to guide men towards spiritual harmony.

And is Hinduism really so ideal? Does it not mask poverty and social injustice?

Hindus, caste and society

Truly there is injustice, corruption, starvation and other ugly sides to Hinduism. We should expect it up to a point, for men are not much given to perfection. Even so, it will be argued that one point of a religion or an ideology is to raise men to higher levels of conduct and aspiration than their own nature might warrant one to expect. And it might be argued that Hinduism does not offer spiritual incentives for the reform of an unjust society. There is some truth in all this. But caste, which is the frame for social action and aspiration, has a positive message as well as a negative, dark side. The dark side is hierarchy. The positive side is the provision of a structure of custom and tradition which allows men of startlingly different moral, religious and other beliefs to live in the same society. It makes tolerance, if not always justice, an institution and we should recognise it as containing a possible pattern for the future of an increasingly plural world, in which men of different races, cultures and creeds interpenetrate each other's societies.

Hindu myths

I have stressed the visionary and devotional side of Hinduism, and given some explanation of gurus and caste. But Hinduism is also the religion of multitudinous stories. It is shot through with myth. It is not all philosophy and yoga, *bhakti* and Rāmānuja. It is also more image-conscious, symbol-drenched, story-haunted than, perhaps, any other great religion. It therefore seems appropriate to tell a story or two, and who better than Krishna as the hero of such tales? The story of his life can be found in the great epic, the *Mahābhārata*, and in other collections of myths; his legends rouse some memories and pose some challenges.

Krishna, whose name means 'Black One', was son of Vasudeva, and was born in North India, his mother being Devakī. His elder brother, who shared in a number of his more important exploits, was Balarāma. They were numbers seven and eight of a large family, but all the other siblings were killed by the cruel king Kamsa, who had been told that an offspring of Devakī would usurp his throne. Kamsa ordered a general massacre of children (reminiscent of the New Testament tale of Herod's killing of the innocents), but miraculously Krishna escaped, and was brought up by foster-parents, who were cowherds. His childhood was spent in the meadows by the banks of the river Jumna at Brindāban, now a great centre of the Krishna cult. Many tales are told of his delightful naughtiness – stealing the milk and butter of the *gopīs*, the cowgirls. His parents did not know of his divinity, but once his mother made him open his mouth to see whether he had swallowed some mud, and briefly perceived to her stunned astonishment the three worlds in his throat: heaven, the atmosphere and the earth itself. As he grew towards manhood his pranks and amorous affairs with the milkmaids justified his later title (one among many) of Kanhaiya, or lover of virgins. He maddened them with his handsome looks and magical flute-playing: he loved to steal their clothes when they were bathing, and mingled naughtiness with a cheerful promiscuity.

Not edifying? For the pious Hindu the young Krishna reflects the miracle of childhood and the love of God for the soul. The cowgirls are like men's souls, with whom God dallies and who are maddened thus by love of God. Earthly love is a symbol of divine love.

Kamsa still jealously plotted to kill Krishna, and in a series of adventures Krishna and his brother Balarāma defeated the emissaries of the evil king and finally slew him. However, this led to an attack on Mathurā, near Brindāban, where Krishna was now based, by Kamsa's father-in-law, the king of Magadha. Eventually Krishna had to withdraw to Dvārakā, a city of Gujarat, and now a centre of pilgrimage. Various adventures followed, including participation in the great civil war described in the *Mahābhārata* and in the great battle which served as the backcloth of his teaching in the Gita. On his eventual return to Dvārakā awful omens and portents appeared. The person of Death was seen in the city, haunting households; hurricanes whirled over the city; the animal kingdom was topsy-turvy and camels gave birth to mules, storks hooted like owls, goats bayed like jackals; worms infested food, men became maddened with drink and Krishna's son (by his beloved Rādhā) was murdered in front of him. Rebellion flared, and Krishna fought back, but vainly. He and Balarāma retired to the forest to find peace, where Balarāma died. Sad, Krishna mourned by a river bank, and was shot in the heel by an insouciant hunter who mistook him for a deer. His heel was his vulnerable spot. Dead, he ascended to paradise – glorious, amorous still, yet also tragic.

It is a strange tale and a collage of many things, including perhaps an echo of the death of Achilles – Greek influences in India, after Alexander's invasion, were not negligible. Its symbols and sentiments cover a wide spectrum of human life, and the marvels and miracles scarcely conceal the human side of the godman Krishna. By such legends is the religious imagination of India nourished.

Hinduism's relevance

The Hindu world is so complex, colourful, cheerful and austere that its main messages are hard to discern. But motifs can be picked out. First, that the many gods point to the one reality, and yet at the same time feed different desires and ideals in a plural human world. Second, that the Hindu, though aware of history and rhythms of time, is not too much worried about the historical truth of his myths. Did Krishna really do all those things? The question is not one which seriously arises. What is important is that we can identify with different aspects of his career. Third, that it is the genius of Hinduism to bring together elements arising from its federation of cultures, and that it thinks of itself as prefiguring a new world synthesis. Fourth, that the Hindu spirit is made into stone, wood and clay in a fabulous gallery of images and temples. Its contribution to the art of the world is hard to underestimate. Primitive themes, Greek techniques but above all Hindu and Buddhist traditions of making sculptures and icons have blended in an amazing collage. Fifth, that Hinduism has fervent devotion, to gods like Krishna and Shiva, but also contemplation and yoga. The contrast between the devotee and the yogi is a creative tension throughout India's history. Sixth, that the fabric of Hindu society though in part unjust (what society can escape the accusing finger?) nevertheless manages to tolerate a mosaic of different lifestyles. Seventh, Hinduism is a pioneer of peace, expressed most of all in the life of Gandhi. Of course, there are wars and riots. But Hinduism has absorbed lessons from the Jains and Buddhists, and stressed non-violence and respect, too, for the animal kingdom.

Yet in the end perhaps the greatness and delight of the religion is seen most clearly in places – in the smoky evening in a village in northern Bihar as wiry men come back from the fields; on the floating magic of the Ganges at dawn in Banaras, as men and women wait for the sacred sun to rise; in the labyrinthine temple of Minakshi in Madurai in South India where the green water of the sacred bathing pool dimly reflects the ornate cloisters; on the hill above Mysore, sacred to the gods and rising above the hot tree-dotted plain. Such places where Hindus seek truth assiduously reflect the inner thoughts and hearts of men. The Hindu world fuses the sights of the great land of India and the inner woes and joys of men.

BUDDHISM 2

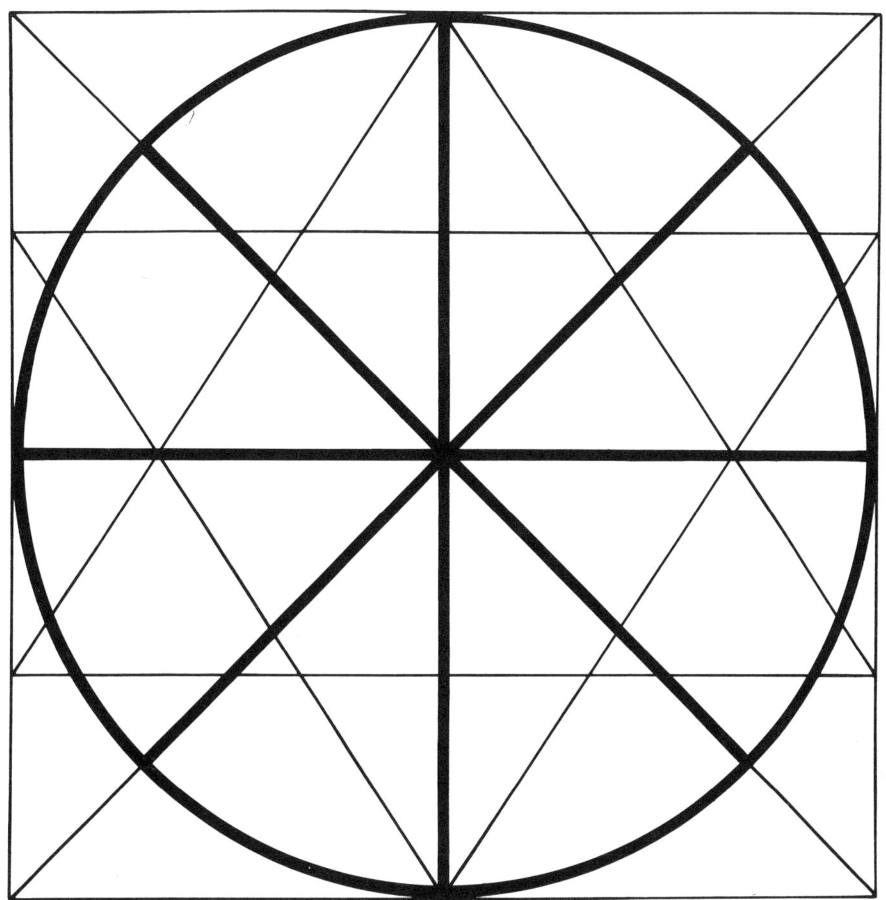

The religion of the Buddha has been enormously effective, and takes many forms. The Buddha himself, who lived perhaps from 563 to 483 BC (I say perhaps because of obscure aspects of the Indian records), was evidently a person of great subtlety, intellectual power, psychological insight and holiness. In due course the religion spread through most of India, and from there into Ceylon, South-East Asia, Central Asia, China, Korea, Japan, Tibet and Mongolia. In this century it has been drastically curtailed in those countries with Marxist governments, but it has begun to make a vital impact in the West.

When Western scholars first encountered Buddhist texts, they tended to look upon Buddhism as an ethical philosophy, rather than a religion in the more popular sense. Philosophy there is in Buddhism, but it is geared to practice, with a view to bringing men to liberation from the round of rebirth. Further, Buddhism would never have been so successful as a missionary enterprise if it did not adapt to the cultures through which it spread. It does not repudiate the local gods and myths, but tempers them and uses them. To understand the spirit of Buddhism it is therefore vital to see how it deals with the gods. We shall begin at that point, and observe Buddhism as a living and rich system of practice. It is also a means of beginning to understand something of the variety of the faith – a variety which is expressed through its differing main movements: the Theravada or Doctrine of the Elders in Sri Lanka and South-East Asia; Mahayana or Greater Vehicle Buddhism in the Far East, and the Diamond Vehicle, sometimes known as Lamaism, in Tibet and Mongolia.

After fifteen hundred years Buddhism faded away in its native India, the final blow being the Muslim invasions. As we have seen it is under pressure in much of the East. Some think its future strangely will lie in the West. How will it adapt to the Western technological and scientific gods?

The Buddha and his message

Some time in the sixth century BC (about the date we cannot be sure) the Buddha achieved enlightenment. It was from that momentous experience that the religion called after him flowed. It not only affected deeply North India, where Gautama the Buddha lived, but spread eventually into most of Asia north and east of the Indian subcontinent. It moved into Central Asia, China, Korea, Japan, Mongolia, Tibet, Burma, Thailand, Cambodia, Laos, Vietnam, Ceylon, and Indonesia. It has left its imprint of tolerance and peace on the civilisations of Asia.

Put simply, the message of the Buddha is this: in order to achieve liberation from the ills of the world you need to tread the Path he trod. Above all, put away the craving for what is in the world that binds you to the round of birth and rebirth. Although Buddhists recognise the basic teachings of Gautama, the freedom he gave his followers to interpret the message has led to splendidly different kinds of Buddhism. But all schools look back to that Indian teacher who acquired the title 'Enlightened One' or Buddha.

We cannot be certain of the truth of the accounts of his life, for they have become overlaid with legend, but the main outline of belief about him is as follows.

He was born, perhaps in 563 BC, son of a chief or king in the foothills of southern Nepal, among the people known as the Sakya, for which reason he was later to be known as Sakyamuni or the Sage of the Sakya. He married and had a son; but already he had come to see something of the suffering and unsatisfactoriness of the world, and he longed to find the secret of liberation from it. Feeling the call to the spiritual life, he slipped away from home, and spent a number of years as a wandering recluse (such seekers after truth can still be seen in India today). Finally, after various experiments, he attained enlightenment and a vision of the true nature of reality, while seated beneath a tree, the so-called Bo Tree, at a place called Bodh Gaya in North India. As a consequence he went to Banaras, holy city on the Ganges, where some other recluses with whom he had associated were gathered. In the deer park there he preached his first sermon. He continued travelling, teaching the truth, the Dharma, and gaining disciples. His mission went on into old age: he died at the age of eighty not far from his birthplace. He left behind him the Sangha or order of monks

Continued on page 59

TEMPLES

Men do not just house themselves: they also house their gods. Often sacred buildings are lavish and glorious, as a way of saying something about divine majesty – as with many a Hindu temple or Gothic cathedral. The temple sometimes is seen as a meeting point between heaven and earth, hence the idea of height is often stressed. Also it is a sacred space set apart from the rest of the world – even in the plainest Protestant chapels there would be resistance to worldly activities, and it would scarcely be thought right, say, to play billiards in a church building. The temple is thus both heavenly and screened off, in such a way that it becomes the proper place for the enacting of the sacred dramas of religion, such as the Eucharist.

The mosque is, like the synagogue, less a home for sacraments than a congregational meeting place. It ranges from the splendid beauties of Mughal architecture in India to very simple structures, as in buildings used in England for the Islamic community. Here something of the variety of Islam is seen: this West African mosque attests to a grandiose conception in local style. It also shows how Islam is making itself at home in sub-Saharan Africa, riding down the trade-routes across the Sahara from the Muslim shore of the Mediterranean.

The building of St Peter's cost a fortune and a Reformation, for it was partly revolt over the selling of indulgences to pay for the basilica that sparked off the upheaval. Luther's doctrines spread widely through northern Europe and signalled a return (as at least it was seen) to New Testament values. Simplicity often replaced pomp. This Lutheran church in Norway is eloquent on this score – yet it retains the spire, northern Europe's chief symbol of aspiration towards heaven.

Left: The architectural centre of Catholicism, and at one time of all Western Christendom. St Peter's expresses both faith and the Renaissance – in short it shows forth the continuity between Roman civilisation and Christianity. The approach to it also reminds us of the grandiose architectural style of Mussolini. But for all the criticisms that might be levelled at the pomp of Rome, St Peter's remains the focus of great devotion, and its very scale symbolises the awesome responsibilities of the Pope, Vicar of Christ.

The Golden Temple at Amritsar is the headquarters of the Sikh faith. It is a blend of both Hindu and Muslim motifs – note the golden domes, characteristic of Mughal architecture in which Indian and Islamic ideas merge. It thus shows forth in stone the spirit of Sikhism, which tried to cut through the differences separating Hindu and Muslim, and yet ironically ended up as a third faith, acquiring the outer symbolisms to show its apartness.

The architecture of Eastern Orthodoxy is more mysterious than much of that of Western Christendom. The golden and blue domes (seen, left, at the famous monastery at Zagorsk in Russia) point to heaven, but seem too to enclose heavily the space below – for it is inside the church that heaven is really to be found, in the divine Liturgy.

If Zagorsk encloses liturgy, synagogues above all enshrine talk – the talk about the Law which is the great preoccupation of the Jewish tradition. The synagogue is a community talking-place, in which words mediate the relationship between God and man. Here a Paris building shows clearly that the synagogue rarely is altogether grandiose. It often, as here, has the style of a meeting hall.

The Church of Jesus Christ of the Latter Day Saints, otherwise known as the Mormon Church, always paid much attention to sacred buildings – the temples in Kirtland, Ohio, and Nauvoo, Illinois (scenes of their early and ill-fated settlements) testify to this. But the crowning architectural expression of the faith is to be seen in Salt Lake City, that promised land which the faithful reached after their long trek westward under the leadership of Brigham Young. Somehow the building reflects the closed nature of the faith and yet also mysteriously its missionary ambitions.

Here is a good blend of motifs in Buddhism and Hinduism. The style of this temple is Hindu, but the spirit is Buddhist. The towers represent artificial mountains – for the mountain is a symbol of the way to heaven and the transcendent world. Below the main tower is a small stupa, or reliquary. One function of temples is to house sacred objects, and relics are one means whereby Buddhism celebrates its great men.

and nuns who would carry on his message. By his enlightenment and his final decease he was liberated from the world and would no longer be reborn in the round of reincarnation to which living beings are subject. That, briefly, was the Buddha's life.

The Buddha diagnosed the world's ills. I use the term 'diagnosis' deliberately, for the original teaching of the Buddha, the Four Noble Truths, was cast in the form of a diagnosis and prescription, in accord with ancient Indian medical usage. First, you see what the illness is, then you enunciate the cause of the illness, then you consider if there is a means of removing the cause, and then if there is such a cure, you formulate the prescription for it.

In the first of the Four Noble Truths, the Buddha states our trouble: that everything is *dukkha* or 'illfare' (to coin a word – the term in Buddhism means the opposite of *sukha* or welfare). The second truth gives the cause of this condition: our craving for the world and for good things, all of which contrive to disappoint us, but bind us further to the world. The third truth states that there is a way of removing craving. The fourth, that this means of removing craving is the Noble Eightfold Path, which leads to nirvana.

The Eightfold Path

The Path as preached by Gautama has eight elements and these can be put into three groups. One has to do with attitudes; another has to do with moral behaviour; and the third has to do with the contemplative life. In order to start the quest, one needs right views and right aspiration – these are the first two elements of the Path. Thus the disciple needs a preliminary understanding of the Buddha's teaching, for example the Four Truths; he also needs to aspire towards the higher life. A preliminary trust in the view of the world taught by the Buddha will be verified in experience. That is why Theravada Buddhism claims to be a 'come-and-see' religion. Each man can see for himself, once he treads the Path. The major difference between the saint who sees for himself and the Buddha is that the Buddha discovered the Way (or rediscovered it, for there were previous Buddhas in ages gone by), rather as Einstein discovered Relativity Theory, although many graduates in physics can come to understand it and see its truth.

The next three elements are: right speech, right action and right livelihood. The emphasis on speech shows how important Buddhism considers it to be not just truthful but economical and harmless in the use of one's tongue. The need for right livelihood arises from the fact that some occupations are necessarily in conflict with Buddhist values: those jobs involving bloodshed, the sale of intoxicants, prostitution, and so on. Sometimes the moral aspect of Buddhism is summed up in the so-called Five Precepts, which indicate that the good man should refrain from stealing, killing, wrong sexual behaviour, wrong use of speech and the use of drugs or intoxicants. In addition to these five precepts which apply to everyone, monks are supposed to follow a further five, which control their daily lives in a pattern of austere poverty.

The other parts of the Path are: right effort, right awareness and right concentration. These are of the essence of the Buddhist life, for they represent aspects of meditation. Briefly they amount to the striving to eliminate bad mental states, the cultivation of self-awareness at all times, and the practice of the higher stages of contemplation. This last part of the Path is vital, and later I shall try to indicate something of its character. But meanwhile let us note that the main term used in Pali for one of these stages of meditation is *jhāna*. In Sanskrit the term is *dhyāna*. When the faith moved to China, the Chinese tried to reproduce the Sanskrit sound as *ch'ān*. In turn when Buddhism migrated to Japan the Japanese represented the Chinese *ch'ān* as zen. So Zen Buddhism is literally meditation Buddhism, and though the methods differ greatly from those in Sri Lanka, yet at either end of the Buddhist world of Asia we see the same adherence to the central value of contemplation as the means of liberation.

Buddhism and God

For many people in the West, Buddhism is a puzzle, for unlike Christianity, Judaism and Islam it does not demand belief in God. It does promise a kind of salvation, but this salvation does not depend upon a Creator. Although, in Mahayana Buddhism, there is belief in heavenly Buddhas who are to be worshipped, meditation, not worship, is the essence of Buddhist religious practice; and it is meditation without God. Though the Buddhist teaching can be reduced to a brief set of principles, such as the Four Noble Truths and the Noble Eightfold Path, which I have just described, it is rich in religious legend, myth, ritual, parable, and imagery. Thus if we read the Pali scriptures – the records of the faith written in the Pali language and regarded as normative in Theravada Buddhism – we get a strange perspective on the person who in our age (for other ages had other Buddhas) taught the liberating doctrine.

In these scriptures the Buddha is not God, but he is not just a man either. His life is shot through with strange and magical occurrences. Before his birth he descended from a heaven, the Tushita heaven, and entered into the womb of his mother Queen Maya in Kapilavastu among, as we have seen, the Sakya people. His arrival on earth was fixed for a time when it was ripe to preach the liberating Dharma, for from time to time, when living beings need it, Buddhas come to restore the true teaching. And when, seated under the Bo Tree, he gained his great vision all nature seemed to reverberate with awe and joy. There were, as well, portents and signs at other great junctures of his life and at his death. There is a transcendent aspect to the Buddha's nature that eludes the full understanding of men. He is thus entitled not just the Buddha, but the Tathagata or 'Thus-gone', one who has gone beyond ordinary human existence. He is also seen as the Jina or Conqueror, who has overcome the sufferings of the world. Though he is not God he is referred to as 'beyond the gods'.

The Buddha taught in a milieu of religious movements, including many which were to enter later into the make-up of classical Hinduism. He contended with, among others, Brahmins, the custodians of an ancient sacred tradition orientated towards the gods, including the great creator Brahmā. In the Buddhist scriptures even he takes second place to the Buddha: he may think himself creator, but this is an illusion. Buddhism deflates the gods with irony. In modern times the Christian God is treated by Theravadins with reserve and scepticism. Thus K. N. Jayatilleke, a noted philosopher of modern Ceylon, could argue that Freud was right to see the

Western God as a projection of the father-figure; he thought the Buddhist need not take such a God with too much seriousness. It is easy for Christians or other believers in a personal God to feel hurt by such disdain; but it is easy, too, to miss the reason for the Buddhist preoccupation with other matters. The Buddha did not deny the religion of others, but instead insisted that the Dharma, the Truth, should dominate, even if men otherwise retained their customs and beliefs.

Is Buddhism pessimistic?

The Buddha's teaching about suffering and dissatisfaction has struck a number of Westerners on first coming to Buddhism as being pessimistic. Does not Buddhism tend to negate the world, to take a negative attitude to the good things about us?

Pessimism means being unrealistically gloomy. It is not pessimistic to say that in a world where there is tooth decay, dentists are needed. It is not pessimistic to say that we all die, for indeed we all do die. By contrast, if I think that whatever I do I shall be sick and poor, that most likely is pessimistic. If I think there is bound to be no cure ever for cancer, that too is pessimism. So we need to judge the Buddha's message by the following test: Is his diagnosis of the world's ills – the basic teaching I have described – realistic?

The Buddha's skill

The Buddha is not portrayed in the scriptures as the great Teacher, though they certainly describe him as that: he is also the skilful diplomat and perceptive psychologist. He does not try to ride over men's concerns roughshod. This idea of dealing with men's cultural and psychological condition lies behind Buddhism's toleration of and taming of the gods. There is a key term in Buddhism which means 'skill in means', and it represents the idea that the faith needs to be adapted to the condition of those with whom it comes in contact. At the individual level it means that Gautama had knowledge of men's motives and constitution. At the cultural level it means that Buddhism spreads gently, not by destroying the gods but by making use of them. The commanding heights of a Buddhist society must be occupied by the Teaching, but men can retain their beliefs and customs, which then become subtly changed by the Buddhist environment. It is a method of mission which has proved highly effective throughout Asia. Today, in Sri Lanka, which preserves many aspects of early Buddhism, we can see something of this tolerance.

The gods in Sri Lanka

Ceylon, a strategically placed island, has always been liable to invasion. Indeed the Sinhala, who are the majority on the island, and who largely practise Buddhism, themselves originally came by sea from India. The second largest element in the population, the Hindu Tamils, came across the straits from India's deep south. In more modern times, the Portuguese came, as such names as Fernando and de Silva, frequent now in Ceylon, amply testify. Then came the Dutch, who built canals and developed trade. And finally the ubiquitous British who not only managed to control the coastal plains like their predecessors but also conquered the highland kingdom of Kandy. Through all this Buddhism survived successfully, especially in the mountains, and continued to give shape and spiritual substance to Sinhalese culture. The white temples scattered through the green landscape, the cave temples, the ancient cities of Anuradhapura and Polonarruwa, the monuments of Kandy – all these are eloquent of a deep-rooted Buddhist civilisation. Although more than two thousand years have passed since the Buddhist Dharma came to the island, the monks have maintained, first by oral tradition and then by writing, the scriptural norm. More importantly they have also kept up the tradition of meditation and preaching to the ordinary people. Monks, meditation and morals – these in a way seem to be the essence of the Buddhist faith. The Order or Sangha indeed flourishes; in monasteries and hermitages the higher reaches of consciousness are explored; the people are instructed. But there is much else. For one thing, there are the gods. In the complex of buildings which make up most Buddhist temples you will find one building devoted to the gods. Buddhist culture accepts them. Astrology persists, and spells to ward off evil – monks chant parts of the Pali canon, scriptures used for anxious ends in partly magical disguise. There are great processions to parade the Buddha-tooth, an efficacious relic kept in the so-called Temple of the Tooth in Kandy. It seems as if monks, meditation and morals are surrounded by a cloud of gods and magic. That cloud can tell us a lot about the nature of Buddhism. What, then, is to be made of the gods so hospitably entertained within the ambit of Buddhism? Perhaps the most popular and powerful of the gods these days is Kataragama, in the south-east part of the island, where annually at the chief festival men walk on fire and daily pilgrims come from all over the island. Indeed the god's popularity has been greatly enhanced by the buses, of which Ceylon has more per capita than any comparable country in the world. Poor people, cabinet ministers, students, even sometimes monks (who strictly should not) make the trip, and bathe in the little river below the temple before attending the service, loud with jangling bells. For everyday crises and the pursuit of the goods of this world, the god is thought to be powerful. So it is useful to make offerings to him. The student who wishes to pass an examination, the trader about to do a deal, or the young man soon to marry may gain something from Kataragama. Yet for more spiritual benefits, for serenity and liberation, it is to the Buddha's teaching that the faithful turn. Such at any rate is the distinction usually made by the Sinhalese when they wish to explain the relationship between the gods and the Buddha. They express an important point about the gods, which Westerners could apply to their own secular deities. The point can be seen through an analogy.

If the gods are like a stretch of luxuriant jungle, then the attitude of Islam and Christianity as missionary religions is that the jungle must be cleared so that the single tree of the one true God can be planted. The Hindu by contrast thinks of the trees as divine, so that by wandering through the jungle you may indeed come across the one true tree. For the Buddha, the eightfold path which leads to nirvana runs by, but not through, the jungle. You can wander in the jungle if you wish, but it does not bring you onward to liberation, and it may delay your spiritual progress. So the Buddha does not deny the gods. They are psychic forces which impinge upon men, and symbols of men's worldly hopes. But they must take second place to the true search, which is for release from the round of rebirth and the ills of the world.

Buddhist meditation is supposed to bring peace and insight. Such elements are essential to nirvana, and thus to freedom from the round of rebirth. Buddhist meditation aims for a state where there is no consciousness of anything else, a kind of blissful unity, but not a union with anything, even God, 'out there'. It is a form of yoga, or purification of the mind, but it is not a conscious relationship to anything or anyone. The Buddhist sees such contemplation as bringing the highest peace and is no longer concerned with individuality, whether it be the worries of his own ego or the need to enter into communion with the supreme individual, namely God. Enlightenment itself is, if you like, divine, and from it flows serenity and wisdom; there is, thus, in the higher Buddhist experience, no need to bring in God. Under the guidance of the Buddha's teaching we can, by following the Path, achieve our own liberation.

Thus Buddhism does not focus on the idea of a God, and proceeds from a different root from those religions which express the thunderous majesty of the object of worship.

Buddhist meditation in the Theravada

Looked at from one point of view, and in the simplest manner, meditation is a way of stilling the mind. Just try closing your eyes for a moment. Now try to shut out the ordinary thoughts and pictures running through your mind. Just let it go blank. You know what begins to happen? All sorts of stray ideas crop up willy-nilly. Try it with your eyes open and you are even worse off, and worse still if the radio is on. The fact of the matter is that we are all of us trained from the very earliest days of our lives to organise things round about us, to give them names, to see them in a special way. I cannot look out of my window at a tree without thinking of it as a tree, and in particular as a holly or a willow. We impose our active minds upon the world. But does the holly think of itself as a holly or the willow classify itself as willow? The world around us just is: our classifications are conventional and convenient, to us. In a way the Buddhist ideal is to break down all our names for things and the cloud of words which we impose on reality. They distort, however useful they may be. So it is that because I use the word 'I' I came to think there is a permanent I; and so it is that I carve up the seamless fabric of nature about me. This project of breaking through language and thought is a bold and arduous one. That is why it is necessary to adopt techniques of concentration, and why you may need the guidance of a spiritual master. You cannot get it from reading a book, though you may learn from a book why it is you cannot get it from a book. To climb Everest you need to be a mountaineer, but at least a map can tell you where it is. So in trying to indicate something of the nature of Buddhist meditation here, I can only try to point in the right direction.

The stages of meditation

The idea of Theravadin meditation is not, as we have noted, communion with God; but this does not mean that it is merely a negative operation, though there is a certain dazzling blankness about pure consciousness, so reports testify. It is not even a very individual quest. Buddhists, some poems apart, are not too much interested in autobiography, and the texts on meditation are almost clinical in their detachment, and have a rather pleasing air of efficiency. So let us briefly look at the eight stages of *jhāna* as depicted in the Theravadin tradition.

It is an eightfold path of its own kind – Buddhist texts are fond of grouping things by numbers. But instead of being in three sections, like the Eightfold Path, the *jhānas* essentially fall into two groups of four. The first four deal with the realm of form, and the next four deal with the formless. What does this mean?

Only that in the first group the person meditating is still concerned with worldly appearances, with the colours and forms that he perceives around him. As we shall see, he is only so concerned in a highly restricted way. In the formless stages, however, he leaves even this restricted concern behind him. He goes beyond the visible into a more abstract dimension. But first, let us attend to the meditator in the realm of form. He should seat himself in a pleasant and quiet place, which is free from distractions. Within easy reach he places before himself what is called a device, namely an aid to meditation – a simple object such as a blue flower or a circle of clay. He now concentrates on the blue shape in front of him, and gradually excludes all other sensations and thoughts. He gradually comes to lose himself in the blue shape, and the first four stages represent more and more refined successes in producing the image of the patch of blue in his consciousness at will, and smoothly, so that the process, requiring great effort at the beginning, becomes effortless. All this prepares the way for the next four stages.

In these, certain formulas are used. In the first of the formless stages, the meditator repeats to himself, 'It is all infinite space'. The words repeated internally help him to remove from his consciousness all visible forms. The blue flower and all other images dissolve, and the world is pictured as just empty, just space. But in conceiving reality thus, the meditator may be aware of his own consciousness contemplating the blankness of space. So the next formula is 'It is all infinite consciousness', and the words help him to subtract from his mind even the blank space, so that nothing is left but consciousness, not even differentiated into his own and others – there is just one boundless consciousness. But even this highly refined state is not enough. The next formula, at stage three of the formless *jhānas*, is 'There is nothing'. Here even the preceding tenuous awareness of consciousness is supposed to disappear. Finally the adept reaches the top stage, known as the stage of neither perception nor non-perception, where the individual though vigorously awake and alert rises beyond all the distinctions, however tenuous, which the mind may make. Even the thought that there is nothing is transcended.

It sounds blank, like a dreamless sleep, and that image has been used in mystical writings, notably in the Upanishads; but if darkness it is dazzling, like the cloud of unknowing and the dazzling brightness of the soul to which Christian mystics have alluded. It is supposed in its own mysterious way to bring the saint into a state of insight into the Transcendent. It is a foretaste of the bliss of nirvana. If indeed there is a realm beyond the world, then it is logical that the mind should try to reach it by emptying itself of all worldly images and thoughts; and if that process can seem from our point of view negative, it is undertaken on a positive assumption:

Continued on page 71

PRIESTS

Religions have their professionals. The priest or monk is one who is ordained to serve the faith through ritual and other kinds of expertise. Though the priest is expected to live a life somewhat apart from other men, and to maintain certain standards of holiness, his authority comes primarily not from the quality of his person, but rather from the community who commission him to perform the relevant sacred acts.

Followers of Amos Shembe, leader of an African Zionist movement, listen to his preaching. His brother, Moses Shembe, was the prophet. The death of a prophet creates the need for a priestly successor.

Traditionally, Catholic priests have heard confession, a means whereby guilt is dealt with before God. Above, in Communist Poland faithful folk line up to have the priest listen to their expressions of sin and contrition. The confessional box is meant to serve the aim of anonymity.

Again, the priest has special authority in regard to the sacraments. Above all in Catholicism he mediates God through the communion, the Mass. Below, he administers communion.

Strictly speaking, Islam has no priests. Yet there are those specially trained to teach. Here in Turkey an imam addresses the faithful (men) in a mosque, expounding the message of the Koran. Islam does not have priests as such because the relation between Allah and man is direct and does not need mediation other than that found in the holy Koran.

There is an echo of the Islamic emphasis, right, where a Swedish pastor preaches to the congregation. The pulpit is rather gloriously decorated, symbolising the vitality of the Gospel which the pastor has authority to preach. Still, Swedish Lutheranism also retains much of the outward air of Catholicism, even if the centre of gravity has shifted. Because the pastor is professionally a preacher much care is taken to ensure a long and thorough education as the basis of his priestly expertise.

MINI

However, theology is not everything. Shinto has its own special rituals and priests, but is remarkably unconcerned with any kind of systematic theology. It lies at the opposite end to Protestant Christianity.

that pure consciousness can tell us about what transcends our usual experience.

The meditator, having reached the bright summit of the *jhānas*, comes down them, as down a ladder, till he reaches the ground again; and he lives now in the dusty plains with a refreshing easeful awareness and memory of the insight-giving peaks of consciousness.

Other things to do

Perhaps the *jhānas* are not for everyone. But Buddhism is full of other helpful exercises, such as dividing up the world in one's mind's eye into the four quarters and thinking in turn of the living beings inhabiting each and suffusing them with compassion. And in daily living there is the practice of mindfulness or self-awareness (the seventh element in the Eightfold Path) through which one practises continuous knowledge of one's own bodily and mental states. More grimly, there is the practice of meditating in the charnel ground where bodies are burnt, to remind oneself of the pervasiveness of death and impermanence. Or again one can in one's mind analyse oneself or other human beings into the various physical constituents, in order to overcome too great a sense of charm in the delights of the body.

In brief, the Buddha set forth a way to purify life and consciousness so that one might ultimately overcome the illfare implicit in the world and prolonged through the ceaseless round of rebirth (ceaseless, that is, unless one took the right action). In all of this he underpinned his teaching with subtle analysis of the human condition and a wealth of illustrative teaching.

Indra and Brahma

To some extent the irony with which the Buddha created the notion of a supreme Being stemmed from a scepticism about that kind of religion presented by a privileged priesthood, and Buddhism although hospitable to popular gods emerges as a kind of enlightened atheism. But one needs too to see meditation, as a means of liberation, against the background of belief in rebirth or reincarnation.

Buddhist rebirth theory

At the popular level, joys and sorrows, luck and disasters can be explained through rebirth. If a person does well, most likely he did good in a previous life. If a man falls seriously ill, then probably that is a consequence of some prior evil deed. These ideas still prevail in many countries, and give a kind of rational explanation of the vicissitudes and injustices of this life. The Buddha's doctrine went beyond such popular ideas, but before we consider the subtleties of his teaching let us glance at the cosmic scene against which the dramas of rebirth, as individuals wander from one life to another, are enacted.

The belief that a person may be reborn of course includes the idea that he can be reborn in a different form. Thus he might be a god in the next life, entering some celestial realm, such as the Tushita heaven from which the Buddha descended to earth (for he too had wandered through countless previous lives), and where the future Buddha Maitreya dwells. He might be reborn as a human being, though one passage in the Pali scriptures makes out that that is unlikely for a long time to come. If a blind turtle living at the bottom of the ocean rises to the surface once every hundred years, and if floating on the surface is a wooden yoke, the chance of his coming up within the yoke is about the same as a person's chance of being reborn as a human being. A person can be reborn as an animal or lower form of life, such as an insect. Or worse he may reappear as a ghost, or even worse go to one of the hells or purgatories through which individuals work off the deadliest sins. According to this picture our destiny is determined by our deeds, by karma. But whether one is in the bliss of heaven or the pains of purgatory, the state is not permanent. In due course the god-like person will descend to earth and the tormented individual rise up out of purgatory. Everything is in flux, and the only way the changes from life to life will stop is through attaining final liberation. It is only then that the flame of desire which burns living beings will go out. It is only then that the bonds which tie us to existence will be broken. So it is against this scene of rebirth or reincarnation that the aim of Buddhist meditation is to be understood.

The picture of an immense seething and changing universe in which individuals migrate from life to life at all levels of existence is reinforced in traditional Buddhism by the belief that there are many world systems (other galaxies as it were), each like our own and each replete with heavens, hells, worlds and Buddhas. The virtually infinite scale of the universe in space, with its innumerable world systems, is matched by its virtual endlessness in time. The universe expands and contracts over vast ages called kalpas, each millions of years long. The great ages roll on, almost defying human imagination. The whole vast and daunting picture appealed strongly to the Indian imagination, and the Buddhist cosmology was taken up into traditional Hinduism.

Of course, we are not certain how much of this picture was in the mind of the Buddha, and how much it has been expanded, but certainly from early times Buddhism has conceived of rebirth and karma against some such cosmological backcloth. Others of his time may have had similar ideas, but the Buddha gave a rather special analysis both of the individual and of rebirth. Though adept at parable and no doubt charismatic in his presence, what strikes one above all is the original philosophical stamp he gave to the system of salvation he discovered.

Rebirth and the soul

It is easy in one way to think of reincarnation as a matter of the soul leaving one body at death and migrating into a new one. That, roughly speaking, was what a number of religious thinkers of the Buddha's time believed. Suppose my son George was Winston Churchill in a previous life: does this not mean that there is a soul which survives from the one life to the other, first of all occupying Churchill's body and then now my son's? How can we say that Churchill and my son are the same person unless there is something which carries over, a single soul which exists in the two different individuals? This is why in the West the doctrine of rebirth has sometimes been called transmigration and sometimes metempsychosis (from the Greek). The idea of transmigration implies that there is something permanent which transmigrates, while metempsychosis means, literally, the transfer of the soul (into another body). But the Buddha taught differently. This was partly because he saw, in his Enlightenment, that nothing in the world is permanent, that all is shifting and transitory. (That is one reason why nothing can give true, permanent satisfaction, except nirvana.) In consequence there is no permanent soul – the Buddha was very insistent on the dangers, both intellectual and moral, of belief in the soul – and thus nothing which can migrate from one body to the next. (Incidentally as there could be no eternal soul, so there could be no eternal God behind the universe.) These ideas he summed up in the teaching known as the three marks of all existence: everything is impermanent; everything is without eternal soul; and everything is full of dissatisfaction (the term is also commonly translated 'suffering', but this goes beyond the Buddha's intention).

All this made the Buddha's doctrine of rebirth original. There is no permanent me: just a swirl of events conventionally referred to by my name. When this swirl of events ceases, then a new swirl will begin, in some other form. Death therefore merely marks the boundary of a particular bundle of impermanent events. But the actions which have taken place during the swirling onwards of my life will generate new events in the future, and that is what is meant by rebirth or reincarnation. What occurs between one life and the next is, after all, similar to what occurs within what we regard as one life.

When a man first comes into the world he is a tiny baby bearing little resemblance to the grown adult. What connects them is that the baby events give rise to child events, the child events to youth events, and so on. The very substances of the body are changed over. Only the form and the connection of causes remain. So similarly, though after death a person's form may change, there is a continuity in the operation of causes. And the name given to the law governing those causes is karma. Nothing, then, carries over. This was the difficult and original doctrine of the Buddha. In many ways the Buddha's analysis is in accord with modern science, for physics sees the apparently solid and durable table or tree as a cloud of short-lived events. This cosmological and metaphysical aspect of Buddhism, together with its subtle psychology, leads modern Buddhists to see in their ancient tradition a great anticipation of modern science. Be that as it may, the Buddha's teaching on impermanence and karma was not just of theoretical significance, it also provided the practical underpinning of his method of liberation.

Nirvana as the goal

If the individual is just a bundle of events, then, when all such events cease, we can speak no more about the individual. This is why the Buddha himself and every Buddhist saint (*arhant*) who attains nirvana eludes further description. That is why the Buddha is 'Thus-gone' – we can point in the direction in which he went, but we can no longer say anything about him. Strictly speaking the woman in Sri Lanka who goes into the statue room of a temple and lays flowers as an offering in front of the great statue of the Buddha is not worshipping the Buddha or entering into relationship with him, for he is no longer an individual to be addressed in praise and prayer. Yet though nirvana seems, from our side of it, a kind of extinction, positive things can be said about it. For nirvana is not just what occurs as the saint or Buddha finally breathes his last. It is also what occurs at and beyond the moment when enlightenment is realised here and now in this life. Thus when the Buddha gained Enlightenment beneath the Bo Tree he gained nirvana, living liberation and the assurance of continued serenity and insight for the rest of his earthly career. Thus the beauties of liberation can be seen in the peaceful, blissful, wise behaviour of the saints. Something of this is expressed in one of the early Buddhist poems:

> While the wind blows sweet and cool
> As I sit upon the mountain top
> I'll break up the power of ignorance
> In the flowery wood and in the cool cave:
> I'll enjoy myself on Mount Giribajja,
> Ecstatic at the gaining of release.
> My purposes are granted like
> The moon on the fifteenth day.
> I have rid myself of spiritual poisons,
> And now there will be no more rebirth.

We picture here a monk who has been dwelling in the forest on a mountain side, no doubt near enough a village so that he could beg for his food daily. And there too no doubt he would preach the saving doctrine, and men might see from his mien that he had indeed thrown off the poisons of selfishness and sensuality, and of grasping and ignorance, and had gained a deep and abiding understanding of reality and its impermanent nature.

The notion that the saint is liberated already in this life is part of a wider Indian tradition, that of *jīvanmukti*, meaning 'living release'. The yogi who has gained supreme clarity of consciousness and is assured of no more rebirth is held to be saved already in this life; he awaits only for his decease, and his life is like a potter's wheel which spins on even when no more force is being applied to it by the potter. The saint is like an engine running down, with no more karmic fuel to keep it going.

On this side of final nirvana, it can, as we have noted, seem like extinction. Why should one strive for that? If nirvana means the loss of individual being, its achievement is the opposite of self-fulfilment, and is it not natural and right that a person should fulfil himself? Does not nirvana amount to some kind of spiritual suicide? The Buddha's answer is simple, yet subtle. If I still struggle for survival as me then I have not gained true peace. If I have gained true peace I shall not worry about the future. But this does not mean that the saint chooses the opposite of life, or rejects it. He is on the Middle Path, the path between affirming life and rejecting it. As for suicide, here is another poem from the *Songs of the Elders*, the *Theragāthā*:

> A quarter of a century ago
> I left the world, but not even for a moment
> Like a snap of my fingers did I know
> True peace. In despair at the lack of purpose
> And still gripped by sensuality, I left
> My cell. Should I take up the knife or not?
> What's the use of living? Rejecting the discipline,

How should a man like me die?
Taking the razor, I sat on the seat
And the razor was poised to slit my vein.
It was then that insight arose in me.
The danger was vivid, and distaste for the world
Entered into me. My mind was liberated.
I see the essential truth of the Dhamma,
And so the Buddha's teaching has been realised.

So suicide is as wrong as clinging to this life. Hence there was some dispute during the Vietnam war when monks and nuns burned themselves in protest. A wise monk of Ceylon, when asked about it, replied: 'It is better to burn oneself than to burn others.' In brief, nirvana is not suicide and only perhaps seems like it to those who are still on this shore. It is a cause of calm joy to those who have crossed the river of life.

The spread of Buddhism

The inspiration of the Sage of the Sakyas gave an impulse to the Sangha, the order of monks that he founded, which bore great missionary fruit. Perhaps in its early days in North India, in the regions round Banaras and Patna, it was assisted by a growing urban prosperity. Princes and merchants helped the faith, by granting facilities to the monks and nuns. It may have been helped by the relative lack of strength of the Brahmins in the region, compared with the Aryan heartland to the north-west of modern Delhi. Further, it may be that the Buddha latched on to something of earlier tradition, a Buddhism before the Buddha, so to say. Thus the cult of cairnlike monuments, later developed into the stupa of the Buddhist temple, seems to have pre-existed Gautama, but to have been taken up by his followers, and certainly Gautama did not claim, precisely, to be the founder of the faith but rather the rediscoverer of an ancient truth. But there can be little doubt that the main agent of the spread of the faith, as virtually always through its history, was the Sangha, which symbolised by example and impressed by preaching, and drew on the respect of the masses for the sincere holy man who could see beyond the world and could transmit merit to those who saluted him and gave him food and water.

It spread along the Ganges and westwards to the Indian ocean. From the coasts it migrated to Ceylon, the first great Buddhist missionary endeavour beyond the land mass of India itself. Much later the sea routes could carry the faith to Burma and South-East Asia, down as far as Java, and even up to the coasts of China. But its most significant route was to the north-west, up into Afghanistan and beyond, where it came into contact with the rich cultures of Central Asia athwart the silk route into China and west to the Roman world. In the first century AD it had begun to percolate into China, and would thus be carried into those areas where Chinese civilisation was influential – Vietnam to the south, Korea to the east and across the sea to Japan, where it retains to this day a strong presence. So Buddhism was destined to embrace Asia with two arms. The one, the Theravadin arm, went round through the southern lands as far as Vietnam; the Mahayana arm circled round through the north and came to meet the Theravada beyond the bounds of China.

The great emperor Aśoka, ruler of most of northern India some three centuries after the Buddha's decease, patronised the faith; guilty at the massacre of his enemies in a bloody campaign in Eastern India, against the Kalinga, he embraced the ethic of non-violence so far as his position permitted. In recognition of the truth of the Buddha's message he sent missionaries in various directions, including his younger relative Mahinda to Sri Lanka. He sent some in the direction of Europe, but though Buddhism was to be spectacularly successful in Asia, little came of the Western contacts. Only in the twentieth century has it made real headway in the West.

The rise of Mahāyāna

Already in the time of Aśoka, those tendencies which were to coalesce into that kind of Buddhism known as the Great Vehicle or Mahāyāna were beginning to show themselves. Although other traditions were carried East, it was predominantly the Great Vehicle which flooded East Asia. There it too, in accord with the Buddha's attitude of skill in means, was to develop further.

Of the schools of the so-called Lesser Vehicle, the Theravada remains the living survivor, while a variant on Mahāyāna Buddhism, the Diamond Vehicle, later on came to permeate the culture of Tibet and the Mongolias. Today, because types of totalitarian Marxism, impatient of older religions, have for various reasons, both good and bad, come to dominate the lands of the Diamond Vehicle and much of the territory of the Mahāyāna in China and its neighbours, it is to Japan largely that we must look for the living messages of the Great Vehicle. The countries of the Theravada such as Cambodia and Laos have also been overrun by revolutions indifferent or hostile to the Buddha's message. But it is unwise to forget that the Great Vehicle played a formative and creative role in most of the civilisations of East Asia, and left a powerful imprint upon India and the cultures influenced by that civilisation.

The Mahāyāna was called so because those who espoused its ideals thought that it was a greater, wider means to salvation than the narrower conceptions of the more conservative monastic schools – that is, those who like the Theravadins tended to think that salvation was chiefly, even exclusively, reserved for monks. The Mahāyāna gave a new perspective on lay participation in Buddhism, and though undoubtedly much Great Vehicle teaching moves far beyond the original Buddhism of the Buddha, much of its vitality is due to that early teaching. (Though we must remember that much is guesswork about what is earlier and what is later: the ancient history of a religion more than two and a half thousand years old, whose traditions were handed down for a number of centuries orally, must necessarily be a matter of speculation.)

The Buddha image: a lesson

One of the impulses lying behind the formation of the Great Vehicle can be seen in the image of the Buddha. Perhaps the most striking aspect of Buddhist art and piety are Buddha-statues, often of transcendental beauty, like the wonderful sandstone carvings of Mathura and Sarnath. At Sarnath, just outside Banaras, and near the deer park where the Buddha preached his first sermon, there is a museum. Though

Continued on page 88

HOLY TIMES

Just as religions so frequently separate off places as holy, like places of pilgrimage and church or temple buildings, so too there are times of holy significance, whether it be the Sabbath or festivals. During such holy times men and women may have to undergo special purification. At any rate holy times recreate the great events expressed in the stories of a faith – for example, the Sabbath reminds us of the seventh day of the creation, the day when God rested; while Easter recreates Christ's rising from the dead.

Here Greek Orthodox worshippers carry an icon in procession to commemorate the Annunciation, virtually the first act in the amazing drama of the incarnation, when Mary is told of the great honour she is to undergo, because to her will be born the saviour of the world.

Islam chose Friday as its weekly special day. Here the faithful are to be seen in festive mood on a Friday outside Delhi's most famous and popular mosque, the Jama Masjid.

Buddhism from one point of view is a philosophy with a vital ethical outreach. But it is also a method of persuasion, to help folk on the path to liberation. Part of that persuasion has to do with festivals and worship, in which ordinary folk can express their aspirations concretely and with feeling: so, right, in Ladakh, for example, where a form of Tibetan-style Buddhism prevails in this remote North Indian area, worship defines a holy time when men and women are reminded of the transcendent values of Buddhism in symbolic form.

Judaism is strongly anchored to its perceived history. The Passover meal is a potent way of remembering, and up to a point re-enacting, the awesome event whereby the Jewish people were liberated from bondage and precipitated upon the path to the Promised Land under the leadership of Moses, with such momentous results. The candles, the wine, the kinds of food, the Torah, the actions and prayers – all are carefully defined and means of giving meaning to family and group loyalty to the Jewish tradition of relationship to God.

One of the great holy times of India is the religious fair known as the Kumbh Mela, held principally every dozen years at Prayag (Allahabad), where the rivers Yamuna (Jumna) and Ganges join. A Kumbh Mela is an occasion for the auspicious pilgrimage of the laity in their millions, and for the gathering of yogis and ascetics, who use the festival for the discussion of the varying interpretations of the Hindu tradition.

For Christians the most vital feast is Easter, for at this holy time people see again the vision of Christ's resurrection from the dead and hence his victory over the forces of death and evil. Something of the awe and strange joy of the occasion is brought out in this picture of the celebration of Easter in Guatemala.

If the ritual re-enactment of auspicious or seminal events is a feature of traditional religions, it is also in its own way to be found in secular ideologies. This picture (right) shows May Day in Red Square in Moscow. Here at the heart of the Soviet Empire, in the vicinity of the old centre of Russian power, workers and others parade in order to celebrate the values of Socialism, where work is seen, as it were, as a sacred activity. Hence the spirit of Labour Day.

ЗАВЕТЫ
В ЖИЗНЬ

Sometimes times become holy because they repeat events of general significance for human beings. This picture shows an aspect of the Anglican Harvest Festival, in which God's gifts to men through the bounty of the earth are celebrated and some of the fruits of men's labours returned symbolically to the Creator.

All kinds of festivals abound in India – not just the Kumbh Mela seen earlier but also local and particular days of festivity. Left, in northern Bihar the villagers praise Sarasvati, goddess of learning. It is a day of rejoicing for schoolchildren and their parents. The image is itself bound by time. The goddess, in cheerful and decorated clay, is made for the day in question, and here is, after the rites and procession, being drowned and broken up in a nearby lake.

Holy times are defined sometimes by the scriptures which incorporate the central truths of the faith. In this picture Jews in Djerba, an island off the coast of Tunisia, ritually give reverence to the Torah or Law, the essence in effect of the Bible and therefore the divine way of defining the direction of Jewish and universal life and history. It is thus a festival about what holy times there are.

Birth is always a matter of celebration; but the Nativity of Christ is a specially holy anniversary, seen (right) being enacted in the ritual of the Syrian Orthodox Church.

the sculptures there of the Buddha are damaged (alas the Muslims failed to see that Buddhism could not commit idolatry) the spiritual force of the Buddha's message shines through. Many sculptures remind the Westerner of the Greeks: not for nothing, for Hellenistic art, in the wake of Alexander the Great, sowed seeds in the Indian mind, and helped, through the Gandhara school of art, to produce a beautifully proportioned and peaceful synthesis between East and West. The Buddha-image was to migrate throughout Asia, taking on different features, but always with the same underlying sense of the spiritual. But it was more than art, and it represented something of a revolution, vital for Mahāyāna piety.

For in the earliest days of Buddhist carving, such as the friezes which decorated the Buddhist temple at Sanchi, the Buddha just wasn't there. Trees were there. Seductive female spirits were there. Elephants and disciples were there. But where Gautama himself should have been, there were only traces – for instance his footprint. His Bo Tree was there, but he was like a man Friday, seen only by his traces in the sand. What did such a positive absence mean? Why was Gautama not himself portrayed, but only the symbols such as the Wheel of the Law? Scholars are divided as to the answer. One theory is that the absence of the Buddha is a way of representing his disappearance in nirvana. He is there but not there. He is no longer an individual. He is the mysterious 'Thus-gone', the Tathagata. Whatever the explanation, later Buddhist art came to represent the Teacher directly. In doing this it helped make concrete the devotion to the Buddha which grew in succeeding centuries. It was also the period when, in the Hindu environment of India, there was developing a more permanent and direct representation of the gods. The new Buddhist art provided one impulse towards a devotional attitude to the Buddha. He now became a visible being, who could be addressed in worship.

Devotion and the Buddhas

The new emphasis on *bhakti*, loving adoration, also was a factor in the multiplication of the Buddhas. Attention was not just directed to Gautama, vital though he was. The idea of heavenly Buddhas, corresponding somewhat to the Hindu gods and partly influenced from outside India, from Zoroastrian and other sources, came to pervade Buddhist piety. Thus among the most important of these great objects of piety was the Buddha Amitābha (known as Amida in Japan, where he retains his magic and his compassion), who creates a heavenly paradise for the faithful, sparkling with gems and lambent rivers and all kinds of delights. If a person calls on his name with faith he will be translated to this paradise on death, to the Pure Land, where everything is not merely lovely but also propitious for the final attainment of nirvana. The ideal of the Buddha's compassion for living beings is elevated to the sphere of grace; the otherwise unworthy faithful can gain the highest reward through the creative power and favour of the celestial Buddha. Such an ideal relates to, but seems far removed from, the austerer doctrines of the Lesser Vehicle, and it met with much resistance from that quarter. Yet it may be that the forces of devotion in religion are irresistible, and the Mahāyāna was merely using skill in absorbing these tendencies within its own fabric. In brief, not only were there earthly Buddhas, above all Gautama, whose teaching could save, but the Buddha-principle had a heavenly dimension which could liberate through faith and devotion. Still another motif to enter into the Great Vehicle was that of the Bodhisattva, the person destined for Buddhahood.

The Bodhisattva ideal

Before his Enlightenment, both in this life and in previous innumerable existences, the Buddha was the Buddha-to-be, the Bodhisattva. He was destined for Buddhahood, yet his motives were those of self-sacrifice and compassion, not pride in his future glorious status. After all, according to the legend Gautama had to come down from heaven to help living beings. There are in the Pali scriptures a whole series of birth-stories known as *Jātakas* which described the Buddha in previous lives. Often they depict him as sacrificing himself for the good of others, for example when as a hare he threw himself on the fire of a lonely starving old man in the forest, to provide food. The Great Vehicle began to build on this idea and to give it a new dimension. For it conceived that a Bodhisattva could put off his own salvation, which is the ultimate sacrifice, in order to work compassionately for the salvation of other beings. So the Bodhisattva became an incarnation of compassion. Thus did the Mahāyāna come to terms with what they saw as the paradox of compassion in the Lesser Vehicle.

The paradox of compassion

According to the formulas of classical Buddhism, a person must cultivate morality in treading the Eightfold Path. A person will not achieve true insight unless he conquers his own bad impulses and substitutes in their place the corresponding virtues. Since men are so often consumed with mutual hatred and antagonism – a hatred which can result in killing, warfare, brutalities, the slaughter of animals and humiliations inflicted on the unfortunate – not surprisingly love and compassion are seen as central virtues. If one attitude above all sums up the essence of the Buddhist ethic it is *karuṇā*, compassion – yet here we come to a paradox. For the very cultivation of compassion serves a person's interests, since it helps to take him along the path to nirvana. So on the one hand, Buddhist compassion, like Christian love, tells us to have regard for the welfare of others; it tells us to forget our own interests in order to serve others. But on the other hand, how can the saint who is on his way to nirvana be forgetting his own well-being? Is he not, even through his compassionate acts, pursuing his own higher happiness? It is, in brief, in his interest to cultivate compassion: self-sacrifice becomes self-centred. This is the paradox of compassion as perceived by Mahāyāna critics of the Lesser Vehicle. The Theravadin will reply that the criticism rests on a misunderstanding.

The Theravadin sees the matter almost from the opposite end. The aim is not to transform the person, whether in God or in nirvana, but rather to abolish individuality in the process of liberation. The very pursuit of happiness, the very concern with self-interest, the Theravadin would say (partly in reply to the Mahāyāna), is a misunderstanding of the realities of the Path. There is no substantial 'I' to gain anything. There is indeed a Path but no one to tread it, and there is liberation but no one to enter it. If nirvana is the highest happiness it is a happiness belonging to no one. Thus the Buddha abolishes both pain and pleasure, and that is true serenity; he comes to destroy not to fulfil the ego. Still, the appearance of selfishness was there in the Lesser Vehicle, and to combat it the Bodhisattva ideal was elevated, for he sacrifices even liberation in order to work for suffering mankind and indeed for all living beings.

Bodhisattvas, faith and merit

It was a short step to seeing how it might be that the Bodhisattva could suck up others in the train of his heavenly progress. On the one side, the very giving up and putting off of liberation, and the attendant trials and heroic acts through which the Buddha-to-be works through many lives for the welfare of the world – all this is bound to generate an immense store of merit. Thus great Bodhisattvas such as Avalokiteśvara (the One who looks down on the world with compassion, his name implies) have amassed boundless treasures, from which they can give to the faithful. Thus, on the other side, the struggling folk immersed in the world can look to supplement their own meagre merits by calling on the grace of the Bodhisattva. So by calling piously on the name of Buddhas and Bodhisattvas, people may be granted the blessings earned by those celestial beings. The logic of the Bodhisattva ideal led to a kind of devotionalism not distant from that of the Christian faith and Hindu *bhakti*. Buddhism in effect grew its own gods in the shape of Buddhas and Bodhisattvas, but effective gods, unlike the secondary beings we have already explored in the context of Sri Lanka. Yet before we jump to the conclusion that somehow the spirit of Buddhism has through these developments been so changed that the faith has become distorted, let us look to another, subtle and abstract, ingredient of the Great Vehicle.

Philosophy and emptiness

If the Mahāyāna was wide, and threw salvation open to all, it was also subtle in its central philosophical thinking. The most vital aspect of its philosophy we owe to the second-century AD sage Nāgārjuna, who propounded the doctrine of the Void, or Emptiness, known as the *Śūnyavāda*. Briefly it means that everything is empty, and it involves a radical extension of certain motifs in the Buddha's teaching. The Buddha had, for instance, argued that the idea of *things* is misleading. As we have seen he perceived the world as a swirling mass of impermanent events. What we take to be solid is fluid and changing, a cloud of instantaneous separate events. But our ordinary language conceals this, and so it is necessary for us to break through our ordinary ways of thinking and speaking. So much we have already observed as part of the teaching of the Theravada and of the Buddha himself. Nāgārjuna used intellectual arguments, running in parallel with the practice of meditation, to break up our ordinary view of the world, and so to see it as in essence empty. His argument ran somewhat as follows. In living in the world we have to treat it as governed by laws, by regular sequences of causes. When I rub a match against a rough surface it bursts into flame. When water cools enough it turns into ice. If I let go of a heavy object in my hand it will crash to the ground. Indeed, we generalise and suppose that every event has a cause, that there are underlying regularities which govern everything. This is the basis, after all, of scientific investigation. If we observe a certain effect we want to know why it has occurred. So then: the world is governed by causal laws. But, and here comes Nāgārjuna's astonishing argument, all ideas of causal processes, of causes and effects – all such ideas rest upon contradictions. Consider a cause which is supposed to bring about a certain effect. It is, as we have noted, a short-lived event, lasting some would say but the tiniest fraction of a second. Thus it goes out of existence as the effect comes into existence. But that means that when the effect occurs the cause no longer exists. How can that which is an effect be caused by something which does not exist? So that model of causation breaks down.

Nāgārjuna then goes on to apply criticism to other possible models of causation. In brief, all causal theories are contradictory, and since all theories about the world involve some account of causes, all theories about the world break down. Moreover, the very language we use to describe the world itself rests on assumptions involving regularities – when I use the word 'cat' of an animal I do so on the assumption that it will not turn into a shrub the next moment, so in other words I assume a certain causal tidiness about reality in order to be able to use language. Hence, Nāgārjuna's critique means that the whole fabric of our ideas rests on self-contradiction and absurdity. So nothing can be said about the world as it is in itself. If we have to use an expression to indicate the situation, we say that the real nature of the world is Void, Emptiness. It was this truth that the Buddha perceived in his Enlightenment, and there is a convergence between philosophy and contemplation. For the Emptiness which Nāgārjuna arrives at by intellectual reasoning coincides with the bright Void which is perceived in the higher reaches of consciousness. This then is the higher truth, and one that cannot properly be spoken but only indicated. Naturally, we still live our ordinary lives. For practical purposes we use language and make assumptions about the world's regularities. But for Nāgārjuna all this represents the conventional, worldly level of truth, something merely provisional. It is not the higher level to which we may aspire. It follows, by a paradox, that the Buddha's own teaching, in so far as the Dharma is put into words, is provisional and ultimately even contradictory. It is but a means of trying to get people to look in the higher direction. His words are fingers pointing at the moon.

Buddha-aspects

These different sides of Mahāyāna Buddhism – the cult of Buddhas and Bodhisattvas, the philosophy, the meditation, the teachings of Gautama – all these are summed up in what is sometimes referred to as the Three-Body or Three-Aspect Doctrine of the Buddha. This was a means of giving coherence to the various ideals through which the Great Vehicle combined piety, compassion, intellect and mysticism. According to the doctrine, the Buddha can be seen at one level as an earthly figure, for instance as the Gautama who in our age propounded for our welfare the Dharma. This is the Transformation-Aspect of the Buddha (in which he is, so to say, transformed into the human condition). At another level, Buddhas are celestial beings, worthy of our worship and dispensers of merit, creators of paradise. But third, at the highest level the Buddha is the Void. The true heart of Enlightenment, which is the true essence of the Buddha-nature, is the perception of Emptiness, in which there is no distinction between perceiver and perceived. So at the highest level there are no distinctions, and all Buddhas are united in the undifferentiated Void. And in that we all may gain the ineffable vision of the Void we are all in principle Buddhas-to-be. Part of this message is conveyed by a famous Mahāyāna parable, which has been compared to that of the Prodigal Son, though its message, naturally enough, is rather different.

The Buddhist Prodigal Son

A young man, on attaining manhood, leaves his home and emigrates to work in another country. But as he gets older he falls on worse and worse times, and wanders about seeking odd jobs. Eventually he comes to his own land and to a city. Now it happened that in the meantime his father has made good in business and has amassed a great treasury of wealth. He lives in that very city to which his broken, hungry son has come. He has long brooded about his long lost son. He would love nothing better than to have a son and heir to whom he could bequeath his wealth and his business. If only he could get back his errant son! And the son indeed arrives begging at his gate. It is no wonder that he fails to recognise his father. His father reclines upon a magnificent couch, surrounded by priests and other citizens, and clad in fine and precious clothes, hung with jewels, attended by handsome and delicately proportioned servants, while overhead there is a brocaded canopy, adorned with fresh trailing flowers, shielding him from the sun, and swaying gently in the perfumed breeze. The son is worried. Perhaps this fine man is a king: and you know what these rajas are like – they pressgang you into their service if you don't watch out, and cause you to be beaten up if you don't work hard enough. So the son slopes off. But not before the father has seen him.

He sends attendants to arrest the son, who is brought struggling back to the rich man's palace. In terror, he faints. The old man orders his servants to revive him with water and to free him. The son is overjoyed to get his freedom, and sets off to a nearby village to beg for food and shelter. Later the father sends some servants to him to persuade him that there is a job awaiting him, for which he will get double wages. The son is agreeable. The work is mean, but he has some security. The job is shovelling manure and refuse.

The rich man puts on some old clothes and supervises the refuse-clearance, as an excuse to get close to his son. And he tells the son, who still does not recognise him, that he shall adopt him as his own son. He gives him a new name. But the job stays the same for many years. Still, the younger man is growing in confidence. Eventually he is promoted to become the old man's accountant and so familiarises himself with all the business and all the items in the old man's millions. He cannot believe his luck. But there is more to come. As the old man feels his end approaching, he summons his retainers and advisers and publicly announces that his son is indeed his son. And the son, whose ideas have gradually become enlarged, recognises the truth. He inherits all those riches, yet it was not through his own efforts that all these blessings have flowed upon him. It is all through the gracious wisdom of the old man that the son has been brought to gain the riches which he did not himself compile.

Continued on page 101

MEANS

Religion is not just theory: it is importantly practice. And in the practice of religion various means are employed to assist the devotee to reach the higher life. Such means range from sacred rites or sacraments to the performance of spiritual exercises. At a very simple level, lighting a candle is a means of expressing a religious aspiration, and it is in such outer ways that religion often seeks to make concrete the inner life.

A Tibetan monk with prayer wheel. The prayer wheel is from one perspective a mechanical contrivance; from another it is a means of manifesting the Buddhist message, often itself symbolised as a wheel (the Buddha is supposed to have set the wheel of the Law in motion). Also used in Buddhism are other material symbols of prayer, such as flags.

Even gurus can be seen as means rather than ends in themselves. The rapture on the faces of these devotees as they venerate their guru indicates that a spiritual teacher can be an instrument of elevation. As with other means used in religion to advance higher in the path, the guru can be dangerous as well as helpful.

In many religions the most important means of conveying the message is through pictures, or through buildings. This Eastern Orthodox woman (right) is kissing a holy picture. The act of kissing an icon is a discipline of a kind in which affection and respect are shown to the visible representation of the unseen, angelic world. Note too how here, as often elsewhere, vertical height is used to symbolise the transcendent. Our language is full of this symbolism: consider 'higher things', 'superior' and so forth.

BANKERS
TRUST

Sacred Dance. Here we see the slow rhythmic dance of the dervishes – that is, Muslim mystics who use gyrations as a means of becoming wrapped up in the higher experience of Allah. Many religions use dance as a controlled way of inducing ecstasy.

Left: Hare Krishna. The Hare Krishna sect, stemming from the devotional movement founded by the Bengali saint Chaitanya (born in 1485), stresses above all the chanting of the divine name as a means of expressing love for God. Rhythmic repetitions help to convey the devotee to the divine realm. The chanting is a variant on the use of singing to elevate men's minds towards heaven.

Above, on a train in Israel Jews perform traditional prayers. Note that there is wound on to the person's arm the object known as a phylactery – a small box containing a text of the Torah. This is a material manifestation of the orthodox Jewish devotion to the Law handed down through Moses from God. Also, covering the head is a method of expressing respect for the almighty (oddly, in Christianity, the reverse applies – men at least uncover their heads in church).

A Buddhist monk of Japan (below) finds the formal garden, austere with mysterious rocks, a visible mode of conveying calm and harmony with nature. In part the tradition here stems from Chinese Taoism, where a kind of communion with nature is seen as important in training oneself to attain a sort of immortality.

Folk praying at an evangelical crusade in London. Note that a very simple means used in Christianity is to close the eyes. This indicates a certain turning towards the invisible world. Clasping the hands in prayer also is symbolic, and a method of showing that worship goes beyond the daily use of one's hands as tools for earning one's living and so forth.

The parable has a secular meaning: note how the old man gradually prepares the younger one for inheritance. Too sudden success is a danger, as many of those who have won huge sums through football pools or by lotteries have bitterly come to see. But more particularly the parable expounds the Greater Vehicle theory of the Buddha's plan of salvation. When the old man dresses up as the foreman and gives him guarantees and a promise to treat him as a son, this is like the Buddha's taking on himself human form, as Gautama. It is easy for the younger man to take a narrow view of his good fortune. In fact there is a wider way to the glories and riches of the liberated state, to Buddhahood itself. That way is the Great Vehicle.

Note too how in all this the various values of Buddhism are integrated. Since the heart of Enlightenment is the Void, nirvana just is that Void. From this point of view liberation means becoming a Buddha. So he who accepts the Mahāyāna teaching treads a path towards Buddhahood, and that is nothing other than being a Bodhisattva himself. He should therefore reflect the compassionate concern displayed by the great Bodhisattvas whom he worships. In worshipping Buddhas he is worshipping his own ideal condition. And since the Void is also the underlying nature of everything, he can find nirvana even in the flux of everyday living. From this point of view the round of rebirth, *samsāra*, is simply nirvana. This apparent paradox means that it is not through retreat from the world that the truth is gained, but through it. And though the monk and the Sangha remain key institutions in the developing and spreading Mahāyāna, the quest for liberation is thrown open to everyone here and now.

Despite the innovations of the Great Vehicle and its sense of imaginative extension of the original earthly Buddha's teaching, it retains contemplation of the Void as its central value. The commanding heights are still controlled by that ideal of insight and wisdom which permeated the life of the Buddha himself and to which the Theravada gives a rather different testimony.

The Mahāyāna as a major force in East Asia

As we have seen, Buddhism began to spread into China from the first century AD onwards. Both Lesser Vehicle and Mahāyāna works were translated into Chinese, but it was the latter that came to make the most profound impact on Chinese culture. It was, thereby, also highly determinant of the culture of Japan. One reason for its success in China was that the promise of the Pure Land presented a powerful appeal to the masses. Another was that Confucianism, one of its rivals, was a largely ethical doctrine suitable for the ruling class and the theory of emperorship, but of less appeal to the ordinary cultivator. Another rival, Taoism, contained many notions similar to those of Buddhism. It had as it were prepared the Chinese for the Buddhist invasion. Indeed, a fusion of the Tao and Buddhist meditation produced the Ch'an school, better known in the West through the Japanese version of its name, Zen. Again, there was less stress in some Mahāyāna schools on the whole business of rebirth and karma, for one might go straight to Paradise: and belief in reincarnation was not native to Chinese culture. Still another reason for Buddhism's success, especially in the Mahāyāna form, was the subtlety of its philosophical ideas, and the fascination of its metaphysical claims. Though previous Chinese philosophy had its moments of profundity, it was less complex and penetrating. So Buddhism not only appealed to the heart of the peasant: it could also appeal to the mind of the educated classes.

Finally, the monastic organisation of Buddhism proved a powerful means of propagating the new faith across the Empire. Buddhism gained so strong a grip on the Chinese imagination that it is often classed as one of the Three Religions (the three strands of spirituality and ethics which make up the fabric of Chinese traditional thinking about the world) and brought about a cross-fertilisation of Indian and Chinese cultures which was fruitful in religion, thought, art and literature. Wherever the spirit of China ran, downwards into Vietnam, eastwards into Korea and across the sea to Japan, there also ran the spirit of Buddhism. We will see, in chapters on China and Japan, how Buddhism became the most successful missionary religion in Asia, perhaps in the world. Meanwhile, Buddhism was destined for two other important successes and one tragedy.

Buddhism and India

The Buddha was an Indian. Nowhere other than in North India was Buddhism in its Mahāyāna heyday more gloriously instantiated. The rich cities and agricultural areas stretching eastwards and northwards from the land round where Delhi now stands supported innumerable temples, great monasteries, huge study centres like the university of Nalanda, and shrines and places of pilgrimage, such as Bodh-Gaya where the Buddha reached Enlightenment and where the original Bo Tree was venerated.

Its art was magnificent, breathtaking even in its audacious and successful attempt to put wisdom, serenity, insight and compassion into stone, and delicious in its portrayal of the luscious and sensuous glories of the world which the Buddha penetrated in order to bring about a transformation. Even now, chipped and fragmented, these art-works inspire awe and affection. To see them, often noseless, in the setting of the museum at Sarnath or in Mathura is to re-enact in one's own eye the essential preaching of the Buddha; and yet I am always struck by sadness and bitter regret that so much has been smashed (in the name, as it happens, of religion). The noseless Buddhas are symbols of the vanishing of Buddhist India, of the tragedy that overtook Buddhism in its homeland.

Buddhism virtually vanishes from India: Why?

There were various reasons why Buddhism almost disappeared from India, only remaining to cling round the Himalayan foothills and in Nepal, to the skirts, as it were, of the Tibetan Lamaism which was well established beyond the high ranges. One was from the eleventh century onwards, the incursion of the Muslims into North India. The establishment of Muslim kingdoms in North India robbed the Buddhist monasteries of their patronage and protection, while Muslim piety led to the destruction of many Buddhist and Jain temples, and the dispersal of the monks. As recent events in the Communist countries of Asia have shown, Buddhism is, because of its monastic base, very fragile in the face of hostile rulers. But Islam apart,

Buddhism was in decline. For one thing, the devotionalism of the Mahāyāna had over the centuries coalesced with Hindu *bhakti*. Moreover, Hinduism had itself borrowed much from Buddhism, even the Buddha himself, regarded oddly as an incarnation or *avatar* of Vishnu (his task on earth being mainly to test the faith of Vishnu's devotees). Buddhism came to lose definition, and thus to lose a reason for separate existence, in a way a victim in its homeland of its very success. It has come to share with Christianity the oddity of being weak in its birthplace, though highly influential elsewhere. Meanwhile, in the period of its decline it had a striking success beyond the Himalayas.

Buddhism goes north

The Buddha himself came from the south of what is now Nepal. From early times Buddhism was influential at the boundaries of the Ganges plain and in the jungle and foothills to the north, but it was not till the period between the seventh and twelfth centuries AD that it made substantial progress into Tibet and the regions beyond. (In its migration to China it had passed to the north of the Himalayan massif.) Towards the end of this period Muslim incursions added impetus to the Buddhification of Tibet, as monks migrated to the north. From the twelfth century on, Tibet became thoroughly converted, and to a form of Buddhism known as the Vajrayāna or Diamond Vehicle. It thus became the bastion of the third force in Buddhist spirituality.

The Diamond Vehicle was developed out of the Mahāyāna, but with much emphasis on sacraments and rituals as means of training and self-purification. It also absorbed elements of the indigenous Bon religion of pre-Buddhist Tibet. Yet though its structures are unique, its greatest saint, the guru and poet Milarepa, could write very much in the spirit of earlier Buddhism. Here is a song composed in response to those young folk who had come to learn from him as novices:

> When you are looking to become a Buddha in this life
> Do not take your likes and dislikes too seriously,
> For if you make much of them you will do good and evil
>   of all kinds
> And will fall into a bad condition . . .
> When you are studying the scriptures
> Do not be conceited in your mind:
> Such ideas will give rise to the five poisons of
>   delusion, anger, passion, envy and hatred.
> And thus poisoned your virtue and good inclinations
> Will become confused.

So far, apart from the reference to becoming a Buddha, Milarepa's message is solid with the thinking of the Theravada. But Milarepa knew the higher truth in his own experience, and to this he refers in the following lines:

> The white leopard of the snow-clad peaks
> Who lords it among the white, snowy deserts
> Has nothing to fear from others.
> The leopard who is king in the snow
> Finds his strength there.

The leopard here is the symbol of independence and wisdom. But the Diamond Vehicle also incorporated magical practices, centring upon the use of mandalas – sacred diagrams. In this, Tibetan Buddhism succeeded in uniting earlier peasant-based religion and the higher reaches of Buddhist speculation and contemplation. In addition, it drew upon the sexual imagery of northern Indian religion. The controlled use of sex was thought itself to be a means towards enlightenment.

The adherents of the older sect of Tibetan Buddhism are known as the red hats. After reforms in the eleventh century, a new type of purified Vajrayāna was initiated, and its followers were known as the yellow hats or Gelugpa (virtuous ones); it is from them that the spiritual head of state was drawn. The theory here was that the ruler should be a *bodhisattva*, hence the careful search for a boy showing the right characteristics to succeed the previous Dalai Lama.

The Tibetans managed to live largely in peace and reasonable prosperity under this medieval system, which was shattered when the rulers of red China decided to transform Tibetan society, an event leading to the flight of the Dalai Lama and many other monks to India.

Buddhism – a retrospect

Buddhism adapted itself to many Asian cultures, but, because based chiefly on the monastic life, it is vulnerable to hostile regimes and its future in South-East Asia and in China does not seem bright. It is however now making another of its transitions, as it adapts itself to the Western world, which is, increasingly, fascinated by the richness of Buddhist psychological and spiritual training, and by the splendours of Buddhist art. To that we shall return in our final chapter.

CHRISTIANITY 3

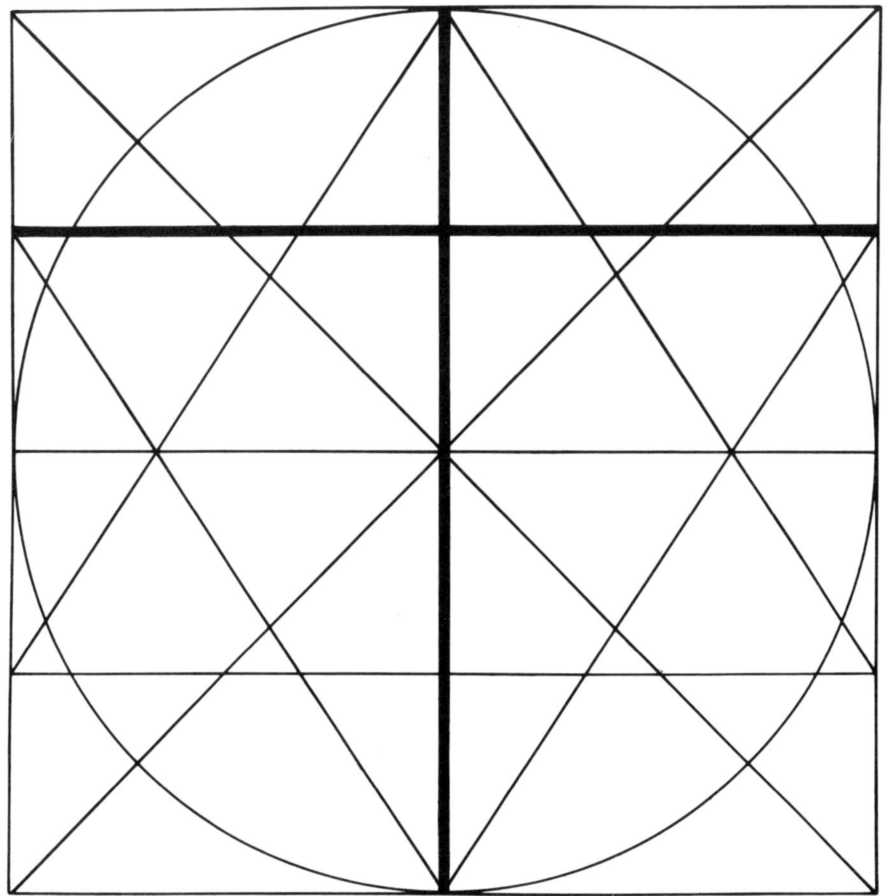

Christianity is the most mysterious of the great religions. We think we understand it. We identify it with certain messages coming out of the Bible. Yet it has proved to be diverse. It ranges from Eastern Orthodoxy, through Catholicism, to a great variety of Protestant churches and sects. At its periphery there are a host of movements claiming to be Christian, such as the Mormons, or Church of Jesus Christ of the Latter Day Saints. So Christianity is by no means as simple as it sometimes seems. It can approve war and pacificism, monasteries and secular attitudes, hierarchy and democracy, preaching and ritual, philosophers and those who reject philosophy.

Perhaps this is part of the logic of the faith. It may be that there are many faces of Christ in the New Testament and that Jesus had differing roles and a baffling resistance to being put into conventional categories. If so it would be surprising that Christianity worked itself out so diversely. What is needed if we are to begin to come to terms with it is to forget for a moment any immediate ideas we have, good or bad, about this stormy mother of European culture and of such unruly children as science and modern humanism. For that reason I start with, for most people, an unfamiliar manifestation of the faith – namely the Romanian Church, surprising in its flourishes in the context of Communism. Is this as much the true faith as the evangelical messages of twice-born Baptists? Tracing the ancestry of Eastern Orthodoxy we are, however, driven back to the events leading to the drifting apart of the Church. For essentially Christianity has had three poises – one the Eastern, another the Roman Catholic and the other the Protestant; and the first great division came between East and West.

That division was perhaps implicit in the early history of the Church. In its first three centuries the faith became widespread throughout the Roman Empire. The Empire, though often hostile, provided the milieu through which the faith could travel. Then, with Constantine, the Church achieved official success. But the Empire itself was beginning to break into two halves, one based on Constantinople, the other on Rome – the one Greek in tone, the other Latin. Moreover, in the succeeding centuries the West was overrun by Visigoths and others from the north. The Church became the vehicle of Latin culture and struggled successfully to convert the invaders. A new Western Europe was born, a synthesis between Latin south and Germanic north. But it was many centuries later, in 1453, that Constantinople was overthrown. So the historic situations of Eastern and Western Christians were very different. Moreover, the sudden conquests by Islam, in the seventh and eighth centuries and after, helped to isolate many Eastern churches from Christendom.

Then, when Europe was beginning to show new strength and to begin its amazing overseas conquests, in the early sixteenth century, the Roman Church was split asunder by the Reformation. Much of northern Europe and through it much of North America and, in the nineteenth century, Africa became Protestant. These events ultimately were to precipitate modern capitalism, the scientific revolution and modern humanism.

In my treatment of Christianity I shall not only retrace vital parts of the history, but also select varying themes from areas and aspects of its development. Christianity will be seen thus in some richness, possessing both a bright and a dark side, and often showing how it is much more surprising and diverse than you thought.

Roman faith: a question

The church and the monastery at Neamț (pronounced Ne-umpts) in northern Romania are set in beautiful rolling country, close by the Carpathian mountains which run like a bent rib or boomerang through the middle of the country. There are hints of the Latin world for the people and language are predominantly, and rather improbably, under the grip of the Roman past. This is where Ovid was exiled and memories of his poems reverberate in the Romanian hills and coast. But it is a country of many traditions – the Ukraine lies to the north, and Turkey to the south. There are Hungarians in Transylvania, and Germans live in the Eastern Carpathians, practising the Christian faith in suitably Lutheran churches.

In Romania everyone seems to go to church. At Neamț there were peasants and suited seminarians, while young and ancient priest-monks conducted the divine opera, the Liturgy, so heavenly that three hours pass in twenty minutes (in heaven no doubt three hours pass in no time at all). Outside afterwards an upstanding peasant, with hat, dark suit and moustaches, declared that the Liturgy meant that the Baptists could not get at him. Another told of his fight in the war against the Germans (the Romanians like the Italians fought on both sides, as memorials discreetly show). A girl, of peasant family, declared that the Liturgy gave her a 'frightening feeling of faith'. God comes in gold and drama to earth, and the Virgin and saints are kissed in jewel-crusted portraits. The heavenly world is here on earth, and the books of Protestants (for Protestants are given to literacy, to their everlasting credit) are nothing too much in the face of the glories of the Romanian liturgy.

But the glories of Romanian Christianity exist in a Communist society where the Party and the images of the Comrade President are pervasive. What does this conjunction between Church and State mean not only for Romania but also for Christendom generally?

I told a Bucharest bishop that in England children are taught Christianity at school and grow up to be atheists, while in Romania they are taught atheism at school and grow up to be Christians. That is all right as a joke. But to understand the growth and present situation of the Orthodox genius we need to go back into the past, and place it in the wider perspective of the Christian experience. From Bucharest the connections run back to Bethlehem and over to Rome and Indianapolis. To study them helps correct the narrowness of Western approaches to the faith, born of a pre-occupation with the early church and the Reformation, and leaving aside many crucial later transitions.

The heart of the faith

Before we see the mind Christianity grew, let us see its heart. We are, perhaps, so used to the Christian faith, those of us who read English and buy books, that we forget how unfamiliar the central myth and ritual really are and were.

The myth was something like this. Man was made by God, but he was disobedient, and so could only partly be reconciled to God. This partial reconciliation came through the covenant or contract which God offered to the people of Israel. The people were miraculously helped by God; he also inspired certain prophets who maintained, on balance, the fidelity of the people. But the people came to see that salvation must lie in the future, with the coming of the Anointed One. The Hebrew scriptures authorise us to seek such a Messiah. And he came, in the form of Jesus. Jesus saved man, for he was actually God, son of God. Only God could offer the perfect sacrifice which could atone for man's disobedience. This sacrifice happened at Calvary, where Christ, the prototype of martyrs, was rejected both by Jews and the imperial power. But Jesus showed his victory through the fact that he got up from the dead and appeared to the disciples. We, likewise, can in Christ conquer death. Christ was the new man, the second Adam, and he will come again to make the final judgment, at the end of the world as we now know it. Thus will be created a new heaven and a new earth.

There are prefigurations and echoes of this myth. Thus the first Adam fell from grace because of a virgin, Eve; the second Adam saved men because he was born of a virgin, Mary. The first Adam died because of a tree, from which he ate the forbidden fruit. The second Adam saved through a tree, namely the cross. The first man was in a garden of bliss which he had to leave. Jesus was in the sad garden of Gethsemane, from which he went to pain and glory.

Jesus was, somehow, the successor of John the Baptist. So the Christians had initiation through baptism, which was itself a re-enactment of death and new life. Likewise through the sacrament of the Last Supper, the faithful were united with Christ, and so with his conquest of death. They were thus assured of being got up by God and given renewal in their bodies when the new heaven and earth were established at the time of the final judging of men. No wonder the early Christians were rather secretive about their rituals. For it was through these rites that salvation came, and this salvation could not be casual, could not exist without faith in Christ and in the God who ruled the world.

This strange story also has the dimensions of a cosmic drama; the Christians believed that Jerusalem was the centre of the universe, and the Cross was the midpoint of heaven and earth and the midpoint in time of the drama of all human history. The Cross was the central act in this cosmic drama which unfolded God's design as creator and governor of men and matter. Thus it was not hard for the emerging Christian mind to try to link the myth of Jesus to the structure of the universe. So philosophy and sacred story were destined to marry, perhaps sometimes uneasily. Whenever, later, there has been a conflict between the two it has been painful.

The Jewish tradition had been feeling its way towards a similar synthesis, a similar binding together of mind and heart. Consider, for instance, the thinking of Philo of Alexandria, who saw in philosophy a special gift from heaven, which could say in general much that could be seen more particularly in scriptural revelation. He wedded Greece to Jerusalem. (Later, in the third century, father Tertullian could ask: 'What has Athens to do with Jerusalem?', but the foundations had been laid for the great marriage.)

Egypt was the milieu of Philo, and the Christian Origen, and other great writers and thinkers. Many scholars are inclined to think that it was through Egypt that ideas from the East were funnelled. The teacher of Plotinus, the greatest religious thinker of the Roman Empire, who shaped the teachings of Plato into a new spiritual form known as Neoplatonism, may well have been influenced by India. Certainly the similarity between the thought of Plotinus and that of some major Indian systems is striking. Thoughts occur in different cultures independently, so we cannot be sure, but there may be an invisible Suez Canal transporting Eastern ideas to Christian Europe.

The identity of Christ

Though we have the Gospels, and other elements of the New Testament, it is naïve to look upon them as bringing to us an authoritative portrait of Jesus. The writers were numerous and the words put together in a kind of liturgical mosaic – it was two centuries before the canon was really decided within the Church.

This does not mean the Christians were wrong to trust the scriptures, within their own setting. They read them out at the sacraments because they presented Christ the saviour of mankind. They read out the good news because they thought it relevant to their condition. They also needed to compile something of the same weight as books they came to call the Old Testament. The scriptures, then, though they pointed, at least in part, to real events, were not primarily history books as we know them today. They were mythic, inspiring accounts of the drama of salvation as seen in the life of Israel and of Jesus. They were nearer Shakespeare than Lord Acton. Above all, they were read out as part of the divine liturgy. But they gave no definitive portrait. Instead from the New Testament and Christian history we get overlapping images: of the teacher, and indeed rabbi, of the moral leader, of the Zealot rebel, ready to overthrow authority and to whip the money-changers out of the Temple, or the divine, victorious Christ of Eastern icons. Christ can be seen as the man hanging on the Cross, nails through his hands (but probably it was a matter of ropes). He can be seen as the founder of a religion.

Probably every image has a certain truth. But we soon see that it is not sensible to look on Jesus in just one way. All the searchlights we illuminate him with have differently coloured beams. So what is the point of asking what his real colour is?

The New Testament

It is, however, vital to see that the New Testament, even if it multiplies pictures, is a kind of test of the faith. Rightly or wrongly (and it really is a matter of judgment) some Christians have seen the New Testament as a virtually infallible witness to the Truth. But we do not need to accept that to see that, if an estimate of Jesus himself is to be made, the primary sources will be the books of the New Testament.

One thing stands out. An incredibly large portion of the Gospel is taken up with the arrest, death and trial of Jesus – the resurrection stories are much more fragmentary. The accounts of the last few days of Jesus' life are continuous and circumstantial. The scriptures seem to emphasise not so much Jesus' moral or even spiritual teachings (though the recollections of parables run like a thread through the accounts of his public career) as his action and passion. The New Testament is about a new series of saving acts. And of course whether Jesus is saviour is not so much a matter of history as of sacred drama or (to use another term) myth.

The upper room

The sacred drama finds physical expression in the words and music of the Liturgy. To find the beginning of it, the origin of the central Christian sacraments, we must go back to the upper room, and the last supper. Or perhaps we should say the first supper. For though it was Jesus' last meeting with his disciples, not counting the resurrected encounters, it inaugurated a new order. The ritual which is recorded in the New Testament was simple, and there have been recurrent attempts in Christianity to resimplify the re-enactment of it, but it held within it the seeds of the golden harvest of the Eastern Liturgy. In Christianity, the most self-critical of religions, the thought that the glories are perversions will arise, but, that aside, the last supper held promises of future dramas.

First, because Jesus, in giving meaning to the bread and wine, was making the disciples see his own death as a kind of sacrifice. He was seeing the bread and wine as what they literally were not, his own body and blood. And he was seeing his own body and blood as what they literally were not, a sacrificial offering to God on behalf of man. He was the new sacrificial animal, maybe. Yet he was not dead: the inner meaning of the last supper could only unfold in the future. That is why it was always in process of (from our point of view) development, and why an end product of that development – the Orthodox Liturgy – was not too surprising. But if Christ was the seed of the sacred drama what was the soil?

In theory it was Israel. Jesus stood in a special relationship to the Jewish tradition, and his predecessor and relation, John the Baptist, was an abundantly Jewish religious figure of the time. But Christianity spread through a Roman Empire and quickly acquired a Greek dimension within that framework. Did Jesus anticipate this? Did his disciples realise what was beginning to happen – that, though Jewish, Christianity was to be spread by Greek and Latin means. Orthodoxy has cunningly wedded the sounds of the synagogue to the music of Byzantium.

Purely Jewish Christianity, those who wanted to circumcise the Christian, and who made up the Jerusalem church, was largely destroyed in AD 70, amid the holocaust which the Romans imposed upon the recalcitrant Hebrew people. It could be said that Islam took over the universalist destiny of the Jewish Christians, while Christianity set its face to the west and north, becoming both Greek and Latin, in the process of being all things to all men.

The pax deorum

Though the Roman Empire contained a medley of religions, it was sustained by the thought that a harmonious relationship between gods and men, the *pax deorum*, was necessary to its wellbeing. Its tolerance had itself a religious or even magical rationale. The real trouble with the Christians was that by refusing to sacrifice to the Emperor, and by rejecting the gods, they upset this heavenly harmony and thus threatened the earthly peace of victorious Rome. If the Tiber flooded or the Egyptian corn failed, Roman citizens, either wet or hungry, were liable to shout 'Feed Christians to the lions'. Pogroms thus abounded, sometimes, as in the great persecutions which started in AD 303, with the enthusiastic approval of the imperial system itself.

Constantine seems to have sensed that the old gods were crumbling and that to this could be attributed the problems of imperial civil war. A new God might restore the *pax deorum*. Now it would be the peace of one God: the boot was on the other foot, and an imperial constitution of 438 could ban Jews, Samaritans, pagans and heretics, whose lack of conformism was the cause of droughts and failures of the harvest. The new peace of God was more systematic and ultimately more ruthless, perhaps, than the older system. Yet paradoxically, Christians won the throne by self-sacrifice, not aggression. Thus Lactantius could write that religion should be defended not by killing but by dying.

Christianity was not, in any event, political even if it offended political powers. The resistance to sacrifice to the Empire was a religious, not a political revolt. So when the faith triumphed a symbiosis between Church and State was easy to arrange. It was not as though Christianity itself had principles contrary to the imperial power, though it might have views on morals and cults. Thus was fashioned the Caesaropapism which became so vital in the East. In other words, emperor and priest could be mutual supports, while in the West Pope and Caesar could work well together – even if the break-up of the Empire under inner and outer forces meant that it was the Papacy that had to carry the main burden of transmitting Latin and Christian culture through that turbulent period known a little gloomily and misleadingly as the Dark Ages.

Caesaropapism

Thus in the Eastern empire, the Byzantine court in particular was also the centre from which Christian authority radiated. Even when the Turks finally overwhelmed the old empire in 1453, they continued to rule the Christians partly through the Patriarch. Thus though the great church was in captivity, its identity was maintained.

Another reason why the Jewish sect, with its odd myth of a dying and rising Christ, succeeded was that it grew a powerful mind. Ultimately it is not possible for a movement to succeed unless it can capture the heads of those who have education. They are in key positions of power and influence within the bureaucracy and technical substructure, which sustains the edifice of an empire or of a modern state. This is one reason for Marxist success: it has a coherent philosophy, and so has a coherent policy: both fire in its belly and direction and plausibility in the mind.

Christianity and the mysteries

Meanwhile what were the secrets of Christianity's success over the mysteries and other cults? First, and this was important, it looked like a mystery religion in the sense that such cults involved some kind of initiation and secret transformation of the individual through ritual and sacrament. Consider what occurred at Eleusis, outside Athens. The replay of the story of Demeter, once a myth heralding the crops and of deep importance for fertility, was now seen in a much more psychological and spiritual sense. The earth that sent forth life after the period of death now created new life in the breasts of the initiates. As Aristotle remarked, the aim of a mystery was *ou mathein alla pathein*, not so we would learn but so that we would undergo change. And there were more dynamic, more universal, cults such as those of Mithras and Isis. About the latter, we have the famous and moving account written by Lucius Apuleius in his book *The Golden Ass*. He was transformed by the goddess:

> 'I arrived at the frontier of death and set one foot
> on the threshold of Proserpine; but I returned,
> steering through all the elements. I saw the sun
> shine at midnight as if it was noon. I entered the
> presence of the lower and upper gods and worshipped
> them from very close by.'

Such were the effects of the divine ceremony. And symbolically his retransformation into a human after being an ass signalises the sacramental salvation from baser things. But the mysteries were a matter of choice. The Graeco-Roman world sustained a federation of cults, only here and there underpinned by a coherent philosophy. It was like today's Hinduism, though even more loosely knit together. But Christianity was in its own way uncompromising, and had in it the seeds of system.

The uncompromisingness derived from its Jewish background. There could be no other gods than God. It is true that Jesus was Lord and worshipped in and through the eucharistic sacrament. But in due course the identity (and yet difference) of Christ and the Father came to be affirmed and given intellectual content through the Trinity doctrine. The Christians could not worship the Emperor, though they might obey him. As for Isis she was neither worshipped nor obeyed. As Christianity became universal the severe monotheism of the Jews was injected into all parts of the Empire and indeed beyond. And though at first the Christians looked negligible – an offshoot of a peculiar minority faith – their uncompromising stand against other gods proved formidable: and blood of the martyrs was the seed of the church.

Catholicism, Orthodoxy and Protestantism

Christianity proved creative. Perhaps the marriage of Jew and Greek, of East and Rome, of charisma and sacrament, of Jesus and his destiny, of one God and the flavour of the many, of mystery and metaphysics, was the cause of the amazing success of Christendom.

Some would say the causation is clear. It flows from Jesus as divine being and centre of the Gospel. What Christian would not in the last resort say this? Still, the faith had to work through human channels. The Christian world broke apart. During the centuries of the first millennium, the Byzantine Roman tradition grew away from that of the crumbling Capitol and the growing Vatican. The waters of Christianity flowed mainly in two mighty channels, one of which later divided to make three. Those two channels are of course the Eastern and Western Church. Their characters formed gradually. By the eleventh century the division was virtually complete, but the Eastern Church had in effect rejected the authority of Rome many centuries earlier. It was partly a matter of imperial jurisdiction (Constantinople versus Rome); partly a matter of doctrine, an argument over the famous *filioque* clause, to which we need to return. The division was helped by the political changes in East and West. Rome succumbed to barbarians, while Byzantium carried on the theory of the Roman Empire. Later the Orthodox world would be substantially overrun by the Ottoman empire (this, as we shall see, is one of the clues to understanding the intertwining of Party and Church in Romania today), while a little over half a century after the fall of Byzantium in 1453, the Western church was engulfed in the crisis that led to the establishment of the Protestant churches which were destined to become dominant in northern Europe and North America.

It is worth glancing briefly at the map of the world to see how the three channels, the Orthodox, Catholic and Protestant, of Christianity have flowed across the surface of our planet.

Catholicism radiates from Rome, but beyond the Alps its influence wanes, except in southern Germany and Austria where it is vital, and in Poland where it is a vehicle of national identity. Through the great efflux of Europeans to the New World, Catholicism was transmitted to America. More importantly the imperial conquests of Spain and Portugal made it the predominant religion of Latin America. This perhaps reinforces the image of Rome as a southern European religion, for it is in the Western Mediterranean that it retains its ethos most spectacularly. In Africa and Asia it has had some success, but basically its strength lies in the territory from Lithuania south-west to Trafalgar, and by another geometry from the Rio Grande to Tierra del Fuego. These then are the main lands of Catholicism. Yet one of its most vital centres lies in the north-west – in Ireland, with its own blend of austerity and warmth, and its wide influence upon the American scene. Naturally one must also recognise the importance of Catholic minorities, often, as in England, of growing significance as Protestantism wanes.

The dynamo of orthodoxy was Greece and from there it reached deep into the Balkans and beyond to Moscow, which long thought of itself as the third Rome. The Orthodox were spiritual rulers of the Middle East till the Church's fabric was shattered by the explosion of Islam, leaving it marginal in the area – but still living in Armenia, Coptic and cryptic in Ethiopia and to the north. It stuck in India, but on a small scale, and its venture into China proved ultimately unsuccessful. In the modern world, most of Orthodoxy is behind the Iron Curtain. It continues the tradition of a Church in captivity, for we must not forget that not only did Islam largely knock out the Church throughout the Middle East, but captured it in the Balkans. Catholic Hungary and Russia stood out – the Russian church was virtually the only independent survivor of Orthodoxy outside the grip of the infidel Turk. The heart then of Orthodoxy is in Greece, but its power lies largely to the north. It is a Church whose powerline runs from Archangel to Crete. Its distant outreach lies in Siberia, Ethiopia, Uganda, India and parts of Canada and the USA.

Protestantism found its pastures in the flatter northern parts of Europe. Perhaps Christianity had not really taken too magical a grip upon the Teutonic, Celtic and Viking lands. At any rate, it was in France, Germany, Britain and Scandinavia that the new shape of Christianity found its best success. And because of that it was the religion which was most effectively transmitted to the new European nations. Thus it was that the Protestant ethic was a matrix of America and much of the white Commonwealth. The rhythm of Europe was echoed in the New World. To the south Latin languages and predominantly Catholicism: to the north Germanic languages and mostly Protestantism.

The way the three streams flow differs also. The Orthodox like autocephaly – each national church having its own head but in communion with Constantinople. The Romans like monocephaly – one head, the Pope in Rome. The Protestants like creative chaos – sometimes being somewhat autocephalous, in the Lutheran and English traditions, and sometimes being self-directed and given to sectarianism, as in the spectrum which lies from Methodism through to the Mormons (or do they count as Christians? A vital question if we are seeking for that elusive substance, the essence of Christianity).

Christianity

The creative chaos is one of Christianity's bequests to black Africa, that highly Christian continent, furiously breeding thousands of new independent movements with a Christian father and an African mother. The ethnic rhythms of Africa may play with a disorganised beat, but there is a thunder in the sound, for it heralds some vast new religious forces to be released upon the world. It could be that a new Christianity is being born in the black world, and it may be that one day the mission will be from south to north, rather than the other way round, as the forces of geography and conquest have hitherto dictated.

Though Protestantism has striven hard in Asia it has not overtly done well. Indirectly, however, its force is felt. For one of Protestantism's unruly children, Marxism, has provided the mechanism for reconstructing post-colonial nations in the East, most vigorously China. And though Marxism is anti-Christian and anti-religious, its virulent attitude towards the traditional faiths is itself an indication of its protesting nature, and only relations could hate one another as much as do traditional Christianity and Marxist ideology, even if sometimes they feel tugs of sympathy.

If the axis of Catholicism runs from Lithuania to Trafalgar and beyond, and the axis of the Orthodox from Archangel to Crete, the axis of Protestantism runs from Prague to Vancouver. In the southern hemisphere, the American dimension is largely Catholic; the antipodes are largely Protestant and secular; while Africa is churning forth new undreamed of kinds of Christianity. Yet from Morocco to Indonesia, Islam lies, largely impervious to Christianity, while from Moscow to Peking Christianity's cousins show their love-hate relationships.

But what about the geography of the Christian mind?

Three poises of thought

We will look at three men – Athanasius, Aquinas and Luther. They achieved three poises of thought. The first was an attempt to use Greek ideas to express a living but difficult truth of Christian worship. The second was a great synthesis of Greek and Christian ideas in the flowering of the Latin Church, which so miraculously survived the smashing up of the Empire it had subtly permeated, and which was now laying the foundations of a new and later Christian civilisation. The third led to a break-up of the new church of Rome which had tried too hard to impose authority upon the centrifugal forces of a Europe whose powers had shifted north from the Mediterranean basin. A new culture was to be born of the Reform, but it could perhaps be said to have been born out of that which it struggled against. A cultural dialectic animated the unseen heart of the Reform. In sampling the three poises of thought we have seen some of the thrusts of Christian doctrine. The doctrinal dimension of the faith remains vital, but it is of course built upon the story which is re-presented in the liturgy and present in the spirituality of the Christians – Christ's story. It took on an extra dimension, and one great extension of the story of salvation was undertaken by Augustine. Augustine was also a formative figure in Christian philosophy, a person from whom, by the way, Martin Luther derived much inspiration. It was Augustine who came up with a theory of history, which Western men have found it natural to carry on. He is thus one of the fathers of Hegel and Marx, one of the genes shaping the unruly children of the Christian faith now stalking our contemporary world. But his own story was interesting, not just the story he told about history.

Augustine and others

Augustine was born in what is now Algeria. The southern shore of the Mediterranean was good Roman territory, before the Muslims struck, and it was in process of being Christianised during Augustine's lifetime – that is in the second half of the fourth century AD. His mother, Monica, was Christian, but though he knew Christian ideas and feelings as a child, it was another religion that gripped him in his early manhood. He had gone to Carthage to study rhetoric and other matters, and lived with a mistress by whom he had a little boy. He had known the scriptures of the Christian faith, but they hardly had appeal for one trained in the intricacies of Greek philosophy. Christianity seemed crude. The Manichaeans seemed more attractive, for they combined elements of Eastern and Western thought which emphasised knowledge and self-discipline – ranging from Christian to Buddhist ideas, and to which we referred earlier (Chapter 2). Yet there were seeds of disillusion in his mind, which germinated when he repaired to Milan at the age of thirty, to take up an appointment teaching rhetoric (or literature as we might put it now). Milan was then capital of the West, and a flourishing centre. It was there that he came under the influence of the amazing Ambrose, and also, more directly, of the Neoplatonic school, who combined mystical insight with certain aspects of the intellectual framework constructed originally by Plato. He was to combine these elements, with his new-found Christian faith, in his philosophy. He was converted rather dramatically, in 386, when he heard a divine voice urging him to read the scriptures – and when he took them up he lighted upon the line: 'But put ye on the Lord Jesus Christ, and make not provision for the flesh to fulfil the lusts thereof'. His baptism followed the next year, and after that his priesting. He was to become a vital teacher in the church, a *doctor*. He returned to Africa, where he died during the siege of Hippo by the Vandals in late August 430. He had in the meantime been ordained bishop.

Meanwhile the followers of Donatus who felt that those who had not been strict in their resistance to previous persecutions should be excommunicated had been strong in North Africa. What about bishops and priests who had given in? Was their ordination valid? The Church decided that even unworthy priests could have validity. The problem thrown up by his struggle with local Donatists was a major factor in stimulating Augustine's greatest work (after his *Confessions*), namely his *De Civitate Dei* or *On the City of God*. In this work he was the great new storyteller.

Augustine's new myth

Why did he tell the story? Alaric captured the sacred and imperial city of Rome in 410, and it was two years later when Augustine began his response to this horrid and disenchanting event. A new theory of history was needed. It took fourteen years to finish, and it provided perhaps the most impressive outline of the drives within history till Hegel. (Although whether either Augustine or Hegel is right is quite a different matter.)

In a way this new story of the sacred side of history went back to the idea of the *pax deorum*. First, Augustine reckoned the replacement of the old gods by the one God (from Constantine and beyond) as a great gain. The older *numina* and divine spirits had ultimately done Rome no good. The *pax deorum* did not assure Rome of strength or virtue or happiness. And this is because of the whole story of man's fall and salvation. When Adam rebelled against God he transmitted his sin sexually to his descendants, for which reason Augustine had a rather gloomy view of sexual intercourse – but till his old age he kept his love of what he called 'the perishable beauty of the body, the brightness of the light, the soft strains of arias, the lovely scent of flowers and the limbs made for embracing flesh'. And thus human history is dominated by selfishness, and by the rapaciousness of power. The rulers of this world are normally bad, though it is true that there are some goods which they necessarily insist upon. From this idea, Augustine developed his contrast between the City of God and the earthly City. They are represented in man's beginnings by the figures respectively of Abel and Cain. The course of history shows forth two great splendours of the earthly city – Babylon and Rome, one dominating the thoughts of the Old Testament, the other the destiny of the New Covenant, for did not Peter and Paul go thither? But both were built on men's power, not on the divine sense of grace which characterises those pilgrims upon earth who inhabit the City of God and who are members of that invisible Church which God has made through his predestination.

So what of the way history has gone? Divine guidance could be seen, despite Alaric's sack of the capital, in the amazing empire to which Augustine owed so much. The evil earthly city needs to produce constraints upon selfishness; and in this it can be influenced by the Church, and so by the City of God. It was this development in history which indicates God's providence in choosing Rome as the place where the two Cities would coexist. If Rome could be prone to plunder, some folk began to argue, it showed its despotism as a weakness. Under the influence of the heavenly City, human history will culminate in a different sort of disintegration of the State when the heavenly City will come in a flash in all its fullness. So Augustine extended the salvation narrative well beyond the Biblical events, and paved the way for theories of history: from Africa there came one seed of Marx. Augustine made myth more universal, and showed a pattern of great events. But apart from historical myth there lies the more personal one; the story of the Virgin took on an altogether more intimate significance in the ongoing life of the Church, as we shall see later.

Athanasius and Christ

Athanasius' day was at the Council of Nicaea, in 325. This gathering of bishops and churchmen was called by Constantine, now master of the Empire, who had used Christ's battle standard as his victory at the Milvian Bridge, and so, reinforced by visions of Christ, had come to think of the faith as essential to the *pax deorum*. He wished the spiritual side of his empire to be as tidy as the bureaucratic side. But deep divisions caused bitterness among Christians. It was the age of the Arian controversy – an age of decision which would leave its mark on the whole doctrinal future of the faith, for the dispute had to do with Christ's divinity. Athanasius the squat, militant deacon, overcame the previously tortured half-martyr Arius, in an assembly of divided, noble, sometimes volatile bishops presided over by an awesome and inspiring Emperor. And no doubt each man's thoughts there ran back to his constituency – his diocese, his monastery, his empire, his Egypt, his Bythinia and so on. Not all spoke the same language – Greek may have dominated but perturbations could reverberate through crossed translations into Latin and the incomprehension of intrusive iotas. For in a sense it was an iota that divided the two main parties.

The issue was monotheism and the Lord Christ. Could the two live in harmony? Many of us in the West are so used to the idea of God being Father, Son, and the Holy Spirit as well, that we miss the tensions in early Christianity. How could one genuinely worship one God, the old God of Israel who created the world and led mankind and the chosen people to their destiny with the resurrected Messiah, if one also addressed Jesus as Lord God, as in the Eucharistic rite? Arius compromised, by saying that Christ was not equal to the Father and was not always there – there was a time when he was not, as the Arian mobs in Alexandria would defiantly chant (for Arianism like most influential movements was political as well as religious). Athanasius fought successfully at Nicaea for a creed which gave the Father and the Son equal power in the same substance. They were of the same substance (*homoousios* in Greek), not of similar substance (*homoiousios* – notice the extra *i* or iota). In brief they were not like me and a fellow Scot, of similar substance, but more like me and the father of my children, the identically same being. Thus were the mysteries and subtleties of the Trinity doctrine born, a doctrine meaning that God is three entities (persons) in one being. Athanasius ultimately spoke for the majority and the creed of Nicaea took form. It certainly stressed faith in Christ. Thus:

> We believe in one God the Father Almighty maker of all
> things visible and invisible.
> And in the one Lord Jesus Christ, the only-begotten
> Son of God, begotten of the Father before all worlds,
> Light from Light, very God from very God, being of one
> substance with the Father, through whom all things were
> made; who for us men and our salvation came down from
> the heavens and was made flesh of the Holy Ghost and the
> Virgin Mary, and was made man, and was crucified for us
> under Pontius Pilate, and suffered and was buried, and
> rose again on the third day according to the Scriptures,
> and went up into the heavens, and sits on the
> right hand of the Father, and will come again with glory
> to judge both the living and the dead, and of his
> kingdom there shall be no end.

We see the great emphasis both on Christ's divinity, and on his being human ('and was made man'). Both were necessary for the full flowering of the Christian idea of men's salvation through the offering by Christ of his manhood, solid with those of us who have faith in him, to God, and achieving infinite power and merit through that humble sacrifice because of his divine nature. Or to put it in another, more Eastern perspective, Christ in his resurrection shows forth the possibility of men becoming through him, and solid with him, divinised themselves. We become like God.

So from Athanasius, under the seal of imperial approval, there issued the definitive doctrine which was to leave its stamp upon Christendom. The rest were heresies, destined to wither. Athanasius fought his sacred battle when the Church was in a period of practical transition. Nine hundred years later, Aquinas, a highly practical Dominican, achieved the most perfect intellectual synthesis between the faith's revelation and the intellectual milieu.

Aquinas and the Greek world

In the earlier centuries, the Christian church came to terms with the Greek and Hellenistic world. Augustine (whom we shall encounter again shortly) had woven the Platonic element into the formulation of a faith that needed philosophy to show the relevance of revelation in the wider firmament of men's intellectual understanding of the world. Augustine's synthesis proved influential, but ultimately it was largely superseded in the new renaissance of the thirteenth century. This was a time when the European world was reappropriating the classical heritage. Partly through the Arabs the great works of Greek thought reached Christian Italy and France (the wonderful living together of Islam, Christianity and Judaism in Spain and elsewhere was a means of mutual enrichment of thought) and Aquinas gave Catholic Christianity a new framework – using Aristotle, rather than Plato – which was earthier, more articulated, more powerful than any earlier system of Christian belief.

Thomas Aquinas, born in Roccasecca near Naples of aristocratic family, was built like an ox, and Dumb Ox was his nickname. But the Ox had a big brain and a passion for truth – above all for the truth of God. He was determined to migrate to the university of Paris, then the intellectual centre of the Western world. His life's work was shaped by his experiences and influence there. Thirty books, many voluminous, were dictated or written by him, the crown being the famous *Summa Theologica*. It is austere in form, but it has in its own way a sort of poetry, the rhythm of logic applied to the divine. It was to become a paragon of doctrine and a norm of Christian philosophy. It matched revelation and reason. Thus Aquinas tried powerfully to establish the reasonableness of belief in God – partly drawing on Aristotle's metaphysics in doing so – through, for example, his famous five ways. The five ways are five ways of arguing to belief in God. Thus he argued, for instance, that the universe must depend upon a first uncaused cause or prime mover; and that the purpose and organisation seen in nature argues for an intelligent governor of the universe. The fact that we find things arranged in degrees of value or perfection argues for a most perfect being. And so on. Such arguments were wielded and formed in a subtle way by Thomas, and have retained a powerful grip, even if many modern philosophers would see flaws or problems in the reasoning. But from the conclusions of such arguments, Aquinas was able not just to argue that God does exist but that his nature must be of a certain sort. Reason could thus take you a long way in understanding God, even if it needed to be completed by the work of grace, namely God's revelation of himself through the Bible and in Christ.

Continued on page 127

Illustration section

RITES OF PASSAGE

Scholars use the phrase 'rites of passage' to mean those rituals which mark a transition in life – a baptism, a circumcision, a wedding, a degree-conferral, a funeral. They are important in most societies because they signal a change of status in the individual, and society needs to know how to treat a person with appropriate regard. They also have important emotional meanings. The priest who is ordained typically feels the weight and significance of the momentous change, just as those at a funeral recognise the emotional loss which the dead person represents to his dear ones. Religion, obviously, is a vital ingredient in most rites of passage, and one of the functions of religion is to celebrate and record the meaningful transitions which men and women must undergo in their lives and deaths.

Birth and death are the most important times for the rites of passage – a person joins or leaves the visible community. This picture shows both the comforting and the starkness of the putting away of a dead man, in County Mayo, Ireland, in 1973.

Generally Hindus cremate. Holy men and little children are typically not cremated, as they lie outside the norms of society, trailing different kinds of glory, as it were. Here we see the burning ghats at Banaras, a holy and auspicious place for an Indian (or anyone?) to die. Bodies are burnt on pires presided over by relatives and best of all the eldest son. The bones are thrown into the sacred Ganges and the ashes scattered likewise. A cow, symbol of sacredness, takes the acrid scene in. Where did cremation originate? It is uncertain, but the Aryans who came into India in the mid part of the second millennium BC *were migratory, and burning rather than burial is more logical for wandering folk.*

In days gone by the good Hindu widow burnt herself in order to go with her husband to the next existence. The British stamped on the custom, known as suttee. The word derives from Sanskrit, and literally means 'a good woman'. Whereas most Westerners look on suicide as a sin, there are occasions in Eastern cultures where it is seen as highly noble – the loving wife, the protesting monk, the defeated Japanese admiral, and so on. It is going out grimly, right, in a blaze of glory.

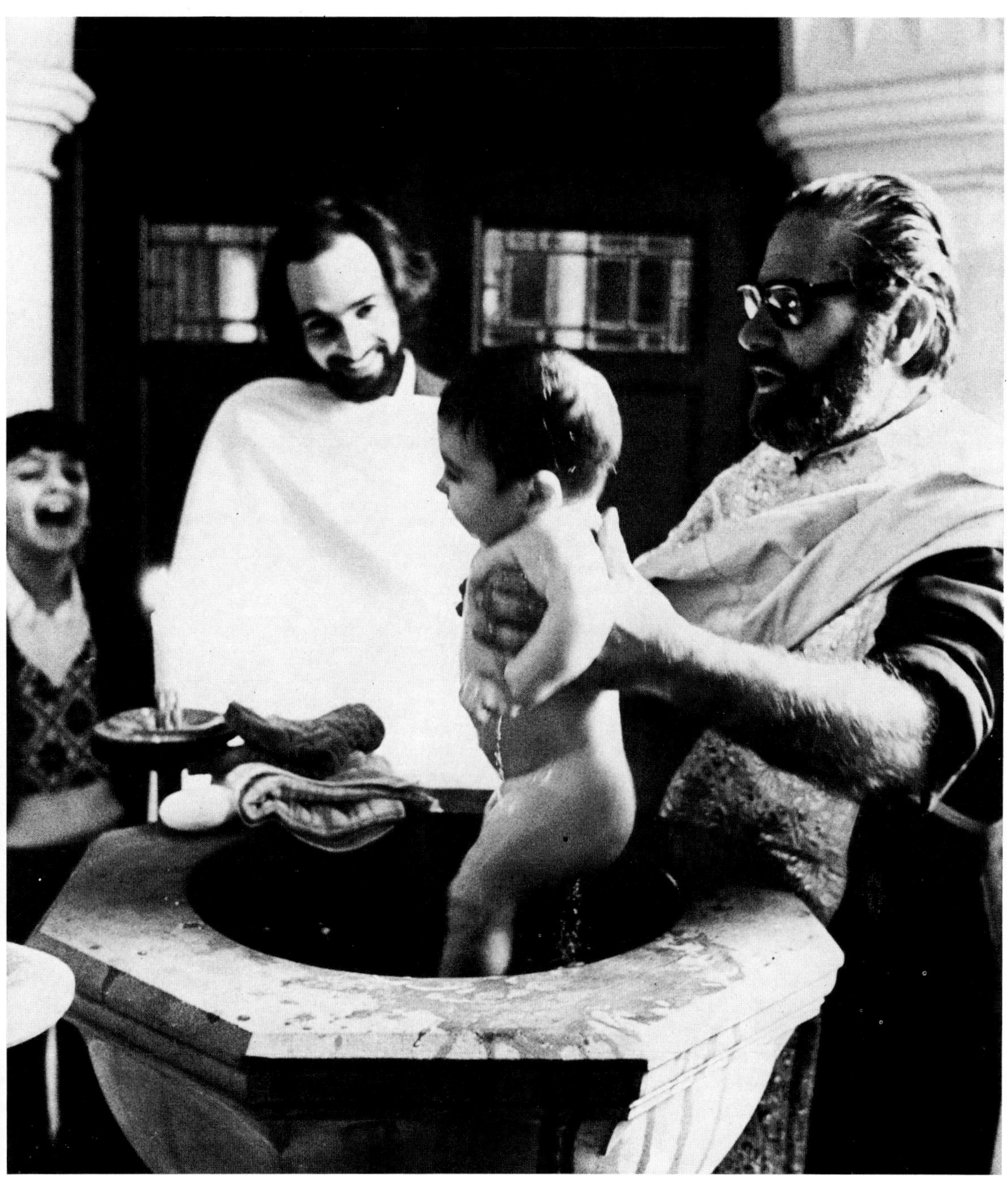

Water is a symbol, partly because it means cleanness, partly because, controlled, it shows God's power over chaos, partly because life depends upon it. Anyway it is used in various cultures in rites of passage. Here, in an Orthodox Church in London a baby is being immersed and given his name and spiritual identity. Though John the Baptist used the river, as many later Christians, it became customary to have a stone font to use in churches for the ceremony.

Left: In Rhodesia an African expression of Christianity uses a pool to echo the river Jordan. African forms of the faith very often match more closely the feel of Biblical times.

For lay people in Christianity there are various transitions, the most memorable in some ways being the first communion. This takes place at a younger age in Catholicism than in most Protestant denominations. See here how the boys and girls are so well got out, and see too how the girls are treated, in their dress, as mini-brides. Often in religious ceremonies new clothes themselves signify a change of state: for clothes are the real human skin, and though the leopard cannot change his spots the human being can.

Dying literally is leaving the visible world: but some rites signify symbolic death, always an important idea in Christianity, for Christ died that he might rise again, and Christians have seen baptism too as a kind of dying in order to gain true life. Left, we see a special dying to the world: priests prostrating themselves during their transition into the priesthood. Their lying down signifies humility and a mysterious prelude to a new sacred existence when they can administer the sacraments of the Catholic faith.

The signalling of the commencement of marriage is important to society, for it is the milieu in which the production of new members of society is ideally carried on. In many traditions it has also a sacramental significance: marriage is an outward sign of an inner, invisible grace. Thus Christianity has sanctified marriage as one of the sacraments (the other important ones being the Eucharist and baptism). This bride in Rotherhithe in South-East England is dressed in the typical bridal dress – its whiteness symbolising virginity. As often in religious rituals the dress is abnormal (she would not go shopping in it, for instance, and indeed may never wear it again). This is itself an expression of the special nature of the event and of the wedding day itself.

The edifice that Aquinas built has deeply affected Catholic thought to this day, for it gave a special precision to the idea that men could know God, albeit imperfectly, by the light of their own natural resources. This means in turn that Christianity can build upon human foundations and does not need simply to reject philosophies and religions which do not have their roots specifically in Christian tradition and revelation.

At the end of his life, sick and his powers beginning to fail, Aquinas had visions, among them an ecstasy during mass. And after that he hung up his writing implements, for what he had seen made what he had written seem to him no more than straw. Perhaps he was right, but I doubt it, for the beauty of his intellectual edifice must remain a wonder, this side of heaven.

The success of Christ

Why should Christ not, after all, be successful? The hankering after that pristine purity, when Christians heard distantly the growl of lions and the guttering of the pitch with which they would be smeared into living and dying torches, might in later times generate the sects. But in the great age of the church, both east and west, a different solution was worked out, unconsciously no doubt, in the fabric of the triumphant body of Christ.

A distasteful consequence of this accommodation with secular authority was that the Church could now turn the powers of the state upon those with whom she disagreed. Thus heresies could from time to time be persecuted. The new *pax deorum* gave, it is true, stability. But it led to excesses, ultimately to the Inquisition. Let us consider the fate of the Albigensians, who in their dying summed up so much of Middle Eastern and European religious history.

Albigensians

Their main strength was in Southern France – the name comes from the city of Albi, being one of their important centres. But they called themselves the Cathari or pure ones, and had roots in Manichaeism, itself a major faith in more ancient days, to which Augustine once adhered. The Manichees were called after Mani, who was a Persian martyred in 276. He brought together ideas from Zoroastrianism, Buddhism, Gnosticism and Christianity. The synthesis proved powerful for many centuries, even if Mani's teachings were somewhat austere. The religion held that matter is evil and the divine spark in the soul of man is trapped in it, and can only free itself by great austerity, though (through reincarnation) ordinary men can work their way up to a position where they can join the rigorous élite. Before his conversion Augustine was a Manichaean; and the faith took root in Bulgaria in the early middle ages. It constituted a so-called heresy under the name of the Bogomils. From there it penetrated Western Europe and had an influence upon the Waldensians in Italy and, most importantly, upon the Albigensians in southern France. Although it was a heresy it attracted the people of the French south-west – and even in Florence it is thought that up to a third of the people followed the teachings. In days of ecclesiastical corruption and laxity, where, despite the attempt to reassert older ideals in the founding of new monastic orders, princes of the church could look like princes of the world, and many clergy lived with concubines, the transparent austerity and spiritual leadership exercised by the Albigensian élite – the holy *perfecti* or perfect ones – was attractive to many ordinary men, who therefore became *credentes* or believers. For the perfect ones, there was no question of marriage (for reproduction brought souls into an evil world), or of killing or war (here the old influence of Buddhism showed), or of eating meat or eggs or even milk, entities that were tied up. with fleshy reproduction. Although the Cathari were theoretically Christians – lay folk often conformed to the outer practices of the Church, much use was made of scripture and there was a return to the simplicity of some early church practices – they were a threat to ecclesiastical authority. Hence it was that in 1208 a crusade against them was proclaimed by the Pope. The king of France was agreeable, for the nobles of the south were too independent. The heresy was crushed after a brutal twenty years' war, symbolised in the massacre of Montségur, one of the main fortresses of the Cathari, where hundreds of the perfect ones went peacefully to their execution by burning. The grim smell of burnt flesh was the final tribute to the steadfastness of those holy folk. Yet military defeat was not enough. The task of uprooting Catharist ideas through the newly instituted inquisition was entrusted largely to the Dominican order, but they were assisted by civil power and later torture.

Strands of religion

How many strands of religious thought were bound together by Mani and the Cathari! The old conception of the world as a struggle between good and evil harked back to Zoroaster and thus to one of the powerful prophetic religions of the ancient Near East, destined to be overrun by Islam in Persia, but keeping its ritual fires lit among the Parsees. The idea of the body as a prison of the soul harked back to ancient Greek Orphism and to those Gnostic movements which were so important in Hellenistic times, and stressed the spiritual gnosis or knowledge of God brought through Mysteries and meditation. Not surprisingly the Cathari prized St John's Gospel above all, for its opening hymn 'In the beginning was the Word' mysteriously echoed Gnostic ideas. The initiation of the perfect ones involved laying St John's Gospel on the brow of the initiate. The doctrine of reincarnation went back not merely to Indian religion but to much of the tradition of the ancient Greek world. Indeed it is interesting that the belief never really took a grip upon the orthodox Christian imagination.

But of course the complex of ideas in Catharism was deeply incompatible with the spirit of Christianity. If it is sad that the Church used soldiers and the rack to root out the Albigensian mind, nevertheless it was correct in perceiving that the doctrine of the evil and fallen nature of the world clashed with that positive valuation of the created order handed down from Genesis and implicit in the life of Jesus himself. Modern 'secular' Christianity itself is a reaffirmation of this positive picture of nature and the world.

Paradoxically, the century which saw the miseries of Montségur also saw the renaissance of Christian spirituality in the West. The thirteenth century was the century of the great Aquinas, the influence of whose massive and magisterial reformulation of Christian philosophy reaches down into the twentieth century. It was at the beginning of the century that Saint Francis received what he saw as a call from God which led to the formation of the Order which bore his name.

The pomp of the great church at Assisi and the frescoes attributed to Giotto represent a pious enrichment of the poverty which Francis preached, yet the Order was one of the vivifying streams of genuine Christianity in an uncertain and troubled era. It was in the twenties that Pope Honorius gave recognition to the Dominican order. St Dominic's mendicant preachers became the *Domini canes* as the pun had it, dogs (*canes*) of the Lord (*Domini*). Those dogs were sometimes employed as hunters, tearing the hares and foxes of heresy in the name of the Inquisition, yet the ideals of Dominic were noble ones, and fed a renewed Roman Catholic intellectual framework. It was the Dominican order that gave to the world not just the fat, mystical, energetically philosophical Thomas Aquinas, but also such mystics as Tauler and Meister Eckhart, and the fierce reformer of the Florentine scene, Savonarola.

Yet there was no doubt about the problems facing both Christianity and Europe. Both the Eastern and Western church were still threatened by Islam. Admittedly they had overcome the thrust of Muslim generals into France more than two centuries earlier, at the decisive battle of Poitiers. Europe in its northern reaches was no longer concerned at the dim memory of the loss of the southern shore of the Mediterranean Sea to Muslims. But Islam stayed strong beyond the Pyrenees. And two centuries later the Eastern empire would finally fall to the rampaging, yet splendid, Ottomans. The Crusades of course had made a dent on Islam. But Saladin had near the end of the eleventh century retaken Jerusalem, and the Third Crusade ended in a draw.

Northern Europe and the Cross

Meanwhile great changes had engulfed north and eastern Europe. The northern nations had in the centuries between the demise of the old Roman Empire and the Renaissance of the thirteenth century become, through various missionary endeavours and political chicaneries and choices, largely Christian. The barbarians, as the Romans thought of them, had become the vehicle of a strong faith. How had this happened? The story is not yet fully figured out. How was it that Vikings and rough Scandinavians even in distant Iceland, and Irish and Saxons and Celts in Britain, and Teutons all over northern Europe, had fallen under the religious spell of a crumbling Rome that some had never encountered as an imperial power? How was it that Greek religion crept up through the Balkan lands and, spiritually, conquered Russia? Christianity's major second wave of mission (that in the Empire being the first) was stunningly successful. It was also the key to the third, for it was ultimately the northern seafarers who took the message round the sea-girt globe (though Spain, the more committed to Catholicism now it had thrown off the Islamic yoke, and sea-oriented Portugal opened up much, above all the lower Americas, to the Christian message).

Britain

The way the second wave worked was complex. Let us look briefly at the pattern established in the British Isles, always a centre of converging and conflicting forces.

The Celts were the first key, the Saxons the second: Patrick, Ninian and Columba at one end; Augustine above all at the other. And in the north-east the extraordinary Bede. Celtic monasticism proved important in Ireland and parts of central and south-western Scotland.

It must be recalled that in the fourth, fifth and sixth centuries and beyond – the great age of the early Celtic saints, such as those mentioned above, together with David and others in Wales – the sea, or rather water in general, was the easiest mode of transport. Indeed it was not till the railway that the speed of overland travel caught up. So the Irish Sea should not be seen as a gap surrounded by land masses. It should be seen as a sea surrounded by interesting coasts. Within that framework there grew up a Celtic civilisation in which Christianity, mediated mainly by monks, travelled relatively fast and effectively. It was a Christianity linked to Rome but not too closely. It came to be a culture which knew something of the Greek heritage, as was shown by the great Irish scholar John Scotus Erigena, one of the early medieval writers on philosophy and faith.

The south and east of the islands were more accessible to the continent, hence the invasions from the Germanic and Nordic peoples which put a Danish and Saxon stamp on England and parts of Scotland. It was that population which came under the spell of the great mission sent by Rome to establish the faith in the south-east – in Canterbury, as it turned out, under the leadership of Augustine. If now in England the two archbishoprics are at Canterbury and York it signalises the dominance of the east and south-east by the invaders from across the Channel and North Sea. The Anglo-Saxons were persuaded through missions to kings: when they agreed whole tribes and nations were Christianised. Among the Celts the preachings were perhaps more arduous, more monk-born. The two movements fused into a British Christianity which was ultimately riven by the Reformation.

North, East and Southern Europe

The astonishingly successful missionary endeavour in northern and eastern Europe, including Russia, in the early medieval period, and the later re-establishment of Catholicism along the northern Mediterranean west of Greece (through the Albigensian Crusade and the gradual destruction of Islam in Spain) was followed by the drifting apart of East and West, and the great explosion of the Reformation which left Europe in a threefold state. The northern lands proved unreliable, from the point of view of Rome. The Eastern ones were lost, beyond Poland.

A great age of Christendom, like the thirteenth century, gave popes worldly glory. This does not necessarily imply that they were orgiastic; they were sometimes cemented to the ideals of the faith, but like establishmentarians everywhere they justified pomp by effect. Consider Innocent III. His ideas were good. He had degrees from Paris and Bologna, and knew both philosophy and law. He was young when elected. He was a JFK of the Papacy, then the best fief in Christendom. When he came to the sacred city to take up his supreme office he rode on a scarlet-decked horse, and had a great parade with stops for well-organised ceremonials. Rome was proud to be the centre of attention. The thirteenth century was almost upon them. The city stank, but still had fantastic things to be proud of. Her seedy inhabitants still thought of Rome as the navel of the universe, and the Pope still had clout. The centre of political power had been shattered, but the centre of sacred power still retained its dynamic. At other times lunatics, dodderers, foolish and stupid popes could occupy the seat of the Vicar of Christ, but that did not mean that the Papacy could be taken lightly. Even now that is so. Stalin's 'And how many divisions does the Pope have?' was a misguided remark in the twentieth century, and more certainly so in the thirteenth. Rome, however, could use its power foolishly: that was, of course, one reason for and cause of the Reformation. But, from a social point of view, the integration of secular and sacred, of state and church, which the Papal arrangement implied, worked. It meant that men could have an ideology to suit their ordinary life, and princes a theory to guide their actions (even if these were often governed by power-hunger and self-interest).

Still there were those who thought Western Catholicism an odd historical deduction from Christ. Was this the kind of social order acceptable to the utterer of the Sermon on the Mount? One of these pre-Reformers was Hus. He was an agent of the Czech reformation, but the antipathy to a pious, yet arrogant and corrupt Rome which he represents was to boil over in all kinds of places, especially in northern Europe. Hus knew Wyclif in thought – he was born about a decade before Wyclif died in 1384. But obviously he was not just a means of transmitting alien English ideas. He was a focal point of social rebellion in his own land, and in particular a lodestar of Bohemian nationalism. Condemned repeatedly, but most importantly by the Council of Constance in 1415, he was burned on 6 July of that year. He showed in his life and teachings that a more Biblical Christianity could attract the opprobrium of an established order.

The conflict between the authority of the organised church and the authority of the scriptures was (and is) a dilemma for Christians. Go back to the Bible and you go back to a primitive way of life, possibly out of accord with that of Jesus himself. To carry on the traditions and develop them may lead to corruption. The church pulsated, and continues to pulsate, with such religious questions. But meantime another rhythm was interior. For Christendom also greatly nourished mystics, men such as Eckhart, John of the Cross and Jacob Boehme and, indeed, much of monasticism was directed to the life of contemplation.

There had been signs before Luther that the fabric of Western Christendom might be torn. The ideas of John Wyclif, for example, were somewhat revolutionary. It is true he worked (naturally enough for someone who died in 1384, in the high tide of feudalism) within the framework of existing political concepts, themselves feudal in character. But he held that God's mandate, to the church and state powers, could be revoked. High positions are matters of stewardship rather than property. Not unnaturally, therefore, he attracted criticism, as a radical. He was only one of the heralds of the Reformation, later unwittingly unleashed by Martin Luther, but his attempt to give the Bible to folk in the vernacular was a great time-bomb left ticking beneath the edifice of hierarchy. The bomb exploded by chance in 1517, when a rather unexciting German seminary professor, Martin Luther, publicly expressed dissatisfaction concerning the practices of a rather mercenary and over-confident church. He is said to have fixed his famous ninety-five propositions (or theses as they are usually called) to the door of the castle church in Wittenberg, and sparked off chaos, reform and the Thirty Years War, and Protestantism as we know it. He bent the course of history. He also helped, unwittingly again, to form the German nation, through his translation of the Bible and the generation of a colloquial literary style. By and large, northern Europe broke off from the Roman connection.

The meaning of Reform

Reform was partly politics. It was partly though to do with faith and religious practice. The Reform stressed grace; harking back, above all, to Paul, it argued that man is not saved by works – even holy works – but by God's grace. It rediscovered the Bible and it saw the New Testament as preaching a Jesus who saves men not through their goodness but out of their sin. It at the same time gave the Old Testament back to the Laity (the Roman Church tended to keep it away from folk). It argued strenuously for the priesthood of all believers. It democratised puritanism. It was not austerity in monasteries, but relative austerity for all. Monks left the order, as did nuns, such as Martin Luther and his spouse. He was earthy, but of the earth heavenly. Naturally the Protestants quarrelled and why should that be denied to those who brought authority down from the Papacy to the local church community? And ultimately why should not each man decide for himself? The paper pope, the Bible, could hold folk together, but only for so long.

Luther and grace

With Martin Luther we find a spiritual revolution starting through a very different perspective on nature and grace, and a very different view of the way men and God interact. People today, in the last decades of the twentieth century, may be surprised how much could turn on theology. They should not be. After all we have new examples of doctrinal infighting – only nowadays we are more used to such disputes in the tradition of Marxism than in those of religion proper. If Mao slangs Brezhnev in the name of world revolution and the Communist tradition, he does so in similar spirit to the disputes of the Reformation, when Christianity in Western Europe began to take on its modern pluralism, creating liberty and anguish, nationalism and scientific thought, kingdoms and communes, and heaven knows what in a series of creative but also distressing turmoils. So Luther's thoughts about grace and nature, rather different from those of the Dumb Ox, are vital in the comprehension of modern Europe. Was it a coincidence he was German? In a way: but he was one ancestor of modern nationalism, and beyond the Alps the writ of Latin Europe ran more feebly, so when he revolted, he found political and cultural echoes, and so achieved a revolution, beyond any dreams he might have had.

Let us begin with the man's thought. When he nailed his theses on the church door, what was he really protesting against? It was a tangle of things. No doubt the final issue was the sale of indulgences to cover the cost of building St Peter's in Rome, but beneath that fairly mundane issue was a deeper concern, which Martin Luther expressed. It is a thought in all our minds regarding religion, I think. Let me try to express its general form. The fact is that, if there is a God, or if there is a transcendent realm of whatever kind (let us not for the moment argue as to whether it be personal or not, whether it be Christ or nirvana, say), that 'other realm' needs to be mediated by folk like us. I can see God, but I have to tell what I saw to others. Do they trust me? Am I good? I am not. So they begin to distrust the mediator. So God has a problem getting through. But if you believe in God you accept that he is mediated. And then the question becomes: What mediators can you accept? Luther got to a point where he could no longer accept the priestly hierarchy of the Catholic Church centred upon Rome. He saw in it a takeover by men of God's power. If God is supreme, the power lies with him not with human institutions, even the Church with its impressive organisation and powerful Pope. The building of St Peter's could put a strain on the economy of the Western Church, and it was through that strain that it broke apart. Luther was the occasion of the break through his doctrine of grace, which ran flat against the theories of the human dimension of the faith as espoused both by the Papacy for practical reasons, and by Aquinas and his successors for theoretical ones. Aristotle and Rome both took a beating from the tiresome, but gritty Luther. God's salvation comes by faith, not by reason; and by God's grace, not by human works. In the last resort no priest can achieve anything.

The author of this explosive doctrine was a miner's son, who gained enough education to be able to enter the University of Erfurt. After graduating he did not go on to finish his legal studies, but instead entered the Augustinian order, which then had a fine reputation of being monasticism at its best. There he was much encouraged by the spiritual and intellectual guidance of Johann von Staupitz, who died six years after the crucial events which led to the whole explosion of Reform. Luther was surprised at the effect of the ninety-five theses when he enunciated them at Wittenberg, where by now he had a university chair of theology, on 31 October 1517. It was a great time of change. The New World was less than three decades old, in Europe's eyes. The older apparatus of the Holy Roman Empire was cracking. But Luther did not act from political motives, though his challenge was to have profound political meaning. He acted out of his own psychology and out of faith. Since university days he had been burdened by a strong sense of sin and of the need for salvation. But he came to see that God is love, not primarily a punisher.

He was especially affected by two experiences. The first was a journey from his own austere monastic environment in Germany to the fabulous city of Rome. The glories of the Pope's life did not seem quite like the poor, if sometimes easygoing, life of Christ and his disciples. Should the Vicar of Christ be carried on a litter? The seeds of practical doubt about the course which Christianity had taken ripened in the ardent Luther's mind. The second experience was where, in a flash, he saw the essence of the Christian teaching on salvation in the words 'The just shall live by faith'. Paul spoke not just to the old Romans but to the new Reformers. As with Augustine, Luther's great perception, conversion we might say, was mediated directly by scripture. He wanted to challenge the scholastic theology of which Aquinas had made such as grand synthesis, but which was now the ideological basis of indulgences, whereby money on earth could seem to assure benefits in the afterlife. Indulgences were the logical extension of the idea that the faithful could acquire merit from Christ through the church. Like many logical extensions in the practical sphere it breached a moral boundary (in our own day folk argue sometimes: If tanks are all right, then H-bombs are).

So, on that eve of All Saints, Luther pinned his ideas up in the public place which acted as a forum for the university intellectuals. And then the troubles came. The Roman power hit back, and a period of debate and confusion resulted in the culminating encounter at the so-called Diet of Worms, where Luther, under safe-conduct, defended his reforming ideas. Though condemned, he was protected by his prince, the Elector Frederick of Saxony, and hidden for a time in Wartburg Castle, where he undertook his influential German translation of the New Testament. How dangerous! Printing now made it possible for any man who was literate to read the scriptures, which had previously been protected by Latin and the ecclesiastical near-monopoly of literacy. Luther not only helped form the German literary style but was also a main parent of the free access to the Bible, and then, more generally, to any literature in the modern world.

Another casualty of the Reform were the monasteries. Where the new ideas spread, monks and nuns left the order. Luther had five children by an ex-nun. For after all even the good work of celibacy must be vain, according to the teaching, in securing salvation. Luther was a more easy-going ox than Aquinas, it turned out.

The Reform showed the vitality of the Bible, but it did not prove an assured way to agreed truth. While it was through deep thought on both Old and New Testaments, about which he had to prepare courses of lectures, that Martin Luther came to question the latter-day teaching and practice of mother Church, it soon turned out that other Reformers interpreted it differently – men such as Zwingli and later Calvin, great founder of stern Presbyterianism. And in any case the success of the Reform in northern Europe, like the earlier success of the faith itself, largely depended on the decisions of princes and kings. Those whose ancestors in northern lands had embraced the Cross and substituted Christ for the Teutonic and Nordic gods now turned to the new Christianity of the Reform. Without them, there would have been no Lutheran churches. Luther indeed preached a convenient thing – for he preached a kind of (establishmentarian) submission to the State that meant that the faith was spiritual and moral, but the princes ruled. No wonder that faithfully Catholic prince Henry VIII in England was tempted! And dissolving monasteries was a good racket for princes in need of money. Eventually, the Reform itself gave birth to new faiths – Protestantism in its amazing multiplicity, a new ethic, and humanism in its modern forms. But let us now turn to more practical aspects of the Christian life before and beyond the Reform.

Pilgrimages

That there are holy places and holy times is no more surprising than that there are holy people or holy books. Modern Christianity has much less of this sense of sacred space and time. The festivals are often decayed.

Canterbury is now more an architectural monument than a lodestar for pilgrims. Tourism is more frequent than pilgrimage. Yet pilgrimage was an integral part of both Western and Eastern Christianity. One can even look on the Crusades as military pilgrimages, for the holy places of Palestine loomed large in the imagination of Christians. But of all places East and West, Rome was undoubtedly the greatest focus. From all over folk piously trudged there, and when they at last reached the top of the last slope from which they could see the sacred city, redolent of Peter, of Paul, of empire and papacy, of sacred Latin and secular law, of churches and Tiber, of promise for eternity, the eternal City itself – when they at last saw it, they chanted in solemn joy the song:

O Roma nobilis orbis et domina
Cunctarum urbium excellentissima
Salutem dicimus tibi per omnia
Te benedicimus salve per saecula.

In other words:

O noble Rome, you mistress of the globe,
Pre-eminent over all cities,
We say our salutes to you for all your blessings,
We hail you, bless you, through all time.

Rome then was a bit like a small Tuscan city now. It had, in medieval times, no great dome of St Peter's. It was replete with towers and battlements, like a mini-Manhattan. Bell-towers as well as defence-towers abounded. It was not too nice, full of faction, gnats, drains, ruins. But it was the holy city of the faith. Rome was not just a place; it was an idea. Although the middle ages were to end with Rome rebuilt, but the Church in spiritual faction, yet as ever Rome survived to see new triumphs. Why did the pilgrims come? Partly because the earthly voyage was an echo of life, which is itself a pilgrimage. We travel through time to eternity, and through space to the eternal city. Partly they came because Rome had replaced Jerusalem as the focus of Christian eyes. They came because Rome summed up all cities seen as founts of wonder and civilisation; the Christian religion itself had first been transmitted from city to city, only it later reached out to peasants and barbarian lands. They came because men in the West saw the bishop of Rome as above all other bishops, and the city therefore worth a sacred visit. And in the manner of men who share in the substance of a thing, by being present with it, the pilgrims came to gain promises of later glory and even earthly welfare. As boys now touch sports stars, medieval men touched, in their minds, the saints who hovered invisibly glorious over the turbulent ancient city.

Rome was the centre. But many pilgrimages were to the outlying parts: man is not of this world, says the pilgrim – spiritual comfort may not always be at the geographical centre. The real Broadway is off-Broadway. The real Rome is perhaps off-Rome. Maybe that is the charm of Lourdes and Walsingham and the Madonna del Soccorso on Lake Como, and also perhaps of the other Romes – Constantinople, mother of Orthodoxy, and the third Rome, Moscow, seat of the Patriarchate and of Stalin. But Rome, the eternal city, retains its grip on the heart, and was of course above all the chief seat of the Papacy.

The monks of war

The twelfth century was crucial. The northern (and even not so northern) nobility were brutal, yet not without ideals, of their own kind. It was not unreasonable for the Church in the West to look with favour upon the creation of new, élitist, monastic orders which could recruit literal soldiers of Christ – sometimes hooded in chapel, but sometimes steel-clad as cavalry; sometimes humble, but sometimes the panzers of the middle ages. They were sacred von Mansteins, holy Pattons, who went down into Palestine on dear crusades, and north-east into the pagan lands which now cover the area from Danzig up to Latvia and beyond. Palestine, the theory was, might be rescued from the Infidel, from the Muslims who, stemming from the lands of Semitic religion, had overrun the Semitic heart of Christianity. The north-east European campaign of the Teutonic knights continued the conversion of northern Europe by new means. There was a large vacuum between the Muscovites and the converted North Germans, where the inhabitants retained a pagan and uncivilised (as their enemies saw it) culture. The Teutonic knights rode like heavy armour into it, but the vacuum was unwilling to be filled and came resisting out of the sacred forests.

The main spark of it all was the crusading impulse: the idea of regaining the Holy Land was, in part, a way of harnessing the unruliness of the time. The concept of a sacred order devoted to war in the cause of Christendom, though it strikes against some of the earlier poises of the martyr-generated early church, was by no means absurd.

The crusades towards Palestine were one motif and we have had a glimpse of the Albigensian crusade, but the crusade in the Baltic regions is perhaps most interesting in showing how Christians tamed, and then unleashed, the dogs of war. It is not uninteresting, by the way, that some of the ideology of the old *Drach nach Osten* passed into the consciousness of the author of *Mein Kampf*. Towards the end of the thirteenth century the Order of Teutonic Knights (of St Mary's Hospital of Jerusalem, to give them their full title) was formed. It flourished mainly under the successor of the first chief of the Order, one Fra Hermann von Salza. The leaders, the brother-knights, had to be of noble birth. The order also had priests and sergeants, but the core was the order of brothers who rode the heavily-armoured horses. It was they who constituted the central force in the military campaigns that won the north-east to Christian (and to some extent German) tutelage. By 1407 these austere warriors had captured what were later the Baltic Republics, the regions of Lithuania, Latvia and Estonia. Earlier they had carved off what was East Prussia. It is ironic to reflect that Russian nationalism, in the guise of Stalinism, and inspired by a different ideology, took all those regions back from the enemy.

Desmond Seward has written of the ideals of the monks of war and shows how they were a strange counterpoint to those of the earliest martyrs:

> In St Bernard's words killing for Christ was . . . the extermination of injustice rather than the unjust, and therefore desirable: indeed 'to kill a pagan is to win glory for it gives glory to Christ'. Any cavalry soldier will speak of the characteristic noises in a squadron, the squeak of leather and the jangle of metal harness, but above all troopers cursing beneath their breath at restive mounts. It was prayerful ejaculations rather than swearing in the ideal Templar squadron. . . . Death in battle meant consecration as a martyr. [*Monks of War*, p. 39]

The Virgin Mary

The story of Jesus and the disciples is in great part the story of a man's world. But the ancient like the modern world found as many mysteries in the fecundity of women as in the potency of men. It was not surprising that by the fourth century after Christ the Virgin Mary came to be a dominant figure among the saints. She was mother of God – and how could one be more fruitful? Yet strangely by repute she had not conceived through human intercourse but received through the mysterious Holy Spirit, the divine seed of the Father. She could thus be a marvellous replacement of the older mother goddesses. For one thing she was no God herself – merely a human vehicle of divine action, and yet by being called mother of God, the Theotokos, she had the numinosity of rivals like Isis. The place she was to play in Christian devotions was clarified somewhat at the Council of Ephesus (415) when the title Theotokos was officially confirmed. It was a title that refuted those who maintained that Mary was merely mother of the human side of Jesus. Much earlier, by the second century if not before, elaborate ideas had grown up about Mary's early life and motherhood. These were expressed in various versions of the so-called *Book of James*, supposedly the word of the brother of the Lord.

These tell that Anna, Mary's mother, was, like Sarah, barren (there are echoes of the earlier tale), and was diffident about appearing with her husband at the feast of the 'great day of the Lord'. But she was persuaded to put on her finery, and in the afternoon went into the garden to lament her lot. But an angel heard her poetical lament, and she was told she would conceive. She offered her baby to the Lord. In due course the baby was born and the book goes on to describe Anna's joys of motherhood and the precocious wisdom and virtue of the little Mary. Already we see here a rhythm running from Samuel through Mary to Jesus himself. Mary's own birth was later thought immaculate – sin did not get transmitted to her, as the theory of the propagation of original sin from Adam might dictate. This foreshadowed the virgin birth. In some versions of the *Book of James*, Mary was both Joseph's ward and his second wife, so that on this view James would be half-brother of Jesus. Eventually the cult of Mary led to the dogma of her bodily assumption into heaven. But really the dogmas and stories are less important than her sparkling, sweet presence in the thoughts and pictures of the burgeoning Church and in the cults which came to surround her sacred name. She could fulfil so many roles. She could be the holy ideal of the virgin, for the Church has always had leanings to celibacy. As we shall see later, different attitudes emerged about the church and sex, but the prizing of the celibate state was an engine of monasticism, and so a powerful current in the spread and spiritualisation of the faith. So she was a virgin for virgins. She was also a mother for mothers, and the love for Jesus she displayed was an example of the holy family life enjoined by the church and tenderly displayed in so many pictures of Virgin and Son. The ideal is summed up in the not so rhetorical question in the hymn: 'Can a woman's tender care, Cease toward the child she bare?' But Mary was also ideal mother for pious men, giving out the mother's love that males especially crave. And also, as we have seen, she was a rival to the mother goddesses of the Hellenistic world, a means of overcoming the other, more earthy, deities. So it is no wonder that her icons glow with sacramental grace in Eastern churches, and the sound of Ave Maria remains a source of delight to so many of the pious in the Western Catholic world. Not for nothing is Italy's great summer holiday, the Ferragosto, timed for the celebration of the feast of the Assumption of the Virgin. As an Italian proverb has it: 'Who goes to Jesus without Mary gets hassled, and prolongs the way.' So the Mother of God also is the chief of saints – and what are saints for? Why, they are good-human intermediates between us and the awesomeness of the divine throne where the human Jesus now sits in glory.

Christians and sex

In older days Christians were, like most people, confused about sex. The creation was good, and therefore bodies were too. Christ was a man, not a mere ghost, and was not Abraham told to get on with multiplying? (Hence one problem about Sarah, and thereafter Mary's mother, as we have seen.) But on the other hand Paul urged virginity if you could achieve it, marriage being all right as a fence against such problems as might arise for those who burn with desire, it thus being 'better to marry than to burn'. Fairly early in the church's life it was thought good to practise celibacy. Early on, too, the Church tried to get women to be very demure: they did not need to be too attractive to men, and sex was chiefly for procreation. The establishment of monasticism, which grew partly out of these attitudes, led to a certain relaxation. For if some people could specialise in being virgins and celibate, other folk could more cheerfully get on with the married state. The Reformation destroyed the monasteries, and became rather unrelaxed on the sexual front.

The ascetic attitudes to sex in the early church attracted favourable comment, in that the Christians practised rather generally what the more prestigious philosophers of the period recommended – in those days philosophy was a kind of intellectual alternative to or superstructure of religion. In a sense Christians democratised an élite ethic – not that they failed to do naughty things, as Paul's scriptures to the Corinthians indicate. Quite early the idea of the celibacy of the clergy began to take a grip, especially in the Western church. In the East the custom grew that clergy should be already wedded, monks celibate, and bishops generally recruited from the latter. No Mrs Proudie could haunt the novels of Russia or Romania. By the time of the Reformation the whole matter was on the agenda again. There were questions about divorce and second marriage. Clergy often had concubines, which showed that the ethic was somehow not matching the ways in which human desires and feelings could be put under discipline. The Counter-Reformation brought reform to the Roman Catholic church and a new sense of discipline. But some radical groups, such as the Münster Anabaptists, favoured polygamy – for after all the Old Testament exhibited the system – just as in modern Africa new Christian or semi-Christian groups have rediscovered the social meaning of the Old Testament. The Reformation was not foreign to new and sometimes alarming thoughts on the reshaping of family ethics.

Yet through all this runs an interesting and positive thread. Marriage was looked upon as a sacrament. It was a sacred interlocking between two people and made holy the procreation of children. As it was the great pre-Christian 'natural' Christian sacrament, so the thoughts of men about it, and their rules and contrivances from times gone by, have always had a disturbing influence. Yet Christianity in essence glorified the married state, and in many varied ways its complement, monasticism, was good. Celibates were holy contemplatives, father confessors, miracle-working abbots and spiritual advisers, breeders of carp, hermits and agriculturists, wine-makers, those who cared for the sick, friars and mendicants, fat men and thin men; and the nuns likewise – though clustering more in gardens and kitchens, on high days scurrying after bishops, and finding joys in incense and liturgy.

But the monastic ideal could take strange turns, as in medieval Japan. And as we have seen medieval Europe also bred the monks of war – the Teutonic knights, the monastic Crusaders and so on give us a new meaning of 'Onward, Christian Soldiers'.

Standing back

Perhaps at this point it is useful briefly to stand back, as we face towards the epoch of modern religion. The monks of war belong essentially to late medieval Christianity, due to be transformed by Reformation and Counter-Reformation. The monks, early Christian ideas about sex and marriage, the cult of the Virgin, the pattern of pilgrimages, the inquisitions, the synthesis between Greek and Jewish ideas, the wedding of state and church – in such facets of Christian life up to the great Reform we have seen something of the complex, even contradictory, character of classical Christianity. There were other facets too – such as mysticism, a current within Christianity too little appreciated, and to that we shall come, for in some respects it spanned the Reformation. The complexity of classical Christianity overlaid by the changes initiated by Luther brought various values into the modern world – European and American culture is haunted and also dynamised by the ethics and austerity of much of the Christian heritage. Moreover, the achievement of Western Catholicism was to provide a continuity with Greece and Rome, allowing a newly prosperous Europe to burgeon first with the Renaissance and then with the tremendous critical powers released by the Reformation. Perhaps, however, in modern consciousness it is the ethical component of the faith which retains the greatest power, while the belief in the Last Things – the consummation of history – has taken a strong grip upon men's imagination, albeit often in a secular form, as with Marxism and forms of national utopianism. Also, Protestantism was to some extent the father of modern European nationalism. However, let us first contemplate Christian ethics and hope as they helped to shape the modern world.

Christianity

The Christian churches made much of sin, for it was a way of integrating ethics, devotion and belief. Christ's saving work was seen against the dramatic background of the first Adam and his sinning aftermath, and ethical rules were perceived, like all else, in the light of God's saving work. Thus the very idea of *deadly* sins is linked to the theology of salvation. For death here is not literal. It is rather the ghastly notion of ultimate alienation from God – of being everlastingly cut off from Him, in hell. Certain forms of moral behaviour, without repentance, could at the time of death project the sinner into ultimate death. And Christendom thought of seven. The very idea that moral behaviour is relevant to God can mean that being good is in itself positively a service to God, and Christ of course can be seen in every man. Thus Brother Lawrence, a simple contemplative and goodly brother, could see life, ordinary activities – dish-washing or whatever – as being a way of practising God's presence. It was a way of worship and of meditation. All religions tend to see the mundane in the light of heaven. Christianity sees goodness as godly. So worship is extended everywhere. But what is worship? At its heart lies the great sacrament – Catholic mass or Eastern Liturgy, and in Protestantism the hearing of God's word. Ethical behaviour projects worship into ordinary life. There lies saintliness.

Space, time and the millennium

If the picture of a saint, above all of Mary, could mediate a sense of what lay beyond the sky and beyond the rite, transcending space so to speak, then the picture of the Last Things could bridge the gap between human hope and history on the one hand, and the timelessness beyond history, beyond time, on the other. Not surprisingly, the images in *Revelation* and elsewhere were taken up in a dramatic way as a kind of story-telling of the future which justified present forms of life (just as stories of the high past could explain our predicament and the nature of the world). If Christ was midpoint, the creation and final salvation for man were the beginning and the end. But as Christ had two natures, divine and human, so creation and consummation had two aspects: God, out of time, making time and then involved in his transactions with Adam; likewise the end is preceded by the resurrection and a thousand-year reign of Christ. Mind you, the long delay of Christ's second Advent made the Church disillusioned with the more dramatic speculations about the immediate future. But the middle ages saw revivals, and with the Reform the images sprang freshly from the pages of the newly open scriptures. And sprang too from the hearts of men, for the Reform also drove anti-Papists towards a sense of the authority of their individual revelations.

One of the movements loosed by the Reformation was that whose members were rather vaguely called Anabaptists – those who believed as the name implies in rebaptism or in other words adult baptism. A favourite punishment of them by Lutheran authorities, who favoured close Church-State relations, in the tradition of Augustine, was to drown them. That was rebaptism indeed. Why was baptising important? For a double reason. First, it meant voluntarism – you chose to become a member of the Church, the true Church: it was not a matter of where you belonged on earth, but where you belonged in heaven. It was not a matter of your country, but

Continued on page 147

Illustration section

THE FACE OF HEAVEN

What is divine, what transcends the world, what is heavenly – this men try to represent by symbols: but because it can only be indirectly represented by earthly analogies, sometimes a religion, such as Judaism or Islam and some types of Protestantism, largely objects to visible representation of the divine, for fear of idolatry. Very often the spirit of a religion can be perceived clearly in its art. The study of what I here call 'the face of heaven' is known usually as iconography.

This great statue of the Buddha in Sri Lanka (Ceylon) portrays him lying down, asleep to the world: in other words it shows him at his final decease or nirvana. Thereafter, since he escapes thus all individuality and possibility of being reborn, he cannot properly be referred to. It is like a flame going out. When that has happened there is no flame to talk about, no trace of it. In early Buddhist sculpture sometimes the Buddha himself was left out of a scene, say of him talking with his disciples, to suggest this final evaporation of the Buddha and his mysterious disappearance into the ineffable.

The Bible gives an impression of the masculinity of God. But most traditional Christianity, both East and West, celebrated the glories of motherhood through the figure of the Virgin Mary. This Bavarian mother and child sums up much of European piety and society: chaste mother and lovely child. But the Reformation brought a widespread rejection of reverence for the Virgin Mary – it seemed to some Reformers a kind of idolatry, setting up Mary beside God. Perhaps psychologically there was truth in this charge; but on the other side of the coin the figure of Mary gave a feminine dimension to heaven.

This African crucifix (right) shows how Catholic Christianity has used as a central symbol the scene of Christ's death. It is his sacrifice upon the cross which atones for sin and heals the breach between man and God brought about by Adam's falling from grace. Eastern Orthodox Christians on the other hand give greater prominence to Christ risen – the triumphant Lord who in his resurrection overcame death.

In Hinduism the female dimension is much more prominent, for the female is regarded as the powerful, creative force. A God is often seen pictured with his consort. In this scene (left) there is Vishnu, one of the two great representations in Hinduism of the Supreme Being, and his consort Lakshmi. Vishnu has a particularly dynamic place in Hindu piety because he is incarnated in various forms, notably in the figure of the amorous and noble Krishna.

However, even in the West Christ triumphant is not absent. Here is a lovely example from Constance Cathedral, dating from about 1000.

In China the divine was often spoke of in terms of heaven. Even in Mao's poems he refers to heaven – but the inner meaning is the people and spirit of China. The cult of Mao's portrait, here seen in Peking, is a socialist and nationalistic translation of the old values – bringing the face of heaven to earth.

of your commitment. This was not the stuff of which Lutheranism was made – for had it not flourished by serving the needs and loves of princes? The exigencies of politics were important. Even the very Catholic prince Henry VIII in England, who embraced reform that he might somewhat bigamously embrace a bosom, retained the Church-State principle. And Elizabeth fought the great zealous Spanish Armada to defend religion as well as political territory. Against all such systems the idea of commitment jarred threateningly. So baptism was important. Second, the question of who underwent adult baptism was vital: it showed concretely who was unreliable. It fuelled martyrdom from both sides. So the Anabaptists were rather miserably tortured, burnt, drowned or at least exiled. Only Philip of Hesse really tolerated them, on the principle, shown to be correct, that violence increases opposition, while gentleness can lead to reconversion. Many Anabaptists in his territory came back to the fold, angry but conforming sheep. So the label Anabaptist was dangerous but, partly for that very reason, the movement flourished.

Amid the upheavals in northern Europe in this heady period of the twenties and thirties of the fifteenth century it was not odd that there should be expectation of the millennium: men sensed an approaching consummation. If Augustine was theorist of the story, and Mary a focus of love in the story, the millennarian hope of Anabaptists and others was the new drama of the story. We can see this in the sad events at Münster. The radicals of the Reformation (precursors of such groups as the Hutterites and Mennonites in the United States and Canada, who today quietly pursue a profitable communal life amid the opportunities and sinful delights of modern capitalism) were men such as Melchior Hoffman and the Dutch baker Jan Mathys, who preached with great and disturbing effect the idea of an imminent Second Coming. A new age was upon us, they urged. And people of the lower classes, particularly, could easily believe them. Mathys was a primitive Lenin, and his revolution in 1534 took over Münster and drove forth opponents. It was disturbing, triumphant and apocalyptic. But conservative forces were not long in mustering. Though the Anabaptists in general were peaceful, even pacifist, the Münster community was impelled into armed warfare. Though Mathys was killed, the new leader (proclaimed as King David, for Münster was seen as the New Jerusalem, against Romish and Strasbourgian Babylon) was able to increase evangelical support for the uprising in many parts of Germany and Holland. Folk were urged to flock to Münster for the inauguration of the millennium – the thousand-year reign of Christ. But the rising in Münster was put down bloodily. The leaders were tortured and their dead bodies displayed in cages. That was an end to disturbing social changes, and communism and a bit of polygamy (the Old Testament hit them powerfully, and it was all right there) were wiped out. It is interesting that radical groups have returned on occasion to such themes when a new social order is seen as a preparation for the consummation of history. For the Anabaptists it was an earthly working out of an old myth. We have millennarians today but in a different disguise.

Christian mysticism

In a way Christian mysticism was a paradox. The testimony of many religions, and many contemplatives, is that in the interior vision of ultimate reality the distinction between what is seen and what sees is abolished; the soul feels that it is absorbed into a greater whole: or, to put it another way, there is an experience of deep identity. Yet the Christian heritage latches firmly onto quite a different conception, namely that God is wholly other. He is set over against man, as formidable creator. It is wrong for man to seek to be God or even to grab for immortality – what else was the story of Adam about? The idea of God as Holy is the notion of God as different. What then are Christians to say about the mystical experience of union with ultimate reality, with, maybe, God himself? Three in one being divine is all right. But two in one with one partner human could be a doctrinal problem. But the experiences went on. How did Christians cope with the paradox?

One of the most striking of mystical movements is that known as Hesychasm, a term derived from the Greek word for quiet, for contemplation involves a quiet and silent concentration upon the ultimate. Yet, though the Orthodox Hesychasts followed the teachings of the early fathers, in the fourteenth century they attracted criticism. The special techniques they used included the control of breath (and are therefore reminiscent of Yoga and the Taoists) and were criticised as being materialistic. Although the Hesychasts were, perhaps, also a menace to the more worldly churchmen of the day, they did pose a real problem for a theology which stresses the distance between God and man – as mystics they saw a Light, but were they justified in identifying it with the Divine Light? They had a great champion in St Gregory Palamas. He saw that mystics might not see God's essence but the energies or offshoots through which his work was accomplished and perceived. After all, the world is God's energies at work. It is good and beautiful, dynamic: and if we can see God in forest and burning bush, why should we not see him in this interior Light?

Eckhart had troubles as a mystic too, in the Western context. He claimed on the basis of his own interior experience a view of God not quite orthodox from the point of view of Catholicism. His reasons were similar to those of the (to him unknown) Hesychasts, and other mystics. He had a view of God as both personal and as beyond personhood. He saw him as ineffable, as beyond being; and indeed the goal of the contemplative life being mystical union when the liberated divine spark in man returns to its origin and likeness. Eckhart is very Hindu, though he did not know this. Indeed, the mystics of the Christian tradition take us East in various ways. It is wrong to look upon Christianity as set over against the so-called Oriental religions. It is quite wrong to think of a great schism existing between the two, especially in the era of Christendom up to the fragmentation at the Reformation. Monasticism, contemplation, Hesychasm, the Liturgy, the Mass, Neo-Platonism, devotionalism, magic, candles, pictures – all these would have been very familiar to the visiting Buddhist or Hindu. And, although it was only when Protestantism came into its own that one could see clearly the difference between Europe and Asia, many Protestants were also committed to the deep interior life: an example is Boehme.

Boehme

He was born in 1575, in Silesia, in an unimportant town called Alt Seidenberg. He was brought up in the Lutheran faith, among peasants, and was to become a shoemaker. When he was about twenty-five he had a penetrating experience which he saw as divine. The bright sun one day fell upon a highly polished pewter dish and in a flash he was transported into a kind of ecstasy. He felt he knew thereby the centre of the universe, the ground of being, the nature of God. He had long sought the Truth in his earlier life, and now it came to him briefly and yet he felt eternally. From then on he was to meditate on his experiences and to wait until he felt ready to write about them, which he did, profoundly, in a number of works which were to be one of the main influences upon the Quakers.

So we glimpse similar inner experiences in East, West, Catholic and Protestant. The mystics highlight the almost universal impulse towards directness in the love of God, which was the point of the outward pomps and ritual offerings of the official church. Beside the mystics, perhaps, the writings of the theologians were, as Aquinas thought, so much straw. But perhaps his perception was just that religion can be better based upon the heart and the experimental dimension than upon a system, however marvellous, of ideas.

Conclusions so far

Christianity, the least understood of religions in the West, has in its classical days centred on three main things: upon sacraments, above all the Mass and the Liturgy; upon monasticism and its attendant contemplative life; and upon the ideal of Empire, the relation of church and state. So it was sacrament, monastery and power. From that the magic flowed, that held the loyalty and awe of the peasants and the masses. It was, thus, the great inspiration of Europe through dark days. It could stand up to Islam. At the Reformation it was bursting with new, violent, and sometimes malignant life: The Thirty Years War showed what lay beneath. Was it fortunate that, at this crucial time, it was spilling over into the New World and New Spain?

National Churches after Luther: Sweden

One dramatic effect of Luther's reformation was the proliferation of national churches in Northern Europe; another was the uncorking of Protestant multiplicity: sects and denominations bred unnervingly. Meanwhile the Roman church carried through its own Reformation just at the time when it was expanding enormously in the New World. Let us use the examples of Sweden and England to illustrate the first of these consequences of Reform.

The early part of the sixteenth century was not a happy one for Sweden. It had come under the Danish crown, and King Christian II, to consolidate his grip on the country, had suddenly and bloodily murdered a large part of the aristocracy. But the move backfired. For a young nobleman Gustavus Vasa, some of whose close relatives had been murdered, and who himself had escaped from prison, raised a revolt with massive peasant support. He became king, and at a time when monarchs and princes throughout northern Europe were adding a political dimension to the Reformation debate by trying to bring the Church under their control. Vasa was impressed by one of the early Swedish reformers, Olaf Petersson, who had been studying at Wittenberg itself when Luther pinned his theses to the door. Further, the chief prelate, the Archbishop of Uppsala, was a supporter of Christian II and had fled. The financial resources of the Church were tempting to Vasa, who was chronically short of cash.

The collision with Rome came over the latter's authority to nominate a successor for the see of Uppsala (the Pope nominated a pliant Italian). In 1523 the tie with Rome was broken, and a national church which, though Lutheran in principle, had a distinctly Swedish stamp came to be established. Olaf and his associates brought out a Swedish Bible, a hymnal and a Swedish version of the mass. Somewhat to Vasa's surprise, the bishops showed much more independence than might be expected, and his mind turned towards more radical reform, but the Church did not undergo further dramatic changes. It is striking that, despite considerable intellectual and missionary vigour, especially in the nineteenth century and the early part of the twentieth, Swedish Christianity reaches but a small minority. Even though it is built into the fabric of society, in that the pastor acts as registrar of births, deaths and marriages, and thus everyone sooner or later has formal contact with him, the churches are largely empty.

Possibly this stems from the way in which Sweden was originally converted and from the nature of the Reformation itself. Though the old Viking religion was disintegrating through the very success of the Northmen in overcoming other cultures which affected them strongly, the actual Christianisation of the northern lands was confirmed by royal decisions. It was kings who took the final step. Though missionaries from England and elsewhere made trips to nurture the new Christian lands, there was always doubt as to how deeply the new faith could really sink its roots without borrowing some of the old magic of living pre-Christian religion. The Reformation not only swept much of that compromise away, but was also, most egregiously, a conversion from the top, engineered by king and churchman. The alienation of the Swedish masses from Christianity was prepared for by these earlier events. In England the issue of the Reformation was in doubt until after the Civil War, but in many ways the general picture was the same.

The Church of England

Though the Church of England's independence from Rome owed much to Luther, the Church is not Lutheran. It claims to be both Catholic and Reformed, and has its own ethos to which the name Anglicanism may be attached. It prides itself on the width of its teaching, the varieties of piety permitted within it, and its relative freedom from dogmatic uniformity. It is what may be called orthopractic. If you stick to the right practices, notably of course conformity to the Prayer Book, you can believe more or less what you like. It is interesting that a doctrinal commission of the Church of England should, before World War II, have published a major report (an excellent one, incidentally), *Doctrine in the Church of England. In*, be it noted, not *of*.

How had this situation come about? The English Reformation was a conjunction of two forces, between which, ultimately, a compromise had to be reached. One force was political: the desire for national independence. Under Elizabeth, for example, to be a Roman Catholic might mean being a secret enemy of the state. Guy Fawkes's plot was Popish. The national Church had to be under the control of the monarchy. Henry VIII, though greedy for monasteries (and the Reforming doctrine that celibacy and monasticism smacked of salvation by works was a useful lever to justify plundering them), was not much of a Reformer. He was Catholic by instinct and, give or take a divorce or two, orthodox. The real issue was Papal jurisdiction and, to complicate matters, the need in Elizabeth's day to fight off a resurgent and expansive Catholic Spain. That was the political dimension. The other force was religious and ideological. There had been pre-Reform movements towards reform; and the new doctrines of Luther, Calvin and others found good soil in England. Life could be dangerous for those with reforming instincts: Thomas Bilney, mentor of the young Tyndale, was burned at Norwich in 1531, and Tyndale himself, energetic translator of the Bible, was strangled in the Low Countries in 1536. But the tide of change was not to be stopped, and through the work, above all, of Cranmer a new shape was given to English piety. If, later on, the Puritans took too radical a line for Charles I, and the Commonwealth under Cromwell could suppress the bishops, it was through the historic compromise reached after the Restoration that the Church of England in its present shape was born. It combined Catholic and reforming elements, and balanced political and religious aspects. But it must not be forgotten that it was an official church. It was not till the nineteenth century that disabilities against non-conformists, Catholics and Jews were lifted. Even then England's first Jewish Prime Minister, Disraeli, had to be an Anglican.

It is interesting that the rest of Britain did not really follow suit. Scotland showed its relative independence by becoming Calvinist; Wales though formally Anglican nurtured its own brands of non-conformism; Ireland struggled to retain its Catholic past, partly to spite the English. Where Scotland, England and Ireland met, in Ulster, bitter divisions were generated which still spawn violence and death.

Varieties of protest

The conception of the national Church sowed the seeds of multiplicity within the northern Reformation. The very idea of appealing to the principles of the early Church was bound to have the effect of fragmenting Protestantism. This is what makes it impossible to speak of an essence of Protestantism, something beyond a tendency to protest, self-examination and revision. It may seem a paradox that some of the most active Protestant groups are fundamentalistic; surely (it will be said) fundamentalism is highly uncritical. The Bible becomes a paper Pope. But rigid acceptance of the Bible in a literal way is, after all, one spiritual option. Protestantism is a vast series of experiments with such options. Once external authorities, whether of Pope or of national Church, are overthrown, it is natural enough to turn to the Bible for direction in doctrine and life, since it reflects the early Church, for which Protestantism is vehemently nostalgic. But the key to the Bible is interpretation. Men and societies being what they are, the interpretations were bound to multiply.

Consider the varieties of the new (and supposedly old) Christianity that sprung up after a century or two of the Reformation. In the early sixteenth century there were those in the Church of England who believed that only adults should be baptised, and they by total immersion. (They harked back to the heroic end of Balthazar Hubmeier, burned at the stake in 1528, whose wife was drowned in the Danube a few days later.) From that group in the Church of England came the varieties of modern Baptists. A person crosses a vital line by his immersion: in Eastern Europe and Russia today the success of the Baptists, despite persecution, comes from the integrity which the act of immersion signifies. In the southern USA immersion and the Bible offer needed assurance of his place to the small man sandwiched between the ex-slave and the rich white.

Also in the early seventeenth century in England, the Congregational movement was born, chiefly through the work of Robert Browne. It showed a sturdy independence of spirit: the democratic arrangement through which each church is an independent self-governing congregation was not one likely to appeal to those who believed in a national Church. It was a good thing for both sides that the New World was waiting – and indeed Congregationalism set the pattern for the New England commonwealths and was thus seminal in the evolution of American democracy.

The mid-seventeenth century saw another movement separate out of the matrix of English piety and questioning – the Quakers, who left an especial stamp upon American Christianity, from William Penn to Whittier and beyond. The Friends stood in the tradition of Boehme's mysticism, and were outstanding witnesses to the pacific side of Christianity. The doctrine of the inner light has made the Quakers especially sympathetic to Eastern religions, and at the same time provided an alternative to the appeal to the authority of the Bible.

Another, but later, offshoot of the Reformation, Methodism, was mainly the creation of John Wesley, but had roots too in German Pietism and the group known as the Moravians, led by the ardent nobleman Count Zinzendorf. Wesley encountered some of these brethren on a visit to America, and the combination of Continental and English motifs generated a new, warm Christianity which made considerable headway both in England and the United States.

And so we could continue. Protestantism bred many varieties – some perhaps toppled over the edge of Christianity, but we shall have to come back to this question of the bounds of Christianity later. Meanwhile let us see how the Catholic Reformation took place.

The Catholic Reform

This was formally summed up in the Council of Trent, which began in 1545 and went on sporadically till 1563. Not only did this Council define Roman doctrine, in particular regarding the Papacy, in a manner which set it over against Protestantism, but it shaped the faith into a classical form which lasted essentially till Vatican II. Moreover, the Council made moral and practical reforms: pluralism was disallowed, better education for the clergy was set in train, the dignity of the mass was reinforced, thought was given to improving church music, the sale of indulgences was curbed, monasteries were to be put under proper authority, bishops were given wider powers, fixed establishments for clergy were to be provided, duellers were to be excommunicated, clerical concubinage was once again condemned, bishops were encouraged to live without too great pomp, the overall administration of the Church was overhauled, and, above all, the supreme authority of the Pope was affirmed. The Church, in short, was putting its own house in order, and strengthening its distinctive hierarchy. Modern Catholicism was born. As it entered the Baroque era, the Church became more splendid and more rigid. Abroad it was an age of great missionary opportunities. The Roman Church had to recognise that most of northern Europe had been lost – even close to Italy some of the Swiss cantons espoused the Reforming cause. Yet as the great Spanish and Portuguese seafaring and colonial expeditions and conquests opened up the New World and parts of the East there was a great expansion of proselytising activity.

There is no universal pattern of Catholic missionary endeavour. In the New World the Spaniards, still living with the memory of the Christian reconquest of Spain from the Muslims, came as crusaders. Alas, the conquerors were often cruel and rapacious, but often too the Church protected the Indians and attacked abuses. In what is today Paraguay and adjoining regions the Jesuits set up a thoroughgoing paternalistic Christian system. The Indians were gathered into model villages, each with its church, beautified as much as possible. The Indians were trained in agriculture, cattle-raising, and useful crafts; militias protected the settlements against the marauding slavers. In this way an Indian theocracy was established under white Jesuit rule. It was one solution to the problems of the New World.

In the Philippines different religious orders participated in the process of conversion, each order being assigned to a different province or region. They were highly effective; in forty years over three hundred thousand Filipinos were baptised. The country was to become largely Catholic; it is the only chiefly Christian country of Asia. Christianity has not made spectacular headway in countries with strong religious traditions such as Hinduism and Buddhism, but the Filipino religions were smaller, more localised: It is in these circumstances that Christian mission does best.

Roberto de Nobili (1577–1656) was an aristocratic Italian, a nephew of the great cardinal Bellarmine, and a saintly determined Jesuit. (No wonder some countries banned the Jesuits: their military discipline for peaceful and evangelistic ends made them formidable, and they seemed like a cross between a crusade and a conspiracy.) What de Nobili found in India, whither the Portuguese in particular had ventured in force, was that most converts were from the poor and the outcast, fisher folk and the like. It was after all better to be a Portuguesified Indian than an untouchable. De Nobili, like other Jesuits, considered it important to convert the upper strata. He was assigned to the city of Madura in the South, with its great Minakshi Temple, splendid in towers and carvings, centre of pilgrimage, famed afar. De Nobili built himself a hut in the area where Brahmins lived, and lived like a Brahmin. He learned the theology of his friends and wrote Christian works for their instruction. He became Indianised, and he allowed his Brahmin converts to continue with most of their customs. His methods on the whole were successful and he was much respected. But his approach was bound to cause controversy. Then as now it is hard to distinguish between Christianity as a faith and Christianity as a Western cultural package. De Nobili's methods, early supported by Rome, came under a ban some ninety years after his death. An extraordinary experiment thus petered out.

Protestant mission

In the eighteenth century, sea power passed into northern hands; in the nineteenth, missionary activity followed it. Protestant missionaries, at first mainly British but in the later nineteenth and early twentieth centuries American, set out to convert colonial subjects in India, China, the South Seas and, with the greatest impact, Africa. Meanwhile, as new forms of Christian religiosity grew among African slaves in the plantations of the Caribbean and the American South, a new black Christianity, poignantly captured in the spirituals and vital in its charismatic energy, was born.

The offspring of the faith: Marxism

Meanwhile, however, in the two centuries since Trent two errant offspring of Christianity – secular religion and science – had been growing up in Europe. Both were carried upon the tide of a new bourgeois culture, itself both a cause and effect of capitalism and the new technologies which made the Industrial Revolution possible.

The poet, William Blake, could wonder about a new Jerusalem as the mills of Lancashire belched. Karl Marx (1818–1883), guest of the English bourgeoisie and protégé of Engels, was to follow different trains of thought. He developed a secular ideology which takes up a number of Christian concerns but in a way that is hostile to the religious style and indifferent to the contemplative dimension of the spiritual life. But to get to Marx we must go through Hegel (1770–1831), an intellectual whose language was barbarous, whose thought was thick and inspissated, whose vision was heavy, whose system was baroque, but who nevertheless had great charm and liveliness and above all immense influence: he was a major maker of modern Germany, of European idealism, of Marxism itself. His effect was great, for good or evil. Karl Popper, champion of modern liberty and a humanely scientific outlook, cannot bear him: he is the devil walking the pages of his seminal book *The Open Society and its Enemies*. Hegel could easily be seen as the ideologue of Prussian militarism, his ideas as strange descendants of the ethos of the Teutonic knights. But he gave a picture of history which updated and made credible the myth inherited from a Biblical past. If God works in history so does the Spirit, Absolute Mind: it proceeds in rhythms of dialectic, like an argument amid the actions and cultures of men. First Jesus, then Paul. Out of the opposition, the Church. Later, the contradictory tensions could produce Protestantism. Thesis, anthithesis, synthesis: then the synthesis becomes a new thesis, and so on goes the living logic of history. It was this idea of pattern that Marx took over, but he began in the opposite way, from matter rather than from mind. He took over Feuerbach's atheism.

Feuerbach (1804–1872) was the main forerunner of those who in the modern age have seen religion as a projection out of the human mind: he is the harbinger therefore of Marx and Freud, of Durkheim and Berger. So Marx, of Jewish Christianised stock, grasped eagerly at Feuerbach's atheism, and adapted Hegel's dialectic. He studied economics in depth, and his thought was fuelled by the appalling sights of an age when Satanic mills gobbled up the thin children of the poor, and deprived men and women of dignity and tradition. Out of moral fire, extensive theory and the revolutionary postures of the mid-nineteenth century Marx fashioned a system, which was to be the blueprint for revolutions and new social orders. The dialectical framework remained, but now it was the classes in creative contradiction. The evolution towards a higher state remained, but now it was revolution leading to a classless society. The means had to do with mobilising the proletariat. The workers were to be the creators of the new order. The theory worked like this. The accumulation of capital made possible the Industrial Revolution. The new revolutionary force was the bourgeoisie, who directed the new capitalism. But since that capitalism depended on the creation and exploitation of an urban proletariat (exploitation because the lower wages could be kept the higher the profits), the situation would lead to a contradiction between proletariat and bourgeoisie, exploding into (hopefully) revolution and ultimately a classless society. Thus the working class was to be the agent of transformation and a new synthesis.

In fact, things have rarely worked like this, for Communism in Russia gained success by a superior sort of coup d'état, in China through brilliant strategy and the mobilisation of peasants, in Yugoslavia through rural wartime guerrillas, in most of Eastern Europe through the Red Army, in Cuba by a guerrilla campaign from the mountains against a comically inept old regime, in Vietnam by bitter civil and international warfare conducted by a tenacious but essentially rural north, in Cambodia by armies. Nevertheless Marx's vision has proved vital and practical. It may not be a good vision; the folk in Communist-dominated societies have little freedom, and the creativity of social democratic societies and more orthodoxly capitalist ones, such as the United States, is often immensely superior to that of the monolithic societies of the East. But still, the vision has in a certain sense worked. Between hunger and Wolfgang Amadeus Mozart there falls the red shadow. Marx brought a new hope to many and, in effect, a new religion. Just how far it can be seen as such we shall see later, in the treatment of Mao's thinking and Mao's China.

British Humanism

The England where Marx worked was also the birthplace of an incipient Humanism, another of Christianity's unruly children, though a much more polite and harmless one in the upshot than Marx's theories. This form of humanism claimed to be scientific, but it stuck, essentially, to Christian moral values. It was Christianity without the superstructure. It struck deep chords in England where to be a Christian is thought of essentially in ethical terms. The sturdy worker often despises those who go to church, for one can be Christian enough in doing good. What does it matter whether I wash my car on a Sunday morning rather than take communion? The intellectual version of this attitude is Humanism, and it was argued in the nineteenth century by some noble figures, like T. H. Huxley.

Eastern Orthodoxy

Meanwhile events had been stirring among the Eastern Orthodox. The nineteenth century saw the expansion of Russian power into Central Asia and across Siberia. This was followed by some missionary endeavour. The Turks were driven from most of the Balkans, and the long-captive churches of South-Eastern Europe could establish national revivals. In Russia itself, there was a period of cultural flowering. The writer Dostoevsky (1821–1881), among others, expressed something of the Slavophil (Slav-loving) spirit, which saw in Moscow a third Rome, destined to liberate the world spiritually after the fading of the mission of Rome and Constantinople. In *The Brothers Karamazov* there is a strong indictment of the Western Church in the legend of the Grand Inquisitor, the message of which is that Christendom would put away Jesus if he were ever to reappear on earth. Dostoevsky gave strong shape to the vision of divinised man – Christ seen in the face of the prostitute and the criminal. Likewise holy Russia, less favoured than the West, might through her sufferings save Europe and the world. His successor in the expounding of the Eastern Orthodox spirit in literary form is Alexander Solzhenitsyn. Russia suffers, it is true, but under the heel of Russian boots. Marx and Dostoevsky perhaps stir uneasily in their graves. If there are sounds of underground rumbles from Highgate cemetery, they may be echoing in fatefully different tones the conversations of the *House of the Dead*, one of Dostoevsky's more macabre tales, where the dead speak to each other from the grave.

America

But the great success story of nineteenth-century Christianity was God's own country, America. After all, most of those, if we except the Catholics and the Orthodox, who sailed in past the Statue of Liberty, and crammed the railroads to the West, were not practising Christians. Many of the Swedes and English, the Germans and Finns, the Scots and Welsh were, like those they left behind, out of contact with the church. Less than ten per cent of those already in America at the beginning of the century had church affiliations. It is true that there was an ethos of piety established by the puritan fathers of the realm, but it was not to be expected that things would be much different in the United States from what they were in Europe. It must be remembered too that the majority of those who came across the grey Atlantic did so in mingled despair and hope. They were poor, and paradoxically religion flourished least among the poor in northern Europe. Yet by the end of the century, religion, especially Protestantism, flourished in the United States. It was partly achieved by the important role religion played in the orientation of the settler. When I was in Madison, Wisconsin, in 1965, I made a point to go round and photograph every church in the place. It opened my eyes to the diversity of American Protestantism (though of course there were Catholic and one or two Orthodox churches as well). The sheer number of denominations gave a clue to patterns of settlement. There were black churches; two heavily German churches, one of them Lutheran, the other harking back to the Moravian connection – the Germans who came over to fight as the King's mercenaries; there were churches looking to Sweden, and to Norway; there was a famous unitarian church, catering in part for less-rooted Jews; there was the so-called Christian Church and there were evangelical temples; there were the staid Protestant Episcopalians – and so it went on. One could write a social history just through those churches. But one flavour came out strongly: the churches made folk belong. They provided islands in the shifting seas of a new world. They provided a moral structure, an underpinning of neighbourliness and a felt sense of Christian democracy. In their diverse and sometimes clamorous ways they continued the tradition of the *Mayflower*. In their Sunday schools, their parish meals, their outings, their particular togetherness they were agents in opening up the land to the drive and ingenuity of men who had indeed mysteriously become free, perhaps too free, through the strange sacraments of Ellis Island. The more prosperous of the churches were garish in their instant antiquity: they were suddenly old in a reshaped wilderness, and brought settlers memories of the glories of lands that poverty had driven them from. God has taken possession of his own country and America has become the dynamic home of modern Protestantism, which, decaying in northern Europe, has found new vigour across the Atlantic. Now in turn it sends missionaries and evangelists across the seas.

New faiths in the New World

America was also the womb of new faiths. There were new denominations as well, such as the Disciples of Christ (they tried to break out from denominationalism, but can it be broken out of? The publication *The Religions of America* puts them on a par with Baptists, Catholics, Methodists and the like). Of the American white religions possibly Christian Science and the Church of Jesus Christ of the Latter Day Saints, otherwise known as the Mormons, were the most vital. There were others, such as Adventists and Jehovah's Witnesses. But the astonishing history of the Mormons is heroic, American, and, redolent of the values of one type of Protestantism, is a good example to take. It is a faith that poses the question of the bounds of Christianity. Is it, truly, Christian? And for that matter, how could one tell? And does it matter?

The Mormons

The story of the Mormons starts with Joseph Smith in upper New York State, a place, in those days, full of the uncertain and hopeful poverty of a frontier. Preachers abounded, Baptists and Methodists mainly, hoping that through conversions individual human atoms would cling together in a viable society. Joseph Smith was born in 1805 and died young, murdered, in 1844. What he saw in his mind's eye was a new Jerusalem, a theocratic society, ordered under God and guided by the visions of himself, a prophet. He was only fifteen when he had his first vision. Later he had others. Angels guided him to the tablets that, translated, turned out to be the *The Book of Mormon*. Its revelations were American, but ancient. They saw the Indian tribes as the Lost Tribes. They saw a meaning in America. Christ, it seems from the daring chronicle which, miraculously, Joseph Smith could read, once visited the Western world. The son of God was once in God's own country, and a new Israel was to be founded in the United States. So on 6 April 1830 Joseph Smith founded his new church, in Seneca County in the State of New York. His following increased, for he had found a myth for America. He and his disciples moved West, to Kirtland, just outside Cleveland, Ohio, where a magnificent Temple was built. (I made a special pilgrimage there not long ago, but was disappointed that the Temple no longer belongs to mainstream Mormons – Protestants, as we have seen, were ever given to quarrels.) From there the trek went on to Illinois, where in Nauvoo Smith, dangerous because theocratic, was killed in the gaol. The Mormons crossed the Mississippi, mainly through the genius and leadership of the polygamous Brigham Young, and eventually settled – the new Israel turned out to be Utah. They were saved by a miracle from a plague of locusts, and there were other signs of God's goodness. The faith multiplied. Welshmen and Germans came in from Europe – all sorts and conditions of men and women, for the Mormons were, from early days, excellent missionaries and active colonisers. Joseph Smith's dream came true. It was a splendid achievement hedged round with hardship and tragedy.

I remember Mrs Moore, wife, and at that time widow, of the Cambridge philosopher G. E. Moore, the most gentle yet also the most sophisticated of men, telling me that she had let her house the previous summer to some Mormons from America, and how they impressed her as true Christians. She herself was, as far as I could make out, an atheist, as was her husband, who mildly regretted it. She was full of *avant-garde* ideas and brought up her children on the wave of the future. Still, she admired these Mormons, particularly because they took their faith so seriously in not smoking or drinking – not even tea or coffee. She had a certain view of the essence of Christianity.

What is Christianity?

Perhaps the question is unimportant: perhaps there is no need to define the faith – let it simply proliferate. But the fact is that most Christian groups wish to define themselves in relation to what they conceive to be the orthodox or authentic tradition. But what can be the criteria? As one who tries to look upon Christianity in the round I find myself baffled. I think I follow a principle I learned in New Zealand. There, one of the important questions is: Who is a Maori? After all, with the meeting of north and south, of Maori and Pakeha (as the white man tends to be called), there has been much mingling of blood. It is doubtful whether there is a single Maori without a dash of English or Scottish blood (just as it is doubtful whether there is a Scotsman without a bit of Viking in his veins, and so we go on). But who is a Maori has to do with rights, heritage, pride. The generally recognised answer is: If you have some Maori blood in your veins and want to be counted as a Maori, then you are a Maori. So I say: If you have some Christianity in your tradition and wish to be counted a Christian, you are a Christian.

So we come to the present. I have not written about modern theology, about the ecumenical movement, about Vatican II, about the heroic feats of revolutionary Christians in South America. I have not written about the present state of the faith in the Western world, or in Russia, or in Asia. Elsewhere there have been accounts of resurgences of new forms of the faith, in Africa and beyond. Much of modern history is familiar, and much of it is irrelevant. Christianity has suffered, one suspects, from assimilation into humanism and other movements. Of that, we shall see more in the last part of this long search. In the present chapter I have only tried to sample aspects and phases of the faith during the main Christian centuries.

JUDAISM 4

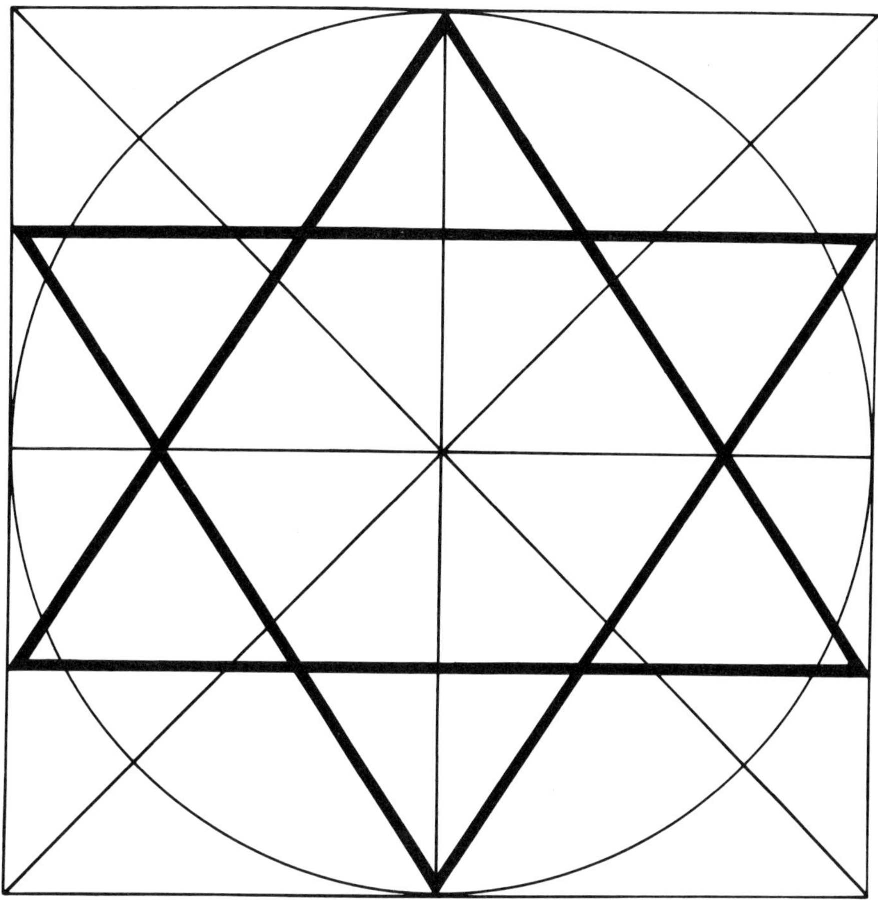

The Jewish faith has proved fruitful, not just because Judaism lives on as a vital religion, but also because it has helped to shape Christianity and Islam. In the thousand years up to the time of Christ it acquired its unique shape as an ethical monotheism, and acquired experience of prophetic renewal and the ability to survive conquests and exile. The destruction of the Temple after a Jewish revolt, in AD *70, led to a wider dispersal of Jews though a continuing population remained in Palestine up to modern times. During this second main phase Judaism survived by the handing on of the tradition through the synagogues and the weekly and yearly round of festivals and holy days. In an often hostile Christendom, and in the lands of Islam, it developed new forms of mysticism, in the Kabbalah and, in more recent times in Eastern Europe, Hasidism. The modern period has seen a Jewish renaissance. The French Revolution proved to be a major factor in the*

restoration to European Jews of their rights, while nineteenth-century immigration into America released new energies. Judaism, adapting itself to the modern world, underwent reforms, and is poised between Reform Judaism and those who maintain a stricter orthodoxy. Zionism has led, too, to the establishment of a Jewish state in Palestine, though the most powerful group of Jews exists in the United States. However, the twentieth century saw not just the creative development of modern Judaism but also the terrible European backlash – the holocaust. This leads once again to the great and terrible question: Why does God bring so much suffering to Israel? Was it for this that the Jews were chosen?

The main question today

Reasonably traditional Jews are like an Indian caste. They intermarry with each other to a great extent; and their dietary regulations can make eating with others difficult. It must have been especially so through the northern, central and eastern parts of Europe, where a large number of Jews lived till World War II. Also, traditional Jews need to be within walking distance of a synagogue. The Christian Church condemned usury (for odd reasons); Jews could practise it. In the rising mercantile economy of medieval and post-medieval Europe Shylock became the caricature and the innocent pursuit of lending money at interest became a further badge. Jews prospered to some degree – though like most men they were mostly poor. But they were different and, as the surrounding population made the Jewish colonies into tighter units, ghettos were born. They became an institution. The Jews lived in Europe as a suspect, unintelligible, perhaps dangerous minority. They were set apart. Which brings us to the main question today.

Hitler

Hitler was the fierce, dangerous, brilliant, narrow, ex-down-and-out spokesman of a humiliated folk, crushed first by total defeat, then by economic disaster. Such people need scapegoats. There were many Jews in Vienna in the days when he hung out in a doss-house. He used his venomous hatred of this minority group expertly, to invent a conspiracy. They were sometimes powerful in money and influence. They were international, while German humiliation was of its essence national. Anti-semitism took on a new and horrifying dimension. Hitler wrote all about it in *Mein Kampf*, but his intentions were not believed, at least not by Neville Chamberlain and many other relatively well-meaning people, who failed to realise that not all gentlemen can understand maniacs. So the holocaust was born; and millions of Jews (though not only Jews) were gassed into paradise or death. Yet the Jews survived and the horrors of Nazism even gave impetus to the founding of a Jewish State of Israel. But what was to be thought about the six or seven millions who had died horribly? How could God have chosen the Jews if this was to happen? What did their mission to be a light to the Gentiles mean in these circumstances? The Jews are an uncomfortable people; they pose also the question of God's work in history, and most of all, through surviving, pose a question to themselves. What is their survival for, and why have they had to suffer so much? Any way we may seek: Why did they survive at all?

Continued on page 170

Illustration section

SCRIPTURES

The invention of writing was a great turn in the history of humanity. Religiously it enabled men to record traditions handed down orally, and to put in objective form what they regarded as revelation from a higher power. It was natural to treat sacred texts with reverence: holy books were beautifully bound, illuminated, or otherwise adorned. So it came to be that scriptures took on the form of art – a motif within the general pattern of beautiful objects through which many religions have attempted to express their feelings of devotion and enlightenment. Of course, for long periods in the past and in some societies even today the written word has been unimportant, and authority has resided in the spoken traditions conveyed by sacred experts. Nevertheless, for most religions scriptures play a vital part, and the differing styles in which they are presented give us a clue to the respective values of the traditions.

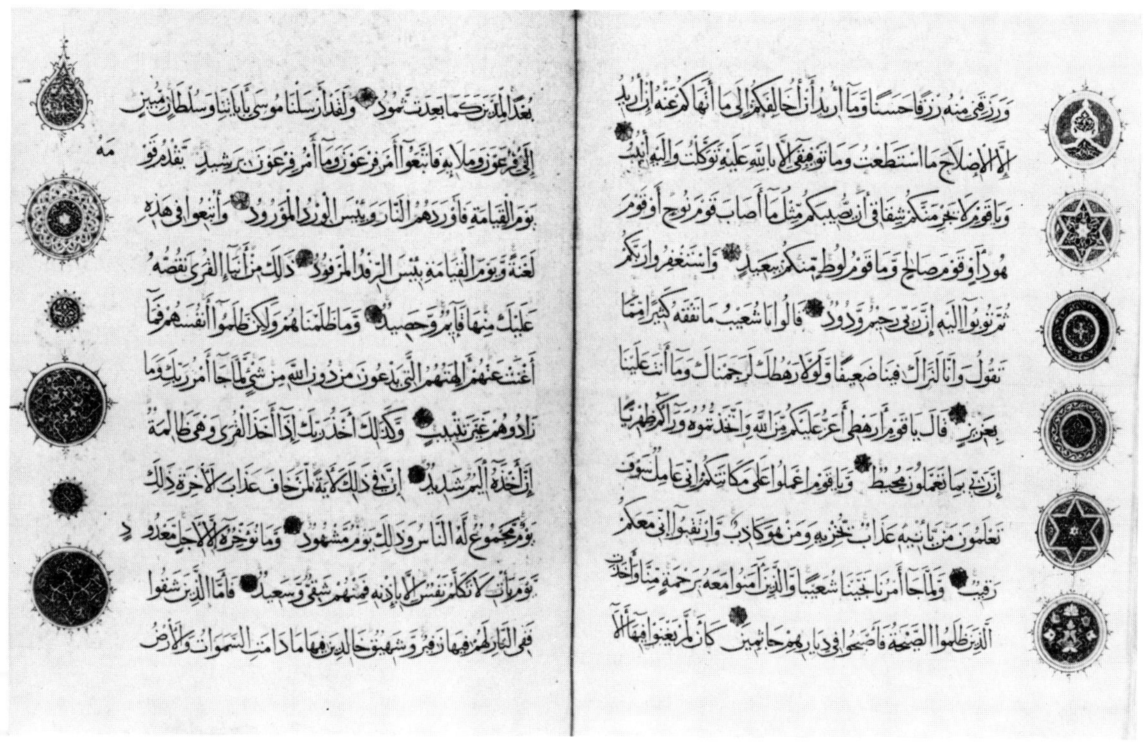

Of all scriptures in the world the one with the highest and most sublime status in the eyes of the faithful is the Koran. This manuscript is one example of the care lavished on the Arabic text. Technically the Koran (Qur'an) is not translated, for any translation out of Arabic to some degree diverges from the everlasting original, laid up in heaven, of which earthly manuscripts are a copy. The Koran as embodying the words of Allah corresponds in Islam somewhat to the incarnation in the Christian tradition. The habit of decoratively developing the Arabic script of the Koran for use in mosques, manuscripts and so on gives us the English word 'arabesque'.

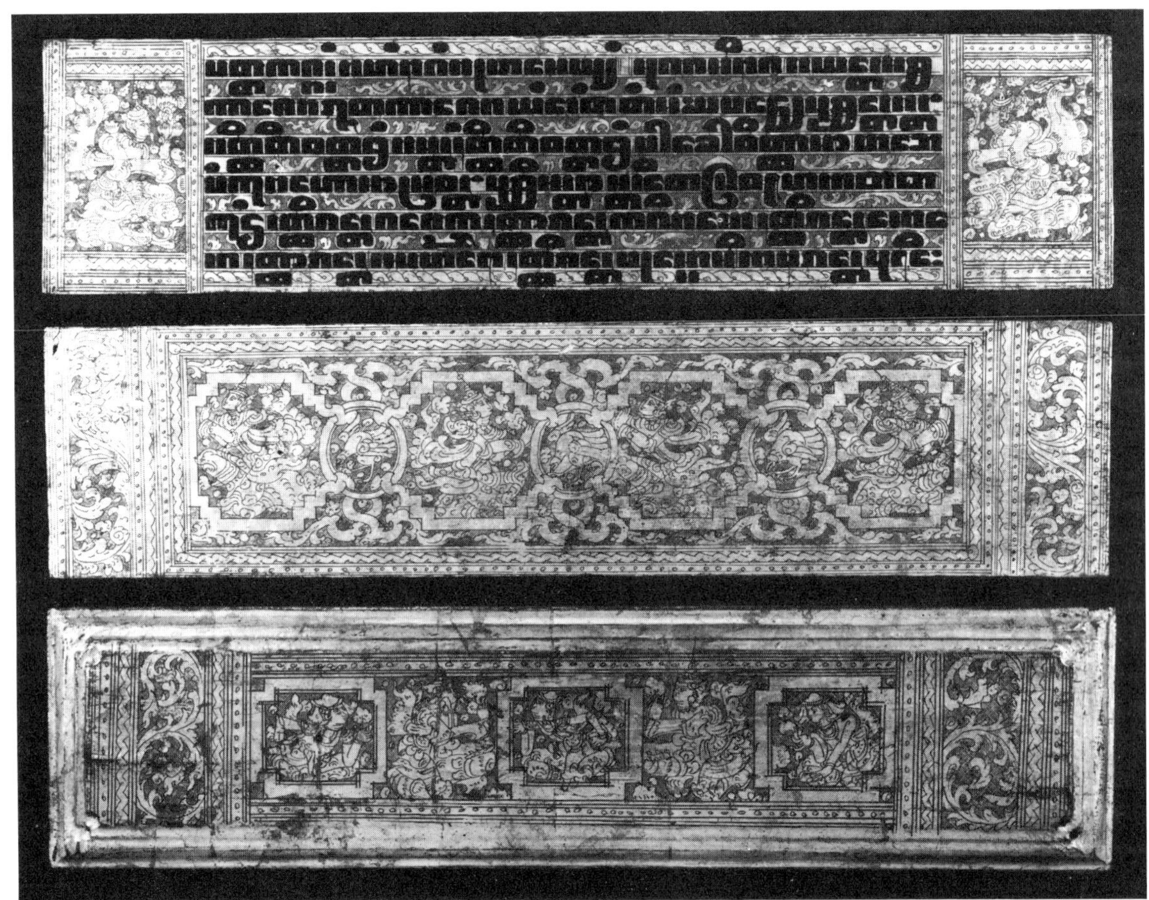

Buddhist tradition was at first passed on orally but came to be recorded in writing. In South Asia and South-East Asia, the principal language used was Pali, a North Indian language. It is written in a number of scripts – the above is Burmese, and is written on strips of palm leaf held together between ornate covers. In the Greater Vehicle other scriptures were evolved such as the famous Lotus Sutra, written in a variant of Sanskrit, and then translated into Chinese, Japanese and so on. Generally speaking the southern or Theravada Buddhists have a less devotional attitude to the scriptures than other Buddhists. But in Buddhism as in Hinduism there are those who give scriptures special status because what they refer to (ultimate reality) is thought of as somehow present in the words referring to it. However, a famous Zen painting shows a monk tearing up the scriptures, to indicate that we must transcend words and really experience what the words are about. Look at the moon, not the finger pointing to it.

The Sikh faith arose and developed through a number of inspired teachers or gurus. Ultimately, however, the scriptures arising from the lives of Kabir, Nanak and others were treated as the ultimate Guru, and called the Guru Granth. It occupies, as the picture (right) indicates, a central place in a Sikh temple, as here in the great mother temple at Amritsar in India. Thus the divine words of the early founders of the faith have become objectified in the scriptural book.

INCIPIT LIB̄
SAPIENTIAE

ILIGITE IUS
tiam quiiudicatis
terram. sentite
dedn̄o inbonitate
et insimplicitate
cordis quaerite
illum. Q̄m minue
nitur abhis quinon
temptant illum.
Apparet autem
eis quifidem ha
bent inillum. per
uersae enim cogita
tiones separant adō. probata autem uirtus. cor
ripit insipientes. Q̄m inmaliuola anima non in
troibit sapientia. nec habitabit incorpore sub
dito peccatis.

II S̄c̄s enim sp̄s disciplinae effugiet fictum et auferet
se a cogitationib; quae sunt sine intellectu. et cor
ripietur asuperueniente iniquitate. Benignus ē.

The Bible came to be translated from Hebrew and Greek into Latin during the great days of the transmission of Christianity from Rome to the outlying parts of the old Latin-speaking empire. This manuscript (left) shows the beginning of the Book of Wisdom, executed by scribes at the Benedictine abbey of St Martin at Tours in France. The revision of the text had been done by Alcuin of York, England, who became abbot of Tours. Whereas in Islam no representation of God or man could be allowed (or used at all religiously), Christian texts came to be illuminated with symbolic and biblical figures. After the Reformation and the invention of printing, the trend has been to produce unillustrated Bibles. Nevertheless the care often taken to print the Christian scriptures on high-quality paper with leather covers and so on reflects ancient reverential attitudes towards the word of God.

For Hindus the sacred language is Sanskrit, thought by many to be of infinite and divine antiquity. It is typically written in the script known as Devanagari, mythically supposed to be of heavenly origin. While the most important scriptures from a theological angle are the Vedic hymns and the Upanishads, the most popular work is the Song of the Lord or Bhagavadgita, which is extensively used and commentated upon by Hindu thinkers. The text here is a good example of Devanagari penmanship, and as elsewhere it has much affectionate decoration lavished upon it.

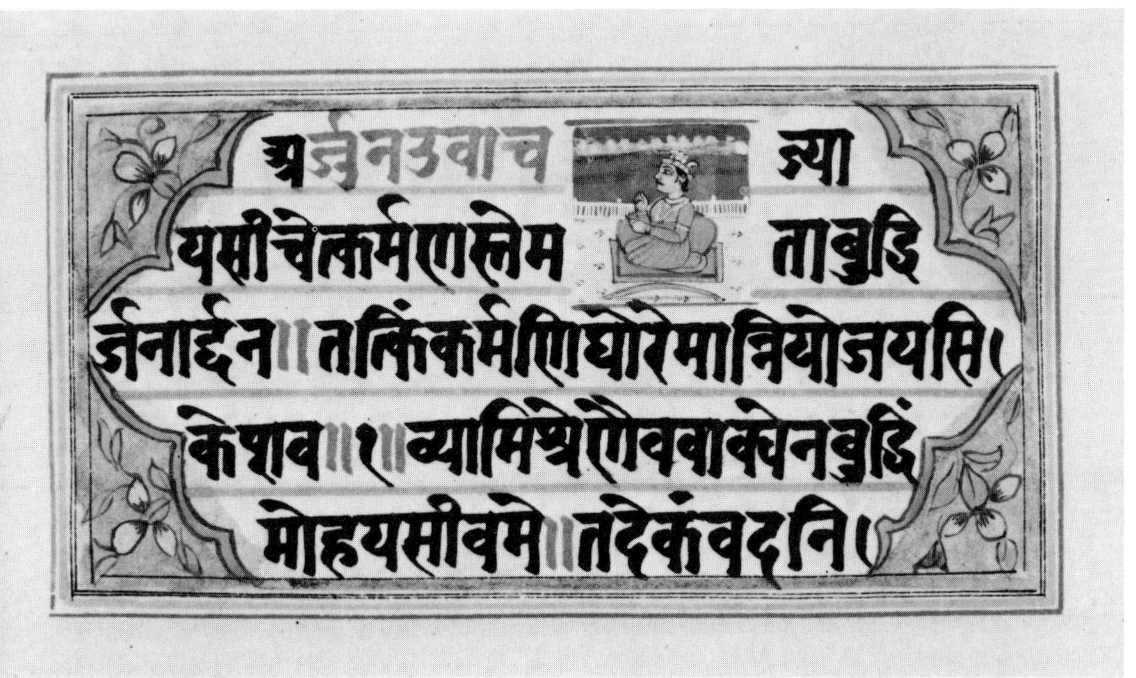
अर्जुनउवाच ज्या
यसीचेत्कर्मणस्तेम ताबुद्धि
र्जनार्द्दन॥ तत्किंकर्मणिघोरेमान्नियोजयसि।
केशव॥१॥ व्यामिश्रेणेववाक्येनबुद्धिं
मोहयसीवमे॥ तदेकंवदनि।

The Jewish scriptures are of course vital to the faith: they record in Hebrew the Torah, that is the law and teaching which God has given to the Jewish people and more generally to mankind. Typically it is written on a long unwinding scroll, often with gold, silver or cashere handles. The pointer assists in reading, and also serves as locking pin when the scroll is closed up. The Torah represents a main focus of pious Jewish intellectual life: the Jews argue strenuously with God about the correct meanings of the complex text.

As we have seen, there is a tendency for religious traditions to treat a particular language as sacred or authoritative – for much of Christendom it was once Latin, for Muslims Arabic, for Jews Hebrew, for Hindus Sanskrit. It thus becomes important to teach these languages. Here, right, a traditional Hasidic Jew is teaching children Hebrew.

ΙΩΑΝΝΗΝ

ΕΥΑΓΓΕΛΙΟΝ
ΚΑΤΑ
ΙΩΑΝΝΗΝ

Christians adopted the Hebrew Bible, but also developed their own New Testament, as they called it. The most vital component was of course the Gospels, written in Greek (though Jesus spoke Aramaic, related to Hebrew: he might of course have known some Greek, for the Palestine of his days was heavily penetrated by Greek culture and customs). The manuscript above is a portion of St John's Gospel and is part of the early manuscript known as the Codex Sinaiticus, from the fourth century. The language is not the classical Greek of the great writers and thinkers of Athens, but so-called Hellenistic Greek – less elegant and more colloquial.

Even secular ideologies can create sacred writings. The little red book (so-called) of Mao, compiled by the later-disgraced Lin Piao, has the appearance of a holy manual. The quotation below by Lin Piao appears in it, and says: 'Study Chairman Mao's writings, follow his teachings and act according to his instructions.' It is written from top right downwards and ends on bottom left. The second character on the right is the name 'Mao'.

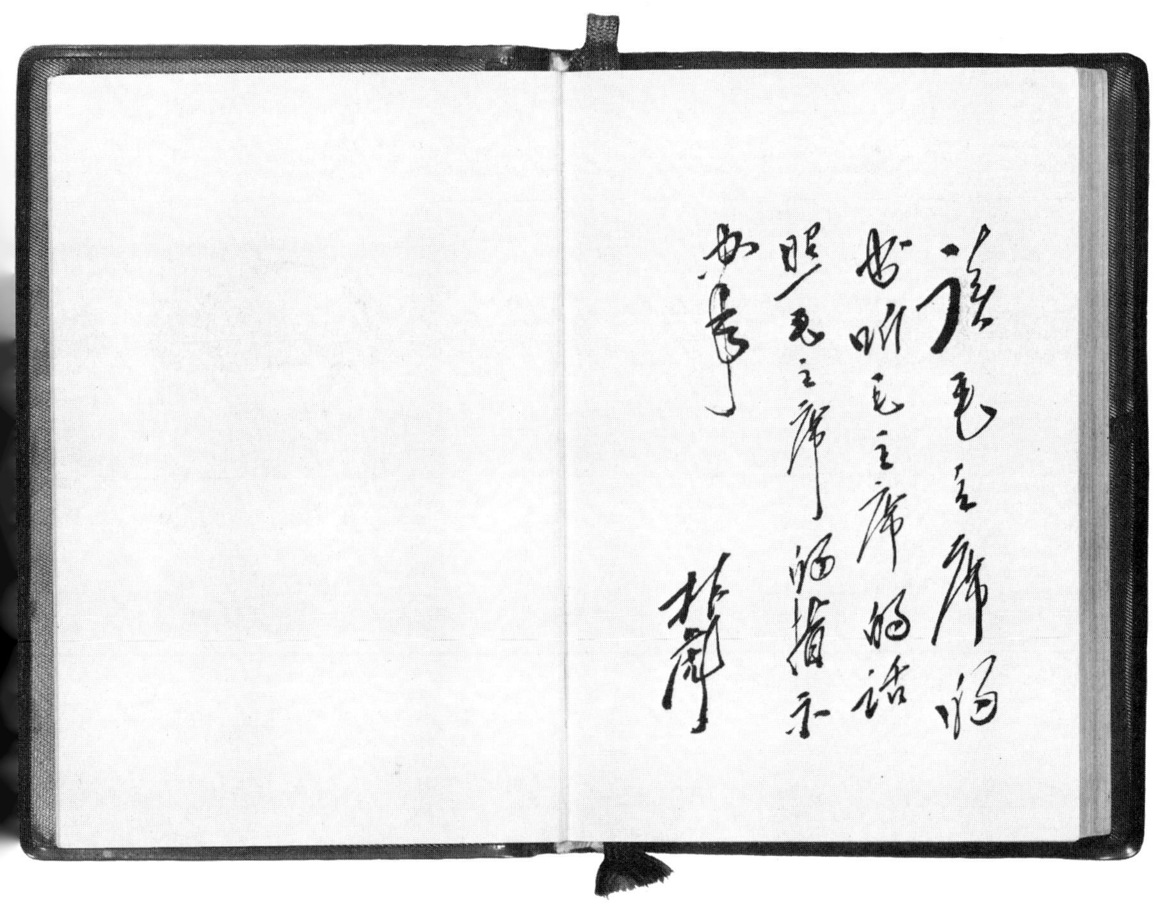

Judaism

We have seen that the Jews are not quite as other men. This is highly important for survival as a group. If you are set apart because of customs and marriage, you can maintain a separate identity. The Law, the Torah, that is the framework of living for the traditional Jew, came to be a means not merely of serving God, for God had a contract or covenant with the people of Israel, but also a means of defining a nation in dispersal. They were scattered abroad: before the fall of Jerusalem in AD 70, but especially afterwards, and through the impact very much later of other persecutions. Thus the Jews were expelled from the Spain of Ferdinand and Isabella, which, having driven the Muslims from the peninsula, was already poised for its amazing conquest of most of Latin America – the New Spain. Jews from Spain came to be dispersed through central and eastern Europe, and Italy. The Torah provided both a focus of devotion and a method of retaining a special integrity. Its existence meant that the destruction of the Temple caused no profound harm. Of course the synagogue – precursor also of the Christian church building – was already in existence before the tragic events of 70. But its importance was in providing a pattern of communal life which was essentially universal. Wherever Jews lived together, within walking distance, there could be a synagogue. There the Jewish sabbath could be communally celebrated; there the Torah could be read; there Jewish families could meet together; there the rabbi could teach the essentials of the faith. If the Torah established the norm, the synagogue was the vehicle of that norm: and to a large extent it remains so to this day. So: intermarriage (on the whole); observance of the Law; the synagogue plus rabbi; devotion to the God who gave them his contract – these gave the Jews the means of survival.

The dream of Israel

Though some Jews continued to live in Israel through the centuries, many pined for it. It was no surprise that in the age of nationalism, the late nineteenth century, the Jews should begin to think about the establishment of a national home. Zionism was born and with it the doctrine that the Jews should set up a state in Zion. That idea and the battle to establish the state of Israel gave a new dimension to the problem of survival. How could Israel, born of bloodshed in 1948, survive the bitter (and to some degree understandable) hostility of her Arab neighbours? The tank replaced the Torah as the survival kit of the Israelis.

The ancient aspect of the same question

Those who live now pose the question of Jewish survival in terms of the holocaust which is a living memory. But earlier survivals were as notable. For, several centuries before Christ the Jews arrived at a national identity that survived the overrunning of the country and exile in Babylon. What was it that was distinctively tough and resilient about these people? For the answer to this question we must ask about the other side of the Jewish equation. For the ancient Israelites were not just a people with an identity: they saw that identity in terms of a contract with God, and their survival was also, mysteriously, the survival of a new idea that of a single all-creating God – it was this that differentiated the Jewish faith from those of the rest of the tangle of Near Eastern cultures out of which the Jews emerged.

Gods in the ancient Near East

The records indicate that the Israelites were originally nomads; but they settled in the land of Canaan or (roughly speaking) Palestine. In doing so they came into contact, and conflict, with the local deities, which were largely associated with fertility. The conflict partly arose from the fact that the Israelites had by now begun to think of God as single, and partly because of struggles with those already settled there and round about. In going to Canaan from Egypt, they were in a sense going back. For those Israelites who settled in Egypt, later to be press-ganged into construction work to feed a Pharaoh's ambition, were descendants of people who had come south, together with the Hyksos, in the migration of peoples from Mesopotamia initiated by Indo-Aryan and other invasions from the north. This was in the nineteenth century before Christ and onwards. They were going back, and indeed there were Hebrews in the promised land who had not continued into Egypt; though mostly Canaan was dominated by the Canaanites, rich in agriculture and with strong walled cities. How had those of the Exodus from Egypt acquired their faith in a single God, Yahweh? Chiefly it seems through the charismatic leadership of Moses, based upon his experience of Yahweh. Moses, a misty figure when we try to sift history and legend, stands out nevertheless as one of the great religious leaders of the world: but very different in style from, say, the Buddha or Jesus. He was a campaigner and leader. When he fled from Egypt to Midian, it was because he had killed an Egyptian oppressor. And it was in Midian that he married the daughter of the priest Jethro; and it may be that it was there that he learned to call God Yahweh. It was there too that God is supposed to have spoken to him out of the burning bush; and so he had the call to lead the oppressed Israelites out of Egypt. They were the chosen people of Yahweh; and they chose Yahweh in turn. That relationship was sealed after Moses' second great experience of God, on Mount Horeb (Mount Sinai) after the people had started their long trek out of Egypt. Thus was born the Mosaic covenant, and the Law which bound Israel and God together.

Is the Law rational?

In its elaborated form, the Law, defined first of all by the books ascribed to Moses which lie before the Prophets in the Hebrew Bible, enjoined ethical, religious and customary rules upon the worshippers of Yahweh. A number of the commandments are straight ethics – 'Thou shalt not steal', for example. But the keeping of the Sabbath and the injunction not to make graven images, for instance, are more directly religious in character. And with such rules went such matters as dietary regulations. Thus the 11th chapter of *Leviticus* declares that certain creatures are unclean, such as swine and shellfish.

The ban on pork and so on seems to have arisen because the pig, for instance, has a parted hoof but does not, like the cow, chew cud. In pastoral cattle-raising people the pig was an anomaly. Eventually, whatever the origins of such rules, they helped to define Jewishness and helped therefore to keep Jews apart and so cohesive among themselves. They were part of the increasingly elaborate and distinctive Law. Sometimes writers, both Jewish and non-Jewish, have tried to make out that the rules are simply rational – pork, for instance, may be dangerous in a hot climate (all meat can be); but this is to miss the point, for then all men would wisely follow the rules, and Jews would no longer have a distinctive pattern of life.

Graven images

The religion of Moses was at least monolatrous even if not monotheist. That is, only one God was to be worshipped by the Israelites whom he led. This did not necessarily imply that all folk should worship this God: the next stage of Jewish discoveries was to be universalism – the idea that one God ruled over all men and indeed over the whole universe. But the God Moses enjoined his followers to worship was invisible, spiritual, and not to be represented by images or sculptures. This set Yahweh apart from the Canaanite gods. Those Israelites who made golden calves (or more properly bulls) were following a more agricultural, earthy, nature-oriented style of religion. But the Golden Calf could not be the true God or even a fragment of him. This ban on images of God had a remarkable impact upon human history.

For one thing, it became the dominant motif of Jewish ways of representing God: he could be imaged in words but not in things. So words, like the words of the Bible and the Talmud, came to be vital, the vehicle of divine truth. Then the ban on images animated Islam, which was in so many ways continuous with Judaism. It has even animated a number of Christian movements, such as Iconoclasm. It has been adapted in Eastern Orthodoxy, where pictures, icons, are permitted, but not sculptures or three-dimensional crucifixes and the like. The relative dearth of great Jewish painting (but compare the riches of Jewish music and novels) is perhaps a reflection of this old tradition. At any rate the best picture of God was entirely blank, and no picture at all – just a reminder of the strange, invisible, power of the one God.

Christianity took a different line, because Jesus Christ was an icon of God. If he was truly man he could be truly pictured, and thereby God could be represented.

Circumcision

Another feature of the Jewish law was the practice of circumcision for males. It is possible that it was from the Semitic cultures that the institution spread through much of Africa, where this form of initiation, e.g. among the Gikuyu in Kenya, is widespread. Again, the custom was passed on to Islam.

It was one of the most potent ways of initiating males into the community, and made a permanent mark upon the body of the individual, binding him mentally to the community. In such ways the Law shaped a community, a people who were to show remarkable powers of endurance and survival.

Conquest and defeat

Moses did not live to enter the promised land, but his successors were successful in conquering Canaan and establishing, eventually, a kingdom. Thus were born two parallel motifs in Jewish history and feeling: on the one hand the divine Law, on the other the political kingdom. Right down to modern Zionism there have been perplexing questions about the relationship of the two. Such questions become, of course, most acute in times of disaster. Two such moments stand out clearly in the history of the people. The second was the Holocaust. The first was when, in the time of Jeremiah, Jerusalem was captured and many leading Jews exiled to Babylon. The Temple was looted and razed. Many fled to Egypt. The southern kingdom was destroyed, nearly a century after the northern kingdom had been overrun by the Assyrians and the ten lost tribes deported and assimilated. What was the future of Judah to be? There was pathos in the famous lines in Psalm 137:

> By the rivers of Babylon
> There we sat down and wept:
> When we remembered Zion,
> Upon the poplars in the midst of her,
> We hung up our harps
> For there our captors
> Demanded of us songs,
> And our tormentors, mirth:
> 'Sing to us some of the songs of Zion.'

But though the exiles were cut off from the Temple and the sacrificial cult through which they had been accustomed to approach God, they developed forms of piety and ceremony which kept their memories fresh and their relation to God lively. It was out of such practices – reading the scrolls of the Law and the writings of some of the Prophets, on the Sabbath day, and praying and singing – that the synagogue style of Jewish faith was born.

The significance of the synagogue

The synagogue or meeting house of the Jews was destined not only to develop on its own, but to provide the pattern of Christian church building, not to mention the mosque. Semitic religions by consequence have tended to be congregational, in the sense that the relevant set of people meet together at fixed times to worship jointly. Though this is not unknown in Indian religion, there the pattern is much looser. Folk go to the temple at festivals, but in a way which tends to depend on individual and family rhythms. The next important meaning of the synagogue has already been alluded to. It was and is a means of nourishing the faith in Community. It became part of portable Judaism.

For the Exile was only a forerunner of the Diaspora or dispersion, intensified from AD 70. Egypt, Exile, Diaspora – these were three phases of banishment from Israel. The Torah was lodged in the synagogue, and the synagogue in the community, and the community in non-Jewish culture. Assimilation was easy, but the synagogue was an anchor against such drifting, and indeed a magnet, for proselytes kept coming in, in the Hellenistic period especially. As the great teacher Hillel said, 'Do not separate yourself from the congregation.' If the Law and the synagogue were anchors, nevertheless a chart was also needed for sailing the stormy seas of the wide world. From Hellenistic times, around the beginning of the Christian era, Judaism came to terms with Greek philosophy and then, much later, with Arabic and European thought. There was always need to look beyond the community, and even if Israel could be a light to the Gentiles, the Gentiles could shine and flicker in their own ways. Synagogue and philosophy, Torah and world, represented a tension. Indeed by implication a triangular tug of war: Synagogue and mysticism; Zionism and pugnacity; assimilation and Reform. Let us examine the parts of the triangle, but let us remember too that the elements I have listed can be shaken into different combinations. Zionism has led to a largely secular, 'assimilated' Israel. Torah has often been integrated into philosophy, into specifically *Jewish* philosophy. But let us look at the trinity which creates tension in Jewish history. Some of the same tensions were apparent in New Testament times. Pharisees and Essenes, communal and perfectionist in desert communities, stressed personal and collective holiness. Sadducees kept the Torah but had accommodation with Rome. Hellenists were on the point of assimilation, through their acceptance of powerful and attractive Greek values. Zealots were ready to fight and were forerunners of Moshe Dayan.

Hasidism

I have linked synagogue and Hasidism, partly because some of the most intense spirituality in the Diaspora has been mystical – it has been seen in the medieval tradition of the Kabbalah and in the much later Hasidic (or Chassidic) movement, two centuries ago. Note that Judaism, though highly ritual and devotional, replaying history and the hand of God in weekly and festal rhythm, has also nourished a mystical, contemplative side comparable to much in the Christian, Buddhist, Hindu or Sufi heritages. Inner light is discernible in the outer observances. The Hasidim were firm in legal, customary and religious practices but revolutionary in their pursuit of inner meaning. Originating in the Ukraine, they came to be vital for Eastern European Jewry, and quite prevalent, therefore, in the USA, whither many migrated. Persecutions have been powerful in East Europe, to this day. The father of Hasidism was the mystical movement known as the Kabbalah.

The Kabbalah

The picture of the world in the Kabbalah is found above all in the book known as the *Zohar*, sometimes seen as a third authority beyond Bible and Talmud. The book is about splendour, and splendour is the meaning of its title – the splendour of God of course, and yet gleaming in man and through the veils and the darknesses which the creation has brought. It was a book supposedly put together by Moses de Leon, who lived in Granada. Spain was a glorious meeting place of Islamic, Jewish and Christian thought and spirituality, before Crusading became endemic. He died at the beginning of the thirteenth century – although there were those who ascribed the *Zohar* to Talmudic times, to the second century AD. And the picture it paints?

God is the Boundless, the *En Sof*, the Infinite: but in him all things exist, so he has two forms – the primary form, the Infinite and Unmanifest; and the secondary form, the creation at all levels, the Manifest. This is the frame of the picture.

To take an analogy – a person has thoughts and feelings that are at base hidden, deep, hard to describe, perhaps indescribable, yet acts, smiles, or frowns, has a body, clothes, relations, a job. He is manifest in these, unmanifest though in his soul. Likewise with the En Sof.

And you think it presumptuous of man to make such an analogy, as if we are like God? Well, according to the Kabbalah the splendour shines in the soul, in our Unmanifest – so do not mistake my analogy for arrogance.

The En Sof is like the hidden and manifest Brahman, and is like that which is seen in the sayings of the *Iśa Upanisad*: 'It moves, and it moves not; it is far and it is near.' Similarly with some thoughts to be found in Eckhart and Shankara.

God, the En Sof, is so hidden that he cannot be understood or spoken of, except in so far as he clothes himself in creative attributes and worlds – four worlds or universes, of which ours is the lowest. But even here he is present, for he is everywhere present, and most luminously in the soul of man. The way He or It manifests itself or himself is through Aspects called *Sefiroth*, who radiate from his creative power and create different levels of manifestation.

In this complex picture of the emanations of the *Sefiroth* from the One, a strange thing is noticeable. Every one of the creative aspects and their effects is connected with every other. It is like looking at a marine engine where pipes run from one part seemingly to every other. Indeed the imagery of the pipe is used in the *Zohar*. So if something happens here it will affect what goes on there. More particularly what happens below will cause an activity on High. So the saint on earth can be a means of inducing the harmony which, through Adam, the world has lost and yet, of course, yearns for. For achieving this unity, Israel has also a cosmic destiny. Every element of the Torah was thus subjected to scrutiny by the Kabbalists, to penetrate to its hidden meaning; and every festival and custom was seen as an outer form of inner significance. The whole of life was alight with divine signs.

So man, though apparently insignificant, can in his contemplation, prayer, obedience and joy help to promote universal harmony. The pipes channel the universal spirit. So the picture was both a chart of the cosmos and a chart of quiet action. Both the intellectual and the ordinary Jew could delight in it and could use it.

Israel Baal Shemtob Besht

This, then, was the picture made use of, in general terms, by the Eastern European Hasidim in the eighteenth century to recreate a blossoming of Jewish spirituality. The key figure in this movement was Israel Baal Shemtob Besht (1700–1760). He taught with immediacy and power, partly because he saw that redemption always goes on here and now – there is no need to wait for a Messiah. In Eastern Europe, right over into the Ukraine, Messianic expectations had run high, partly because of persecution, such as the massacres by the Cossacks in 1648. Though despair roused spiritual hope, that hope should not be projected always into the future – such was the effect of Besht's teaching.

Among the Hasidim there was great stress on the practice of the presence of God – of seeing the divine, not just in the Torah and on the Sabbath, but all the time and everywhere. The love of all men was essential both for life and redemption, and that love was fostered by humility. So the mysticism of the Hasidim was also in an important sense life-affirming. Not for nothing do the Hasidim dance on festival occasions. Interesting too was the idea of the perfect person, the saint or *Zaddik*. Like the holy guru, the marabout in Algeria, the Zen master, or the *pir* in Sufism, here was a living embodiment of redemptive harmony, and in Eastern Europe such holy men soon abounded. They were not necessarily learned, but they had charismatic power. Thus Judaism latched on to one of the most potent forces of spirituality.

There was too a directness about Hasidism. Access to God was easy: the Infinite could be known at once. Self-emptying, and so humility, were a matter of attitude, and there were no barriers to divine enlightenment.

But was the humility of the Hasidim and their gentleness the right training for Jews in a modern age? They did not, happily I suppose, dream of Hitler, though they knew evil well enough. Their destiny was more American than Zion. And they met a sentimental destiny thereby in *Fiddler on the Roof*.

The ghetto, Napoleon and the Jewish renaissance

More sophisticated Jews than the Hasidic holy men were to animate Europe and America. They were released into creativity once the post-medieval trap of the ghetto was sprung. The dark ghetto era was to last till Napoleon and beyond, but the ideals of the French Revolution included equality for all citizens, and so, incidentally, the Jews were released from the legal confinements of the past, a liberation extended beyond France by the explosive success of Napoleon's armies. The liberation was the trigger of an amazing Jewish renaissance; Jews were not merely able to participate in European creativity but also in some areas to lead it. The fascination of the marvellous culture of European intellectuals, the opportunity to swim again in the main stream, the opening up of new social possibilities – such forces led to another wave of assimilation; or at least to radical compromise. While many Jews in the modern era became secularised (though readily aware of their identity as of Jewish descent), there also emerged the movement known as Reform Judaism. Meanwhile, let us note how much part Jews played in nineteenth- and twentieth-century intellectual and artistic life – Mendelssohn, Marx, Freud, Einstein, Chagall – these are just the peaks in a very high range.

Reform Judaism

Part of the ancestry of this new movement lay in the philosophical past. Moses Mendelssohn, who died three years before the French Revolution which was destined to realise some of his hopes, had been freed from the mental shackles of the ghetto by reading Maimonides, the great medieval Jewish philosopher, and John Locke, the English exponent of toleration and empiricism. In a way he saw himself as a new Maimonides, though his approach was more rationalist in character, for he thought religion could be built upon reason, or at least that its essence could be so established. He shrank the essence of the faith to three articles – belief in God, the operation of Providence and the immortality of the soul. Just as the Hasidim simplified the *Zohar* and the Kabbalah, so Mendelssohn simplified Maimonides.

Maimonides

Moses ben Maimon, better known as Maimonides (Greek for ben Maimon) was born in Cordova in 1134, but settled in Cairo, where he wrote his famous book *The Guide for the Perplexed*. This masterly treatise was in the same class as the later *Summa Theologica* of the Catholic master, St Thomas Aquinas. It also used logic, to integrate religious belief and the philosophy of Aristotle, which, transmitted largely through Islamic channels, was coming to be seen as the great intellectual and scientific system for understanding the nature of things. To Maimonides' work Aquinas and others were indebted. One of its most original features was its combining the Aristotelian idea that the world is eternal or everlasting with belief in creation out of nothing by God. Since I share this view on the matter, let me be a little prolix about it. You cannot appreciate philosophy without doing a bit, and so getting a taste for it. We shall be coming back to Maimonides, of course, and through him to Mendelssohn and Reform Judaism. One trickle of Jewish streams runs from Cordova to Highland Park, Illinois: from medieval thought to Reform.

The creation and philosophy

If you take *Genesis* literally it looks as if the world started at a given point in time. First there was nothing, then behold! God made it. Also he didn't begin with atoms, clay or whatever, and shape them into the articulate world as we know it. No, first there was nothing at all (other than God) and then behold there was light and creation. In modern times some astronomers think the world started as a dense blob and then exploded outwards to form the universe as we see it now. This is usually referred to as the Big Bang theory. It is like *Genesis* only you don't have to have God. But there have always been those who for various reasons think the universe has always been there. Most Indian religions and many modern astronomers take this view. There are variations of course. Some think (as do most Indians) that the universe expands, collapses into torpor, re-expands and so on in an endless rhythm: that it pulsates over vast ages and immeasurable distances and that before the primeval atom, the dense thing, exploded at the Big Bang, there may have been a previous era, when a previously expanding system started to contract again and eventually ended up as the big atom, waiting for the next Big Bang. And some have believed simply that the world is everlasting, without bothering with pulsations. But most Jews and Christians have resisted the idea, on the ground that it is incompatible with *Genesis* and also incompatible with the idea that God is creator; for if it was always there how could the cosmos have been fashioned out of nothing by God?

How do we disentangle some of the problems here? Well, consider the first point of all: the idea that *Genesis* tells us that creation was in time. Need we take such scriptures literally? A lot of scripture speaks of God talking, or otherwise acting, like a human being. These anthropomorphic descriptions, however, aren't to be taken literally. People on first hearing of radio waves might expect to hear the thunder of surf or hope to bathe in them. Obviously, though, we quickly learn not to take such scientific language literally, so why should we take religious language literally? For Maimonides, the answer is to see that language about God and language about man exist at two different levels. Later Aquinas was to work further on the problem, and produce his famous doctrine of analogy. When someone says he sees God, it does not literally mean that he uses his eyes, it is more like his seeing the solution to a problem or even seeing a joke. Anyway, if we were literal about God, we would bring him down to our level, which is both a foolish and a blasphemous thing to do. In brief, it would be wrong to be literal about *Genesis* (but think how many men have been!). So you can't simply argue from the picturesque and mythic language of *Genesis* to the finitude of the world. What you *can* say is that *Genesis* expresses the thought that God is sole creator of the world and created it out of nothing – needed nothing outside his own powers to do it.

Now God himself is everlasting. One might suppose therefore that if he creates at all he was always creating, as an everlasting violinist might play an everlasting melody, without beginning or end. And out of nothing? How is this to be understood? First, a reply to those who think that God could not have gone on creating out of nothing, but are happy to suppose he did it once, as in *Genesis*: such people seem inconsistent. If creation out of nothing is intelligible at all, then it must mean that God simply does not use any material. Plato, on the other hand, thought that the divine Designer had to work with difficult material, hence the evil in the world. But the Christian and Jew have never accepted this: the created world is basically good and there is no limit to God's powers. Nothing for him is intractable.

Perhaps an analogy for creation out of nothing is what happens when you have an inspired idea, or a composer suddenly creates a new tune. It does not quite make sense to think of an idea as made up of material, however ghostly. That is, perhaps, why we use the term 'creative' for artists, musicians and writers – their likeness to the divine.

So I conclude that Maimonides' notion of an everlasting created universe is quite in accord with reason and not inconsistent with the meaning of the Jewish revelation. It also, from the point of view of astronomy, seems more logical. If things started with a Big Bang you will still need to think of what went before: of what produced the Primeval Atom, densely ready to explode.

Maimonides worked out his doctrine of creation with great acuteness and richness. But he always wedded ideas to practice. Contemplating the knowledge of God's goodness as revealed in his actions leads us to the love of God and this is expressed in our own actions, wherein we follow his commandments and the deliverances of the Law. Some of the Jewish observances, such as the old sacrificial cult, might by some be thought to have no rational basis: but for Maimonides the system was given by God as a counterpoise to pagan sacrifice, and so to make sure that his believers retained a pure worship.

Mendelssohn was the forerunner of those who hammered out a new form of Judaism which would allow cultural as well as legal emancipation. The ghetto Jew could enter the fashionable salon only on two conditions, either by baptism into Christianity, or by shedding phylacteries and shawls (such as the orthodox wear) and the strict entanglements of the Talmud. To be baptised was tempting and many fell. It might be blackmail, but the riches of Christian civilisation in its latest and most critical phase were glittering, and secular jobs and university education, where restrictions of religion applied, were important. Reform Judaism shocked the Orthodox; but it was a new means of survival, for it presented a modern, though sometimes too slick, version of the ancient faith that a modern young man could accept and cherish. The flight from the synagogue amid the siren songs of the nineteenth century was largely stemmed by the new presentation of Judaism. But if philosophy and new knowledge were a bridge towards a compromise Judaism, affirming the heritage while modernising life, they could also by the same token be the path to Jewish secularism. If Maimonides and Mendelssohn followed in the path of the Greek yet Jewish Philo of old, others followed in the path of the old Hellenisers who merged into Greek culture. One thing, though, could cut across the religious divisions, even if it did not win universal acceptance, and that was Zionism – the movement towards an independent Jewish state in Palestine. It was a dream born of ancient faith; it was a dream which could replace the nightmares of the pogrom; it was a dream which could transcend the thoughts both of the ghetto and the salon intellectuals; it was also a dream which could combine growing socialist ideals among the Jews and the rich hopes of a rising Jewish bourgeoisie. But before we go on to the history of modern Jewry, which dates from those fateful days at the end of the nineteenth century when Theodor Herzl called the first Zionist congress in August 1897 in Basel (Switzerland) – let us pause to reflect on the ghetto, Israel, and the customs which sustained the Jews.

The ghetto and Israel

Jews are of course an argumentative lot. It was not for nothing that the Hebrew Bible included the book of Job, for Job argued strongly with God, and with good reason, even if God could silence him with awesome accounts of how he fashioned the crocodile. Being argumentative, the Jews are not agreed, even about Israel. It is true that the land is an icon and a focus, an aspiration and a memory, a reality and an anxiety. But whether the State of Israel is the true Jewish destiny is itself a matter of debate. It can be seen, in its own curious way, as an extension of the ghetto. Mendelssohn thought that church and state should be divorced, that religion and politics should be separate. He would have thought of Israel as itself a kind of holy enclave (though in fact it is largely secular). But it is of course a fighting ghetto: more like Warsaw, though of course largely successful; while Warsaw ended in blood and rubble Israel has managed to retain a reasonably secure, though always threatened, foothold in the Arab world. But the danger is its being cut off from its milieu. Israel looks greatly to America and Europe. It has not seriously settled down as a Middle Eastern country, though that is by no means its own fault. From the Diaspora and ghetto it has taken people to live in a wider, freer, more beautiful and tougher community. But it is still surrounded by hostility. Only now the anti-Jewishness comes from a Semitic ethos. It is a sad irony that Israel should be viewed by the Arabs as an outpost of colonialism, an expression of that white arrogance which itself has so often been the breeding ground of terror.

Zionism as a dream

There is a sense in which Zionism has always lived among the dispersed Jews, in the longing for Israel expressed in the prayers and ethos of the synagogue. Sometimes Israel was a spiritualised icon, but sometimes a very concrete one. Just as the Jews continued in their rites to think concretely about the Temple sacrifices, and went on writing commentaries about the requisite rituals long after the sacrifices had disappeared from the religious life, so Israel too was never quite in the sky, never quite sublimated, as in some Christian hymns like:

> Glorious words of thee are spoken,
> Zion city of our Lord.

In that hymn, Zion is a sort of heaven; certainly it is not the new Russia or the United States, both promised lands in their different ways. There was always a certain literalism about Israel, the beautiful icon of the faith: the land itself became especially sacred. The blue lake of Galilee, the lovely trickle of Jordan, the orchards towards Jaffa, the awesome mountains, the marvels of Jerusalem, the shimmering coast, even the Crusader castles and Muslim mosques, the olives and oranges, the snows and distant cedars, the reverberating names of ancient times, the tanned people – all these seemed somehow to echo the divine presence. So Zionism latched on to the literal dimension of Judaism's understanding of the promised land.

Zionism was a dream which came in the sleep after persecution and disdain. The dream, as Freud saw, is a means of adjusting the balance of life. And though Jews found emancipation in the nineteenth century, under the impact of Napoleon and the European Enlightenment, there remained deep troubles. Russia stayed intermittently devoted to the pogrom. In France the Dreyfus affair marred the closing years of the nineteenth century. Anti-Semitism might be thought to be abating, but in fact more awful craziness and destruction were brewing. No wonder, in such a world, Jews should tell themselves that they must find their own nation, as European Nationalism, a dominant motif of both the nineteenth and twentieth centuries, to some degree bred anti-Semitism.

It is said that at the first meeting of the Israeli Parliament (the Knesset) David Ben-Gurion, the first premier of Israel and the tough patriarch of the return, allowed each MP to say his piece, right down to the most junior. It was a wordy celebration of a new nation in dark times, but it was the dream come true. When it came to the turn of the most junior, he got up and said that Israel should declare war on the United States. 'Why?' said Ben-Gurion. 'So we would lose,' said the young man, 'and so get massive aid from the USA.' 'But', someone shouted from the back, 'suppose we win?'

In modern Judaism there is a tug of war in three directions. Though Orthodoxy and Hasidism are not for the majority, they are still vital. Though reform and accommodation have given Jews the benefits of emancipation, they have weakened tradition; while Zionism has brought about a new generation of toughened Israelis who are largely national and political in their allegiance and have gone far in the direction of making Israel a secular state.

There is another polarity that needs to be seen – that between Diaspora and Israel. For centuries, and typically, the Jews of the Dispersion have outnumbered those in Israel. There are more Jews in New York City than in the whole of Israel. There are about as many in the Soviet Union as in Israel. France, Britain, the Argentine and Canada have sizeable numbers. There are a hundred thousand or more in each of Brazil, South Africa and Romania. There are still 50,000 living in Arab countries. (But the large numbers in Germany, Austria, Poland, Czechoslovakia and other parts of Eastern Europe were victims of the Nazis and war.) Dispersion and return are two poles which can live creatively. Without the Diaspora, Israel could become a narrow nation state; without Israel the Diaspora could be atomised, have no earthly focus.

And the customs?

The political and social dimensions of Judaism are, as we have already seen, interwoven with Jewish legal and customary life.

For men to refrain from certain foods, from many activities on the Sabbath, to wear strange little black boxes on forehead and arm (phylacteries so-called by outsiders), to wear head-covering at meals and in synagogue, and shawls or shawl-like vests, to get circumcised – these customs which Talmudic Judaism has generated might, from the outside, seem irksome. And in many ways they have proved so to those Jews who have modified them by Reform or left the traditional fold to become assimilated, thoroughly 'emancipated'. If then, for many, the rules are irksome, why do so many others keep to them? For there is no Jewish Pope, and no KGB to enforce conformity. In brief, many Jews practise the traditional ways because they are meaningful, enjoyable even. Inconvenient, perhaps, but still generating peace and fun. So it is that the Jewish Sabbath is not just prayers but eating, and not just eating but wine, and not just inactivity but lights, not just spiritual remembrance but family togetherness, not just walking to the synagogue but chat and gossip in communal fellowship; and the synagogue is not just words but strangely familiar music; not just talking but procession. And then the rhythm of the weeks is supplemented by the rhythm of the year – the great festivals.

The Sabbath

How is the Sabbath traditionally celebrated? Like this: the men of the family would be off to synagogue. Have you noticed? Men. Not your latter-day nuclear family, two parents and two children in a semi-detached house, worker's apartment or ranch-house. Jews have, longer than others, and certainly traditionally, kept to a more extended gathering of the family. Anyway the men go off for a service. The women light the Sabbath candles. How the light of the candle is prized in Judaism! Light is one of the great symbols. Jews are light, God is light. The world is light. Light is the lovely medium which makes us see, and it is the burning passion of faith. It is one of God's icons upon earth. No picture fits him, but light serves to see him. So when the men return, the scene is set for family rites.

Before eating, singing. The blessed and blessing song celebrating the Sabbath, the holy day when the whole creation is in effect commemorated. *Genesis* is at the family table. Then the dinner, a bit formal, and presided over by the father, who blesses wine, and passes the cups around in order of seniority. A kind of sacrament, but of very different meaning from the Christian mass, even if it resounds with echoes of the Last Supper. The special bread is cut, and chunks left for possible strangers. But the bread is salty, a bitter reminder that even in joy Jews recall suffering, for being a light is also self-sacrifice. Then the meal, and then afterwards cheerful Sabbath songs, something between a hymn singing and a family sing-song. Saturday morning is a matter of going out, nicely dressed, to the synagogue. After this, there can be a congregational get-together. Then visiting and an afternoon meal to round off the Sabbath, with a final service to complete everything. It can all be merry, gossipy and holy; it is togetherness and matiness. For restless souls it could perchance be boring. But it is important to feel its attraction. For in that, and in festivals such as holy Yom Kippur and the Passover, lies the magic of Jewish time and the reinforcements of a cheerful solidarity which none of the trials of Judaism could dim. Though we are only scratching at the surface of the customs, they tell us not only about Jewish family and social life but also about the story or 'myth' which has sustained orthodox Jewish thinking over so many centuries.

From Abraham to Messiah

It was vexatious, to say nothing more, of the Christians to purloin the Messiah under strange and even suspicious circumstances. The Jews are perhaps proud of Jesus as rabbi, maybe prophet, but puzzled that he should be thought Messiah. Was his ancestry from David forged? The Messiah was to be the latter-day king of Israel and of mankind. Yet this strange Jesus diverted much faith into a quite different stream from the river Jordan, which has flowed through Judaism's veins down the centuries. Jews have not seen history as having a centre point in Christ, but rather as having its beginning in Abraham and before him Adam and Noah, and bringing about the Jewish call, through the covenants with God and the promise not just of the Land, but also of a special destiny. Jews thus have seen their tradition as a meaningful golden and brilliant thread running through history. They have seen it as a special calling, so that they could both be an example and a help to the others, the Gentiles, whose whole life would be fertilised by the Jewish divinely-inspired creativity and love of mankind. And they came to treat their history not only thus, but also very concretely through the special warnings of prophets, such as Isaiah and Jeremiah, who could recall Jews to their destiny while also seeing everything in its own time. So born auspiciously if oddly in the migration of Abraham and the events leading to Moses, the faith looks forward to a completion, which would make history symmetrical. The idea of the return of kingship through a universal king, the

Messiah and Prince of Peace, was not unnatural, and gave the Jews a picture of a great, solemnly enjoyable, future. The Messianic hope came, in the two or three centuries before Jesus, to be built firmly into the masonry of Jewish life and expectation: predictions about the time scale varied, but it was central to the Jewish myth of history, and their perception of their own place in the divine plan.

And because the myth concerned the land of Israel, the future must somehow lie there. The myth was all pride, and yet open to humility and suffering. It echoed, and, transposed, through Christianity, it became one myth of the west.

Judaism and the world religions

The history of Judaism is much bound up with the story of Islam and the branches of Christianity, but what of the wider world? There were of course Jews from ancient times in India, in Cochin in the far south. They were not unknown in China and Japan. But they never quite entered into the league of world religions, except in Europe and the Middle East, and have never been strongly missionary. What are other faiths beyond their historic horizons to make of them? And what can Judaism say about them?

My answer is this. Judaism is the primeval monotheism. It challenges the images of India and the agnosticism of Buddhism. It raises questions about loyalty to one God. It is not without mysticism, but its emphasis is prophetic. It is in this a mirror image of Buddhism. And though many might prefer the subleties and variations of the Buddha's tradition, no religion has surpassed Judaism in heroic, and usually gentle, determination to survive and to accept suffering. If the Christian thinks of Christ as the sacrifice, perhaps he can also reflect that the Jew has been collectively sacrificed. Israel has in its own way been a light to the Gentiles. Judaism at its best seeks not so much to argue with others or to convert as to show by life and practice a certain sort of faith and holiness. Good luck to such a venture! Why should anyone disturb life with too many questions? Well, of course, Jews are terrors for questions. The modern Jewish philosopher Martin Buber collected some Hasidic stories. One of them was this. A man came to the rabbi of Kotzk and complained that he kept brooding and brooding. The rabbi asked what he tended to brood about.

'About whether there's a judgment and a judge,' the man said.

The rabbi asked, 'What does it matter to you?'

'But rabbi, if there is no judgment and no judge, what's the creation all about?'

'And what is that to you?'

'If there is no judgment and judge, what's the point of the words of the Law?' said the man.

'And what does that matter to you?'

'Why, Rabbi, ask all the time "What does it matter to you?" What else could matter to me?'

'Well,' said the rabbi, 'if it matters that much to you, then you are a good Jew after all – and it is fine for a good Jew to brood: nothing can go wrong with him.'

Is that where we should leave the matter?

5 ISLAM

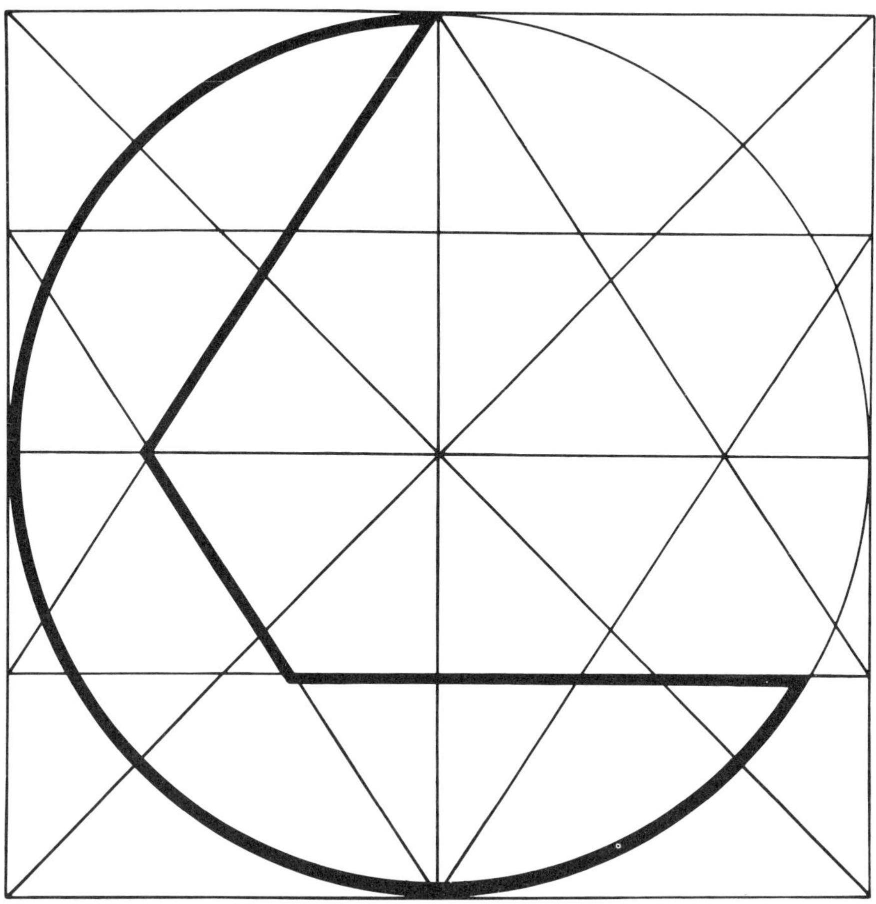

Islam had a sudden and widespread effect on Europe and Asia. Stemming from the revelations of Allah to the prophet Muhammad in the then rather obscure trading centre of Mecca in North-West Arabia, it exploded outwards into the countries of the Fertile Crescent and west through North Africa. In a few decades the new culture stretched from Spain to central Asia. It permanently sliced in two the old Mediterranean civilisation welded together by the Romans. Christendom was forced to look further north, and to abandon the old easy contacts between the Mediterranean and the East.

Muhammad's message was religious, but also political. The Koran taught that men should live in community under God: if so, then that community had to be forged realistically. Using a new technology of warfare, a new administrative and tax system, and a capacity to absorb much of the Greek-saturated culture of the Near East, Islam created a new empire – Arab-based but transcending the Arabs. In due course, from the eighth century onwards, it drifted into different forms – notably the Sunnis or Orthodox, and the Shi'as (dominant from Iraq eastwards to modern Pakistan), differing somewhat in piety and law. Another development was the growth, gradually, of mystical orders, known as the Sufis, who reinvigorated Islamic religion which, paying the price of success, had slipped into worldliness.

Though as a result of arduous campaigns Islam was driven from Spain by the fifteenth century, and though its successes in the Balkans were later stemmed, it remained long active in mission – it spread to Malaysia and Indonesia through trade contacts and it drifted down into black Africa. But in the period of European expansion it suffered political humiliations, and began a painful process of adaptation. The problem remains: Can a robust faith built on an unalterable Koran change with our times?

The map of Islam

When the Prophet Muhammad died in 632, ten years after his migration from Mecca to Medina, an event that marks the founding of Islam, the new religion controlled the Arabian peninsula, an area greater than that of India. The population was sparse, but newly united. Mobile, tough and well led, the Arabs, armed with a new technology of warfare and a new creed which contained the outline of a legal and political system, were ready to move north out of the desert. They rapidly overran the nations of the Fertile Crescent, from Syria to the Persian Gulf, and they swiftly conquered Egypt. A quarter of a century after Muhammad's death Islam had reached the marshes of Afghanistan, having taken the heartlands of the old Persian Empire, and it was reaching into Tunisia, half-way westwards along the southern Mediterranean. It ruled from Tripoli to the gates of India and from the Nile to Armenia. By the time of the emperor Charlemagne, in the early ninth century, it had reached down into Morocco, and had swept through Spain to the borders of France. It was deep into Central Asia and into Sind (now part of Pakistan). It had conquered the North African Berbers and had consolidated its grip upon what we in the West call the Middle East. So it covered countries known today as: Spain, Portugal, Morocco, Algeria, Tunisia, Libya, Egypt, South Yemen, Yemen, Saudi Arabia, Oman and the Emirates, Kuwait, Israel, Jordan, Syria, Lebanon, Iraq, Georgia (USSR), Iran, Afghanistan and parts of Soviet Central Asia and Pakistan. Much later, Spain and Portugal were, after much blood and effort, to be reconquered; while Crusades and immigration were to dent Islam in Palestine. But virtually all the rest remains Islamic. That early rapid expansion was thus not just a military achievement: Islam took a grip on the imagination and the structure of all those societies through which it passed.

Its spread was to go on. The Ottoman Turks, who took Byzantium in 1453, had established their own Islamic empire, which was to dominate the Middle East and the southern Balkans right into the nineteenth century. This gave Islam an Eastern European dimension, still surviving in pockets and folk-memories. Traders took it down the East African coast, to Zanzibar and beyond, and down the Saharan routes into Nigeria and the southern fringes of the desert and thus across the frontiers of black Africa. More adventurously still, trade carried the faith to Malaya and Indonesia, and even to the coasts of China. In the far west of China, Arab mercenaries had settled and created a Chinese Islam. In the Indian subcontinent, the increasing power of the Mughals, from the twelfth century onwards, and the establishment of a Muslim empire based on Delhi, were a factor in the penetration of India by the Faith. Equally important was the missionary work of many holy men or fakirs, imbued with the spirit of Islamic mysticism, in making converts.

But the heart of Islam is the Middle East. What lies beyond turns on that axis. Geographically Islam is like a wedge lodged between Europe and Africa on the one hand, and between Europe and South Asia on the other. To avoid that wedge, Europeans sailed round southern Africa and came at South Asia, unexpectedly, from the sea.

Islam and its varieties

The message of God conveyed by the Prophet was spiritual, but it was strongly political too. The new faith was not just to do with the individual's relationship to God, though it includes that very powerfully; it was centrally also about the community's relationship to God. Individuals might convert to Islam, but in doing so they were joining a new social order. In theory, therefore, Islam should have stayed politically united, as a single empire. But the successors of Muhammad could not agree, and as a result the newly-won empire started to crack and divide. Moreover, regional differences were bound to make their mark, despite the wonderfully unifying effects of the use of the Koran and the Arabic language. Thus divergences in faith and law made their appearance. One result was the general division of Islam into two main versions, the Sunni and the Shi'a. The Sunni, more traditional, form dominates the heartlands of Islam, while the Shi'a is powerful from Iraq eastwards. Later, other offshoots and varieties of the faith were to make their appearance. There are diverse schools too in the interpretation of Islamic law. Yet of all the great religions, Islam remains the most cohesive. What are the sources of this powerful unity, which stamps a sense of worldwide brotherhood upon the Muslim heart and mind?

Sources of unity

First, it has a single source of truth, a single sacred text, the Koran. You can buy an English translation, but it is not the true Koran: *that* is the Arabic Koran, and translations are mere interpretations and probably distortions of the purity of the original word of Allah. Indeed, even the earthly version of the Koran is only a copy of an eternal original laid up in heaven. So Muslims everywhere look to the same fount of divine truth and to God's word manifest in the Arabic language. This is a first source of unity.

Second, every Muslim should, if circumstances permit, make the pilgrimage to Mecca. It is in the direction of Mecca that Muslims daily and repeatedly pray. It is the place above all where Allah's revealing work was done, and thus is the earthly centre of his final and perfect word to men. Thus Islam has not just unity in the mind, but a geographical lodestar.

Third, Islam is uncompromising in its faith in one God. The Koran, itself inerrant and unchanging, is devastatingly clear on this point. No deal with other gods is possible for the Muslim, and idolatry is the supreme sin. Not surprisingly, the Muslims have smashed idols and images in many of the areas where they have been strong. No picture of the one God can be made, and idols are a symbol of men's falling away from true worship. Even Christians, with whom Muslims share much in common, come under suspicion of polytheism through the doctrine of the Trinity, which can seem to Muslims to mean the worship of three gods. So Islamic lack of compromise imposes sharp edges upon the faith and a clarity of belief.

Fourth, the Muslim is also a citizen of the community: he is bound by its sacred laws and customs. We shall see later more particularly what his duties are. But the practice of circumcision, the refusal to eat pork or to drink alcohol, the obligations of daily prayer, the use of Arabic in religious practice – these already are sufficient to differentiate the Muslim from his neighbours. In brief, the source of revelation, the tie to an earthly centre, the clarity of belief and the special duties of the Islamic citizen, are strong bonds of unity in a world which stretches from the West African coast to the far islands of the Indonesian archipelago. Looked at from a human point of view, the achievement of an Arabian prophet living in the sixth and seventh centuries after Christ is staggering. Humanly, it was from him that a new civilisation flowed. But of course for the Muslim the work was divine and the achievement that of Allah. Muhammad was the earthly vehicle through which the divine message passed. Who then was this messenger?

Muhammad and his times

Muhammad was born about AD 570 in Mecca, a relatively rich trading centre through which the caravan trade passed from southern Arabia to the Mediterranean lands. Muhammad himself was involved in trade, and his late marriage to the wealthy Khadija gave him security. About his fortieth year his first apparent revelations came. He could scarcely believe that the visions and messages he received were genuine. Why had God picked on him? Yet the messages remained insistent, they were brought to him by the archangel Gabriel, and proved irresistible. He recognised that he was to be Prophet of Allah, the one true God. Though men laughed at him at first, and it required both courage and the support of his wife to see him through a dispiriting period, his wisdom and powers of character came to be recognised. It was eventually his astounding achievement to forge a new nation out of warring factions. For consider the world into which he was born.

The Arabs' religion was a complex polytheism, interwoven with threads of animism – for example, the cult of sacred stones. Though religious festivals at Mecca and elsewhere might give a fitful unity to the tribal groups, mutual hostility was more usual. Society was polygamous (Muhammad was later to control and reform the custom), while some habits, such as the buying alive of unwanted infant girls, were unpleasant. The Christians and Jews settled in North Arabia were not unnaturally contemptuous of the pagan and barbarous-seeming Arabs. Yet the Arabs were, like the Jews, Semitic, and it was Muhammad's destiny to graft a new faith upon the older Semitic religious tradition of Judaism.

It was both as Prophet and reformer of Arab society that Muhammad made his appeal. The legal provisions of the Koran struck at the root of Arab pagansim, yet they also had some continuity with preceding tradition. So the Koran's limitation of wives to four only, and these moreover to be treated equally, controlled and elevated existing custom. Child burial was banned. The happy-go-lucky life of drink and gambling, so popular in the past, was banned; yet the martial spirit of the Arabs was to be given new and astonishing outlets. Idolatry was forbidden, but the sacred centre of Mecca was kept as a focus of pilgrimage. The sacred black stone of the Kaba was given Islamic status, and some other religious customs given a new interpretation. The latent Arab energies were put into a marvellous adventure of conquest in the name of Allah. The whole fabric of life was given new vigour and texture. All this portrayed considerable talent, charm and foresight on the part of the Prophet. European detractors in the past have seen him as a polygamous epileptic; but the Islamic view of him as the very pinnacle of human leadership and virtue is given immense weight by the enormous changes which he brought about in Arab society, and that too in a brief time. Yet he himself, as we have seen, doubted his call. How did that call take place?

The call of the Prophet

Muhammad was given to spiritual reflection before the drama of his first call. He used to retire to meditate in a cave on Mount Hira, in the harsh ranges near Mecca, a forbidding and awesome landscape. One night he was confronted by the Archangel Gabriel, at the distance, he said, of about two bows' shot, who commanded him to read from tablets he displayed:

> Recite in the name of the Lord who created,
> Created man from clots of blood.
> Recite. For the Lord is most beneficent,
> Who has taught by the pen,
> And has taught men what they did not know.

This thunderous command was at first rejected by Muhammad, for though he was a reasonably successful and shrewd businessman, he could not read. But afterwards Muhammad was able to recite the whole of *sura* (chapter) 96 of the Koran, as it is now numbered. He was surprised and excited, but still full of doubts. How long the period of uncertainty lasted is a matter of conjecture, but another revelation (recorded in *sura* 53) confronted him:

> By the star when it sets
> Your compatriot errs not, nor is he led astray.
> Nor does he speak of his own caprice.
> The Koran is nothing other than a revelation revealed to him,
> Taught to him by one of great might and power.
> He stood poised on the
> Highest level of the horizon.
> Then he approached Muhammad and drew near
> At the distance of two bows' length or nearer,
> His heart lies not concerning what he saw.

What we now know as the Koran is the whole set of revelations transmitted to Muhammad. They range from the short rhymed-prose utterances of the early Meccan period to the more complex messages of the time when the Prophet was founding the new community in the city of Medina. Because of the beauty and power of the original, and because of the testimony of Muhammad about his striking visions, Muslims naturally see the Koran as the utterance of God. The verbal inspiration of the scriptures is the cornerstone of the Muslims' certitude about the faith. It was when Muhammad to his own astonishment felt the thunderous waves of God's revelation swirling through him and out of his lips that, in trepidation, he knew that he was a Prophet.

At first his career as a religious teacher was distinctly unpromising. His own tribe, the Quraysh, were largely hostile to him. The few companions who supported him were subjected to abuse, for Muhammad had begun to preach against the traditional religion in which his compatriots had a vested interest. But providence came to Muhammad's rescue, after this testing and depressing period.

There were those in the city of Medina, some three hundred miles to the north of Mecca, who were looking for a leader from outside who might do something to reshape the social order in a period of sickening tribal faction and bloodshed. For reasons that were not perhaps at the time too clear, but which later were seen to have brilliant justification, the leading citizens' choice fell on Muhammad, and they secretly prepared for his arrival. In 622, Muhammad and his companion Abu Bakr left Mecca in perilous circumstances and rode swiftly to Medina (renamed *Medina al Nabi*, 'City of the Prophet', in his honour). This pivotal change in Muhammad's life has come to be seen as the date of the beginning of Islam as the new faith, and it is from 622 that Muslims date the years. It was in Medina that the revelations were given concrete spiritual and social expression. It was there the first mosque was built, and, under his leadership, a new community created.

Thus after only eight years he was able to turn out an army of ten thousand men. His old city, Mecca, was able to offer only token resistance, and Muhammad's triumph led to the establishment there of the new theocracy. Images were destroyed; the holy places were rededicated; pilgrimage was given a new significance; the laws were changed; by diplomacy and success, by toughness and charm, Muhammad managed to win over the majority to the new way of life. Within a decade of the *Hijra* or migration to Medina, most of Arabia was conquered for Islam. The stunning success of the new order was added evidence of the divine character of Muhammad's inspiration, although, as we shall see, the Islam which Muhammad bequeathed to his successors was not without its problems.

But Muhammad himself was also a successor of a religious past. Islam is consciously a faith which looks back as well as forward. It looks back to vital elements in the Jewish and Christian heritage. Muhammad saw himself as the Seal of the Prophets, the culminating point of a series of revelations which stemmed from the ancient past.

Islam

Spiritually Abraham and Jesus were, so to speak, ancestors of the Prophet. This is no outside judgment, for it is in the Koran itself. It is part of the logic of Islamic teaching. In other cultures questions of historical ancestry are relatively less vital, but in the Semitic milieu they have proved to be decisive. Jews, Christians and Muslims – all see themselves within a certain rhythm of history, which is also the story of divine action. The latest, though secular, manifestation of this way of thinking is to be found in the historical dialectic of Marx: for Muhammad, there was a pattern of divine history, reaching back to Abraham and beyond.

Abraham in the Koran is not just a Jew or even just a proto-Jew. He is *muslim*, that is to say, faithful, devoted (that is to God). He is the prototype of the later Muslims. We may note that the word *muslim* is often better used as an adjective than as a noun. Religion is not only, or perhaps chiefly, concerned with those who count as Christians or as Muslims, but more with those who are Christian or *muslim*, Christ-like or devoted. At any rate, Abraham was seen as the great figure at the dawn of history who is truly *muslim*. But he was also the one who set in train those events which in due course brought Muhammad on to the stage of history, the culminating actor in the great drama of which God is author. Maybe Muhammad had a special affection too for Abraham, as one who knew the desert. For though Mecca and Medina and other settlements were thriving towns, not mere bedouin encampments, the ethos of the desert was never far off, and for Muhammad both trade and his rock-bound meditations on the mountain were filled with the drama of desert solitude. Abraham, migratory, conversant with sacrifice, patriarchal, founder of nations, was thus no unfamiliar figure for those Muslims who joined Muhammad in the great new religious adventure.

Through Abraham, though he was not just a Jew, Jewish traditions show in Islam. For one thing, Muslims do not eat pork and follow similar kosher regulations. They carry on the tradition of circumcision. They worship the one God and, like the Jews, eschew idolatry. Islam inherits the Jewish message, mediated partly by Christianity and given an Arabian taste. But unlike Judaism Islam has a powerful universal ambition. In some ways it is reminiscent of that early community of Christians in Jerusalem who kept to Jewish rules yet preached a new outgoing message. Perhaps Islam is the successor of that community gone universal.

Jesus, Christianity and Islam

Jesus too is highly regarded in the Koran and in the Islamic tradition. It is true that he does not have the status of Muhammad, but he is a great prophet nonetheless. In some particulars, the Koran gives a different emphasis to what we find in the New Testament. There can be no question of Jesus' divinity (or of any man's – such would be blasphemy); and in a somewhat obscure passage the Koran seems to say that Jesus did not die through crucifixion. This maybe reflects the sense of success in Islam, of divine favour. How could a great prophet have an ignominious end?

Much of the territory overrun to the north of Arabia in the first decades of Islamic conquest was Christian. Islam's positive evaluation of Jesus, but rejection of the assumptions lying behind the sickly theological debates about Christ's nature which had helped to debilitate Christianity in the East, meant that many could perceive Islam as a clean new religion. It could bring both social reform and a new simplicity of belief. It is astounding to reflect how successful the new religion was in converting what had been a largely Christian area. Nevertheless, once the boundaries came to be drawn between Islamic and Christian civilisation, from the Middle Ages onward mutual conversion has not been frequent. Perhaps in absorbing much of Greek culture and a Mediterranean style, Islam came more to resemble Christianity, despite the hostilities and frictions between the two cultures. And because of such resemblances, combined with enmities, special problems of mutual understanding have been created. Each is too close for comfort to the other, yet too different for its peculiar excellences to meet the eye. So let us try to see the delights of Islam. When I say 'us' I am thinking that many readers, and certainly myself, come at Islam from Western assumptions, and too easily fail to understand the magic of Islam. My catalogue of the delights is just one attempt to conjure up that magic, as seen somewhat from the outside. In doing so I shall also be trying to depict some of the main teachings of the faith. For apart from the authority of Muhammad's revelations from Allah, and his own dexterity as a human leader, it was the content of the faith which inspired early Muslims to heroism and piety and still inspires those who have inherited their legacy.

Delights of Islam: the Koran

From one angle, the Koran is a compilation of 114 *suras* or chapters, written, as we have seen, in Arabic. The order is inconsequential, save that the *suras* occur more or less in order of length. Those who look to read it like a novel, hoping for drama and plot, are going to be disappointed. It is more like an anthology, but an anthology by one author (whether Allah as Muslims would say or Muhammad as secular scholars might claim). But from another angle it is divine poetry, giving an intoxicating focus for Muslim piety and praise; and it is poetical power, for it was the charter for a new age that came into being. In essence it provides the blueprint of a new community under God. True, there are aspects of law and social order which need to be deduced, for they are not fully stated. To be sure, the Koran may have to be complemented by the traditions with which Muslims attempt to interpret it. Further, it is not just a charter, but incorporates a theology. Once again, the poetry of its vision of God needs to be systematised, in that questions about God's will and nature crop up in the developing world of Islam through the ages. But its impact in presenting a picture of the Transcendent is without question. Even in translation it can thunder beautifully and give poetry to awe, as in the following passage:

> When the sun is folded up
> And when the stars fall
> And when the hills are set in motion
> And when the she-camels are abandoned
> And when wild animals gather together
> And when the seas boil
> And when souls are paired with their bodies
> And when the female child that had been buried alive is asked

For what crime she was put to death,
And when the leaves of the Book are unrolled
And when heaven is stripped away
And when hell is made to blaze
And when paradise is brought close,
Then every soul will know what it has produced.

So, dramatically, is the end, when God's judgment is to burst upon history, depicted.

As we have noted, the Koran cannot strictly speaking be translated. It stands to Islam like Christ to Christianity, for it is the concrete manifestation of God's word. This doctrine of the untranslatability of the Koran has had a pervasive affect upon Islamic art. Since the Prophet forbade the use of images, particularly of the one true God, and even of men (though not all Islamic art follows this latter rule), the visual genius of Islam has predominantly been channelled into architecture and the arabesque. The latter is the decorative art of the Arabic script, drawing above all on verses from the sacred Koran. The holy book's impact is reinforced by the poetry of the eye. Throughout the Islamic world the delights of the curving and dotted convolutions of the script have been used to decorate mosque and painting. And so even if the Koran contains much law and much doctrine, it does so in a sense of total integration with the delights of language, both spoken and written. God's word must be seen and heard to be beautiful as well as commanding. Those who listen only to the commands of Islam may forget its delights.

Delights of Islam: Paradise

Being faithful to God's law brings the Muslim to Paradise, while faithlessness leads to hell. The Koran paints Paradise in vivid colours. Its language is frank and luscious, and its meaning can easily be mistaken. It is to be taken literally, and yet not so. For there are ways in which the Paradise is an allegory, but there are other ways in which the Muslim must take it as totally real. Some of the flavour of heaven reaches upwards from the Arabian milieu:

The pious will be in a safe place
Amid gardens and fountains,
Clothed in silk and rich robes . . .
On inlaid couches,
Reclining on them face to face.
Ever-blooming youths go in among them
Bearing goblets and bowls and cups of flowing wine
From which they get no headaches or loss of sense,
And bearing such fruits as they find most delicious
And the flesh of such birds as they long for.
They shall have the houris, with large dark eyes like pearls
enclosed in their shells,
In recompense for past labours,
Ever-virgins. . .

It is notable that though the Koran bans alcohol on earth, on the ground that its disadvantages outweigh its advantages, in heaven its use is a delight, and from it flows no hangover. The frankness of this Paradise is attractive; and so our dreams after a life of toil will be fulfilled by the kindly will of Allah. Muslims were indeed inspired by the picture of heaven to create its mirror image upon earth. The formal gardens of Islamic Spain, the fountains tinkling amid sun-bathed courtyards, the intricacies of Arab gastronomy, the sherbet and the rich fruits, the concubines, the rich couches and cool flowing robes – many an Islamic potentate has striven to create such a scene. Some thus hope to have their rewards in advance of heaven. The dream, though sensuous, is also beautiful, and has its own nobility. Do we take it literally? Indeed, what is strange and moving about the Koran is that it shatters us with the words of an anthropomorphic God, yet tells us he is unknowable in himself: the Koran has a surface grammar and a depth of meaning. So we can take Paradise as we think; but surely it is beautiful and fulfilling.

Delights of Islam: certitude

Islam is practical and the believer need not be in doubt as to what is needed of him. Of course, external observances are not enough: each duty must be pursued with right intention. Still, the duties are plain. They are the so-called five pillars of Islam – to confess the faith, to pray daily in the prescribed way, to give alms in accordance with a formula, to observe the annual fast and, circumstances permitting, to go on pilgrimage. Consider what the obligation to pray means, if faithfully observed. It involves praying five times daily, at dawn, at noon, in mid-afternoon, at sunset and at the fall of darkness. Thus is Allah kept in daily consciousness. Though men are proud and upright in the brotherhood of Islam, before God they must prostrate themselves. Moreover, they pray in the direction of Mecca, and thus constantly are reminded of the scenes of Muhammad's life and the place where God's action so dynamically entered into human history. The call to prayer in Muslim countries issues most dramatically from the tall minaret, from whose height the haunting call of the muezzin floats. The sound is a noble start to the day, even if now the human muezzin is often replaced by the tawdry electronics of a recorded message. Prayer also has not only its sound but its tapestry, in the weave of the prayer rug, which separates the pious person from the dusty earth or the grubby surrounding floor: it defines a sacred space in the midst of life, and in the divine moments of prayer the worshipper is in the world but not of it. Let those who idly glance at such marvels in the windows of dealers in London or New York reflect that the crooked fingers of the Persian rug-makers worked originally for the certainties of the faith, not for the casual footprint of the well-heeled Westerner.

If prayer is a practical expression of certitude, the first pillar, the recitation of the brief creed, is a reminder of intellectual assent. In its simple resonant form the confession is summed up as *La ilaha illah Allah; Muhammad rasul Allah*. 'There is no god but God and Muhammad is his messenger.' It is almost hypnotic in its Arabic form, in the alliteration and interplay of syllables. The simplicity of the faith means that there is no need for an intervening priesthood between the believer and his God. Thus Islam has no body corresponding to the Christian church, beyond the body of those who believe and worship together. In so far as there is communal worship, as distinct from individual devotions, this most typically occurs on a Friday when the adult males gather in the mosque. After their ablutions, meant to purify the body in sacred preparation for prayer, they follow the leader or *imam* in communal devotions, again facing towards Mecca. The *imam* will also preach, expounding points of the faith. In the hinterland of his mind will stand the whole tradition of Islamic scholarship based on the Koran and on the ancillary writings through which doctrine and sacred law are interpreted.

But prescribed duties go beyond daily and weekly observances. The faithful Muslim will wish, as we have noted, to go on the *hajj* – the pilgrimage to the geographical centre of the Islamic world, to Mecca. A man who makes the journey gains pious reputation and earthly reputation. In the old days the expense could be great and the journey dangerous. Nowadays things are easier, for cheap charter jumbo jets fly the faithful in to Arabia from Nigeria and Indonesia and even from Chicago. But this very fact means a strengthening of the solidarity of Islam in a world where other forces may be acting against traditional religion. If the trip to Mecca is a sacred journey in space, there is also an annual journey in sacred time, during the lunar month of Ramadan, when the faithful are forbidden, unless sick or journeying, to eat or drink between dawn and dusk. Perhaps this scarcely counts as part of the delights of Islam? Well, fasting can in a perverse way be enjoyable, and once again the faith lays upon its devotees a strong bond of certainty in communal practice.

At any rate, in these various matters – the creed, daily prayer, fasting, giving alms – Islam is clear about duties. The delight is that you know what to do and how to please Allah. Do such things with sincere intention, and you are acceptable to God. Muslims rather dislike the too easy-going confusions of contemporary Christianity. But what are we to say about the 'sixth' pillar of Islam, the duty to take part in holy war?

Delights of Islam: warfare

Islam has never been in two minds about the use of force (it was built in the first place upon conquest), and rightly so, for a political community is in part about power. The sword can be used in the service of Allah, and sometimes it has to be. It is rightly used when the *jihad* or holy war is proclaimed. This militancy gives a certain pride to the Muslim: he has not regarded his religion as a demand for humility before his fellow men, however deep his abasement before God may be. Indeed it follows from the nature of the faith that there should be no grovelling before anyone save Allah. Thus there is an enduring toughness about Islamic civilisation, and the picture of Muslim decadence often encountered in Western jokes and stereotypes is very wide of the mark. The martial spirit of Islam is summed up at its best, for the Westerner, in the nobility of Saladin. It has thus been a great source of sorrow for Arabs in modern times that frequently their arms have proved so ineffective against a waspish Israeli David. But if Islam, being theocratic and so political at heart, cannot neglect the use of force, very often the *jihad* has been seen, not as a literal call to war, but as an inner battle, an inner *jihad* – namely a struggle to make society more truly Muslim, and to cause men to conform more strictly to the social and religious ethos of Islam.

The outer observances, so clearly laid down, must be accompanied by the right inner intention. There is much in the religion which might at first seem ritualistic and legalistic, but the sacred law is but the outer skin of an inward fruit. The discipline of the Islamic life must be developed in an inward direction. One major way this happened was through the growth of Islamic mysticism – the so-called Sufi movement – through which men reached God in the depth of the soul. Shortly we shall trace the history of the Sufis. Thus, though the faith teaches that there should be a divine order upon earth, a new society under God, there is within each individual a possible depth of spiritual knowledge which complements the outer, communal life. It is a paradox of much religion that often the firmness of external rules is a condition for inner freedom.

Delights of Islam: Allah

Islam is nothing without Allah, and its glories mean nothing without him. No religion has so emphasised the majesty and otherness of God. The numinosity of Allah, the amplification of the worship of God as found in the Jewish heritage upon which Islam partly drew, the stunning sense of man's destiny under God – all this symbolises God's creative control over the world and over human history (though Iblis, the Devil, creeps into a few cracks and fissures in the fabric of life). Allah is frighteningly unique, but full of mercy and compassion. It should be a deed of love to follow his will.

Allah, in the Muslim consciousness, is much more than a human figure writ large. He is creator, source of meaning in life and beyond death, maker of paradise, punisher of men in hell, a guide and friend to those who suffer, scourge of the unjust, ruler of the angels, the one to reward his faithful slaves, the one who spoke to and through his Prophets, from Adam through Abraham and Moses and Jesus down to Muhammad. When the Arabs overran a world imbued with Greek philosophy, Allah was seen too as the supreme Being of whom the wise Greeks wrote; he was seen as well to be the goal of the Sufi mystic. Yet he lies beyond all descriptions. If the words of the Koran are direct, they also indicate that Allah in his mysterious otherness lies well beyond the meanings which we mortals ascribe to the words themselves. And however forbidding this great God may at times seem, yet the mystic could also say of him, 'Hail to thee, love, sweet madness: thou can heal all our weaknesses'. So God has, from the human perspective, two faces, as also in other religions sometimes: he has the face of awe and the face of love, of majesty and sweetness, of law and grace.

So in God are summed up all the delights of Islam – the call to prayer, the hope of paradise, the charter for a new order on earth, the brotherhood of a worldwide community. His footprint is found in Mecca and on the prayer rug, and his voice heard in the Koran and from the minaret. It is God that creates in men, made from clots of blood, that dignified certitude which is the mark of the truly pious, *muslim*, person.

Islam

Such was the faith and order flowing from the great events of Muhammad's life. But the Islam he bequeathed was not without problems. His rather unexpected death left the question of succession. Who should be the caliph or ruler of the new, divinely chartered nation? Further, the very rapidity of early successes posed problems of assimilation and administration. Different patterns of piety began to emerge, and different political forces. A thousand years before, Alexander the Great had shown that the Middle East could be conquered from outside, but no one had shown how to hold it together. Initially, the new conquerors were not worried. They had divine sanction for what was to many of them a heady new life of booty, power and delight. The spoils of fractured empires were theirs. The men who rode swiftly on camels from far oases could now occupy the thrones of great rulers and steep themselves in the loveliness of ancient cultures. They were men who found to their astonishment that their military tactics were virtually irresistible, while the populations they overran were disaffected and ready for a change. The camel may or may not, as rumoured, have known the hundredth name of Allah, but he surely knew the secret of war. As older, wearier nations crumbled, the Arabs need not, then, have felt too worried by problems of the future.

But the death of the Prophet was a powerful shock, and brought the first traumatic reappraisal of the nature and direction of the new faith. There were ominous signs that the new nation would split apart. The centrifugal nature of Arabian tribalism was too ingrained to have disappeared entirely, even under the magical guidance of Muhammad and the Koranic revelations. It was fortunate that Muhammad's early and faithful companion, Abu Bakr, was seen as natural successor. For though he only lasted a year after Muhammad's death he did some crucial things.

First, he put the Koran itself into systematic and authoritative form. For clearly there had to be a proper definition of the source of revealed truth which all Muslims could agree upon. Second, he stamped hard upon those dissident chiefs who saw Muhammad's death as an excuse for breaking away. Third, under his leadership the tide of conquest swept on into Syria. The Byzantine emperor Heraclius was decisively defeated. In these acts, Abu Bakr pointed the way forward to those who came after, and by the time of the third caliph, 'Uthman, a final agreed recension of the Koran was prepared, circulated and accepted.

But after Abu Bakr's death, some of the disadvantages of success began to be felt. The wealth flowing into the treasury at Medina was vast. 'Umar, who was Abu Bakr's successor, decided to distribute some of the new wealth in a way which would cement loyalties. So some went to the relatives of Muhammad. Some went to those of his followers who had been loyal since early days, the so-called Companions, who had been with him in Medina and at the conquest of Mecca. Some went generally to the Arab soldiery. However, the latter were forbidden to own land outside Arabia, and in this way were tied to the home base. The monetary advantages of retaining Arab identity were tremendous, and in this way, however much Islam also stressed brotherhood under God, a new aristocracy was born. If the caliphs thereby became strong in power and patronage it was not necessarily for their good. 'Uthman, son-in-law of the Prophet, next after 'Umar, was assassinated in Medina, and outrage and

Continued on page 205

SYMBOLS

Visual ways of representing the essence of a religious or spiritual belief are central to men's search for self-expression. They are the eye's equivalent of parables and myths and show the mood of a faith.

This silhouette depicts a Jain saint who stands nakedly as if to show his total independence of worldly goods. He is austere and serenely heroic, a symbol of ahimsā, *or non-violence.*

Here is indeed a garden to symbolise paradise. It is a product of the blend between Spain and Islam, as found above all in the Granada. The careful arrangement of buildings, paths, plants and trees is a formal way of trying to find on earth a visible analogy of the delights awaiting the faithful in heaven. The carpet (right) shows, in more symbolic form, a heavenly garden.

In Hinduism the creative power of God is to be seen indirectly in the lingam. It is sometimes referred to by Westerners as a phallic symbol, and in a way this is right, but the description would offend most Hindus, for the upright stone object (here seen in the Shiva temple at Banaras Hindu University in North India) is not to be equated literally with the human generative organ. Rather it is an austere representation of power, to be revered and garlanded in ceremonial acknowledgement of God's creation.

For Jews there is no representation of God visibly. But there is after all one supreme symbol of the destiny of the Jewish people and that is the land of Israel, the promised land, and always the focus of Jewish yearning. So its hills and valleys, right, remain the earthly centre of piety and hope.

Sometimes symbols are a special kind of shorthand. Here Hindu cosmology is summed up, at least in one of its forms. The God Vishnu sleeps. This points to the idea that the universe rolls through great phases or eons. Sometimes it is unfolded by God and eventually relapses again into a quiet, dreamlike period. That is, so to say, the might of the world, when even God sleeps. Note that he is resting upon a serpent, symbolising eternity, for behind the pulsations of God's everlasting creative and destructive activity there lies timelessness, that eternity to which men aspire, and may indeed gain, through God's grace or by their own selfless efforts.

Right: Another scene of the everlasting round, but now in the perspective of a Tibetan Buddhist painting. Here there is an emphasis of the way in which the wheel of life is shot through with sufferings. At best all worldly joys are fleeting, and always there is the vision of death. But in the background there remains the figure of the Buddha who can lead men beyond suffering to timeless freedom.

Sometimes emptiness itself is a symbol. This thirteenth-century Chinese painting is eloquently blank, and owes much to the traditions of Taoism, where non-action is the best action, and where the best life goes beyond human definition. In this picture the very emptiness of most of the scroll is essential. So with life: emptiness and harmony are the values which enable men to live rightly in tune with the universe.

scandal followed from the apparent decay of the high ideals of the faith. 'Uthman was an Umayyad, a clansman of the Prophet in effect. The election of his successor Ali was the occasion of the great split in Islam.

Ali's election was contested, and he set up his main power base not in the homeland of Arabia but in Kufah in Iraq. He had incurred the hostility of the Umayyads, and it was one of these, Mu'awiyah, now governor of conquered Syria, who moved against him. This was the first overt clash of forces in Islam. Ali, soft perhaps, as his supporters later thought, agreed to settle the conflict by arbitration, was assassinated as a consequence, and so became the focus of the rather tragic legends of the Shi'a. These looked to the dead Ali and later the defeat and death of Husain at the battle of Karbala in 680 – the event which gave rise to the commemorative festival of 10th Muharram, so prevalent in the Eastern Islamic world. It is almost as if the lands of former Christians looked to tragedy as a symbol of salvation. Meanwhile, Mu'awiyah's success led to the consolidation of a great dynasty, that of the Umayyads, which was destined to lord it over half the known world, splendid in Damascus, heir to great empires, fabricators of a great new Islamic civilisation, in which Arabian seeds bore fruit in the rich soils of the Eastern half of the decaying Roman empire. Their even more splendid successors, the Abbasid dynasty, ruled from Baghdad, and Islam proved to be a hammer that could weld together the metals forged in different imperial and cultural pasts. The questions of dynastic succession were sometimes unedifying, but the new faith was partly about political power and could not escape the problems that that dimension of its existence posed.

A new succession

The Umayyad victory and consolidation of power led the Shi'ites to fix upon a rival theory of succession to the Prophet. This focused on the idea of the leader or Imam. Ali was supposed to be the first leader; Hassan (whose leadership interposed briefly between that of Ali and the tragic Husain) the second; and of course Husain the third. Most Shi'ites think of the number of leaders as twelve, ending with Muhammad al-Muntazar who died in 878. This notion of an alternative strand of Islamic guidance, one which repudiated in a sense the manifest power of those who controlled the caliphate, whether in Damascus or in Baghdad or much later in Istanbul, coincided with certain more mystical emphases in the Shi'a. It also led up to the theory of the secret leader or Hidden Imam, as he is often called. This theory sees the last Imam as having gone into hiding, to return as a kind of messiah known as the Mahdi. Again it is interesting to speculate as to the way Christian forms of thought may have entered into the evolution of this hope. The Mahdi, it is said, will return and bring in a period of justice and peace in preparation for the Last Judgment by God. If some traditionalist Muslims look a bit suspiciously at Shi'a belief and custom, it should be recognised that in their hospitality to mysticism, acceptance of local custom and willingness to accept the cult of holy men and saints, the Shi'ites proved to be an adaptable form of Islam destined to have profound missionary impact. Still, the split, both temporal and theological, signified that the dream of a holy Islamic empire was never fully to be realised. On the other hand, the continued recognition of the main principles of the faith, both legal and scriptural, meant that Islam never cracked apart as Christianity did. Meanwhile, from the eighth century onwards new spiritual forces within the fabric of Islam were at work. The most potent was what was to be known as Sufism. It was the mystical element in Islam come to the surface.

The mystical in Islam

We have seen how God in the Koran is numinous. He is other than men, awe-inspiring, majestic, seemingly 'out there', even to the Prophet through whom he spoke. But the stress on the inner was not absent from Islam either, and Sufism came to be the main vehicle of the quest for Allah through the inner path. It corresponded to the Christian mysticism, pioneered by such figures as St John Cassian in Egypt (a main source of the monastic life). But Islam did not seek the contemplative life in the monastery or the convent. That life was foreign to it, for various reasons. First, Islam was not without its own exuberant sexuality, somewhat at variance with the sexual hauntedness of much Christianity. Second, marriage was vital in many ways to Islamic law, because of problems of descent, property and so forth. Similarly one notes the importance of descent in the matter of who were the true successors of the Prophet. Also, the ethos of Islam was largely against withdrawal from the world: it pointed, rather, to control of the world, through obedience to God's faith and law. But although Islam was not favourable to monasticism, there were elements in Christian mysticism which might be taken into the new faith. This process, to a large extent unconsciously, occurred.

It was no surprise, either, that religious and ethical problems attended success. Despite the clarity of the faith, corruptions could occur. The law, however detailed and well fitted to the condition of the first Muslims, might be bent in the rich milieu of the non-Arabian world. Partly as a reaction against the apparent decay of the old ethic, new austerities stirred, and there was a new interest among the spiritually-minded in the inner life. More positively, the riches of Greek culture were open to the Arab intellectual, and new knowledge of the mysticism of the Platonic tradition did not fail to attract attention. New impulses were born within the body of Islamic religion and Sufism in particular came to be a new dimension of it.

The term itself is derived from the word *suf*, literally wool. It was thought that the early followers of the Prophet, simple, pious and austere, as yet uncorrupted by the riches of looted empires, wore woollen garments as a sign of their simple tastes. So those who harked back to an older austerity took wool as their badge and came thus to be known as 'woolly', Sufi. Thus in English (how we love the -ism) the movement is known as Sufism.

al-Hallaj

Perhaps the most famous of all Muslim mystics was al-Hallaj. He was a man in conflict with authority: this was not altogether a surprise, for sometimes the inner vision of unity with the Supreme could look to be in conflict with the otherness and majesty of God as depicted in the Koran and insisted on by the orthodox. His life can help to show the tensions which Sufism could cause and prepare the way for understanding how a synthesis could be achieved between the newer, Sufi, spiritual life and the older structures of Islamic piety.

al-Hallaj became something of a legend, and it is hard to disentangle fact from fantasy, but it is agreed that, no doubt as a result of an inner experience of unity with the Transcendent, he uttered the fatal words 'I am al-Haqq', that is 'I am the Real'. It sounded as if he was saying that he was god, and this was of course seen as blasphemy. He was by no means the first or the last mystic whose ecstasy has led to such extravagant utterance. In addition, it appears that he admired Jesus and may have seen Jesus' claims to being one with the Father as an echo of a similar kind of experience. It was therefore ironical and appropriate that after an imprisonment lasting eight years he was condemned, after a trial, to crucifixion. It is equally appropriate that he is reported to have said, on the cross: 'Father, forgive them. . .' No doubt the authorities in his native Persia were exercised about other things than his apparently heretical talk; being Shi'a they probably wished to establish themselves as being more orthodox than the orthodox. Ultimately, Sufism came to be accepted as a normal part of Islam, but in its earlier manifestations it could be alarming to the pious, particularly in that it drew upon underlying strata of religion in the lands proselytised by Islam. Perhaps the main credit for the normalisation of the new mysticism should go to the philosopher and theologian al-Ghazali.

al-Ghazali

al-Ghazali, or Algazel as he was known to medieval Europe, was not only trained in the rigorous traditions of early medieval Islamic scholarly theology, but also had experience of the Sufi way. He was well versed in Islamic law, a natural adjunct of Muslim theology, but also strove to understand the spiritual meaning behind the doctrines and the legal requirements. He wished to get at the inwardness of Islam. For this reason he was eminently suited to come to terms with Sufism. In his autobiography he wrote: 'Ever since I was under twenty, and I am now over fifty, I have continuously explored every dogma and belief. I have never met an Ismaili without attempting to explore his secret doctrines. I have not met a Zahirite legalist without wishing to explore the basis of his literalistic interpretations. I have never met a Platonist without trying to learn the essence of his philosophy. I have never met a dialectical theologian without striving to ascertain the object of his enquiry. I have never met a Sufi without trying to penetrate the secret of his Sufism. . .' So eager was his quest, so restless his mind, that he gave up his teaching post in the university of Baghdad and set out as a wandering ascetic on a religious journey of exploration. By experiencing something of the Sufi life he came to appreciate its spiritual riches, as well as its dangers. On his return to Baghdad he wrote his masterpieces – the *Revivification of the Sciences of Religion, The Golden Mean in Belief, The Incoherence of the Philosophers* and other works. He was an Aquinas of Islam and left a lasting stamp upon Islamic thought. He saw Sufism within the framework of Islamic orthodox law, as a method of coming to its inner meaning; and he used Greek sources to enrich his theology. In so doing he became, in medieval Europe, a main source for the transmission of Greek ideas to the Latin West, which had become largely cut off from its classical roots.

What then was al-Ghazali's synthesis? It was largely to do with the experimental dimension of religion. He did not deny the requirements of the law nor the worth of philosophical ideas. But he was very critical of those who could write about law or philosophy as though the inner life were unimportant. Rules and conceptions could only have meaning in lives and in experience. Thus the law expressed and channelled men's humility before the Creator, a humility which could lead to the emptying of the self of which some Sufis spoke. Indeed there is a marvellous congruence between the Sufi contemplative life and the needs of devotional worship as in traditional Islam. The interior quest of the Sufi was a way of putting God at the centre. Everything else, including one's own ambitions and needs, was quite secondary, a mere nothing. Likewise the thunderous poetry of the Koran hammered home the need for humility in the face of Allah. The God at the centre 'out there' was also to be found at the centre 'in me'. The synthesis of al-Ghazali echoed similar thoughts in the Upanishads and elsewhere in the mystical traditions of the world.

Sufi orders

The Sufi movement was not a matter of just a few spiritually gifted individuals, though such individuals had a decisive role to play. The methods of prayer and meditation were typically, as elsewhere in mysticism, passed on from master (*shaikh*) to disciples, and in turn from such initiated disciples to further disciples. Groups of Sufis would often live communally, together with their families, in convents, sometimes endowed by sultans or wealthy men. In such ways there grew up separate orders of Sufis, many of which remain in being to this day. Though they have sometimes been looked on with suspicion by orthodox lawyers and teachers, their grip on popular feeling and their undoubted effectiveness in permeating the spiritual life of Islam gave them a vital role to play in the faith from the eleventh century onwards. To them also was due the innovatory use of music and dance in Islamic religious practice – hence, for instance, the slow gyrations of the so-called 'whirling dervishes' of the Mevlevi order, once powerful in Turkey and beyond.

Islam in India

There were, as we have noted, clear affinities between the thinking of some of the Sufis and ideas prevalent in the indigenous Indian heritage. Moreover, the respect of Sufi disciples for their *shaikh* – a respect which could generate saintly legends and the cult of such holy men – echoed the Indian feeling for the sacred authority of the guru. It was not therefore surprising that the Sufi orders should have played a major part in the proselytisation of India. However, more immediately conquest helped. In the eleventh century Muslim raiders were already striking down into northern India from Afghanistan. By the end of the next century the Mughal dynasty became established with its capital in Delhi. At times it was to control most of the subcontinent, but its chief imprint is to be found in the north, especially in the region east of Delhi down to Bihar known as Uttar Pradesh: beautiful in the wonderful grace of Mughal architecture, such as the fort of Agra, the red city of Fatehpur Sikri, and of course the Taj Mahal; but destructive in that so many Hindu, Jain and Buddhist temples were ransacked, so many images smashed, so many monks and holy men dispossessed or killed.

It is one thing to conquer and another to convert. Since the Sufis could encourage devotions at the shrines of saints and other practices familiar in a different context to the indigenous population, and since the Hindu social structure encouraged the lowlier to take up a new and brotherly faith, Islam became deeply rooted in the country. Indeed, so successful was Islam in conversion that in the twentieth century a whole state, Pakistan, could be created on the basis of an Islamic ethos.

When two great religions meet, there are bound to be attempts to synthesise them. One such impulse gave birth to the Sikh religion (see chapter 6). Another highly remarkable episode was the reign of the great emperor Akbar (1556–1605). It was he who built the new capital of Fatehpur Sikri, not very far from Agra. It is still virtually complete but deserted, for the water supply failed and the place had to be abandoned. But one can still see the ingeniously built conference chamber. Here Akbar used to preside over debates and dialogues between exponents of the great religions, for he sensed that there must be truth in each one of them. He even promulgated his own religion, incorporating such tolerant ideas; but religions flourish through saints rather than emperors, and it never caught on. But he was a key figure in developing dialogue, and a forerunner of the modern age.

The Ottoman empire

Meanwhile, Asia had contributed to a decisive shift of power in the Middle East. China, Central Asia, the Middle East and Europe were always somewhat exposed to the forces which controlled the steppes and the great trade routes running to the north of the main Asian mountain ranges. Great empires were built on the steppes, none greater than that of Ghenghis Khan who controlled, through his mobile and well-equipped armies, a kingdom stretching from Russia to China. His grandson Hulagu inflicted on Islam its most terrifying disaster: he took and sacked the city of Baghdad, seat of the caliphate. But as with the barbarian conquest of Rome the conquerors were in turn conquered by the faith and culture of the conquered. In due course, after the fall of Constantinople in 1453, the Turkish Ottomans established there the caliphate, and a new and splendid era of Islamic history supervened. But the balance of power had shifted unmistakably north, away from the old Arab dominance. If the sack of Baghdad was cause of despair, the conversion of the great church of Santa Sophia into a magnificent mosque was a symbol of new Islamic hope. The fall of the Byzantine empire was the culminating revenge for the bitter wounds inflicted in earlier centuries by the Crusades.

For over four centuries the 'Turkish question' was to be vital in European politics. The Turks roamed the Balkans and threatened Vienna. Only in the nineteenth century were they decisively pushed back. The memory of earlier Islamic threats to Christendom was revived. Yet as we shall see the balance of power was to tilt decisively towards Europe, and against the Islamic world, chiefly through the exploitation of seapower. This weakness of Islam in the nineteenth and twentieth centuries was to prove traumatic for a faith which sees success in terms of divine providence. Meanwhile, let us look further at the developing forms of Islam, many of them born out of the matrix of the Shi'a, and, to get a taste of a religiously extravagant version of the faith, begin by observing a major Shi'a festival, the festival of Muharram, as found in India.

Islam is, as it were, a sandwich. At the top is the theology and refined spirituality of the religious élite, at the bottom the local customs into which Islam integrates. In the middle is the world of characteristic Islam – the mosque, the Koran, the law. The festival of Muharram relates that middle layer to local custom.

Muharram

Muharram is the first month of the Muslim year, which is calculated in moon months of twenty-eight days, for which reason the seasons of the Muslim year, and festivals such as Ramadan, wander across our solar calendar. It is during this month that Shi'a Islam celebrates and mourns the martyrdom of Hassan and Husain, in that fateful and bloody sequence of events that saw the first great division of the faith. The tenth of the month is central to the festival; it was on that day too that Adam and Eve appeared on earth, and that God made the heavens and hell. For the festivities standards are prepared and portable biers to represent the tombs of the martyrs; each such cenotaph is likely to be beautifully decorated with strings of glass bangles, paper flowers and saffron and red cloth, and lit up inside and outside with innumerable blue and yellow lights. On the seventh night of the festival the people bring out the Buraq, a griffin-like animal representing the being on whose back the Prophet is supposed to have made his famous night journey, referred to (according to prevailing interpretation) by the following *sura* of the Koran:

> Glory be to Him who carried his servant by night
> From the holy mosque to the further mosque
> Of which we have blessed the precincts
> That we might display to him some of our wonders;
> He is the all-hearing, the all-seeing.

According to legend, the Prophet was transported miraculously one night to Jerusalem, whence under the guidance of the Archangel Gabriel he ascended to Paradise, and there talked with the Prophets. His experience culminated in being granted the ineffable vision of God himself. Some interpreters take the story literally (he actually flew from Arabia to Jerusalem); others see in it a record of a visionary experience. There are, it must be said, parallels to such mystical ascents to heaven in the experience of religious figures in other contexts. At any rate, for the folk celebrating Muharram, there is the Buraq to carry in procession. The processions and other events during the period of the festival are accompanied by much jollification and buffoonery, as in the Mardi Gras; men dress up in various costumes and guises of a traditional kind. Thus there is, most beloved but causing frissons of fear, the fellow dressed and painted like a tiger who runs around with a piece of meat in his mouth, making sudden mock attacks on children and chasing them.

The culminating procession brings the cenotaphs and banners and crowds to the open space of maidan which represents the field on which the battle of Karbala was fought. The sweetmeat sellers are there and all sorts of sideshows. The biers are submerged in the waters of a nearby river or bathing tank – a custom which is a direct reflection of the Hindu practice of drowning in water the temporary clay images of the gods carried in procession at a feast. For the Hindu this shows that the image itself is not the god. Indeed, Muharram borrows much from Hindu custom, though what is borrowed is suitably Islamised. It is not therefore surprising that Hindus and Jains often join in such festivities. However, the vagaries of the lunar calendar can sometimes entail that a big Hindu procession coincides with that of Muharram. With rival groups celebrating in the streets, there can be riots and clashes. Despite mutual assimilations, the assumptions and badges of the two religions are in sharp contrast, and violence between the two groups is never totally ruled out.

Forms of Islam

Muharram in India symbolises one type of variety of expression in Islam, as the faith adapts itself to a particular cultural milieu. Variety also characterises the theory of Islam. It is true that all Muslims agree about certain essentials, but particularly in their expectations of the future there is divergence of belief. Let me illustrate this through looking at world history from an Islamic point of view.

Adam, as we have seen, was the first messenger of God, and to him God conveyed the right pattern of living, and thus the promise of Paradise. But Adam was disobedient in such a way that the message God had conveyed became clouded over. Mankind no longer could see the truth. But God is merciful and repeated the message through various prophets, including Jesus. The trouble with the Jews and Christians was that they failed to remain faithful. Though in a sense they were privileged and above pagans, who in their ignorance worshipped idols and indulged in the primordial spiritual sin of *shirk*, setting up gods beside God, they distorted God's teaching. The Christians in particular failed to heed the words of their prophet and came to treat him idolatrously as son of God. Though Jesus, as we have seen, was given high status in the Koran, Christians had clearly fallen away from the essence of his message. Hence it was necessary for God to send another Prophet as the culmination of his gracious teaching of mankind, and that messenger was Muhammad. The Koran was to be the foundation of a new divine community on earth, and Allah's blessing on that community was signalised by the amazing successes of the new religion. But the community was to be under the leadership of a caliph, and at this point the theories of history within Islam begin to diverge. If chapter one of human history was from Adam to Jesus; and chapter two was Jesus and his message; then chapter three was Muhammad and the foundation of the new community. Chapter four concerned the succession and chapter five the future of human history. The Shi'a theology agrees with the Sunna in regard to the first three chapters. It is chapters four and five where the problem lies.

As we have seen, the Shi'a recognise the succession through Ali, down to Muhammad al-Muntazar. This succession of twelve leaders means that those Shi'a who accept this theory are called the Twelvers. And since God gives hope, the day of the Mahdi, the hidden Imam, will arise. Many pretenders have latched on to that title, not least the Mahdi defeated at the battle of Omdurman.

If the Twelvers believe in Twelve, there are others who believe in seven. Again a question of succession was at stake. The group take their name from Ismail, son of the sixth Imam, who they claim was passed over in the succession in favour of his brother Musa al-Kazim. It is said that Ismail, who would normally have succeeded, was rejected because of his fondness for the bottle. At any rate, the dispute over the succession was occasion for the elaboration of a system of belief far removed from orthodoxy, and based upon a theory of the secret meaning of the Koran. The elaborate Ismaili theology is not unlike ideas found in the later stages of Greek philosophy, to which it owes something. It postulates belief in a whole series of beings arranged in a hierarchy which has at the top the unknowable One. That unknowable One creates divine beings, beginning with the so-called First Intelligence, ranging down to the Tenth. This last is identified with Allah. So for the Ismailis the thunderous, majestic Allah is relatively low in the order of being. Allah, however, is creator of the world and of animals and men, and also of the Perfect One, a primeval man whom the Ismailis believe to have lived in Ceylon (a number of legends link Adam to that island). He is the First Adam who is reincarnated in successive Imams and will reappear in the last days, as the sinless and infallible leader, superior even to the Prophet Muhammad. Belief in reincarnation and an esoteric interpretation of Islamic law mean that the Ismailis are far removed from traditional interpretations of the Koran. Conquered cultural forces have, in this movement, welled up through the Islamic framework. The movement came to be headed by the fabulous Aga Khans, top-hatted at Ascot, weighed against gold, champagne-drinking, Eastern denizens of the jet set, earnest in the United Nations and holy to millions of followers. It was out of a similar milieu that the Assassins (so-called because they used hashish to give them courage to kill) and the Druze, still potent in the Lebanon and in Syria, arose.

The Druze

The Druze are based chiefly in the mountainous parts of southern Syria and the Lebanon known as the Jebel Druze, though some can also be found in Jordan and Israel. They represent a remarkable offshoot of Islam, with beliefs reminding one of the Albigensians (see chapter 3). The faith is secret, with a division between the elect and enlightened ones on the one hand and the 'ignorant' ordinary people on the other. Each village has a hall for meditation, usually away from habitations, in which the elect go through various forms of contemplation and prayer. The number of the faithful (and they are confined to the Druze people) has been fixed since the creation, so that it is strictly forbidden to preach or to give the secrets of the religion to outsiders. The faith incorporates elements from a wide band of Middle Eastern sources and includes belief in reincarnation. In order to safeguard the exclusive character of the divine message, Druze who die are only reborn as Druze. Just as the Ismailis exalt the last Imam over the Prophet, so the Druze exalt their founder al-Hakim, a caliph ruling from Egypt in the eleventh century. We have come right to the edge of Islamic orthodoxy if not beyond. No longer is Islam seen as universal and outward-looking, but rather as cloaking a secret, élitist religious revelation. Often, in the history of religions, older impulses come up through the crust of orthodoxy, as though men find uniformity of belief irksome.

Nevertheless, despite these and other divergences from the Islamic norm, there is no doubt that Islam has preserved a greater degree of unity than other great religions. We have already noted some of the factors which may explain this. However, new forces have come to challenge Islam in the modern world, and perhaps, above all, to challenge its legal framework and its sense of divinely-guided success. The beginnings of the new era date from the opening up of the sea-route to India and the East.

Islam and Europe

By the end of the Middle Ages, the relationship between Christian Europe and the Islamic Middle East was fairly stable. Though Islam had come north of the Mediterranean, into Spain, it was being driven back. The southern shore of the Mediterranean was lost to Europe. And if later the Ottoman Turks were to threaten the south-east flank of Christendom, they were nevertheless contained. Conversely, Europe's attempt to conquer Palestine had been beaten off by the Muslims. It is true that such warfare had left bitterness and misunderstanding. For a while in Islamic Spain there had been a brilliant symbiosis between Jewish, Christian and Muslim culture, but, on the whole, relations came to harden. With the Renaissance, Europe gained a new self-confidence and vitality, and Islam's creativity and richness of civilisation no longer outshone that of Latin Christendom. The stage was set for a great reversal of fortune for Islam, as Europe gathered itself together at the beginning of its imperial age.

The first main victim in Asia of European seapower and cannon was India, invaded this time from the sea, and not out of the north-west (ironically it was the north-west which the British found greatest difficulty in conquering). By the late eighteenth century the Muslim power in North India was virtually broken, and in due course the British came to rule India from the old Mughal capital. Meanwhile Islamic Indonesia was being taken by the Dutch. In the nineteenth century, the Islamic countries of central Asia were coming under the sway of expanding Russia. Napoleon's daring expedition to Egypt struck a telling blow near the heart of the Islamic world, and prepared the way for occupation by the British. Late in the century most of North Africa fell into European hands. The Turks were mauled by the Russians and driven from much of the Balkans. Parts of West and East Africa with Islamic populations were taken by colonial powers. Finally, the collapse of the Ottomans after World War I allowed the West to occupy or overawe most of the Middle East. The whole belt of Islamic lands from Morocco to India and beyond now felt the impact of industrial powers, conscious of the superiority of a European civilisation, woven partly from the Christian religion. Out of the traumas occasioned by European success, new forces in Islam were born. Already, one type of development was being prepared through the reform movement led by Muhammad ibn 'Abd al-Wahhāb, who died in 1787.

The Wahhabis, as his followers are known, and who are specially strong in modern Arabia, look to a return to original Islam. Various aspects of Shi'a Islam, especially the veneration of saints, and of Sufism were denounced as innovatory and decadent. Worse, they conduced to the sin of *shirk* and were in contradiction with the teachings of the Koran. The Wahhabis proved militant both literally and in propaganda. They built up an Arabian empire at the beginning of the nineteenth century, and though ultimately their military power was destroyed through a Turkish and Egyptian expedition in 1818, their ideas survived and exercised a strong influence through the main body of Islam, already deeply disturbed by the encroachment of foreign nations and ideas. To maintain that the troubles of the Islamic community stemmed from lack of faithfulness to Allah's teaching provided a theory of history, a reason for reform and ultimately a hope for the future. Partly because of the impact of the new conservatism, the Sufi movement underwent a decline, and until very recent times lost much of its vitality and influence.

The conservative revival also had nationalistic and Pan-Islamic aspects, and in a number of countries the formation of groups such as the Muslim Brotherhood were attempts to defend the old Islam against the pervasive forces of modern Western civilisation. But though the conservative reaction was better at explaining why it was that Islam's success-story had run out, the quest for reform, above all in law, was seen by many as the chief hope of establishing independence from the West. And here we come to the whole problem of Islamic law, the *Shari'a*.

Islam and the law

Because Islam is predicated on the creation of a community, the system of law laid down in the Koran and further deduced from it is an integral part of the message. Islam cannot make that distinction between private piety and public law which has become a commonplace in the West. In this Islam is more like orthodox Judaism, but yet with a difference. The divinely ordained Torah of the Jews proved able to define a mode of life which gave the Jews a distinct character throughout the dispersion, and through long centuries when to all intents and purposes the Jews had no homeland. The Law was woven into the fabric of Jewish identity. Though this is true of the Muslim too, in the latter case the law defines, for most of Islamic history, the shape of actual Islamic states and empires. So the decisions of doctors of the law, interpreting the revelation and subsequent traditions, had obvious political and social relevance.

Some Westerners, encountering this side of Islam, find it hard to see law as essential to revelation. Does God really worry about pork, systems of divorce, inheritance, punishments for theft, testamentary rules and the hundred and one details of a human religious and legal system? The Muslim reply is straightforward. Given the premiss that God wishes men to live in faithful community, then the rules of that community are his concern. Besides, what you do is quite as important (perhaps more important) than what you believe, and it is naïve to think that God is just interested in implanting truths in men: he must implant actions, too, and these presuppose rules. Human nature and society being complex, the rules need sometimes to be quite detailed. It is not therefore at all odd that, especially in the phase of the Prophet's life after the migration to Medina, Allah should have revealed a whole set of legal requirements. In brief, the *Shari'a* is divinely inspired. The schools of law and the courts are thus vital institutions in transmitting God's will.

All this is dynamic and effective in the creation of a new society, as the early history of Islam showed, and preserves the new community from disintegration. Nevertheless, it is a structure which poses deep problems when the fabric of the community has already been penetrated by powerful new forces. Thus the modern age has seen a major crisis in Islamic law, a crisis which could do more to change the nature of Islam than anything else. It is worth noting, however, that modern knowledge has not posed severe intellectual problems of belief.

Islam and modern knowledge

One of the main problems of Christian belief in the modern period has revolved around the scriptures and their inerrancy. The New Testament contains much that is miraculous, and it contains much about Jesus himself which may or may not be historically accurate. Knowledge of Jesus' actions is vital to the Christian, for the faith is, after all, about Christ, and historical scepticism can thus be damaging to belief. A great deal of modern Christian theology revolves around this issue, while modern scientifically-trained people tend to reject the miraculous elements of the New Testament story. But these problems scarcely affect Islam. The main aspects of Muhammad's life are clear, partly from the Koran but above all from the traditions: and in any event the faith is not absolutely centred on him, but on Allah and his message. If you accept the inspired status of Muhammad's record of the Koran, there can be no further historical doubts. That the Koran emanated through Muhammad is undoubted, and it contains little if anything that need be interpreted miraculously. Thus as we have seen Muhammad's night journey may just be a record of inspired experience, not an aerial miracle. In the past, moreover, Islam has incorporated much science into its cultural fabric, so many of the difficulties in the way of Christian belief do not exist for Muslims and, although a number of writers in modern Islam have attempted a new synthesis between revelation and modern knowledge – men such as the great Indo-Pakistani writer Sir Muhammad Iqbal, it is not in this area that the crisis of modern Islam has taken place, for Islamic fundamentalism has not the characteristics a western observer might expect.

The scriptures are, to be sure, treated as inerrant. But Christian fundamentalism is different in that it usually rejects aspects of modern knowledge, such as the use of historical methods of investigation or certain conclusions of modern science; it is thus a reaction to a particular challenge. Since that challenge scarcely occurs in relation to the Koran, it is wrong to think of the Muslim in the same light. Further, to say that the Koran is inerrant is not to say how its utterances are to be taken. This saves Islam from anthropomorphism, or making God literally in man's image. One prominent school of Islamic theology declared that we know that the things said about Allah in the Koran apply truly to him, but we do not know *how* they apply. The mystery and otherness of God remain.

Islam

The incursions of the West in the colonial age posed at least three questions to the Islamic world. One was how a new form of education could be devised which would train up new functionaries, engineers and teachers to cope with an era when science and modern administration were needed for survival. Another question was whether ultimately resistance to the West had to be based on a national series of identities, rather than the hopes of Pan-Islam. Third, did the modern era not require a new style of society involving severe changes to the old *Shari'a*? All three questions were interconnected, and their answers speak volumes about the future of Islam.

The educational question resolved itself, on the whole, by the general acceptance of European models, whether of universities or of high schools. This meant that prestige tended to pass from those learned in the Koranic tradition to the new Western-type intellectuals. Only here and there – for instance in the Islamic universities of the Indian subcontinent, and in the new dispensation in Cairo's great international seat of learning, al-Azhar, where traditions and the test-tube live side by side – has a synthesis been tried. The trend towards the devaluation of the old learning facilitated moves to change the law. It could also erode the Pan-Islamic ideal, which still depends greatly on international institutions such as al-Azhar.

Western values injected into the Muslim world included the most easily acquired of ideologies, that of the nation state. As the Islamic regions faced the colonial powers in a piecemeal way – encountering British, French, Dutch, Italian and other powers, and in diverse areas – the fragmentation was to be expected. It was encouraged by the forces of regional and linguistic identity, and, consequently, the era of emergent nationalism produced a jigsaw of states. Sometimes the more insecure a state was the more it insisted upon its special character. All this came to fruition after World War II and it meant a domination of the nation over the ideal of Islamic federation. From the point of view of the Law, the results were serious, for when the state took over the main administration of the Law it was not to be controlled in its legislation by the older organs of the *Shari'a*, even if it was bound by public opinion to respect the tradition up to a point. The extreme modern and traditional positions can be seen in Turkey and Saudi Arabia.

The Saudis, imbued with the resurgent spirit of Wahhabi reform, maintained the Law, though not without strain in a nation grown unnaturally rich through oil. Turkey went to the secular extreme. The defeat in World War I, the loss of empire and the end of the glorious Ottoman epoch, led, through the impact of Western ideas and economic forces and the need to reassert national pride, to the secular revolution led by Kemal Ataturk. The model of the new Turkey was the Western state. Islam no longer held any state function. Sufi orders were suppressed. Modern, that is Western, customs were imposed. The flat cap replaced the fez, and the veiling of women was abolished. Turkey opted out of the caliphate into Europe. Most Islamic countries tried to steer a course between these poles of modernism and traditionalism by adapting the Law.

Perhaps most dramatic and interesting are the new laws which control marriage. New minimum ages for marriage, restrictions on divorce (the husband cannot repudiate his wife so smoothly as under the ancient Law) and rights for wives in relation to the annulment of marriage are now normal in many traditionally Muslim countries. Though polygamy retains its scriptural basis, it is hedged about with legal constraints and is gradually dying out. Rules of inheritance have been changed. At a more informal level such customs as the veiling of women (doubtfully prescribed by the Koran, but widespread among Muslims) are becoming less common, and elsewhere the old Law is being overtaken not only by new legislation, but by new social habits as well.

As the nation state takes over the old *Shari'a* and the latter loses its old sphere of influence, monolithic Islam is cracking into nations. The ideal of the divine community, tarnished maybe by the conflicts of the past, has retreated before the ideal of the nation, even if (as in Arabia and Pakistan) that ideal state is Islamic.

All this entails a weakening of the old forms of Islamic Law, and a future for Islam as a spiritual force within each state, rather than as the determining force of the state. The old Law, under the triple impact of new education, modern nationalism and the forces demanding adaptation, no longer is strong, and Islam is in a deeper crisis than it knows. Yet in other ways, Islam can face a more confident future.

The tide of European domination has receded. Oil has given prosperity, and there is justifiable pride in the great heritage of a spiritual civilisation. Flanked by the West, influential in Africa, fearful of Red atheism, uncertain about the East, the old heart of Islam, in the lands from which it sprang and which it so early conquered, pulses both with excitement and apprehension.

6 RELIGIONS WITHIN HINDUISM

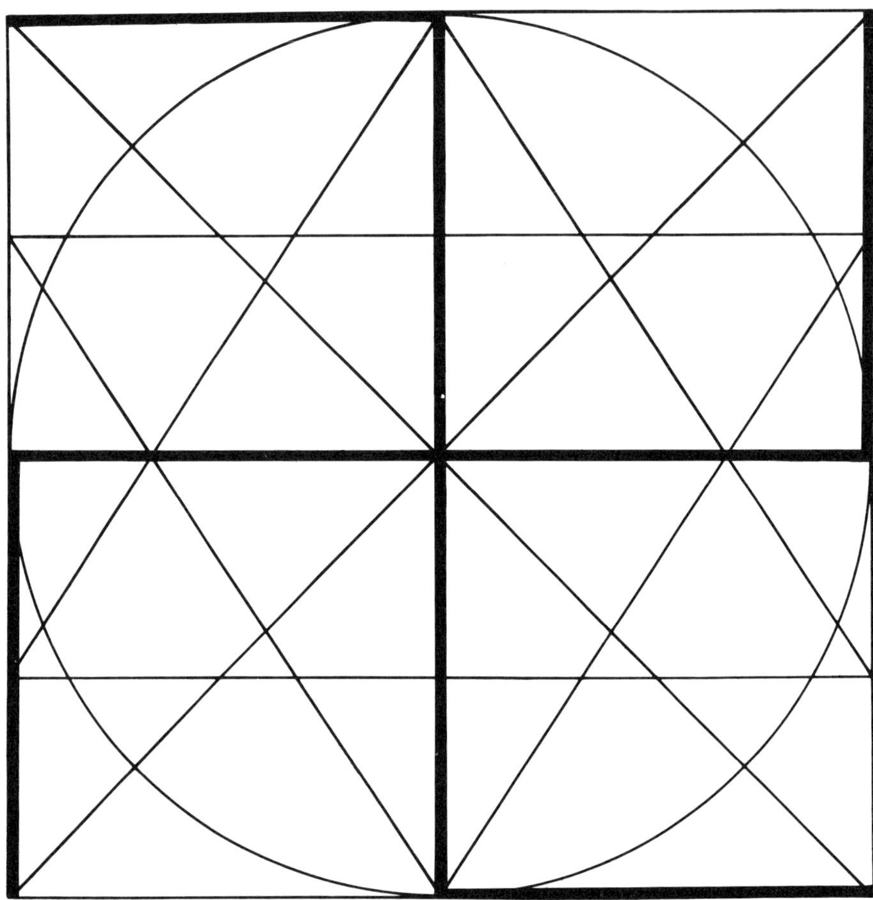

Though Hinduism supplies the frame of Indian culture (though Islam and Christianity have also been influential), there are three religions or traditions which are different from it and yet have had a distinctive life within this environment. They are Jainism, stemming from ancient sources and the teachings of Mahavira, contemporary of the Buddha; the Parsees, refugees from Persia and transmitters of the ancient faith of Zoroaster; and the Sikhs, stemming from deep attempts to unite Muslim and Hindu in the worship of one God, through Guru Nanak in the fifteenth century and his successors as leaders of the movement. The Jains were highly insistent on austerity and non-violence to living creatures – leading them to take up employment in business and so on (farming and the military being ruled out), and though they number only a few million they have had a powerful influence on Indian society. Likewise the Parsees, emigrating to Western India

in the eighth century and following, keep alive in archaic form one of the seminal religions of the ancient world, which influenced Judaism, Christianity, Buddhism and the Manichaean religion which for a time was a rival to Christianity and to which at one time St Augustine belonged. The Sikhs, though trying to bring men together, were for various social and political reasons forced to become a third force in their homeland, the Punjab. In 1699, the last of the Gurus or leaders created a special community known as the Khālsā. As a badge of membership Sikhs came to wear special dress and to abstain from cutting their hair and so on. They remain a dynamic group both within India and in the countries to which they have emigrated, from Fiji to Canada. Each of the three religions teaches us something. But being so particular in tradition, can they give men universal messages?

Three religions

Hinduism, as we saw in Chapter 2, is a federation of cults, held together rather loosely by a priestly class who maintain Sanskrit orthodoxy and knowledge of Vedic rites. Within that framework India harbours less populous faiths which, though they fit into the mosaic of Indian and Hindu society, have a certain independence. Liable to be forgotten, in a world too apt to judge by statistical norms, they represent three extraordinary motifs in human spirituality. One of these faiths, Jainism, is of extreme and awe-inspiring austerity, a moving testimony to constructive pessimism. The second, also ancient, is the faith of the Parsees, who, clinging to complex rites which stretch mysteriously back to that wonder of the ancient religious world of Persia, Zoroastrianism, continue a prophetic religion which was once one of the globe's most influential faiths. The third is Sikhism, an attempt to weld together the insights of Hinduism and Islam, in an age when strife and suspicion exist between them. The three religions represent then austerity, antiquity and synthesis. They all provide lessons for those embarked upon the long search.

The spirit of Jainism

The spirit of Jainism can be perceived in statues, to be found in various places in South India, but notably at Śravana Belgola. A stone replica of the hero Gommateśvara rises huge, stony and naked. So rigid is his stance, so austere his stillness, that creepers are growing up his legs. On his lips is an expression of total impassivity. His nudity of course symbolises possessionlessness. It is a sign of indifference to the good things of this world. It is not even a matter of laying up treasures in heaven. The Jain saint should be indifferent even to those. Any sort of treasure binds us to this world, and even the heavenly world should be transcended. Karma which weighs us down, like weights which depress balloons, must be got rid of, destroyed. This is a supremely hard task. The saint is the culmination of a struggle which has continued over many, many lives. He gazes, unseeing, over the dry South Indian landscape, a spiritual Gulliver among dark-skinned Lilliputians. Every twelve years, the Jain faithful have a great festival in which innumerable pots of milk and curds and sandal paste are poured over the head of the stone hero.

The faith celebrates those who have through heroism and insight gained liberation and thus shown the path to others. Notable among them is Vardhamāna, supposedly a contemporary of the Buddha and the great Jain hero of our world-epoch, usually known as Mahāvīra (which means, precisely, 'Great Hero'). He and others like him are also known as *Jinas*, literally 'Conquerors', 'Victors', and because of this second title the followers are termed Jainas, those who belong to the Jinas.

The Jain universe

In the archaic Jain picture of the universe the cosmos itself is like an enormous person, the head at the top and us at the waist. Above us rise various heavenly levels, below us lie so many purgatorial and hellish levels. The universe consists of souls or life-monads (*jīvas*) and non-living matter. Souls are innumerable, and often inhabit tiny organisms which we cannot see with the naked eye but are peppered through things about us. From bacteria up through animals to humans, the living world is rich, multifarious, pulsating. But souls would fly free if they could. My soul is like an invisible bag, corresponding to the dimensions of my body, but it is weighed down by all the karmic matter which I have accumulated through my actions both in this life and previous innumerable existences. Even good acts produce little dollops of karma further to weigh me down. But if I can cleanse myself, through austerities, self-sacrifice and meditation, then the light bag of my soul will fly upwards to the top of the universe where it will stay motionless for all ages, immune to the vagaries and sufferings of this lower world. This archaic picture of the cosmos sustained Jain austerity.

Jain ethics

About the worst thing the saint or anyone can do is to take life. The faithful Jain is not supposed to eat any meat, or even eggs – they are most strict vegetarians. Oddly enough, the Jains, who have been and are relatively prosperous, may owe it precisely to their worries about taking life. Warfare and butchery are ruled out as occupations. Likewise farming is discouraged, for it too means taking life, as fields are harrowed and paddies are flooded. The Jain laity have thus been nudged into becoming clerks, officials and, above all, merchants. Their standard of education has been high and they have formed a vital segment of the Indian middle classes. Thus vegetarianism has its rewards, and austerity can promote affluence. The very powerful emphasis on not taking life, *ahimsā* or non-violence, has been Jainism's great contribution to the modern Indian ethos, through the life of Gandhi. Gandhi came from Gujerat, and in particular Kathiawar, an area permeated by Jain influence. Gandhi took up *ahimsā*, and gave it political meaning.

The statue of Gommateśvara is perfectly still. Perhaps stillness is a value in its own right, in a restless age. But for the Jain stillness means not treading upon the ground. The Jain if he moves should tread softly, and the Jain monk will sweep the path in front of him so that he does not inadvertently tread on any living thing. The lay person treads softly, when he remembers, reflecting that there are little living things wriggling and jumping in the soil and he must not harm them with brutal crushing steps. Better still to be quite motionless, breathing carefully so as not to damage insects that might be ingested. The saint shows the most heroic way.

But though he is heroic and of awesome proportions, he is no god. Gods are not denied in Jainism (the religion is like Buddhism in this), but they cannot achieve perfection. They have no impulse towards the highest state. They are too fortunate to be blessed. Only man can achieve the highest. He lies creatively between the blind instinct of the animal kingdom and the insouciant felicity of the gods. Man is the potentially omniscient animal.

Jain philosophy

Which brings us to an interesting aspect of Jain philosophy: we, in principle, know everything already, but our minds have become cluttered up and confused by impressions and desires. Karma darkens the clear mirror of the mind. In our degenerate age (for the world is on its way downwards from a one-time period of golden harmony when all men were noble and equal) only a few souls can achieve omniscience by wiping the mirror clean – the Jinas, and above all Mahavira. Such souls are reverenced in the Jain cult – not as gods, for they cannot in any case help us, being motionless in splendid isolation at the top of the cosmos, but rather as exemplars of the holy life and inspirational models for more ordinary mortals.

Jains in India

There are only about two million Jains in India. Yet temples and statues like those at Mount Abu, Śravana Belgola are found in many areas of the subcontinent, and testify to the prosperity of the faith in days gone by. Up to a point it still prospers. The Jain laity are generous in their support of the monasteries. The ideal of monkhood is still clear to behold, for one can see some of these wandering ones in holy places of pilgrimage. The monk's life is hard: begging for alms, wandering (save in the rainy season), no possessions beyond bare essentials. Among the Digambara or so-called 'Sky-clad' branch of the faith the monks literally are bare, nude: the sight of a group of such stark, rapt men in Banaras was for me an unnerving, yet also in a strange way inspiring, experience. Here were men judged, not by what they had but by what they did not have.

Their *ahimsā* may to some seem overscrupulous. It goes beyond the bounds of common sense. But it is a counterweight to the sort of common sense which sees it as 'rational' to destroy whole schools of whales, whole herds of bison, whole stretches of living vegetation. The Christian might think that God put the atheistic Jains in the world to serve as a prophetic warning against those who triumph in Adam's mastery of the world about him. Gentle, scrupulous, starving, prosperous, ingenious Jainism is a living reproach. Starving? Sometimes, yes, literally. For it is the ultimate ideal of the saint, if he is ready both in psychology and karma, to end his life by self-starvation.

The Jains are not inclined to proselytism, though they are proud of their art and the philosophical and spiritual heritage. Herbert Warren, the great Orientalist and student of Jainism and Buddhism, founded a Mahavira Brotherhood in London in

1913, but it did not catch on. A religion resigned to decline by its very theory of history is only going to attract odd souls through karma, not preaching. Sir Ellis Waterhouse told me how he admired his father-in-law, the noted scholar F. W. Thomas, who among other things translated the seminal Jain text, the *Syādvādamañjari*, or Flower Spray of Relativism: Waterhouse approved of the old man's embracing Jaina principles whilst utterly refusing to try to convert anyone. There is a certain heroism about that attitude too. Yet heroism can lead to death other than by starvation. I remember noting in Mangalore, where the dread phyllaria mosquito infects by night, that many houses had not been sprayed by the DDT squads (who marked houses with each date of spraying). These were pious Jaina households. They preferred their own death to that of the insects.

Of the three religions we are examining in this chapter only Jainism really is within Hinduism. Very often the Jains make use of Brahmins for their ceremonials, and the Jains look just like another caste to many Hindus.

The Parsees

The case of the Parsees is different. Though they are well integrated into Indian society, and like the Jains rather prosperous through trade, education and mutual help, their overseas origin is embedded in their name, which really just means Persians. The Indians gave them hospitality in days of persecution, and lived not to regret it for the Parsees have made a distinctive contribution to Indian society, especially in Bombay and on the West coast.

Only a few Parsees have settled outside the two centres of Zoroastrianism today – Western India, chiefly Bombay, and Persia or Iran, in Tehran and the outlying townships of Yazd and Kerman. In the early sixties, there were something over 17,000 in Iran, and about 120,000 in the Indian subcontinent. There are also about 5000 Parsees in Pakistan. Not many people, but they have brought Zoroaster's religion with them through the long reaches of a tragic history into the contemporary world. We criticise conservatism and encourage folk to change; but often sheer conservatism protects a whole species of thought and life from extinction. The modern world has seen too many old cultures wiped out in the name of other ideologies or religions or shibboleths, so let us praise the Parsees for their strong, ritual grip upon an ancient past, and thus on the teaching of Zoroaster, one of the great prophets of the ancient world.

Zoroastrian influences

Consider the influence of Zoroastrianism. The Hebrew Bible was deeply influenced by Iranian ideas about the end of the world, and that fascination with things to come was taken up by the early Christians and, for that matter, Jesus himself. So in a sense Zoroaster walked by the Sea of Galilee. The pietism of the Pure Land owes something to the world of boundless light, the Iranian paradise. So Zoroaster gazed too much upon Mount Fuji. The prophet Mani, whose teachings made such a strong imprint on the Roman world of Augustine, blended Iranian elements into his great religion Manichaeism. So Zoroaster walked the streets of Carthage and Hippo. Mithraism was born in the womb of the older faith. So Zoroaster fought with the legions and stood on Hadrian's Wall. And the Iranian religion gives majesty to Persia's past, remembered well in modern Iran. So Zoroaster's voice is heard in the palace of the Shah and on the ski-slopes at St Moritz. We often forget all this, for Zoroastrianism is no longer a world religious power; but for the Parsees and the remnant in Iran, it would be a dead faith. Yet even if Zoroaster's faith were wholly dead, in the formal sense, we could learn from it.

Zoroaster in history

It is hard to penetrate the thoughts of a great man who only appears in the records a long time after his death. Western scholars have tended to separate Zoroaster teachings from later accretions. But it is sometimes safer to trust the testimony of those who have kept the faith alive. At any rate, the essentials of the faith as it is held today obviously go back a long way. So let us describe them, briefly, even if they are not precisely what the young Zarathustra began to preach, probably just before the Jewish exiles were deported to Babylon.

Parsee teaching

The universe is created by a good God, the great Ohrmazd. The world is good, but (we must be realistic) it is infested with evil also: this is the work of the Evil One, Ahriman. But though Ahriman commands legions of evil spirits and struggles most powerfully and ingeniously against God, God will win in the end. In the beginning, there was goodness; at present there is the struggle between darkness and light; at the end, when God's victory is gained, we shall be restored to goodness. Such is the drama of the universe in which man is destined to play a central part. The aim of every man must be to please God and to seek to further his work in overcoming evil. Yet Ohrmazd is so exalted that men often turn to those lesser beings who serve him, the courtiers as it were around the great king. These are the *yazads*, the 'worshipped ones'. Generally speaking the Zoroastrian cult is directed towards these beings rather than directly to the supreme Ohrmazd. It is like this in many faiths – God seems too exalted; we approach the great king through his servants. Chief of the *yazads*, and the one who has attracted most attention in various contexts, is the judge and friend, the fighter against evil, the dynamic Mithra. He is the one who specially looks after the central rite of the Parsees, the fire-service, and the temples in which the ceremonies are performed, the fire-temples, are referred to as the courts of Mithra. Other *yazads* have specially to do with rain, travel, the earth, justice and so on. To some extent these spirits reflect natural forces, or rather are entangled in them; to some extent they represent those things that make men anxious and animate them in their quest for both safety and salvation.

Though man is the best of God's creation, the old scriptures also speak highly of ox, ass, sheep and dog. Man's job, as we have seen, is to help in the long struggle against evil. Evil is not just moral evil (though that is regarded as important, and the Parsees lay great emphasis upon good moral conduct as a way of serving God), it is also to do with defilement. The purest element, and the symbol of righteousness, is fire, and the Zoroastrian cult centres upon the fire-ceremonies. By contrast, there are evil things which defile. Cattle, birds like the cock, which sets darkness to flight, health – these are good: thirst, disorder, animals of prey, reptiles – these are bad. Morality and a ritual and symbolic sense of what is right and integral are interwoven. The good man is also the healthy man.

One reason why the Parsees do not cremate bodies is that it would defile fire. Hence there are in Bombay the famous Towers of Silence where the bodies of the dead are exposed to the sun and the rain and picked over by convenient vultures. Exposure of corpses is quite an ancient and widespread practice and used to be common in northern India. But of course the dead live, for they live not in their bodies but their souls, which stay at the place of death three days, then take off for their perilous passage across the Chinvad bridge. That bridge is like a sword. If the soul is good, it turns its broad side and the soul passes over to a wondrous Paradise. If it be bad, then the edge stays uppermost, and the soul in trying to cross is toppled into Hell below. There are echoes of this in the modern song, 'Sliding down the razor blade of life'.

So Zoroastrianism makes room for both individual destiny, which is highly dependent upon moral conduct, and that global destiny which is worked out in the last days. Some of these notions – the Bridge and the Last Judgment – appear in the Koran. So we can say that also Zoroaster walked by the walls of Mecca and Medina.

The Parsee story

Zoroastrians are very few, when one thinks of the glories and successes of Darius and Cyrus, the pomps and powers of the Persian empire, the great monuments built by the Sassanians. The empire was vulnerable – Alexander showed that – but the religion remained powerful and fertile over long centuries, until it was virtually wiped out by Islam in those first heady decades of conquest, when the Arabs, in many an empire, put their religious seal on a transformation of former values. The old state religion of Persia was replaced by a new one, and followers of the old way were persecuted and taxed. Very few stayed loyal to the faith – a sufficient number to ensure the continuance of Zoroastrianism, but only in impoverished and poor circumstances. Some were driven to seek refuge beyond Iran, notably in India. Iranian traders may have preceded them, making a possible base for renewal. Possibly the first settlement of Zoroastrians seeking refuge from Islamic persecution landed in Kathiawar in the eighth century. But certainly there came to be a settlement in southern Gujerat (also the home of many Jains, and so almost a centre of the periphery, a focus of the unusual). Islam came again in the late thirteenth century when Gujerat was invaded under the auspices of the increasingly powerful Delhi sultanate. The Zoroastrians fought on the side of the Hindus, but were driven south. Akbar listened tolerantly, and even with some enthusiasm, to the doctrines of the Parsees, but the break came with the British. Many Parsees settled in the region of Bombay, the island annexed by the British, destined to become the great emporium of Western India and gateway, in effect, to the subcontinent from the West. The Parsee destiny was made. They had the educational drive to adapt. They had a religion to match that of Europe. They were fairer skinned than the Marathi. Their daughters might marry the European. The Parsees, though few, could claim to hold much the same values as the Christians, who came with ships and ledgers to found a new economy in the subcontinent. The Parsee journey had been a painful one: Muslims (though not only Muslims) had ravaged the Zoroastrian communities, and the riches of the old religion in Persia were shattered, yet the Parsees in India keep the fire (literally) of their ancient faith alive and are even optimistic.

The Sikhs

The antiquity of the Parsee inheritance in India matches that of other traditions in the subcontinent. But the third of the religions contained within Hinduism, though its elements go much further back, is very recent in terms of world history. The religion of the Sikhs stems essentially from the fifteenth century. From one point of view, it is a product of the encounter between Islam and Hinduism in the North Indian environment, from another a product of a more general human dissatisfaction at the external divisions between faiths. Yet the social and political roots of the new movement caused it to become a third force between two ways of life: an example of the way any faith that embeds itself in society and defines its structure and its doctrine is going to become separate, even when its intention is to embrace opposites. Synthesis of two leads to the definition of a third. The process is both noble in origin and fascinating in development. (It is the story of Sikhism.)

Islam and Hinduism

One sometimes regrets that Islam ever went to India. World history cannot be put into compartments, but the Khyber Pass was a dangerous conduit: the water of Islam and the oil of Hindustan did not mix and took long to comprehend each other. The genius of the one was the anathema of the other; the vigour of one was a threat to the other; the mosque could not merge into the temple. Arabic is written from right to left: Sanskrit from left to right. One celebrates the lingam; the other is given to circumcision. It has through to modern times led to misunderstanding, bitterness and tragedy. It was not possible for the British to leave the Raj without dividing it, and in the process many Hindus, Sikhs and Muslims were massacred – all in the name of religion and devotion to God. But as a friend of mine remarked perceptively: 'Do not ask a man whether he believes in God; rather enquire into the footnotes.' Yet it should not be thought that bitterness always characterised relations between Muslim and Hindu in India. It is naïve to think that so many in the subcontinent became pious Muslims just by force, fashion or coercion. There was much genuine proselytisation by, among others, Sufi teachers – congenial of course to the Hindu ethos. There were, too, black features of the Hindu social framework, and many an outcast found the brotherliness of Islam greatly congenial. There were faults and virtues on both sides, and good reason to think that, sooner or later, some synthesis between the faiths might be achieved. One attempt made by the egregious and magnificent Akbar, taster of religions and great emperor and patron of comparative religion when he constructed his own faith, did not work; it came too much from above and too much from the mind. Yet a true synthesis, from below, had already been initiated before Akbar's time, through Kabir, Nanak and others. It was among the winding streets and bright riverside of the holy city of Banaras, between the silk-weaving and the ablutions, that the thought of unity came to the mind of Kabir.

Kabir

Kabir (1440–1518) followed Islamic feeling about idols. He extended that thought to other externals. He condemned not just images of Ganesh or Krishna but also caste distinctions and circumcision. For after all, circumcision was as divisive a badge as the sacred threads of the Brahmins. Kabir tried to cut through the web of externals and rituals. Both Arabic and Sanskrit were too removed from the people: he wrote forcefully in the vernacular. He argued that the love of God alone could free man from the round of rebirth. He was clearly deeply influenced by the *bhakti* tradition within Hinduism. He no doubt felt in his bones that this devotionalism was also the stuff of which Islamic piety is made. It was only a pity that the goodness in each religion was covered by irrelevant loyalties and commitments. He thus became a forerunner of the Sikh religion. He also had a following which took off on its own, more or less independently of the Sikh tradition – the so-called Kabirpanthis (those taking Kabir's path, as the name implies) who became a movement within the flux of Hinduism in the medieval period. Indeed it is worth stressing that the line between the Sikhs and the Hindus has never been very clearly drawn, and the Sikh synthesis of Islam and Hinduism leaned, as it happened, more on the Hindu side. Maybe this is not surprising, for Islam has always itself been more clearly defined. A field lying between a road and a marsh will more easily become part of the marsh than the road. And after all, Hinduism itself is more syncretic, more hospitable, vaguer in many of its requirements, more federal. When the tragic partition of the subcontinent occurred the Sikh destiny has proved to be on the Indian side of the frontier.

Nanak

If Kabir was a sort of John the Baptist, the Jesus of Sikhism was Nanak, born in 1469 in a village some thirty miles from Lahore in what is now Pakistan. He was the first Guru, as it turned out, of the Sikh religion. He was, in the ancient class system of India, a *ksatriya* by birth, like the Buddha and other ancient illustrious leaders, but his father was poor. It seems that the young Nanak was a disappointment to his father and rather incompetent as a husband. The cause was partly to do with his abstraction from ordinary concerns. He was intent on deeper things, and this preoccupation with the spiritual culminated in a vision of God. He proved to be a new prophet. Under the influence of his vision he composed the great prayer repeated daily by the modern Sikh, the *Japji*: 'There is but one God whose name is True, the Creator, without fear or enmity, deathless, unborn, self-existent, great, bountiful. The True was in the beginning, he was in the primordial age. He was, is and O Nanak will be.' Nanak was not just a prophet. He was an original. He went about preaching the faith by singing, accompanied by his companion Mardana, whose stringed rebeck was in a sense part of the message. Nanak wore a mixed garb, to show he was both Hindu and Muslim or neither. But Nanak was the first of a line:

he and his successors formed a spiritual dynasty, which was to culminate in a separate community, for various of Nanak's successors were persecuted, principally by the Mughal emperors, who found their success in recruiting followers a political and religious threat. The last of the human Gurus who headed the Sikh community, Govind Singh, cemented the transformation of the synthesis into a new and concrete expression of separate identity. He formed the faithful into a community, the Khālsā. Males took the name of Lion, Singh. Every Sikh was enjoined to wear his hair uncut, to keep a comb to tidy said hair, to wear shorts under his trousers, to wear a steel bangle, and to sport a short dagger. His followers were to give up alcohol and tobacco. And Govind named the scriptures, The Granth, as the final Guru or Teacher. Such were the external marks which defined the Sikh community and gave it force against its threatening neighbours. For some time in the late eighteenth and early nineteenth century the Sikhs were masters of the Punjab, and are again today, politically – at least of the Indian half of it. In achieving these ends the Sikhs recruited heavily among the Jats, agriculturists of the Punjab, proud and tough peasants. The religion turned out to be congenial to the militant, though it was born in other feelings. The militarism of the Muslims combined with the theology of *bhakti* Hinduism to create this new and dignified religion; yet despite the earlier dream of synthesis, it is a separate one.

Sikh theology

As we have seen, the main principle animating the fathers of the Sikh religion was that God, the True, is one, and that the differences between Islam and Hinduism are to do with externals. The invisibility of the Divine, however, does not mean that we cannot enter into warm relationship with him. Nanak thus drew on the springs of Hindu *bhakti* devotion as well as Muslim fervour in prayer. Yet despite Islamic influences, the framework of life was depicted in a Hindu way, through belief in reincarnation. But since God is everywhere all men can turn to him in love, in the hope of paradise. The Sikh theology was a noble attempt to bridge the gap between the two major faiths of medieval India. It was hardly the fault of the Sikhs that they were driven politically into a strong militancy fortified by the adoption of so many signs of religious identity.

The austerity of the Jains, the antiquity of the Parsee vision of God's part in history, the attempt at synthesis of the Sikhs add diversity to the rich pattern of the religions of the Indian subcontinent.

7 BEYOND THE WHITE FRONTIER

One of the major forces in the world is that range of rather small societies which retain an incredibly rich mosaic of different cultures and spiritual values: in much of Africa, in Papua and New Guinea, in the Americas, in parts of Asia – in many areas of the world. Probably over 250 million people belong to such groups lying outside the major world religions and outside modern secular societies. However, they are now under pressure from, mainly, northern cultures. A cultural frontier exists, what I here call the white frontier, between the West and such societies. They are in a process of adapting or succumbing. Many new religions are being created, some part-Christian but harking back to older values, others more consciously re-creations of the past values. Often smaller groups go through tragedy, as with the North American Indians or Brazilian tribes. But new psychic forces are often released by the terrible challenge. Other groups

may be just large enough to keep their own indigenous cults with dignity. The Torajas in Indonesia, for instance, fall into this group, though the encroachments of missions cause questions about the adaptation of the old tradition to the present situation, while well-meaning attempts to develop the economy through tourism bring about a new white presence and a new frontier between the old culture and the new visitors – at its worst between the antique exhibitionist and the jet-born voyeur. Still, the many societies of this 'other world' have many riches. Can they survive? Can large cultures learn?

European dominance

Sails, compasses and cannon made Europe master first of the East and then of Africa. Ships took Europeans to the empty Americas and the emptier Pacific, to the whole world accessible from the sea. And even landlocked Tibet was to fall at last: and Europeans took their culture with them. We have seen some of the effects of this in India, China, Japan and the Middle East. The early history of trinkets and barter, spices and gold, was followed by modern capitalism, arising in Europe from forces obscure and, in part, religious. And beyond capitalism lay technology and science. The European did not just conquer: he instructed. He was not just the missionary, but also the man of a new and confident age of science, construction, education and truth. He was almost irresistible. How was what we now call the third world to respond?

If the country was big and had a strong culture it survived. India, though conquered by the British, kept her identity, and Japan toughened itself in the face of the foreigner. But even countries like these suffered, so it is not surprising that smaller societies were deeply traumatised. What happened to such societies in the last two centuries or more is a major part of the modern spiritual condition of men. It is unfortunate that the impact of the West on smaller societies is not better appreciated. In many parts of the world there are mini-nations, tribes or groups which have their own refined and highly idiosyncratic cultures. Some hunt and gather. Some scratch out subsistence in bad lands. Others cultivate well and hunt too. Others again are nomads, herding flocks, or agricultural nomads growing crops in jungle clearings and then moving on. These societies could not easily stand up to the diseases and rifles of the white man, particularly when, as in the Pacific, South America and Africa, large-scale colonisation followed trade.

The responses of the third world

Transactions between such societies and European and, more generally, northern hemisphere imperialism are across what I call the White Frontier. It is a boundary drawn between cultures and in minds, a frontier where ways of thinking meet. The transactions across this frontier must be understood if we are to see man's present spiritual condition for what it is. For we must not see the world only through the windows of the larger cultures and larger religions. Moreover, the overwhelming, liberating, yet oppressive character of European expansion has affected even the great traditions. For China, for example, it meant convulsions. How much more so for smaller, less self-conscious societies!

Most smaller groups possess in an acute form what is evident too in larger cultures, namely a lack of universality. The ideas and customs of a culture are adapted to that culture, and if a society is enclosed, self-regarding, it must have problems when it meets values which are claimed to be universal, especially if it comes from a culture having powers undreamed of in your own. There are various responses. I put them perhaps frivolously in the form of a game, but the lessons are meant to be serious.

I imagine an invading large culture (in principle the white West, though one can think of other examples) meeting a rather small culture. The one I shall call Strong, the other Small. How does Small respond to Strong. My examples are of course religious; but it is worth noting that any study of meetings on the frontier must make religion an important element in the analysis.

A way to small-scale disasters

One disastrous move that Small can make is to act as though he is as big as Strong. This kind of response can be illustrated by the rise of the Ghost Dance among the North American Indians, which had its tragic culmination in the virtual destruction of the Comanche. It began in 1869 when a certain Wodziwob, a Paviotso (a member that is of the Paviotso tribe on the Western edge of Nevada), had a vision. The Great Spirit revealed to him that a major cataclysm would hit the world shortly. The earth would open up and into its maw would fall all the whites, though their buildings and tools would be left for the Indians to use. This was the seed of the movement which spread to other tribes and was known as the Ghost Dance. The ceremony, based on traditional cults, involved dancing round a totem pole, and chanting songs taught by the prophet and learned by him in a trance. It was a variant on Wodziwob's prophecies that animated the Comanche. They lived in the south-west part of the great Plains, and were aware of the spreading dance cults in other tribes. They devised their own Sun Dance, and in the context of the new movement there arose the prophet Isatai, a shaman of great power and a bold warrior. He proclaimed that he had been taken up to heaven to commune with the Great Spirit, and the knowledge he there gained gave him the power to raise the dead, and an immunity to the white man's bullets. Indeed he could render every Indian immune to them. Isatai led a force of fighters into Texas on a large-scale raid. His force was mown down by the white man's guns, and in succeeding battles the Comanche suffered so severely that by 1875 they were nearly wiped out. In various areas, Burma, New Guinea, parts of Africa, similar fatal confrontations occurred.

Another possible move by Small is simply to take over Strong's culture and religion – to try to become as Westernised as possible. This often takes the form simply of converting to a relevant type of Christianity and gaining Western knowledge and technological expertise through the mission school. This was a pattern over large parts of Africa. The move has much to commend it, and in an age when many countries have become politically independent the inheritors of power have often been those members of society who adapted most successfully to Christian and Western values. But there are some disadvantages: there can be a period of tension, for Strong will not recognise the equality of Small even when the latter looks so much like Strong. And what about the traditional values of Small's society? It is very difficult to disentangle purely cultural elements and graft them on to Christianity. Indigenous culture, religion and ethics are intimately intertwined. What, for instance, is to be done about female circumcision, which goes with a whole pattern of initiation into adulthood? Or polygamy which is part of a pattern of marriage involving the roles of property and sexuality? In parts of Africa, for instance, marriage was very different from the conventional Christian form brought by nineteenth-century missionaries. And behind these questions are deeper issues about the spirituality and symbolism of the older religion which Small, as he becomes assimilated, may feel he must abandon.

African ideas

It is hard to generalise – but one can make a collage which gives some notion of the total picture of the religions of a group of small societies. To take Black Africa, for example – one can make up a kind of African credo.

Men are at once part of, and set over against, nature. They must depend upon their own resolve and skills; but they also depend upon the way the rains come, the rivers rise, the herds of beasts move, the way the flies multiply and diseases come. They must look inward upon their own resources and outward upon the bounty, such as it is, of nature. To understand themselves men look at each other as they are now and back to the fathers and the forefathers. Religion is part of the very fabric of the nation, the clan, and the family. Rites perpetuate solidarities. By puberty, the boys of the group must be brave and strong, for the circumcision with its fast and trials will make them into men, and they must be ready to work and fight and shoulder the cares of their elders. Ready too to wed, to found a family, and to carry on the life of the wider family. But a man must recall not just the wisdom and experience of those who live now. The land echoes with the voices of ancestors. It is as if the elders of the clan are all around, in the shadows by the homestead, in fields, in thickets where men and women work and hunt; and hovering over the streams from which men and beasts draw their water. So in our African credo we acknowledge and honour the ancestors, with rites, libations and memories. They are part of man's ongoing life, for they are part of society – a society, though, which transcends the visibly present group. In the West we make do with a sense of history; in the African credo there is no need of history, for the ancestors are with us. When the land was taken the tribe could no longer look upon what an African poet has called 'the whimpering rocks and groaning wood', in which the ancestors have their being. As the wry African protest to the white man has it: 'First, we had the land and you had the Bible. Now we have the Bible and you have the land.'

But the ancestors are more than invisible members of the ongoing social order. They are the living-dead and as such they are interpreters, intermediaries, ambassadors even. For they are closer than we to the spirit world and can the more easily commune with divinities and with God. Yet they also speak our own tongue, and we know them personally. There is an old man here who knew my great-grandfather (a man may muse). So in our group we have good contact with the living-dead and they will help us in our transactions with the spirits of this world, on whom so much depends. The living-dead are most useful and loved when they are half-way gone. The libations and food offerings which are set out for them, the rituals whereby they are made secure from troubles that can befall them on their further way – these gifts and acts are like cheerful parting feasts. The dead must not be too close, nor yet too far. And thus they are good ambassadors to the transcendental world, which also moves around us. They are half-way between here and there.

The world is a hierarchy. Beneath our feet are the rocks and the earth and the grasses. These are the least animate, though not without their own life. Around us are the birds and beasts, the fish, the insects: a whole range of living things, but less than men in craft, knowledge, wisdom and spiritual power. Then there are men, some of course with more charisma and power than others, some nearer God, some more chieftainly than others. Then there are the living-dead, those we remember, persons fading upwards toward the spirit world; then there are the spirits and divinities; and above them all, sometimes seeming very, very far away, is the supreme Spirit, God, creator and first maker of men.

It is often thought by European theologians and philosophers that most small-scale societies were somehow primitive intellectually and socially and thus also primitive in religious belief. It was thought that men in small societies were either polytheists or animists, believing in many spiritual forces, which were conceived in a rather magical way. They did not credit such peoples with belief in God. That was an 'advanced' concept, something uniquely bestowed through the deliverances of Israel's prophetic genius and the European heritage. Even atheists held a like view, though for them the highest stage of evolution, beyond theism, was, of course, atheism. Theism had its uses, in knocking out polytheism and animism and preparing the way for modern scientific atheism, they sometimes argued. It is much to the credit of Father Wilhelm Schmidt that in a magisterial work, *Der Ursprung der Gottesidee* (The Origin of the Idea of God, volumes appearing from 1912 onwards), he assembled evidences against this picture of evolutionary upward progress. He showed in some detail the prevalence among primitive peoples (i.e. those with primitive technologies) of the idea of a High God. He turned the usual picture upside down.

Perhaps belief in a single God came first, and was later overlaid by polytheistic and animistic traits, but the evidence of prehistory is too fragmentary for us to argue satisfactorily about what came first and what did not. There are severe limits to what we can know about early beliefs. Dead men's skulls do not betray their thoughts, and it is fallacious to argue from present-day 'primitives' to early man, for all our contemporaries have had as long a history as we have. Perhaps one can make valid comparisons between modern and ancient hunting rituals – the hunt today may be close enough to the hunt of prehistoric days for us to guess about the magical pictures in the caves of Lascaux. But we cannot safely picture any evolutionary progress. Perhaps early man believed in one God and maybe he did not: theories of the origin of the long search are fallible fancies of over-orderly minds. But the fact remains that in very many small-scale societies there is belief in a high God, a supreme Spirit, and it is a motif in the African credo, the collage I am now assembling. And what is the African God like?

He is thought of as one who sees over all. He is seen as like the sun, seeing the deeds of men, seeing into their hearts too. But he is not like us, for he (to quote a Gikuyu saying from Kenya) has 'no father, no mother, no wife, no children; he is all alone; he is neither a child nor an old man; he is the same today as he was yesterday'. Or putting the negatives in another way, as the Ila do: he has no when and no where, he comes to no end. God then is the endless, all-seeing Spirit. But his place varies. Sometimes he is so high that there is no traffic between him and men. Sometimes he is in a more intermediate position. Thus Jomo Kenyatta (Kenya's first president and an anthropologist by training) wrote about the Gikuyu supreme being, Ngai, as follows:

> He has no father, no mother or companion of any kind.
> He loves or hates people according to their behaviour.
> The Creator lives in the sky, but has temporary homes
> on earth, situated on mountains, where he may rest
> during his visits. The visits are made with a view
> to his carrying out a kind of general inspection,
> *Koroora thi*, and to bring blessings and punishments
> to the people. . . . Ngai cannot be seen by mortal eyes.
> He is a distant being and takes but little interest in
> individuals in their daily walks of life. Yet at the
> crisis of their lives he is called upon. At the birth,
> initiation, marriage and death of every Gikuyu, communication
> is established on his belief with Ngai. . . . It is said that
> lightning is a visible representation of some of God's
> weapons which he uses on ahead to warn people of his
> coming and to prepare and clear the way. His approach
> is foretold only by the sounds of his own preparations.
> Thunder is the cracking of his joints, as a warrior
> limbering up for action.
>
> [*Africa* X: 1937, pp. 308–328.]

God, in creating the world, provided men with animals and fruits and other necessities of life, so that basically he is benevolent, even if he is, because so different from men, mysteriously and dangerously unpredictable. This comes out in stories which repeat from different perspectives and using different symbolisms the story of early men's alienation from God, so that God moved up higher in the heavens, increasing vastly the gap between himself and the men he had made but who had been foolish or disobedient. In one story, from West Africa, the mother of the first men was preparing food in a mortar and in moving the pestle up and down kept knocking God, who lived in the sky but very close to men. To avoid the knocking he moved up higher. She did not like this, and set the men to pile up mortars to make a tower so that they could reach God again. They got very close, but still could not reach him. One more mortar would do the trick. So the foolish mother told them to take out the bottom mortar to put on the top. The tower came, of course, tumbling down and many of the men were killed. Those who survived gave up the ambition of reaching God. The myth like so many others is both naïve and subtle. One of its lessons is a recurring motif in the world's religions – that one cannot grasp at immortality, at the divine substance. Men who try to do so meet with strange incidents, a sign of God's anger. Was not the Tower of Babel a rampart to reach heaven? For it is up to God to give, not to man to take. The African tale shows how man is too ambitious, and all the while stupid. It brings out in its strange way the majesty of God, always higher than our hands and minds can reach. Yet in the African credo there is often a nostalgia for that happy early time when God indeed lived close to men. It was a golden age. And mingled with the nostalgia is a sense that God is too exalted now to bother with the small disasters of men, thus it is best to make sure that we are in the right relationship with mother earth, or the wild spirit of the storm, or the divinity of steel, or the spirits of the rain, and those ancestors who help to promote the fertility of the crops. Because of God's distance our shrines and open-air ceremonies of sacrifice and offerings, our dances and our prayers are directed on the whole to those emissaries of the Supreme who control the immediate world about us. Here and there we see how the ancestral spirits can possess our prophets and shamans, and so guide us in the perilous track of life, where transgressions can bring calamities, and where the world of man and spirit is a seamless whole so that our moral transgressions can reverberate through nature. This closeness means that men can control forces for good or evil, so our world is also one of healing and sorcery, and our specialists in the sacred have wondrous powers. This is the world that was rent by the White intruder, with his own different powers and different outlook upon the world. For him, man is set against nature which must be tamed. For the African, nature – the spirits of the world – is in communion with us and we are part of the savannah and the rain forest.

The small nation and power

While such an African credo can be sketched, it must not be allowed to hide the fact that most tribes feel differences more strongly than similarities. Africa is a country of mini-nations, tribal worlds, where groups speak their own peculiar tongues and have their own gods and God, rites, customs and sense of belonging. The coming of the white man may have helped to unite the blacks of differing groups, but the groups remain, as the tragic events of civil war in Nigeria and Angola proved. Africa is a richer mosaic than its political frontiers would indicate.

Another strand running through African religion is the sense of power and powers. The hidden powers of nature and of the social world have to be harmonised, coped with, struggled against and harnessed for our good. The erosion of the power of the older culture therefore poses a deep problem of adaptation.

Having seen the sacrifice the African may be making if he simply adopts the religion of the invader, it is not surprising that he has sometimes tried one of Small's other moves. Beyond assimilation is the move of new prophecy: in effect the Africanisation of Christianity.

I do not know whether to believe the following story, but it was told me by a priest. He was chaplain at a university where I once taught, and he had acquired a record of a famous African Mass which was composed for talking drums. To his delight he found an African student from the relevant part of Africa who understood the talking drums. He played the record to him. Was the African delighted with the sound of it, enquired the priest. 'Of course,' said the black man. 'And did you understand it?' asked my friend. The African shook his head sadly. 'No,' he replied, 'it was all in Latin.' That, if true, would be superficial Africanisation at work. The new religious messages throbbing across the White Frontier have a much deeper meaning.

New African Christianities

These new forms of Christianity both naturally and paradoxically place stronger emphasis upon the Old Testament. Paradoxically because the New Testament is redolent of love; the Old could seem more attuned to the arrogant behaviour of Strong (the Hebrew God is not really thus: but the Old Testament can be interpreted as a justification of realpolitik). It is the New Testament that contains the beatitudes, and Small might easily identify himself with the meek who will reinherit the African earth. But the stress on the Old Testament is quite natural in terms of the African credo whose collage I assembled. While the Old Testament is against the gods, the Baals – and a lot of African spirits are Baals in function – consider these other motifs from the Hebrew Bible.

God once dwelled close to man, for did he not walk in the garden with our first ancestors?They foolishly transgressed, and had to live a harsh life of toil, though God provided them with the wherewithal, for there were the beasts and the trees and the soil to cultivate. God dwells in the sky, and is manifested in thunder and lightning. He also helps men in war. He appears in visions to prophets, who guide the people and help them survive the trials of bondage and exile. God is pleased with sacrifices of animals, and commands men to be circumcised. He sanctions polygamy. His favourite resting places when he visits the earth are mountains. His early followers were herdsmen, and their life was simple.

It would seem that the African values could easily be joined to those of the Old Testament. Sometimes there are more than hints in African preaching that the New Testament is the book of the White; and that the preaching of humility has been used to inculcate submissiveness in the conquered peoples of Africa. Though it has to be said in fairness that nationalist movements, and not just in Africa, received support and gained impetus from missionary sympathisers. In the nineteenth century the British Foreign Office recommended that Bibles always be accompanied by commentaries, lest the peoples of the East get the wrong message. The Bible is a dangerous set of documents! A friend of mine, then a young Anglican priest, was startled when he arrived in South Africa, just before World War II, to hear an Afrikaaner saying that the Church of England was a dangerous organisation. My friend was cheered by this, as its reputation for tameness in England seemed both justified and depressing. But much of the explosive charge the Christian Churches brought into Africa was concentrated in the Bible; it could blow up in the 'wrong' hands. Ironically White missionaries themselves experienced the shock waves when Black prophets began interpreting the book in all sorts of new, and for the orthodox Christian unnerving and heretical, ways. Let us not exaggerate it: these movements do not turn their back on the New Testament, but quite clearly the new faiths take the step beyond Westernisation to adaptive Africanisation. Let us look at two examples in more detail.

Kimbangu in the Congo

One of the most powerful of the new movements stemmed from the preaching of Simon Kimbangu in the Congo, starting in 1921. He had been taught in a British Baptist Mission. He had received a call through visions of the Supreme Being. He preached against idolatry, and so at one level was hostile to the African religious tradition. But his preaching in other respects struck deep chords in African consciousness and hope. He had the charismatic power of an indigenous shaman, or ecstatic prophet, and effected miraculous cures and, it was reported, other miracles, like raising the dead. He preached baptism and the confession of sins, and the imminence of a new age, in which foreign rulers would be thrown out. No wonder many of his followers thought of him as a black Christ. He was also a David raised up to fight against Goliath. His predictions of a new golden age for the African expressed a strongly nationalistic spirit, while his promise of the return of the dead in the new age restored a sense of ancestral solidarity to societies which had been disrupted by conquest. Simon Kimbangu, however, died before any promised age, in 1950, in a cell in an Elizabethville prison. He was a martyr, to his followers perhaps divine. But another prophet was, even then, giving the new movement impetus, partly because he also died a martyr – and so was living beyond the grave. This was André Matswa, who had fought in France in the First World War and who tried to enlist French aid for Congolese freedom. He too ended in gaol, and died in 1942, still retaining faith in the Free French, whose Cross of Lorraine formed part of the symbolism of his church.

The Kimbanguist drive was in what is known as the Church of Jesus Christ on Earth through the Prophet Simon Kimbangu. It eschews native religious cults and attacks all forms of sorcery and magic, yet is hostile to orthodox white Christianity and especially to the Roman Catholic missions, for the missionaries were believed to be a strong factor in the arrest, and so ultimately the death, of Simon Kimbangu. Kimbangu's Baptist background amplified this hostility, and the rituals of the Church are strongly influenced by the austere liturgy of Biblical Protestantism. There is little doubt that the Church of Jesus Christ on Earth has been an agent of resuscitation, modernisation and dignity for the African peoples of the Congo among whom it has spread. Kimbangu, the crocodile of God, has twisted the tail and bitten the trunk of the intruding white elephant.

A Zulu Zion

The Zionist Church, emanating from the experiences and teachings of the prophet Shembe in South Africa, though less overtly nationalistic was not so different in principle. Indigenous black churches were bound to arise in South Africa because of the evident contradiction between racial segregation and the central ethos of Christianity. However, the New Testament once again suffered in the estimation of the blacks precisely because it formed the core of the whites' faith. It was a perverse and ironic situation, and remains so; one can see why the Africans found it easy to identify with the Jews of old, and look towards the new Zion. Could they build it in the beautiful and tragic land?

Continued on page 246

STORIES

Religious traditions are largely based upon stories about the way the other world impinges upon this one. Often doctrines can be seen as attempts to bring a more abstract understanding to bear upon the stories: for instance, the doctrine of Christ's nature, as both divine and human, is a way of making sense of the story of his incarnation as related in the Gospels. Sometimes writers refer to the central stories of religion as myths – and here the term is used in a technical sense which does not imply (as in everyday language) that what is a myth is false. A myth tends to have different layers of meaning, which is a reason why the interpretation of religious stories is a vital ingredient in the ongoing life of a religious tradition.

Christ at Cana. *The Gospels are a record of what were taken to be the significant acts of Jesus' ministry. The stories recount among other things the miracles or 'signs' which he performed – miracles being signs of his power and of his attitudes towards men. The first miracle, here depicted by Giotto, was to turn water into wine at the wedding feast in Cana in Galilee. The story symbolises among other things the transformation awaiting Israel under the new dispensation when the historic destiny of the Jews is transformed through the coming of Jesus as the Messiah. But also it signifies Jesus' involvement in human affairs and the blessings bestowed by him upon marriage, such a central concern of human society. Incidentally, the quantity of water transformed into wine runs to well over a hundred gallons, if we follow the Biblical account: it must have been a good party.*

The Buddha and the corpse. *Though Buddhism does not imply belief in God, yet there is a sense of mystery about the way in which the transcendent world is seen in the life of the Buddha. His career was very different from that of Christ, for the Buddha lived to a serene old age and did not undergo the brief storms of Christ's ministry. Yet there is drama in the Buddha's story. Here he is depicted as seeing a dead man – an event which, among others, persuaded the young prince that the world is full of suffering. It was ultimately for this reason that he forsook his wife and child in order to pursue the spiritual quest which would lead to Enlightenment and thus a solution to the problem of suffering.*

The Buddha's farewell. *Here is a Chinese version of the farewell of the Buddha to his faithful groom and horse, who helped him flee away secretly in order to take up the spiritual path. It was to lead him to practise austerities and various types of self-control, part of the time in the company of five ascetics who were conversant with the various streams of Indian thinking of the period.*

The Buddha's sermon. *The ascetics could not ultimately help the Buddha, who eventually achieved the highest spiritual insight, Enlightenment, on his own. But his first act thereafter was to preach to his former companions in the deer park at Sarnath outside the holy city of Banaras. That first sermon marked the beginning of the Buddha's teaching mission, which lasted some fifty years till his final decease.*

Demeter and Persephone. *Not all myths or stories have to do with historical personages. This picture shows Demeter (the earth mother) and her daughter Persephone. The story was re-enacted as part of the mystery-cult at Eleusis, near Athens. The Eleusinian mysteries, like other similar kinds of religion in the Greek and Roman world, were a powerful ingredient in the spiritual life into which Christianity was injected – in an important sense Christianity itself could be looked on as a mystery religion, meaning that it emphasised the transformation of individuals in the setting of the sacred re-enactment of the divine story.*

jheronimus bosch

Krishna being naughty. *One of the most loved of all Hindu figures is that of Krishna, incarnation or avatar of Vishni. He was brought up, according to tradition, in Brindaban in North India, near Agra, by foster parents. He there indulged in his youth in various endearing and even naughty pranks, the most famous being his stealing of the clothes of the milkmaids, bathing in the river. His amorous exploits are seen as symbolising God's love of human beings.*

The Wise Men. *The story of the baby Jesus and how wise men came from the East to worship him perhaps sums up the essence of myth, for through this story people understood something of the way in which the heavenly world impinges on this world, and of the way in which human concerns are invested with divine significance.*

Rāma. *Another important incarnation of Vishnu is Rāma, a noble warrior and king, whose exploits are related in the Ramayana, one of the two great Indian epics (the other being the Mahabharata), which are recited both for entertainment and for their spiritual meaning. One of Rāma's exploits had to do with the demon king of Ceylon, who had made off with Rāma's beloved Sita. Rāma enlisted the help of the monkey god Hanuman and his followers in rescuing her. Hanuman is a favourite god in India, the monkey being accorded high status and protection in the Indian milieu. Here Rāma waits upon Hanuman at his court – the picture being an illumination of a manuscript of the Ramayana.*

Ascent of Muhammad. *It is unusual for Muslims to portray Muhammad – typically such portrayal is looked on as blasphemous. But in the rather relaxed atmosphere of Persian Islam we find cases of such pictures of the Prophet, here seen ascending to heaven. The story of his mysterious night ride, culminating in a miraculous visit to the holy city of Jerusalem, has a spiritual significance, especially for Muslim mystics, who see it as a symbol of the way in which the soul may ascend to God.*

چو آن سلطان عرش آرای بر جست
براقش همچو برق از جای بر جست
ز بطن وادی بطحا قدم زد
ببام مسجد اقصی علم زد

Isaiah Shembe, founder of the Ama Nazaretha Church, was a great visionary and a new Moses. As a child and again when he was older he had visions. Such visions occurred, appropriately, during thunderstorms, as with the prophets of the Old Testament. There was a man, a landscape, and God speaking from clouds: his visions had context and impetus. In 1911 he founded his church, and during the First World War he established shrines in high places, somewhat in the style of the ancient Israelites – first near Ekhuphakameni and later on a southern Mount Zion, Mount Nhlangakazi. They became centres of pilgrimage, and Shembe became famous among the proud and shattered Zulus. He was for them a kind of Messiah. 'I am Shembe,' he would claim, in deep and moving tones, 'the servant of the Lord, who has come to wipe away the tears of the people. The peace of God be with you. I come among you from afar, sent by the King.' From afar: thus was summed up the transcendent origin of his call together with the echoes of distant Zion. He was king of the Nazarenes, and a prophet for the Zulu nation. So was founded another breakaway church, but one serving the aspirations of those who had to rethink in anguish the meaning of their existence under the pressure of all those forces both for good and for evil which poured ineluctably over the White Frontier.

Oddly, although the Zulus had fought, Shembe was not a warrior; while amongst those who had slept in the Congo heat when their lands were snatched by the Belgians and the French, Kimbangu preached war. It is too early to say if these moves beyond assimilation work. But even if they do, they still evade the challenge of universality which is one characteristic claim of the ideas that pour across the Frontier.

Syncretism and the Cao Dai

Another move that Small can make in the face of the awesome invasions of Strong is to be more overtly syncretic. The visions of the sort of prophets we have described catch on partly because they correspond to genuine political and spiritual needs. But it is possible to put things together more deliberately, to try to effect, as it were, a formal wedding between cultures. One example of this was to be found in Vietnam, and no doubt it is still to be found there, for the victorious North Vietnamese tread softly in matters of religion.

The Cao Dai has to be seen in the context of the French control of Indochina and the strange adjustments that Vietnamese culture and religion had to make. The Vietnamese were in the orbit of China, but they were definitely not Chinese: indeed there is a cultural hostility to China which far antedates the Marxist epoch, though it helps to explain aspects of it: during the long years of war, the North Vietnamese turned more to Moscow than to Peking, though they wisely kept a good relationship with the latter.

But we are looking further back – to the period after the First World War, when thoughts of Kennedy and napalm did not exist, and hopes of freedom from French colonialism were but a small flame. The immediate problem then was a cultural one. Buddhism and other cults were used to living together and merging somewhat. It was in that milieu that the Cao Dai came to exist – a fruitful interplay between Vietnamese and French ways of life and thinking. It should of course be remembered that the basic Western missionary enterprise in Indochina was Roman Catholic rather than Protestant; we can see that this made an important difference if we contrast the situation here with that in other stretches of the White Frontier.

The Cao Dai grew from the prophetic visions of Van Chioy and the organising ability of his chief convert Le Van Trung. It was a combination of prophecy and ability, like that between Ramakrishna and Vivekananda or between Mao and Chou. The church Van Chioy and Le Van Trung established had Catholic structure, Eastern fillings and elements of Christian doctrine. It tried to indicate a new universalism, and its eyes were on the relation between East and West, between Buddhism and Chinese religions on the one hand and Christianity on the other. Among those reverenced as its saints were Sun Yat-sen and Victor Hugo. Alas, the ideals of Sun Yat-sen are dead (he was a political syncretist). A friend of mine once went to the Cao Dai headquarters, not far from the Cambodian border, north-west of Saigon. He sat at a banquet next to an impressive young man who turned out to be the reincarnation of Victor Hugo, and was busy extending his corpus, as if Hugo had not written enough already. But it is too easy to smile. In many ways the Cao Dai represented an impressive synthesis of cultures. It failed because it was overtaken by a more powerful movement, Vietnamese Marxism, and Victor Hugo could not stand up to the Kalashnikov rifles, nor the minds behind the eyes that aimed them. When Ho and Giap won, after long and bitter civil war, they indicated another option for the third world.

Another solution for the third world

Small found out something: Strong has more than one soul. When you look first across the White Frontier everything appears more or less the same. But on your second look the contradictions and turbulences appear. You see that there are at least two Strongs. Though both are white, one is also, supposedly, revolutionary. There is no need, after all, to come to terms with the official face of empire, you can instead join forces with those working against it. The revolt in Europe could be an ally of a revolt in Africa or Asia. The Bible meant little to most of those who wielded empire: by contrast, revolution had magic, the white man himself believed in it, and it had discipline. It is vital not to underestimate the importance of discipline, the key to many a new religion, many a revolution.

The impact of the West along the White Frontier led inevitably to the disintegration of societies. In traditional societies behaviour is naturally and easily inculcated. But when the social fabric is torn, new, more impressive, means are needed. One of the major traits of Marxism in practice is that it has a theory which can command assent, and so commitment, and a practice which can be harsh but leads to conformity. The new religious movements too impose discipline. Disintegrating societies in the grip of nationalism are natural places for the spread of Marxism. But the nationalism tends to make for Marxism of a rather proud and independent kind. So another move in the game of Small in the face of Strong is to take an ideology from the other, revolutionary, Strong, and use it to strengthen the ideals of a relatively small society. Marxism can thus function like one of the new religions – it did in Mao's China.

Beyond the White Frontier

Another move which can be made by Small in the face of Strong is to try to absorb Strong's values within the structure of his own society and religion. Generally speaking this does not work, but it represents a poignant response to a daunting challenge. It is most evident in the so-called Cargo Cults – these have been prevalent both in the Pacific Islands and in New Guinea. In both cases the societies in question are very small. Papua and New Guinea are a mosaic of little social groups, cut off by mountains and jungles. Small languages abound and diverse customs proliferate. The groups in that big island are like the populations of the little islands of Melanesia to the north and Polynesia. In this region of the globe Strong is very strong and Small is, indeed, small.

In its simplest form the cargo cult was preached in 1914 in the Torres Strait. It was said that a large vessel would reach the island of Saibai with a big cargo of money, flour, tools, clothing and so forth. These items had been filched from the inhabitants by the Europeans but would now be restored. With the coming of these goods a new era of justice and prosperity would begin.

The cults were, to the islanders, a rational response. During the American war against the Japanese in the Pacific, they saw great metal monsters bring goodies (and for that matter bad things too) out of the sky. They were faced with new realities, and reacted to them according to their own theories and values. Thus the new cargo cults could involve laying out ritual airfields, where invocations were made to suck from the sky and from far away good things in magic aeroplanes. That they did not work was perhaps just as well. The goodies were going to come anyway, but when they did traditional life was disrupted, pleasure traded for happiness, and marvels for order. The good things in life, in other words, are never free.

For a society to absorb an alien culture within its own rituals and system of values it must be pretty big. The Indians managed it many times, but India is amazingly rich and absorbent. For the Melanesians and Papuans the task was too hard. The trumpet sounded on the New Guinea shore, but the ship was never seen on the shining horizon; green spaces in the bush heralded, ritually, the arrival of who knows who (perhaps LBJ himself, for that was one myth circulated), but the skies only showed black, uninteresting birds that had been around all the time.

Another solution? Struggle and the Toraja

Another possible move is no move at all – survival without concessions. Conditions of course need to be favourable. Perhaps the enemy is divided, and your region hard of access. It does not happen often, but it can happen.

The buffalo-sacrificing Toraja, full of class and anguish about death, inhabit an area within the Celebes, Sulawesi. Because Indonesia is diverse, scattered and decentralised, the Toraja, despite missionaries and administrators, have substantially retained their identity and their religion. Half, perhaps, are Christian, a few are Muslims, but there is a solid core of those who keep to the old tradition and at the same time have become part of the complex politics and patronage of the Indonesian system.

An aristocratic people, living in hilly regions in southern Sulawesi, the Toraja are given to an elaborate cult of the dead. Buffalo sacrifices mark great festivities of death in which the ancestors are celebrated and a complex range of deities invoked. The religion genuinely contradicts the Christianity of the missions – Dutch Calvinism does not favour slitting the throats of buffaloes and Islam is not cheerful about the Toraja gods, or for that matter the Toraja. Existing in an environment permeated by Islam and controlled, until 1953, by the colonial and missionary Dutch, the Toraja people were at a disadvantage. What they have tried, more or less successfully, to do is to fight for a stake in the school system. The key to advancement in the modern world is education, it is thought. But that education is mainly in the hands of Christian missions and an ambiguous government. Christianity and Islam are the religions 'taught'. So by political pressure, for they are an important piece in the mosaic of Sulawesi and of Indonesian politics, the Toraja now have achieved status for their own religion and traditional beliefs in their schools. I called this at the outset the move of doing nothing, the move of no move, but to keep what you have may involve something of a fight. In this case the fact that the outside forces were divided favoured the Toraja struggle (the missions tended to be Christian, but the government was dominated by the prevalent Islam). So amid the steaming glens of Toraja Land the great funeral rite is still frequently celebrated, the blade strikes the underpart of the neck of the buffalo, the ship-like houses rise amid the greenery, men celebrate the dead amid the favour, hopefully, of the gods, and the old dignity of man in Toraja terms is maintained, despite the pressures of Calvin and Muhammad, felt distantly from beyond the blue surrounding hills. Would sacrament or circumcision serve them better? Who can tell? Certainly the move that is no move can serve an independent folk well.

It should not be thought that the moves in the game between Strong and Small often have cheerful endings. On the whole they do not. Many small-scale societies have gone to the wall. Others, like contemporary Cambodia, have become strangely convulsed. The White Frontier has been a dangerous stretch of country in the field of human history. The search here has not been so much for a real future as a decent identity. Out of the turbulence may come new insights and creativity but they are hard to discern.

There are some 250 million people living in small-scale societies. They are a large section of the human spirit; but they are not unified, they have much in various ways to teach, but they do not speak in chorus and their voices are not easily heard.

8 CHINA

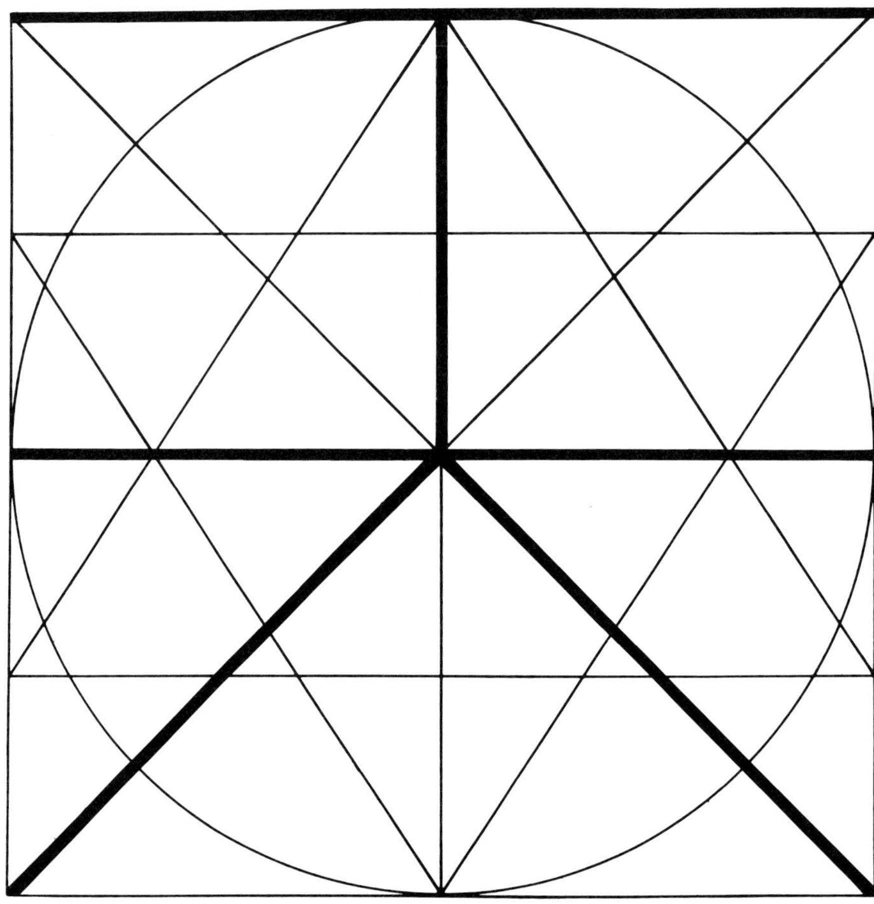

It used to be said that China had three religions – but now perhaps we can speak of four. The three are Confucianism, Taoism and Buddhism. The fourth is Maoism. Other faiths exist, of course, in China, such as Islam and Christianity, but the main body of Chinese culture has been permeated by ideas and practices going back to the sixth century – the period of Confucius and of the legendary Lao-tzu, supposed founder of Taoism. Confucius claimed to restore older values, and moulded a classical inheritance of ritual observance and literary culture. Much later he came to be revered as an ancestral figure of focal importance for those who adhered to the old ways. What we know as Confucianism is a blend between the tradition and cults deriving both from state ceremonial and folkways involving reverence for ancestors and a respect for the dictates of providence, or Heaven.

Taoism proved more anarchic. It started with a protest against formalism. Be natural

– live in accord with the principle animating the universe, the Tao. Much later it acquired the trappings of a popular religion, with a hierarchy of gods and spirits.

From the first century AD *Buddhism came into China and made substantial advances, alternately patronised and repressed by the imperial administration. The T'ang dynasty saw its greatest flowering. It settled in as one of the three spiritual forces of Chinese culture, through which it was to be transmitted to Korea and Japan. The three forces lived in a kind of symbiosis. But in the twentieth century their influence was breaking down, and ultimately Maoism came to power, hostile to the old ways, and yet borrowing some of the forms of religion in its evangelical attempts to reshape Chinese consciousness. In Taiwan and among the overseas Chinese the older culture persists somewhat, but the centre of gravity of Chinese belief has shifted. Yet will the new faith be able to supply the inner meanings the old ones provided?*

The story of the Middle Kingdom proceeds from an ancient past, the world of the Tao, to the new (or is it new?) world of Mao. China runs from north to south, and it looks over its shoulder towards the upper part of the Asian land mass: significantly it was on that shoulder that the Great Wall was built. It has taken the Chinese a long time to appreciate the significance of the sea: classically it has been invaded from the land. Muslims, Hindus and other distant voyagers came to the long, curving Chinese coast, but they were of little importance until European sea-borne cannon in the nineteenth century shocked the Chinese out of their complacency. The land invasions by nomads led to Chinese culture being periodically invigorated by rude conquests and subsequent infusions of new cultural values. But the huge, usually united, Chinese empire was able to convey a written language, a literature, a set of spiritual values, over a vast area. They were the Roman Empire of the East; but with fewer legions and more scholars, and not so divided. China came to look upon the countries of the geographical periphery – Manchuria, Vietnam, Korea, Tibet, Sinkiang, Japan – as cultural satellites, owing homage to the Chinese Emperor, somewhat detached from the heart of the world, seen essentially as a Chinese world – but given some of the blessings of superior Chinese culture and civilisation, and indeed religion. The spirit of Confucius went out to the world from a secure and massive heart.

The shock of the ships

It was an almost unimaginable shock for the Chinese when Western ships arrived. They had to rethink their position in the world in a very painful way. Here were red devils from the sea, men with cunningly contrived sailing ships, later steamships, armed with guns which could blow junks out of the water, arriving on the coast, demanding trade and then concessions, filtering in missionaries moreover, who tried (as the Chinese saw it) to subvert older Chinese values. And the Emperor and his court recognised the peril, and yet despised it and in despising it underestimated its ultimate impact on the Chinese way of life. The Chinese tacked rather incompetently against the wind from Europe. There was the Taiping rebellion, a crude forerunner of Mao's, but it was not until the mid-twentieth century that China was able to reassert its ancient power and grandeur. The Communist revolution in China was nationalism writ red, and writ Chinese.

The Revolution drew mysteriously upon ancient Chinese ideas and practices to which we must now turn. They are commonly referred to in the West as the three religions of China – Confucianism, Taoism and Buddhism. The last of course came from outside but became not only thoroughly assimilated but also strikingly developed in its Chinese phase. It was from China that it came to be transmitted to Japan, eager for new ideas then as now.

Some characteristics of Chinese culture

In the middle of the second millennium before Christ, the Shang dynasty was a matrix in which the written language was developed. That language proved to be characteristically different from Western and most other Asian tongues. It is not based on an alphabet. Each word has its own written character. The scholar thus needs to memorise thousands of these and, as a consequence, literary education has never been easy. The educated became an élite and, not surprisingly, a mystique surrounded the figure of the scholarly Chinese gentleman. Right up to the twentieth century the civil service examinations, whereby aspiring young men were recruited into the upper, administrative class, were based upon a thorough knowledge of the ancient classics. Literature became the key to advancement. This is one reason for the high place put upon aesthetic pursuits in ancient China.

The non-alphabetic quality of the Chinese written language, though inconvenient, also has one great advantage. In such a vast country as China, only gradually brought into the ambit of civilisation as Chinese culture spread southwards to Canton and beyond, there are bound to be great variations in the spoken languages. These are sometimes referred to as dialects, but the differences between, say, Cantonese and northern Chinese (Mandarin) are quite as great as those between Portuguese and Italian, or Spanish and Romanian. However, since the written language did not depend upon phonetic spelling, the same ideogram or picture could stand for *dog* or *man* or *tree*, whatever the differences in the pronunciation of these words in the various languages of China. The same character could stand for *ren* (man) in North China and *yan* (man) in South China and the Chinese written language became a formidable instrument in welding together a vast empire; a powerful literary élite became its bureaucratic spine.

A pervasive feature of Chinese society from early times has been concern with ancestors. The reverencing of the dead generated and cemented clan and family loyalties, and secured a good transition for the dead to the realms beyond. More generally, the whole of reality was permeated by spirits. This cult of the spirits, which is sometimes looked on as real Confucianism, is something that has run alongside the more systematic and philosophical side of Confucius' teaching. It is, as it were, a fourth strand in Chinese religion, alongside all three religions. The cult of ancestors was not just a matter of families: it was also a kingly device, and, more significantly, a way of celebrating ancient heroes. One of these was the wise Duke of Chou, sometimes looked on as the true originator of the Confucian tradition (Confucius often represented himself not as a founder, but as one who restored and put in order the deliverances of the ancient traditions). The Chou had overthrown the rich and sophisticated Shang dynasty in the twelfth century BC. It was the Duke of Chou who consolidated power, acting as regent, and organised the empire along feudal lines, showing conciliation and mildness in winning the acquiescence and support of the conquered population.

The morality of rule has remained a vital strand in Chinese thinking. The Chou justified their overthrow of the Shang on the grounds that the last Shang ruler was violent, drunken and oppressive, and thus claimed that they possessed the 'decree of heaven' or 'mandate of heaven' – a divine sanction, as it were, for their rebellion. In Mao's thinking, for Heaven you have to substitute the People, but the principle is the same.

Confucius and his background

Master K'ung, to give him his proper Chinese name (Confucius being a Latinised version of K'ung-fu-tze invented by Jesuits), lived in a turbulent period, some six centuries after the establishment of the Chou dynasty. The feudal system had over the previous two centuries disintegrated. Centralised rule had broken down. There were a number of larger states and some smaller ones, among them Lu, in Shantung, where Confucius was born in 551. His teaching was much concerned with politics: it was concerned with how to restore stability and justice through the revival of older virtues and courtesies. It was about how to make gentlemen who would be fit to rule, and harmonious in their actions. The answer was: Not just by birth (Confucius himself, though by his own testimony poor and without influence, must have been upper-class), but by education. This was not just the training of the intellect, but learning for living and practical and spiritual cultivation. If nowadays we are so used to education, then let it not blind us to the startling novelty of Confucius' revolution, even though it was, in some senses, a conservative revolution. He set up a school for gentlemen and gained his influence through his many disciples. It was they who transmitted the thoughts and ideals of their Master. For he was not otherwise successful. True he was for a time a minister in his native state, but it turned out to be a sinecure, without real influence, and he resigned. For a decade thereafter he wandered from state to state hoping to find a ruler who would implement his teachings. He returned to Lu, unsuccessful, and spent the remainder of his life in teaching. He died in 479. He might have been thought a failure but in fact his subsequent influence proved enormous. For he had put together a philosophy which reinterpreted the ancient literary tradition, and he had thought out a system of moral and political values which was to serve the Chinese ruling classes in subsequent centuries.

The flavour of K'ung's thought

Confucius, in trying to cure the ills of his society, was preoccupied with the social dimension of man's existence. For him, society should be reformed so that it shapes men in harmonious behaviour, but he was no determinist. He saw that society could be moulded by the actions of influential individuals within it, and so it was his desire to create a new élite, where gentlemanliness was a matter not of birth but rather of training and character. Anyone could become a gentleman. K'ung was thus bent on forming a circle of dedicated persons who would revive the values of Chinese society. And central to the whole operation was *li*. Originally *li* meant sacrifice: it referred to the sacrificial acts so important in early Chinese society, whereby right relations were maintained with Heaven and with the noble ancestors who could influence the well-being of the realm. By extension it came to mean ritual: more narrowly the ritual dimension of religion itself, and more generally those rituals and conventions whereby harmonious human relations are maintained. K'ung had a keen awareness of the role of proprieties, rituals of courtesy, in social behaviour. It is something so pervasive in our life that we sometimes neglect it.

If I pass a neighbour in the morning and fail to smile and wish him good day, he will become suspicious – is my surliness or coldness due to some grudge which I have against him? Neighbourly relations break down without such courtesies. If I insult someone by telling him he is an idiot, this is a gesture which is disruptive of good relations. For good relations, then, we use smiles, greetings, compliments, handshakes, osculations and the like. So for K'ung there was a continuum running from a religious ritual right through to saying 'Adieu'. More particularly, the wise ruler or high official should look upon courtesies and good behaviour towards the ruled as an extension of sacred sacrifice. Of course, the danger of such a teaching is that it might become superficial. The courtesies and ceremonials of life and of religion are too easily manufactured. It is the thought which counts, the sincerity. So though *li* is a vital ingredient in the betterment of men, sincerity is also crucial, and that should rest upon fellow-feeling or *shu*, sometimes translated reciprocity.

Confucius was once asked whether there is one word which could serve as the rule of one's whole life. He replied: Is not *shu* such a word? 'What you do not want done to yourself, do not do to others.' Thus K'ung enunciated the golden rule. The fact that he stated it negatively rather than positively ('What you would want others to do to you, do that to others') has sometimes attracted criticism, but it is just a matter of the way he expressed himself here. Elsewhere he is quite clear that the rule of *shu* has a positive as well as a negative sense. For he states that a son should serve his father as he would expect to be served by his son, and to serve a king as I would expect a minister to serve me, and to act towards an elder brother as a person would expect his younger brother to act towards him, and so forth.

However, it is clear that Confucius here and elsewhere maintained a strong sense of social and family hierarchy. This was a reason why Confucianism was a conservative force in later Chinese society, where the hierarchical nature of the empire was further defined; and why in today's China such strong and bitter attacks are made on the Confucian ethic.

Mao and Confucius

Mao, who was headstrong even in childhood, says that he hated Confucius from an early age. For him the Sage represented feudal and family tyrannies. His own father's tyranny contrasted with his mother's gentleness, and summed up the problems of a less than just social order, which Mao in later life was determined to transform. Mao was much more sympathetic to Taoist and even Buddhist elements in Chinese culture. So in the wake of the Cultural Revolution there has been a renewed attack on Master K'ung. It is interesting to see how many of Confucius' ideas are turned somersault and given different application. Reciprocity is now an equal and comradely virtue, not interpreted within the structure of hierarchical relations. Women are equal. The young can unleash reform against the old. The new China does not look back, as Confucius did, to a golden earlier age. Rather it looks to a future golden age, with the consummation of the Communist way. The whole ceremonial or *li* of China today is a reversal of the old. Instead of the many religious festivities there is national and revolutionary celebration. Instead of sacrifices for the high and mighty there are now praises of the manual worker. Instead of reverence for the elderly there is often the dunce's cap and public humiliation of those who diverge from the true path. Instead of the Classics and the *Analects*, there are the works of Marx, Lenin and Mao. Instead of the mandate of Heaven there is the mandate of the People. Instead of the Emperor there is the Chairman. Instead of the old mandarinate, there is the Chinese Communist Party. Instead of older book learning there are work-oriented courses in schools and colleges. In brief, Mao reversed K'ung. K'ung thus becomes a symbol of anti-Mao. But perhaps the Sage would have shaken his head if he had come back to earth. Has he not been misinterpreted? Tyrannical fathers have nothing to do with the courteous spirit of the reciprocity and ritual which he tried to inculcate. But all teachings can be misapplied. That is why Confucius repudiated dogmatic formulations, and made but rare references to religious beliefs.

Confucius and religion

Confucius' attitude to religion has been a subject of debate. There was a certain ambiguity in what he said. On the one hand, he was not enthusiastic about preoccupation with the supernatural, and preferred to concentrate on the problems of the living rather than the dead. On the other hand, he certainly made use of the concept of Heaven – a concept virtually amounting to what others term God. And he did not repudiate the cult of ancestors and other sacrificial ceremonials. Perhaps the clue to these ambiguities lies in his perception of the role of religion as being a social and ethical one. The court rituals and those of the villages could reinforce men's sense of harmony and fitting conduct. On the other hand, speculative and dogmatic religion might distract attention away from men's practical needs. Such religion was anti-educational, as K'ung understood the matter. His relative conservatism meant that his teaching could in later centuries become the theoretical underpinning of an official state cult, in which Confucius himself was reverenced, so as to provide the ritual and ideology of the Empire.

Confucius and the rectification of names

Another tantalising aspect of the sage's thought was what he had to say about language. Again his orientation was largely social. When he was asked the first thing he would do if he took control of the administration of the state, he answered, 'The one thing that is needed is the rectification of names'. He thought that conceptual confusion could lead to social confusion and disorder. That attitude has much to commend it today. Perhaps Confucius would have enjoyed reading *Catch 22*. At any rate he would have noted with wry astonishment that in modern politics Defence expenditure usually means Offence expenditure; Ministries of Justice are more often than not organisations for administering injustice; equal societies tend to be those where power is concentrated unequally; the emancipation of women means putting them into factories; fashion means obsolescence; social security means bureaucratic dependence; and so forth. We suffer from a great deal of linguistic confusion whereby we are deceived, partly by ourselves. So the rectification of names would be very helpful in social reform. Of course, Confucius' concern with language was partly to do with his literary interests, for by editing the ancient Classics he established them as the normative source of ideas for the Confucian tradition, and to a great extent for the Chinese tradition as a whole.

Confucius challenged

Though Confucius through his disciples came to have much influence on the norms of China, the movement he started was not without rivals. Most important was that movement associated with the name of Lao-tzu, who was said to be a contemporary of the sage K'ung. He was also allegedly the author of the beautiful book the *Tao Teh-ching*, the *Classic of the Way and its Power*, as the title might be translated. That book has been an onflowing source of inspiration to Chinese and other reflective folk. It is poles apart from the Confucian canon: the latter is formal; the Taoist work is poetical. The one is about gentlemen; the other is about mystics. The one is about the rectification of names; the other is about the abolition of names. The one is about morality; the other concerns spontaneity. One is about the fullness of social life; the other about its emptiness. The one deals in ritual; the other transcends, even despises, it. The one is about what men create; the other is about easy harmony with Nature. The one stresses a Way; the other is immersed in a Way. One is establishmentarian in principle, while the other has always looked towards anarchism. The one was generated by a real man; the other by Lao-tzu, whom most modern scholars do not believe to have existed as an individual. Which you could think to be very fitting, for does not the book of the Tao preach acting through not acting? How better to found a faith than by not actually living?

But let us first give a taste of its strange poetry. Its famous first lines have been translated a hundred different ways, for the brevity of monosyllabic classical Chinese leaves open many different paths of interpretation, while the poetical character of the text makes it typically elusive, and difficult to catch in another tongue. But let us try:

> The Way that can be taken is not the eternal Way,
> And the name which can be named is not the eternal name.
> From the nameless come heaven and earth;
> The named is the mother of the myriad things.
> Eternally without desire the one can see the mystery;
> Eternally with desire, that sees the manifested world.
> The two come from the same source, but their names differ:
> Darkness within darkness, the gateway to all mystery.

Further on, we read:

The myriad things of the world wax
And return then to the source
As one watches them.
Quietness: that is the name of the return to the source.
Fulfilling that is eternal nature.
Knowing the eternal is enlightenment;
But not knowing the eternal brings disaster.

What do such mysterious lines mean? It has been a matter of some debate through the ages, but most have favoured what may be called a mystical interpretation. That is, the *Tao Teh-ching* is concerned with inner vision and quietism. It is in many respects similar in its emphases to Buddhism – it lived fruitfully with Buddhist meditation, and gave rise to Ch'ān Buddhism and then Zen. On the other hand, it has some political applications. Historically the Taoists have leaned towards anarchism, and it is therefore not unreasonable to try to see a harder, less mystical line in the book. But in my present account I shall stress the mystical, contemplative side of this poetical anthology – for it is an anthology: one can no longer seriously ascribe the work to a single individual Lao-tzu, supposedly a contemporary of Confucius based in Loyang in Honan province. Rather the work seems to have been the product of a movement of sages, or if you like lots of Lao-tzus.

The first thing to notice in the *Tao Teh-ching* is the repeated emphasis on the eternal, the unchanging. This is the nature of the true Way. The term translated Way here is, of course, Tao. From one point of view the Way is the path trodden by men; but from another point of view it is the rhythm of the whole universe. So man achieves the greatest goal, true immortality, by living in harmony with the Way of the world. This true Way is unchanging, eternal, for it exists within and beyond the world of constant change. It is nameless, for it is the true breath of the universe, not to be caught and entangled by human concepts, by names.

So we ought not to identify ourselves with everyday bustles and concerns, the world that is of names and categories and conventionality. By emptying ourselves we gain the greatest fullness. By quiet we conquer our universe. So the Taoist uses various metaphors: the space inside the pot is its most important part. So:

The softest thing in the world
Conquers the hardest thing in the world.
That which has no substance can enter where there is no room.
Teaching wordlessly, acting actlessly –
This is known by few under heaven.

Later Taoists were to perfect techniques of stillness, including the use of breathing exercises, reminiscent of Indian yoga.

A personal view of the Tao

However, if I were to put the message of the Lao-tzu book into my own words it would be as follows:

> The universe is governed by a spirit: it is that spiritual Way which we must follow, for to be one with the Way, to act as the Way indicates, is to be in possession of the whole universe. Since the spirit moves in the wind and sea, and animates the scene before me, then being one with that Way is to be in harmony with all of life. What is the scene I see? I am a fortunate person, for my house looks upon the estuary of the river Lune, in north-west Lancashire, between the black cities which made the modern industrial world and the borders of Scotland. My garden is replete with elms, beeches, flowering cherries and Australian gums. Beyond it there are drumlins and the hazy river. On a clear day you can see Blackpool Tower, Lancashire's answer to the Eiffel. So looking out I understand the divine togetherness of Lao-tzu's thought. Being one with nature is being one with the Way, the Tao. I see the Tao out of my window. I would be foolish to fail to work with those divine beauties. I would be mad not to see my own unforced need to swim in the sea of nature which I perceive before me. To do that I must cut out preformed ways of looking at my world. Consequently the Tao frowns on decision, categories, ways of carving up the universe. What it frowns on is the ordinary motivations of men. The Tao is peace, harmony, naturalness, anarchy – and it is against militancy, division, uniqueness of religious commitment, and dedication. It is almost the antithesis of how Christianity has been interpreted. It is the opposite of the Protestant ethic.

That, then, is the Tao, thinking of it in its purest form. As we shall observe, Taoism developed beyond the book of Lao-tzu. It became a fully-fledged religion, a set of myths, a hierarchy, a system of anarchy, a search for literal immortality. Perhaps it was typical in this, for after all many a good idea has developed into small men's dogmas. Yet in its pristine form it seems to be a wonderful antidote to Confucianism, and was one pole of the tension in Chinese society. If Buddhism conquered China, partially at least, then maybe it was a kind of compromise between the two opposing moods of Chinese culture. Certainly there was a strong contrast between Confucius' conservative morals and ritualism – all in the service of a stable society – and the basic anarchism and unconventional approach of the Taoists. Maybe Buddhism as foreign could appeal to the latter, while its discipline could win over some of the former. However, in days to come, after the non-existent Lao-tzu, Taoism was to change.

> The person who is filled with the power of virtue
> Like a newborn child can't be stung by wasps or serpents.
> Wild animals will not spring on him
> And he will not be bombed by birds of prey.
> His bones yield and his muscles are weak,
> But his grasp is firm.

Such a person conquers all, it is thought. But it is surely a very different ideal from that of the ritual follower of Master K'ung. Between the artificialities of the ancient tradition and the anarchist quietism of the Tao there falls a great gulf. Though Taoism, as has been said, developed beyond its earlier message (and what religion has not?), it serves as a counterpoise to Confucius and a strong ingredient of Chinese spirituality and culture. From the anthology of the *Tao Teh-ching* through to the collection known as the *Chuang-tzu*, it served as a dynamic and troublesome element in ancient Chinese thinking.

Recently I had occasion to read through a beautiful edition of the Lao-tzu book. It had upon it some words of commendation from the late Alan Watts, an amazed English-Californian guru, flying through the atmospheres of Anglicanism to the strange turbulences of Zen. He was of the feeling that the world needs more of the spirit of Lao-tzu. Yet as a total philosophy Taoism does seem at first to be too radical in its overthrow of the dynamisms and courtesies of life. That is why the dialectical relationship with Confucianism is necessary. Both sides are right, and perchance both are wrong. How do we combine those insights?

The development of Taoism

Taoism did not stay put, but developed a ritual and mythic dimension. The leader who set in train this more organised form of Taoism belonged to the second century AD. He was Chang Tao Ling, and his descendants were to hold, right through to modern times, the title of Heavenly Teacher.

In their teaching the gods and immortals multiplied, but a densely populated pantheon of deities and immortals was given a semblance of order by a hierarchical arrangement under the rule of a supreme Triad or Trinity. It is ironic that Taoism, emphasising spontaneity, should conceive its gods in a bureaucratic hierarchy, reflecting a kind of heavenly efficiency. Theoretically, however, they are so many emanations of one underlying Tao. The Triad consists of Yuan Shih T'ien Ts'un (Heavenly Elder of Primordial Origin), who is the first to interpret the transcendental books which were passed down to the lesser gods and so to man. The next of the Triad is Ling Pao Chün, lord of the Sacred Jewels – the latter being the name of the scriptures. It is he who passes the highest wisdom down to the lesser gods. The third member is T'ai Shang Lao Chün, the Noblest Lord Lao, Lao-tzu himself, who reveals the secret wisdom to mortal men to guide them to the way of immortality. Often associated with the Triad is the Queen Mother of the West, Hsi Wang Mu, who rules over a paradise in the K'un Lun mountains, peopled by tens of thousands of the immortals. In later Taoism, another personage in the hierarchy became prominent, possibly because of imperial patronage. He was a divine reflection of earthly splendour – the Jade Emperor, Yü Huang. But of all these the most vital is Lao-tzu. For he appears in Taoist cosmology as a kind of bridge between microcosm and macrocosm, as a primordial man from whom in some sense the world is formed. Thus in the beginning there is interplay between the forces of Yin and Yang, the female and the male. But out of this interplay emerges Lao-tzu himself, a cosmic man, from whose body is formed the world: his eyes become the sun and the moon; his head is the K'un Lun mountains, mountains of paradise; his hair becomes the stars; his body hair becomes the plant world; his genitals become man; his bones become dragons. Similarly the individual by looking within himself and training the body could gain knowledge of the secrets of the world. In particular he could gain long life, or immortality.

The quest for immortality

Much of later Taoism is concerned with the quest for long life. There was much experimentation with alchemy – gold and cinnabar were used, the cinnabar being transformed into mercury and back again. Drugs of various kinds were tried. But perhaps more important than such material alchemy was the inner alchemy of enhancing vitality through the balance of forces in the body, and retaining within the body the most powerful energies such as those contained in sperm. Techniques not dissimilar to those used in Indian Tantra were employed to practise sex without loss of vital power. Another method was so-called embryonic respiration, whereby the adept limited external breathing to an absolute minimum, causing air to circulate in a closed system within the bodily channels. It was thought that through this he could create within himself an immortal replica of himself. Much emphasised too was the perception of the various forces, spirits and so forth, dwelling within the body which mirrored the forces of external nature. All this seems far away from philosophical Taoism – but is perhaps to be seen as a semi-magical development from contemplative techniques that go back to the original emphasis on being peaceful, spontaneous and quiet.

The richness of the Taoist pantheon and the complexity of Taoist rituals gave the religion a strong, popular impact right through until modern times. However, the advent of Maoism on the mainland of China, and the decline in interest in religious Taoism which is evident in Taiwan, Hong Kong and elsewhere among the Chinese of the dispersal, appear to mean that the religion's future lies in its earlier more spiritual message, rather than its later more ritual aspect. But some of the Taoist meditation techniques also arouse contemporary interest, in line with the general vogue for the yogic aspect of Eastern religions.

Buddhism comes to China

The period of the development of popular Taoism from the first century AD onwards also saw the infiltration of Buddhism into China. It challenged both Confucius and the Tao: but it blended more easily with the latter, and the fruitful interplay between the two streams of spirituality is particularly evident in the rise of Ch'ān Buddhism. Buddhism's relative tolerance of popular cults made possible a living-together with Buddhism and Taoism at the ritual and mythic level. Buddhism and its Chinese counterparts came to represent two sides of a complex religion appealing to the immediate concerns of ordinary men and women. Buddhism and early Taoism were made for one another. Both were quietistic. Both stressed contemplation and illumination. Both held up the idea of the sage, the wise person. If the Tao pointed more towards harmony with nature, the Dharma had the more complex analysis of reality. If the one had the greater appeal to Chinese mentality, the other had long experience with varieties of meditation. It was not therefore surprising that ultimately the two streams should mingle in the story of the famous Indian monk, Bodhidharma, who was supposed to have reached Canton from India in the early part of the sixth century AD. Did he? Did he even exist? The history of Ch'ān goes back to Bodhidharma, but beyond that we cannot penetrate. But perhaps, as in the case of Lao-tzu, the question of his existence is unimportant. It is not the origins of Zen which count, but rather the shape of its special type of spirituality. At any rate, the story of Bodhidharma is instructive, whether true or not.

Ch'ān Buddhism

A famous picture shows him staring at a wall, with a rather fierce expression in his bulging eyes. He supposedly spent years contemplating the stone before him. When he was asked by the Emperor Liang how much merit accrued from good works, for the Emperor was a pious patron of the Buddhist religion and was both anxious and proud regarding his generosity, Bodhidharma disconcertingly answered that no merit at all accrued. But what about karma and the teachings about rebirth? What is the first principle of the Teaching? It is all Empty – nothing holy, replied Bodhidharma. One can see in these surprises a new and original synthesis at work. For in using the term 'empty' Bodhidharma was doubtless harking back to Nāgārjuna's philosophy and his destruction of all theories of reality by the great: all concepts distort reality. That is looking at the matter from one direction. From another direction, the nature in which we are immersed, the Tao in which we live and move and have our being, is just what it is. We cloud it, make it sickly, break it up by not seeing it straight and seeing it in its own being (or non-being). No doubt Bodhidharma came to terms with the real naked nature of his wall, which thereby became no wall, for the very wall-concept was doubtless washed away through his fierce concentration.

Thus it is too that Chinese Ch'ān transcended the scriptures. It is true that this attitude could be misunderstood. The image of the monk tearing up the scriptures could be too shocking. But it was just the image of one who uses the scripture, the Buddha's religion, as a raft to get to the other shore, not as a possession in itself to be clung to. Later the Chinese synthesis between the Tao and the Dharma was given new shape and impetus in medieval Japan. It is perhaps through Ch'ān that Taoism has its biggest impact upon the modern world.

Buddhist schools in China

But the many schools of Buddhism that came flooding into China could be most confusing. Buddhism seemed so complex, so multifarious. There always seemed to be more to discover, more sutras (scriptures) to peruse, more subtle doctrines to disentangle, more rituals to master. It was thus natural that the attempt should be made to provide some kind of ordering of the schools, to provide, that is, a framework into which various facets of Buddhism could be systematically fitted. This was the achievement of China's other great Buddhist product, the T'ien T'ai school, founded by Chih-i (538–597).

The school takes its name from the Heavenly Terrace Mountain, in Chekiang province, where Chih-i taught. His teachings were based upon the *Lotus Sūtra* (the famous Lotus of the Good Law, beloved of Pure Land Buddhism), which Chih-i saw as the culmination of Buddhist revelation. But whereas there were those, such as the Ch'ān Buddhists, who stressed meditation but not learning, and the Pure Land Buddhists, for whom devotion was all, the T'ien T'ai attempted to maintain a balance between meditation and learning, and between ritual practices and esoteric understanding. At one level, Chih-i relied upon Nāgārjuna's doctrine of the Void; but he also made use of the conception of the Absolute Mind, and the interpenetration of all things. The whole world can be seen in a grain of sand. All the Buddhas are present in every element, every moment. This notion of the penetration of the macrocosm into the microcosm was justification for the ritual practices which could reverberate through the world, and which were satisfying and important at one level of understanding for the ordinary man. Religion was a hierarchy, and the Buddhist faith could exist at different levels of refinement and insight. This is because at differing points in the career of the Enlightened One he produces different methods of teaching, in accord with the needs and capacities of his hearers. These correspond to differing sutras and scriptures, and so to the differing schools. These have their apogee in the teachings contained in the *Lotus Sūtra*. Meditation upon this text is given special value.

The Confucian revival

It will be seen that great subtleties were being evolved in Chinese Buddhism. The combination of Indian complexities and Chinese aesthetic and spiritual values gave Chinese Buddhism an impressive and entrancing quality. It was hard for older Confucianism to maintain its influence. True, it provided the core of education for officials; but it was relatively weak in philosophical subtlety and scarcely a fully-fledged religion: it seemed therefore neither appealing to the intellect, nor seductive to the heart. However, during the T'ang dynasty, in the latter part of the first millennium AD, it underwent transformations that gave it a more overtly religious character, and in the eleventh and twelfth centuries, during the mid part of the Sung dynasty, it developed a new and dynamic philosophical superstructure, commonly referred to as Neo-Confucianism. As for the religious aspects of these developments, the emperor T'ai Tsung in 630 decreed that all prefectures and county capitals should establish Confucian temples, in which K'ung was reverenced. These shrines became places where others as well as K'ung could be honoured, through the erection of tablets enshrining their memory. All this gave concreteness to the Confucian tradition.

The Neo-Confucian revival owed much initially to the work of Chou Lien-ch'i (1017–73), who derived everything in the world from a first principle, the so-called *T'ai-chi* or Great Ultimate. This has two poises, one of movement, the other of rest. Through movement it generates the yang, and through rest it generates the yin. Out of these are formed the five elements – water, fire, wood, metal and earth. These material forces are what every phenomenon is made up of, but each thing in accordance with an essential pattern. Pattern and matter, *li* and *ch'i*, are the two aspects of every reality. These ideas, as developed by later Neo-Confucianists, had a moral and spiritual significance, for it is by purifying the pattern in man that one achieves harmony with the rest of the universe, and with the Great Ultimate itself. Since the aspect of pattern in the universe is so important, the wise man studies patterns or principles by whatever means are available, for instance through literary studies. Thus traditional Confucian wisdom is helpful in cultivating the intellect in harmony with the All. Chou also identified his Great Ultimate with the Void of the Buddhists. But the Neo-Confucians tended to argue that this derivation of things from the Void does not mean that they are unreal or illusory. They thus maintained a realistic, world-affirming stance, and deprecated the dream of self-annihilation in Buddhism and the opposite desire for immortality among the Taoists. The wise man is content to let death come in an orderly way, and he does not grasp for too much or too little, but adheres to that mean which was always so much prized in the Confucian ethos. In Lu Hsiang-shan (1139–93) we have an emphasis which assimilated the new Confucianism more to the Buddhist atmosphere. He too identified the human mind with *li*, pattern. There is but one universal mind: therefore, by cultivating the inborn capacities of the mind through eliminating selfishness and the more turbulent passions, the sage gains an insight into reality and harmony with the Great Ultimate. But despite the more contemplative flavour of Lu's philosophy, it maintained the Confucian emphasis upon life in this world. The ideal of nirvana was repudiated with vigour. By fleeing from the world Buddhism could not hope to gain that true impartiality and equanimity which is the high achievement of the Confucian saint.

The changes in the T'ang and Sung dynasties gave Confucianism long-term impetus which, with its entrenched position in the bureaucratic mind, enabled it to survive successfully into the Manchu times, and so into the modern era. But the shocks emanating from the sea-ports in the nineteenth century were too violent for Confucianism, or indeed any of the other older traditions, to cope with. Now of course we are coming on to the era of China's fourth great -ism, that of Chairman Mao, a new religion and a new glue for a disintegrated Middle Kingdom. To understand the success of Mao it is instructive to contemplate the ultimate failure of a dramatic attempt at renewal by the unconscious predecessors of the Reds, the Taipings, under the prophetic leadership of Hung Hsiu-ch'üan (1813–64).

The Taiping experiment

Hung was from a poor Hakka family living not far from Canton, and had enough scholastic ability to enter for the civil service examinations, which he repeatedly failed. On the last occasion he seemed to collapse, and during this crisis he had a vision which he interpreted in partly Christian terms – he had encountered some missionary evangelism and read a few tracts. This was the beginning of a series in which Hung received what he considered to be a call to stamp out devil worship, meaning in effect traditional Chinese religions. As with other prophets in world history, Hung did not set about a public mission immediately. Some seven years later he studied for a couple of months with a fundamentalistic American Baptist missionary. He and supporters began a series of idol-smashing missions, and by the early 1840s Hung was leader of a growing band of God-worshippers, as they were styled. Meanwhile China was in deep trouble, confusion and distress as a result of the disastrous and greedy Opium War launched by the British to force open China to the sale of opium grown in British territories elsewhere in Asia.

Though Hung was harried for his turbulence, he managed to form his followers into a disciplined army, and he then went over to the offensive, proclaiming that he was going to found the Taiping Tien-kuo, that is, the Great Peace Heavenly Kingdom. From the title of the new era came the title by which he and his followers were usually designated. The movement's military successes were rapid and startling. A huge area of central China fell to the rebels. They captured the southern imperial capital, Nanking, in 1853, and renamed it The Heavenly Capital.

The success was substantially due to faith. The Taiping soldiery were required to believe the new creed, and those who deserted from the enemy and wished to join the army, but did not believe, were not generally admitted. Meanwhile, a radical programme of reform was put into effect – the use of vernacular rather than stilted classical Chinese, equality for women, redistribution of land, the banning of alcohol, tobacco and hated opium, the smashing of images and the uprooting of traditional religion, the condemnation of polygamy, foot-binding and other similar practices, the establishment of a Western-style calendar, a ban on slavery, and so forth. There is a wonderful similarity between this puritan reforming spirit and that of the communists in the next century. Indeed, one of the problems of modern Chinese Marxist historians is how to evaluate the Taiping revolution: was it a foretaste of Mao? Certainly, it managed to harness, as Mao did, the forces of peasant rebellion in a genuinely revolutionary enterprise guided by a coherent ideology. But though coherent, the Taiping version of Christianity, with Hung as younger brother of the Saviour, had some tough and uncouth features, especially as viewed from the standpoint of the intelligentsia. Oddly, though initially missionaries thought of it as a way by which China might be Christianised, the idiosyncratic features of the faith alienated the regular missions. Western governments were favourable to the suppression of the movement, which happened after a very long struggle – Nanking was recaptured in 1864, Hung taking his own life in the disastrous last days of the bitter struggle. Not a single Taiping soldier surrendered, according to the victorious imperial general. The faith had taken deep root, and the flower was martial valour of an incredible strength.

But the uncouthness of the ideology meant that the Taipings could not grow an intelligentsia nor therefore an efficient bureaucracy. It was by contrast an achievement of the Maoists that they could present a theory adapted to Chinese conditions which was modern, made sense to intellectuals, and was practical. If the Taipings foreshadowed some of their achievements, this was symptomatic of China's need for drastic reorientation within, if it was to combat the forces outside which were disrupting the once proud Central Kingdom. But her own internal spiritual and philosophical resources were inadequate to the task, hence the need to borrow a Western ideology. The Confucian tradition was too entangled in the imperial bureaucracy and the mandarinate. The mandarins could not cope with the West and modern science. The former they dangerously despised; the latter they did not understand, as their education was more or less exclusively literary. Taoism was too much bound up with popular cults and weird alchemical and magical practices, so that its spirit was alien to the modern technology which China would need to combat the enemy. Its philosophical dimension was too anarchistic to form the basis of a new political discipline for the Chinese people. Buddhism, though subtle and still in many ways vigorous, was too pacific and other-worldly to arm the Chinese soul. Nor was it possible to import Western democracy and John Stuart Mill like so many bales of wool or pounds of opium. Except for Hung's experiment Christian values made slow headway. Sun Yat-sen (1866–1925), it is true, made a valiant attempt at a synthesis between Chinese and Western values, through the three principles of nationalism, democracy and people's livelihood. His boyhood hero had been Hung, and he was strongly anti-Manchu: that China was ruled by a dynasty still perceived by most Chinese as alien, while she was a pillaged hypo-colony (to use Sun's term) of the foreign West, was intolerable. The revolution of 1911 and the subsequent turbulent events led to Kuomintang power under Chiang Kai-shek. But the Kuomintang could not be resolute or clean enough to carry through adequate reform. It leaned on rural landowners and the new business community, who in turn leaned upon Western commercial interests, for there was little truly Chinese industrial and commercial enterprise. And so it was under the pressures from below that the social democratic experiment dreamed of by Sun collapsed, and Maoism became the new Way for China. It could replace the traditional systems because of its various advantageous properties.

The Chinese strengths of Maoism

First, in being Marxist it was against the very establishments and powers which were ravaging China from the West. Second, it had a strong theory of history, appealing to the Chinese sense of rhythms from the past. Third, it claimed to be scientific and it therefore promised the modernisation which was one condition of national independence and dignity. Fourth, in its Maoist form (and Mao quarrelled with Stalin over this) it was heavily oriented towards the peasantry. As such it could use those age-old forces which had stimulated peasant rebellion and turn them into something more, namely the engines of revolution. Fifth, it demanded the disciplines which were needed, and had partly been exemplified in the Taiping movement. In particular it could supply a strong egalitarian ethic and sense of solidarity to replace the hierarchical value-system of Confucianism. Sixth, it could harness some of the old ideas of China, the yin and the yang, the relative materialism of early Neo-Confucianism, the perception of history, into a picture of onward struggle and progress which promised a new kingdom. Seventh, it took over where the Taipings left off, half-way between romantic banditry and religious commitment, half-way between the cannonade and the last things. Eighth, it had a charismatic leader in Mao himself. He could write poems which were not imprisoned in the norms of socialist realism, and construct a new Chinese theory of revolution. Of course he had more than charisma: he and his associates such as Chu Teh had great military insight and boldness, and in Chou and others the Reds had a new and effective mandarinate to consolidate and control the human gains that their ideology, conduct and generalship won. By the end of the 1940s China was Mao's, and a new Great Heavenly Peace

Kingdom was established. From Hung in Nanking to Mao in Peking, ninety-six fateful years had elapsed. Mao's was a splendid achievement, and cannot be ignored for we are here speaking of the destiny of a quarter of mankind. It cannot be ignored in particular in the long search. Maoism is, after all, a kind of religion, even if it be formally anti-religious.

The religious aspect of Maoism

Maoism has a set of doctrines, Marx in effect with a yellowing skin and a Chinese heart. It has a myth of history and a myth of Mao: it has the dialectic, the sense of China's degradation and resurrection in the modern period, the story of the incredible Long March, which those who lived through it can scarcely mention without emotion, as the Red Army and its dependants struggled through the ice and the grasslands and the hells of deprivation, marching, fighting, and more marching. Maoism has a strong ethic, one of solidarity with fellow men in the struggle for human betterment, ideas of the perfection of man, commitment to work and toil on behalf of others. It has its rituals, the raised fist and the rally, the dunce's cap, the flashcards in the stadium, the formulas of self-criticism, the flags and drums, the days of obligation, the filings past the memorial to the martyrs, the party meetings. It has its experiential dimension: its conversions, its sense of dedication, the appreciation of a new dignity, the recounting in awe of the miracles performed in the name of the Chairman, the satisfactions of socialist achievement. It has its new Sangha or Order, the members of the Party and the cadres and the turbulent red guards. It has the marks of faith and church. It lacks God and the transcendent, it is true, but its psychology is religious. And that essentially is why it won. Mao is foremost in holding that it is mental, or as I might say spiritual, forces that are strong, frequently decisive. He fought war on that principle, and he tried to fight the peace thus, with incessant stimulation to new efforts at the right attitude, and incessant assaults upon backsliding party workers, capitalist-roaders and the like. If the mad Hung took something from the West and could explode China's centre, how much more has Mao, more rationally, used the forces of the West to overcome the East and therefore, too, the West in the East. It is an old principle of what the Japanese call Judo, but a principle originating in Chinese Taoism.

The upshot, then, of the collapse of the ill-favoured Manchus was the triumph of the fourth religion of China. Beyond K'ung and Lao-tzu and the Buddha there stands Mao. Beyond the yin and the yang, there moves the dialectic. Beyond the Tao is discerned the mysterious power of Matter. Marx and Lenin are brought into the pantheon of the new China. Mao meanwhile had in modest dress assumed the robes of Empire. But now it is not the Mandate of Heaven, but the Mandate of the People that justifies the rule. Mao then is or was the yang to the people's yin, in a new rearrangement of the mental properties of the Chinese, now though regimented proudly independent. China can never go back to the Manchus, and nationalism more than makes up for the rigidities of life in the new China.

China, then, has given extraordinary moments to the development of man's spirit. I could not here speak of poetry and painting, and the nostalgic beauties of the scholar's contemplations. In the matter of religion, China has, with great originality, thrown up the concept of the Tao and enshrined it in much art and much political action. It has been the womb of Confucius, greatest proponent, I suppose, of the ethical value of ritual. It has transformed aspects of Buddhism and in Ch'ān invented a new form of meditation and a new ethos of contemplation geared ultimately to the requirements of the ordinary man. It has in transmitting much to Japan been father of the islanders' genius. It has produced a new and striking variant on Marxism. In its fourfold religiosity it has been extraordinarily creative.

9 JAPAN

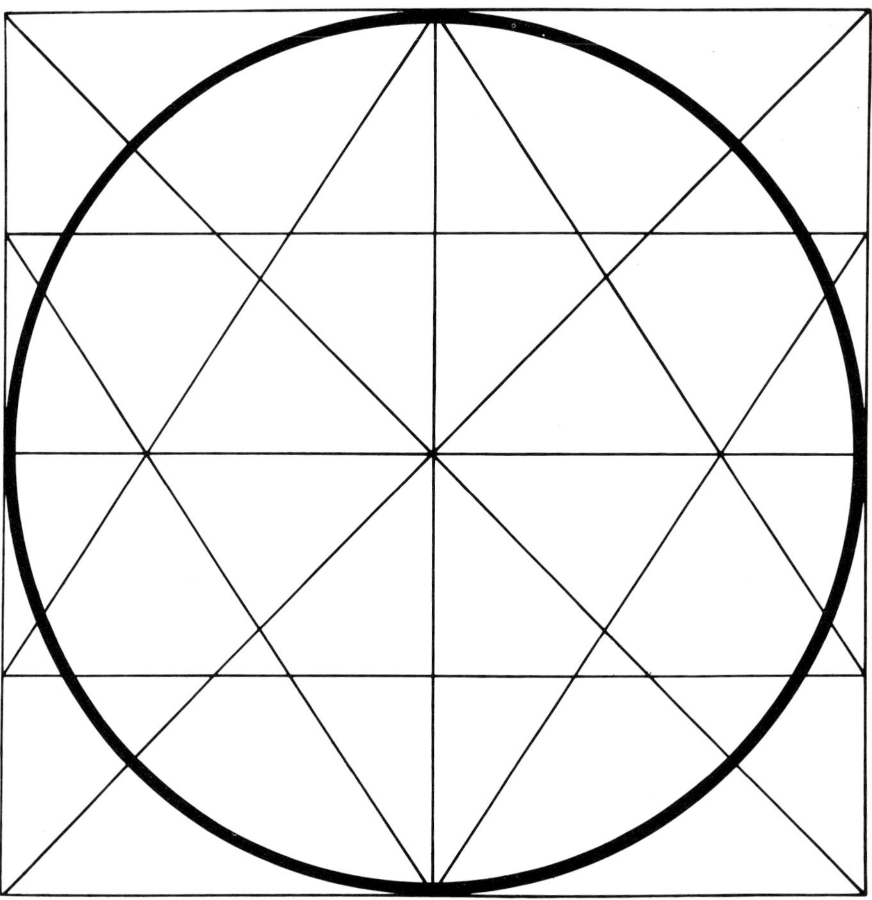

Japan's adaptability to outside influence goes a long way back. Thus in the time of Prince Shotoku (572–621), Chinese culture was patronised and, in particular, Buddhist values were imported. Japan became permeated with China, but adapted it. Likewise Buddhism came to take on characteristically Japanese forms, notably Zen and new dimensions of Pure Land Buddhism. Zen, based on Chinese meditation Buddhism, developed into an ethic and a practice which could combine with secular pursuits. It underpinned the attitudes of the medieval warrior and Bushido. It profoundly affected Japanese art and garden styles.

In the twelfth century the saint Honen introduced a fervent kind of pietism into Japan focusing on rebirth in heaven or the Pure land and on the grace of the Buddha Amida, calling on whose name would give the faithful assurance of salvation. In some ways the

Japanese Pure Land movement developed like evangelical Christianity, stressing faith. In the following century, however, Nichiren led a more nationalistic interpretation of reliance on Buddhist piety, and proved the ancestor of one of the most dynamic modern forms of religion in Japan, the Soka Gakkai. All the while, Buddhism interacted with ancestral religion, the way of the gods or Shinto, which remains a gentle force in contemporary Japan (after its period of militaristic exploitation before and during World War II).

Modern Japan has seen a rise of new religions, some stemming partly from Buddhism. Modern Japan shows spiritual as well as economic resilience. But how Buddhist really is the toughness of Zen and the pietism of the Pure Land? Buddhism has come a long way to Japan and in Japan, yet Japan is bound in the present world to be one of the, if not the, main witnesses to the Buddha on our planet.

Japan and her modern experience

Japan, a string of substantial islands, is an Eastern mirror of Britain, and the history of the two nations forms a counterpoint. In both cases physical isolation explains much, so let us visualise the dramatic effect of the events of 1853, when Admiral Perry, under orders from the then President of the United States, sailed a small fleet into Tokyo Bay.

Hitherto the Japanese had been fairly successful at keeping out the rampaging Western mercantile powers. The Dutch were permitted to trade, but only under strict conditions. Western missions had been excluded and Japanese Christianity driven underground. St Francis Xavier had come to Japan as early as 1549, and there were three hundred thousand Christians a century later, but the Tokugawa rulers in the seventeenth century massacred many of the faithful and closed the ports to Europeans. The Japanese guessed that the West, and the Christian religion as a manifestation of that culture, might undermine and eventually destroy Japanese values and independence. So Japan turned in on itself, in tough but heroic isolation. But Perry's four gunboats were not to be ignored, nor the fleet of ten which the same commander sailed into the Bay in the following year, 1854. The Americans were partly concerned with the ill-treatment of whalers wrecked on Japanese shores and the lack of provisioning; partly with their own imperial dream. Though mindful of its origins, the United States was guilty and so sometimes furtive as a colonial power; it was ambitious for the privileges that European nations were winning. So from Perry's time onward, in the war with Spain when the Philippines were yielded to her grasp, in the period of trade concessions and missions on the mainland of China, right through indeed to Vietnam, America looked out from California to the prizes of the ancient East. Japan's response to Perry was dramatic. If the West could not be kept out it must be used. It was a good principle of Judo, and set in train that fashioning of modern Japan which has brought war, tragedy and prosperity.

Japan absorbed Western values successfully and synthesised them with her own. In 1868, the old rulers, the shoguns, who maintained the formalities of the throne only, were displaced by the emperor. This Meiji restoration accelerated the process of Westernisation, and brought in a constitution, in 1889, which, though it was modelled on Western prototypes, was essentially authoritarian: thus the armed forces were responsible to the Emperor. His prestige was reinforced by State Shinto. Meanwhile Japan was building ironclads and equipping her army with good *matériel* and a fine officer corps. In 1905 the West was staggered to hear of the destruction of the Russian imperial fleet by the Japanese in the battle of Tsushima. Through seapower and trading muscle Japan was now a power on a par with any who sailed in those waters. She looked longingly beyond Korea and Taiwan to China, now ready to be carved up by the great nations.

It was not unnatural therefore that Japan should win her place at Versailles by fighting on the Allied side in World War I. The concessions made to her at the expense of a still enfeebled China, at the Treaty of Versailles, were a main cause of the revolutionary outbursts later welded together under the leadership of Mao Tse-tung. On the other hand, Japan's later maraudings in Manchukuo and in northern China attracted the ire of newly pious Western powers who, rapacious in the nineteenth century, were growling lambs in the twentieth. Japan preferred this time to side with Germany. She struck at Pearl Harbour and in a series of brilliant and unexpected campaigns conquered virtually all of East Asia and the Pacific islands. But she had also chosen the wrong century for expansion. She had underestimated the logistical skill of the USA. Nor did those Japanese military leaders who loved the lightning blow foresee the radioactive lightning which would pour from an innocent-looking sky. In 1945 Japan lay in utter ruin. She was smashed, again impoverished, conquered, occupied, and humiliated. From Perry to Macarthur had been an exhilarating but finally tragic century. Or was it tragic? From the ashes came a new light and a new hope.

The spiritual background of Japanese history

In all these events, vital elements in Japan's spiritual life were at work. Though predominantly a Buddhist country, Japan by a paradox has been most mindful of the military arts, and a skilful blend of Zen and the sword provided the old ethos of the Samurai, while in Nichiren Buddhism Japanese nationalism was celebrated. Shinto could provide a divine pedigree for the apex of the system, the Emperor, while forms of pietistic Buddhism had something of the air of that Protestantism which had provided a main spiritual engine for Western capitalism. But perhaps the fundamental fact is that, in much earlier bringing in and digesting Chinese values, Japan had already in its mind prepared for the swifter and more dramatic importation of Western-style technology, economics and politics. But though it used to be, before the Second World War, a sneer among the British that the Japanese were just gifted imitators, this has never truly been the case. The Japanese leave their own indelible stamp upon that which they assimilate and beyond Ch'ān there is unmistakably Japanese Zen. The beetling and sprouting black superstructures of the great battleships of Nippon were formidably different from the decorated steel tripods of the dreadnoughts of the Western world. Beyond the Pure Land of China, there is the amazing Amida Buddhism of Honen and Shinran. The religion of Nichiren is a strange twist in the fortunes of the Mahāyāna, and its modern derivative Soka Gakkai is one of those new movements in religion so characteristic of contemporary Japan. Heavily Chinese in inspiration at first glance, Japanese art has its own pungency, humour and magic. And if in this chapter there is much to say about Buddhism, it is, after all, Japanese Buddhism and Japan's own special contribution to man's long search that engages us. We must also pay heed to Shinto, the Way of the Gods, Japan's indigenous religion which came to absorb the values of Buddhism and of Confucius as they were drafted into Japan.

Some main factors in Japanese religions

The main motifs in Japanese religion can be delineated as five acts in a Japanese spiritual drama. First, there are the developments of the Pure Land. Second, there are the Japanese varieties of Tantric Buddhism, which I shall exemplify here by the Shingon sect. Third, there is Zen Buddhism. Fourth, there are the modern religions, which I shall approach through the example of the Soka Gakkai. Fifth, there is modern and ancient Shinto. But the drama may not be over and we will try to discern something of the future of Japanese religion.

There remain in Japan the Ainu, until recently technologically a primitive people sustained by food-gathering and hunting. They are the survivors of the early inhabitants of the islands who were displaced, towards the end of the first millennium BC, by the Japanese, a people of Mongoloid stock from the Asian mainland. Japanese is not monosyllabic, like Chinese, but is (or so it has been lately argued with some force) related to such tongues as Finnish and Hungarian, so it looks as if the Japanese may have emanated from the North Asian land mass, i.e. from Western Siberia. However, the Japanese took over the Chinese written language, and many Chinese words. Thus the very term Shinto is a Japanese version of two Chinese words meaning Way (Tao) of the Gods (Shan). This process of assimilating Chinese culture was already apparent in the fifth century AD, but it received great impetus from the policy of Prince Shotoku, whose rule as regent began in 593. And so Buddhism, as mediated by China, spread solidly into Japanese culture. Probably the twelfth century, after the sixth, proved the most significant turning point in Japan's spiritual history. Late in that century, after a time of increasing collapse and despair, a new regime was instituted and the court moved from ancient and fragrant Kyoto to Kamakura. The so-called Kamakura period lasted from 1185 to 1333. It was during this time that characteristically Japanese Pure Land and Zen forms of Buddhism arose. It was a time of creative spiritual and social awakening. It was, so to speak, the Japanese Enlightenment. It was also during this time that the fire of Nichiren blazed.

The new Japanese Buddhism: Honen

The story of the great efflorescence of the Pure Land can be told through the lives of two figures: the saints Honen and Shinran. They were great lovers of Amida – Amida being the Japanese form of Amitabha, whose wondrous compassion and love for living beings we have already encountered as we traced the paths of Indian Mahāyāna, and who was creator of the Pure Land, the believers' Paradise. Honen lived from 1133 to 1212, and despite his gentle lack of assertiveness can be considered the founder of the Jodo or Japanese Pure Land sect. Incidentally I follow common usage in English in referring to Japanese *sects*: the term is misleading in that the various religious movements in Japan are by no means exclusive – in some ways they are like the differing orders in the Roman Catholic church and in other ways they are like denominations within an ecumenical framework; in other words one can belong to one 'sect' without excluding attendance at the rituals of others.

Honen was the son of an official in Mimasaka province who was killed by an enemy but instructed his son, as he lay dying, not to think of revenge but rather take up the religious life. Evidently the father was himself a remarkable man: no less so the son, whose talents soon became clear. He went to study at the sacred mountain of Hiei, near Kyoto, where there were monasteries, colleges and temples, a religious centre stemming from the original hermitage founded in the ninth century by Dengyo Daishi, exponent of the sacramental Tendai teaching (similar to that of Shingon, to which we shall come later). Honen's learning was great and his piety well known. He is said to have read through the enormous Mahāyāna canon (in its expanded Chinese version) no less than five times. He mastered the complexities of Tendai and Shingon and the like, and yet he remained essentially dissatisfied. His was a long search through scripture and experience. Finally the light came to him through the teachings of the Chinese master Zendo, who was third patriarch of the Chinese Amida school. Zendo's writings are not found in the Chinese canon, the *Tripitaka*, but they rang true to Honen's feelings. They had an electric effect upon him, comparable to Luther's 'tower experience' or Augustine's conversion. The crucial words of Zendo were these: 'Only repeat the name of Amida Buddha with all your heart, whatever you are doing, whether walking or standing still or lying down or sitting: do not cease this practice for even a moment. It is a practice which brings salvation without fail, for it is fully in accord with the original vow of the Buddha.' But these words not only rang true to Honen: they were relevant to the turbulent age of civil strife in which he lived.

For consider: Buddhism was often corrupt and even its priests given to warfare and struggles for power; yet in so far as there remained evidence of its true spirit, this was to be found in places such as Hiei, full of learning and the genuine pursuit of liberation. But often this was conceived as achieved through meditation. Was not meditation the heart of the message, the end of the Path? But how was it to be practised amid the troubled affairs of life? How could the soldier or the farmer or fisherman have the real opportunity for peaceful contemplation? As we shall see, Zen offered a way through this problem by taking secular arts into its methods of meditation, but even so it was perhaps not for everyone. Honen saw that the 'calling upon the name of Amida', the *Namu Amida Butsu*, as the formula was called in Japanese, offered hope and a chance of renewal of true religion for everyone. And so at the age of forty-five he started preaching his new-found message. He was not fanatical, and he encouraged the broadest possible vision of Buddhism. He recognised the value of central scripture, the *Lotus Sūtra*, and of all sincere forms of Buddhist practice, but pride of place he gave to calling on the name of Amida. His goodness was the best advertisement for the Jodo, that is, the Pure Land, teaching. Yet he was not lacking in opponents, even enemies. For one thing, if all you need to do is to call on the name of the Buddha in faith, the elaborate practices of orthodox Mahāyāna become superfluous. If they are superfluous so must be many of the monks of Hiei and other centres. For another thing, if faith is all, works are nothing.

You can sin as much as you like provided you keep on with the repetition of the formula, the Nembutsu for short, for is it not a sure guarantee of salvation? Once Honen encountered some fishermen who were tortured by the thought that those who take life will suffer torments in purgatory in the next life. Honen assured them that faith in Amida would bring them surely to Paradise. If you extrapolate from that incident, then surely anything goes. Such were the criticisms voiced by Honen's opponents and enemies. Some of his disciples were punished, and a few killed. Out of favour at court, Honen was exiled, although he was ultimately restored to the centre of things, and died peacefully at the age of eighty, revered by many, and leaving a lasting imprint on Japanese spirituality. Though Luther was an earthy, less gentle, less saintly character, there is a remarkable likeness between his and Honen's central teachings, concerning the vital power of faith.

Shinran

Honen's various disciples tended to differ somewhat in their interpretation of the master's message, for even so simple a doctrine can admit of subtly different applications. The most famous disciple, however, and the one whom Honen is said to have favoured above all, was Shinran, who founded a variant of Jodo known as Jodo Shinshu, literally 'the True Sect of the Pure Land'. It is counted as a separate sect, partly because it differs from Jodo proper in certain customs and externals, notably the marriage of the clergy. Shinran was of aristocratic descent and was born in 1173. He was early ordained, at the age of eight, and rose to become an abbot at Hiei. He was hailed as a genius, but he proved to be a wayward one, from the point of view, at any rate, of the monks of Hiei. For at the age of twenty-seven he heard Honen preach, and found in his words that way to salvation which he too had been seeking, through his studies and exploration of the rituals. He joined the Jodo movement in 1201, and married. This was a sign that external observances are of no avail, and that the barriers between priest and laity should be broken down. His wife, according to tradition, was daughter of the Regent Fujiwara Kanezane, a patron of Honen's (though not powerful enough to prevent the latter's exile, in which Shinran shared). For many years Shinran and his wife lived obscurely in the province of Hitachi, where he preached to the people. The vitality of his faith led him to extend to their logical conclusion the consequences of relying upon the grace of Amida Buddha. Thus he wrote, with charming paradox, as follows:

> 'If even a good man can be reborn in the Pure Land, how much more so a wicked man.' His disciple Yuiembo comments: 'People however usually think it is the other way round: if even a wicked man can be reborn in the Pure Land how much more so a good man. This latter view may at first sight seem reasonable, but it is not in accord with the purpose of the original vow of the Buddha, with faith in the power of Another. The reason for this is that a person who relies on his own power and undertakes to perform meritorious deeds has no intention of relying on the power of Another and is not

> the object of the original vow. . . We who are caught in the net of our own passions cannot free ourselves from bondage to birth and death, no matter what kind of austerities or good deeds we try to perform. Seeing this and pitying our condition Amida made his vow with the intention of bringing wicked men to Buddhahood. Therefore the wicked man who depends on the power of Another is the prime object of salvation.'

Honen and Shinran, then, were two seminal forces in the generation of an indigenous variety of Pure Land Buddhism, which bursts the bonds of orthodox Buddhism. It reaches out mysteriously to Western piety, and the sentiments which animated these gentle and fervent figures could easily be seen as complementary to the love of God and faith in Christ exhibited by Christian evangelists.

There is of course a difference in atmosphere, and also in ideas about what is real. It would be natural for a Western Christian to point out that Amida seems to be a figment of religious imagination, a projection of the Buddhist dream into a Western paradise; while, by contrast, Christ truly lived and truly died for our sins. Christ is historical: Amida is not. Against this one may ask does it matter? Could not the Mahāyāna Buddhist claim with force that he can see Amida for himself? Honen said that in the last years of his life he was continually able to see into Paradise and see Amida. What does historical reality matter beside this? We must come to this question again, towards the end of our search. Meanwhile let us move on to the second act of the Japanese spiritual drama.

Shingon Buddhism

Shingon's introduction into Japan, and its original development in this new context, was due to Kobo Daishi (774–835). He had visited China and was drawn to use the tradition of Buddhist Tantra or sacramental religion. When he returned to Japan, he produced a new synthesis which was to have profound effects. There is little doubt about his theological originality. He used Chinese and Indian ideas to provide a coherent system which at once could appeal to intellectuals, ritualists, ordinary men in search of both other-worldly and this-worldly blessings, and those who still revered Japan's ancient Shinto values. It was he indeed who is supposed to have coined the phrase 'Two-aspect Shinto' (*Ryobu Shinto*), through which he gave a slogan to those who saw Shinto and Buddhism as two complementary forms of life.

At the base of his beliefs lay the notion that macrocosm is reflected in microcosm: every element of existence represents and reflects the whole, just as the whole permeates every single thing. So minor deities are not just minor. The grain of sand is not just an atom on the beach but reflects the nature of the cosmos. My gestures can have significance far beyond the wave of the hand or the curling of the finger. And because Kobo Daishi was a Buddhist primarily he saw the universal as being summed up in the Truth-Body of Buddha-nature. The heart of the Buddha is my heart; it is likewise the heart of the universe. I may have lost myself, as Buddhist doctrine teaches, but I have gained in a sense the whole world. More particularly, though, Kobo Daishi brought in the use of sacred formulas or mantras for controlling the forces of the world. For everything interests, and rituals can bring various kinds of blessings. More, the old Shinto deities which were often identified with forces of nature and geographical locations could be controlled too by ritual means. They too shared in the sacred Buddha-nature. In this way it was possible to unite the Shinto and the Buddhist pantheons. The *kamis* or gods of Shinto and the Buddhas and devas of India and the East could dance together in the great phantasmagoria of this charming, illusory, potent, impermanent, interrelated world. The followers of the Shingon, followers that is of the true mantra, were never afraid to see fear as one of the elements of the universe, and disease and dire suffering as manifestations too of the one Buddha-nature, the *dharmakāya*, or Truth-Aspect of the Buddha.

They saw the mind and human action as clues to everything, and using the twin powers of meditation and ritual wished to heal the individual and to change reality about us. It was not surprising that in its catholicism it proved powerfully attractive to rich, poor, intellectual and uneducated men alike. It was also the Japanese dimension of that great swathe of Tantric Buddhism which stretches across the midpoint between Siberia and the tropic regions skirting Asia to the south. Perhaps hereby it represented an unconscious historic compromise between the cool Buddhism of hot India and the hot shamanism of cold Siberia – between, in other words, the cultural forces which had come to shape Japan and Buddhism there.

Zen

The third aspect of the drama of Japanese spirituality is better known. Zen paradoxes come cheaply. But perhaps the great paradox about Zen is its great orthodoxy. It is Japan's substitute for Lesser Vehicle Buddhism. It is (to put it unhistorically) Japan's form of the Theravada and fulfils much the same function within the overall economy of Buddhism. It is a practical, Japanese way of stressing two vital truths in Buddhism – first that nirvana comes through meditation (how else it comes we need not now enquire); and second that to see the truth we need to abandon views generated by the use of ordinary language and concepts, which mislead us about the true, pristine nature of the world about us and of ourselves. It is true that Zen makes strong use of the idea of the Buddha-nature, a typical and central conception of developed Mahāyāna. It is true also that Zen, via its Chinese dimension, incorporates some of the values of Taoism – the strong appreciation of nature, the felt oneness with the flow of things. But these feelings were not absent from early Buddhism, judging from the poems of early monks and nuns preserved in the Pali canon. The scepticism and mysticism of Taoism were very similar to the ethos of the Buddha, one feels, and the synthesis between Ch'ān and Taoism was a natural one. The Zen emphasis on the transmission of truth outside the scriptures is a healthy reaction against the idolisation of the scriptures and of verbal formulas evident in much later Buddhism.

Where Zen Buddhism is original, over against much at least of orthodoxy, is in its offering hope of enlightenment by lay people as well as monks. It has been seen that Pure Land broke down barriers: the possibility of salvation lay open to all, and monkish good works, though perhaps a symptom of being saved or a spin-off of the sense of redemption, were in themselves useless to bring liberation from the round of birth and death – only Another, Amida, could save. But Zen is not involved in the theory of being saved by Another. It is like so much of Buddhism, and the Lesser Vehicle, a religion of self-help. 'Be lamps to yourselves', said the Buddha, dying, or so tradition states. But because of the arduous nature of release it had been assumed that the contemplative life could only be effective within the bounds of monasticism. Such an assumption is broken down in Zen, whether in the Soto or the Rinzai variety.

Rinzai Zen Buddhism

Rinzai Zen was founded by Eisai (1141–1215), who like Honen and Kobo Daishi travelled to China for inspiration and found it in Ch'ān; it is a form familiar to us in the Western world because of its violent use of paradoxes and contradictions to reinforce its message and to generate a truly meditational attitude. Dogen (1200–1253) also travelled to China and founded in Japan the Soto sect, which stresses less the suddenness of enlightenment – the path to liberation is gradual. Soto is not given to using the koan or riddle so evident in Rinzai Zen (like visualising the sound of one hand clapping), but relies much more on the subtle and voluminous writings of Dogen, by now given the status of bodhisattva. The method of meditation is strongly analogous to the Theravadin method of *sati* or self-awareness, save with the twist that in being aware of my experience I am also aware of myself as Buddha.

Where Zen was original was in its special aesthetic quality which has so permeated Japanese life and its adaptation of secular and even military arts to the practice of enlightenment. Best known perhaps is its use of archery and flower arrangement. By undergoing the discipline of each art a person is brought to achieve a kind of ordered spontaneity. The archer is supposed to hit the target without aiming, just letting off the bow and yet finding it flying direct to the bull's eye. This is delicately described in Eugen Herrigel's justly famous book *Zen in the Art of Archery*. This spirit of spontaneity generated some by-products in the fifties and sixties when Zen was big in California and beyond. The discipline was sometimes forgotten, as in some of the brasher forms of action painting: spontaneity without prior depth and order can become buffoonery, and the *New Yorker* hit the nail on the head (if that be the right metaphor from archery) when it had a cartoon of an action painter throwing blobs of paint at a canvas from ten feet away. The wall is splattered with blobs: the picture remains incompetently virgin. However, the use of the secular arts was a means of incorporating meditation into ordinary life. Zen came to be part of the ethos of the warrior class, strangely, and the peaceful religion of the Buddha had a new expression in a kind of selfless machismo. The frontiers of Zen abutted on the ideals too of Confucius, well suited to the somewhat hierarchic and feudal society of medieval Japan. So the old three religions of China – Confucianism, Taoism and Buddhism – found a new meeting point in a strongly Japanese atmosphere. The Japanese penchant and genius for synthesis triumphed over various contradictions – the tug between anarchy (from the Tao) and order (from Confucius), the tug between peaceful contemplation (from the Buddha) and the demands of active life (from Japanese society), and the tug between other-worldliness and this world, between nirvana and samsara.

Order and serendipity: these are the characteristics of the Zen garden, and they symbolise many things. Thus in the temple of Ryonanji there is a garden, or perhaps better just a space, mainly raked sand white with the faint lines of the rake worked around it. And rising through the sand are fifteen assorted rocks in five clumps. It is a mysterious geological poem; it is a kind of contemplative rock-sound. What does it mean? Any way of telling would fall foul of the Zen destruction of concepts, but for want of silence it is worth commenting that it echoes so much of Zen art – the blanks in the pictures are so many signs of the Void and of that true emptiness of mind which is the fullness of enlightenment. The raked sand is blank; the rocks are whatever may be dredged up, perhaps, in the sea of emptiness and they too are empty.

Shinto and Japan's origins

So we have three motifs in old Japan: the piety of the Pure Land, the extensive ritual richness of Shingon and Tendai, the orderly chaos of Zen, the means of meditation in the midst of life. The counterpoints of Indian spirituality, *bhakti, mantra* and *dhyāna,* find echoes and amplification much further east, in a land not dreamed of by early Buddhists. Alongside the varieties of Buddhism the old plant of Shinto still grew strongly. The Buddha was not jealous of the Japanese gods or of any others. And the gods could come to terms with the Buddha Sakyamuni and with Amida. They stayed important in the Japanese imagination, and in modern times were to play an imperial role, and not altogether a happy one. Shinto myths about the origins of the Japanese archipelago are magical explanations of palpable variety. Japan throws up mountains and volcanic springs. It thunders within, and its rivers are bold. Cherries and peaches adorn it, and snow, and man has made his reflections in the rice fields. Now it also throws up skyscrapers and chimney-stacks, and is green with golf and grey with speeding cars. It is still magical: why should it not therefore have had a magical origin? The myths describe how Japan came out of the sea. It was a long process. There emerged first a reedy mass from the thick brine, and it became a deity. Two other gods emerged and from them other spirits to dwell amid the floating mass. Eventually the gods called on the god Izanagi and his consort (and sister) Izanami to come down and solidify the land. Izanagi stirred the mass with a magic spear and it congealed into an island. There the two mated and their offspring were the various islands of Japan. But eventually she gave birth to fire and died and thus goes to the underworld. As part result death came into the world.

As a result of further events, the goddess Amaterasu is born, the goddess of the sun, from whom the rulers of Japan are descended. Numerous other deities, *kami,* emanate from these early beings, and it is upon them that much of Shinto ceremonial came to be directed. As can be seen, Shinto is not highly systematic. It weaves together myths of explanation and it celebrates thereby the islands and the nation of Japan. It celebrates the forces of nature, sacred mountains, streams and places upon which man depends for his sustenance, both material and spiritual. It is not greatly a doctrinal religion, but centres more upon ritual and experience. It is a religion much taken with shrines, which are as it were the concert-halls of the spirit, where the *kami* whisper and sing music which cannot be translated into dogma and routine ethics.

Japan

It is a rectangular space for the deity, approached through a wooden gateway, the *torii* of sturdy and sacred design – a solid tree trunk supported by pillars and decorated variously. Through the *torii* is found a worship building in front of which the pious ring a bell and bow down, hoping to attract the attention of the *kami*. It is an individual matter, this supplication. From time to time the priests operate within the temple. Men and women leave offerings to the gods, and speculate perhaps about what lies beyond the sanctuary in the holy of holies. For there is kept the so-called god-body, or relic or symbol of the deity: a stone of strange shape, perhaps; a scroll; hair from a saint; a jewel – who knows? The faithful are threatened with stories of awe-stricken death among those who have injudiciously and without due licence peeped into the holy place to see the god-body. The numinous aura of the *kami* is thus preserved. Yet sometimes the god-body is a tree for all to see or some other natural feature. For despite the priests, the *torii*, the buildings, the offerings, the rituals, shrine Shinto breathes the air of nature. Men come to terms with living fragments of the universe. Much of Shinto gives an aesthetic sense of the harmony between man and his surroundings. And like nature itself it is all rather untidy. It was also therefore able to live easily with the subtleties and organisational structures of Buddhism. Shinto did not threaten the *Lotus Sūtra*, and the Buddhist idea of skilfulness in means was able to accommodate the indigenous gods. As we have seen, Shingon provided a theory of synthesis. In the modern period the toughness of Japanese military ethics, the family sense, the feudal mentality (derived from both Japanese society and Confucian ideas) coalesced in a sense of national identity in which Shinto had a special place. It was harnessed to a form of expansionism which was cruel, and doomed to fail despite the glories of the half-century from the Meiji restoration to the First World War. State Shinto, as an instrument of policy, died by that policy. On 15 December 1945 General Macarthur ordered the disestablishment of Shinto, and his words were echoed by the dignified imperial rescript issued a little over a fortnight later on the first day of 1946. The emperor Hirohito wrote:

> We stand together with you our countrymen. Our gains and losses have ever been one. We desire that our woe and weal should be shared. The bonds between us and our countrymen have been tied together from first to last by mutual trust and affection. They do not originate from mere myth and legend. They do not have their basis in the fictitious ideas that the emperor is manifest god and that the Japanese people are a race superior to other races and therefore destined to rule the world. In order to alleviate the trials and sufferings of the people, my government will exhaust all means for devising every kind of plan and programme . . .

State Shinto was dead; but Shinto in its informal and complex way lived on.

Continued on page 283

PROPHETS AND TEACHERS

Individual prophets and teachers give new direction and content to faiths. Secular figures who offer a new way of looking at man also gather a dedicated and committed following. The powers of persuasion and inspiration manifested by such key personalities are sometimes referred to as charisma. Later the new directions became formalised: priests take over the tradition of the revolutionary prophet.

Billy Graham, Bible in hand, in Trafalgar Square, London in 1954. The Protestant emphasis on the conscience of the individual believer gives a particular importance to the preacher who can make manifest the dramatic implications of man's dialogue with God.

Pope John XXIII (right), voted to the papacy in old age and thought to be a stop-gap Pope, proved to be dynamic and saintly in the office. Architect of Vatican II, he showed an independence of mind which was linked with his shrewd peasant goodness (he came from a small place near Bergamo in north Italy). He thus became a modern religious hero, especially in his native Italy. Above: Ramakrishna (1834–1886) was a gentle, semi-educated Hindu ascetic whose doctrine of the oneness of all religions was spread by devoted followers. His contribution to the growth of, and national pride in, the Hindu tradition owed much to this ability to draw people to him: he was both a mystic and charismatic teacher.

The secular world has its sacred figures too. Perhaps no one has done more to change men's perceptions of themselves than Sigmund Freud. There is a sense in which the psychoanalysis of which he was chief architect fulfils many functions of traditional religion: it gives, it is claimed, self-understanding, it cures diseases, it is the confessional updated, it demands loyalty. It also has its heroes.

But Shinto has not had the vitality of the new religions sprouting in postwar Japan. They have come up fast partly because they have represented responses to the traumas of the defeat, and, paradoxically, of the successes of the economic miracle. For that meant dislocations, uncertainties, rapid urbanisation, new forms of life; and that degree of prosperity which could give forward-looking religious organisations economic impetus. Sometimes the new religions that have flowered have old roots. The seed needs, in any case, to fall upon fertile soil. No movement has been more spectacularly successful than the Soka Gakkai. But others have abounded, such as the Konkokyo, a Shinto pietism reminiscent of the Amida cults; the P. L. Kyodan or Perfect Liberty Association, which preaches a strenuous, aesthetic unitarianism; and the Tenrikyo, founded by Miki Nakayama (1798–1887), a charismatic woman, oriented towards faith-healing and a messianic future consummation of history. Such movements have seen their apogee in the postwar period. But more powerful than all these, both in Japan and abroad (mainly California), has been the Soka Gakkai. Its political wing, the Komeito, has also been relatively successful in Japanese politics. The Soka Gakkai hark back to Nichiren who was, at one level, a fiery Japanese reformer and evangelist, and at another, perhaps something more. His teachings and example started a sect or movement, and it is one branch of this which has been strikingly modernised by the Soka Gakkai.

Nichiren: was he a Buddhist?

Nichiren was born in 1222. Records state that he boasted of being an outcaste, a *sendara* – a Japanese version of an old Indian expression meaning an untouchable. Japan still has its untouchables – a strange situation in a predominantly Buddhist country. Nichiren in any event was son of a fisherman, and this class of workers was looked on with suspicion by the orthodox Buddhist, for did they not make their living by taking life? Most folk did not take up the stance of Honen. After years of study as a young man at various important monastic centres, Nichiren realised, at the age of 31, that the secret of salvation lay in the *Lotus Sūtra*, and more particularly in loving devotion to it. He was like Honen and Shinran in simplifying Buddhism, but he did so in a rather different way. The object of devotion was not a personal being but rather the essence of the *Lotus Sūtra*. By uttering the formula 'Namu-myoho Renge-kyo' the faithful could win salvation. Nichiren in exalting the *Lotus Sūtra* meant to supersede all other forms of Buddhism. He was exclusive, apparently proud, nationalistic, given to denunciations of monks and emperors alike if he felt this was needed for the furtherance of his evangelical vision. Such a stiff-necked preacher merited restraint, to say no more. On one occasion soldiers came to arrest and execute him. But just at the moment when the executioner raised his sword to strike off Nichiren's head a ball of fire bright as the moon swooped through the sky. Stunned, the executioner desisted. Nichiren was saved by a miracle, and even though he had to endure exile, imprisonment and other hardships his spirit continued to burn. He was founder of the Nichiren school and its variant the Nichiren Shoshu, which lies behind the modern Soka Gakkai. He looked on the present age, as many Buddhists did, as one of decline – in accord with a strongly pessimistic motif in the Buddhist philosophy of history whereby the teachings of the Buddha are gradually lost, men being no more able to assimilate them. The old teaching could no longer work, but a new Buddha or Bodhisattva could be in the offing, to restore truth to men. There are signs that Nichiren looked on himself in that way.

But he was fearfully direct and harsh. He does not seem at all like the Buddha, still less like the extremely gentle Honen or the unaggressive Shinran. He was also nationalistic in emphasis, for his age. But his writings were subtle and his theories about the tests of truth and value as between differing religious stances were impressive. His was no mean mind, but he was also and still is also controversial. Could such a ferocious figure truly be a Buddhist? Anyway, he struck roots in Japanese national consciousness. It was thus not absurd for his tradition to be revived in modern Japan in a most impressive manner. But the man who had most to do with it died in detention in 1944 because he would not accept State Shinto. He was Tsunesburo Makiguchi, a remarkable schoolteacher born in 1871. He was a reformer, with new opinions in education, leading often to clashes with officials. In 1928 Makiguchi was converted to the Nichiren Shoshu, and out of the combination of his educational interests and the special pietism of the Nichiren sect there emerged the modern movement of Soka Gakkai.

The Soka Gakkai

Dewey and John Stuart Mill met Nichiren, an unlikely but rich conjunction. Nichiren had spoken of his way as a way of happiness. The new movement translated this into modern terms. The theory put forward by Makiguchi is that truth is objective, but values are constructed. So he formed his society for the creation of values, predicated on the notion that a group or nation can make its own values in the light of the truth found in Buddhism as propounded by Nichiren. As a result of its effective postwar organisation, under the leadership of first Toda (imprisoned in the war) and Ikeda after him, the Soka Gakkai has burgeoned. It reckons more than six million families among its membership. It is a new, clean and rather unnerving manifestation of the evangelical spirit. It gives friendship, a strong doctrine, and objects of loyalty to the faithful. It asks them however to destroy any tokens of other religious loyalty. Even ancestral tablets are not immune. It blends East and West, and though in theory neutralist in politics it shows unmistakable signs of a rather conservative nationalism.

Motifs of Japanese religion

These then are some of the acts in the Japanese spiritual drama. What next? Or, to put things differently, what do the differing motifs of Japanese religion mean when put together? How does martial Zen live with gentle Honen? How does evangelical Soka Gakkai square with Shinran? How does the ritualism of Shingon team up with modern industrialism? And does Japan genuinely have messages for the world beyond Japan?

It would appear so, up to a point, when one looks at the influence of Zen in

Western culture in the last two decades or more. And Soka Gakkai is one of the many faiths making strong appeals to the wayward youth of the USA. But perhaps these are marginal, even ephemeral effects. For the true message of Japan we may have to look much deeper. In Japan as in India there is a continual counterpoint between dependence on Another (*bhakti*) and a religion of self-dependent meditation. But what Japan stresses through this is that in either case there is spontaneity: for the Other breaks through to one, as happened to Honen; while in the art of meditation, whether Rinzai or Soto, the results are spontaneous – one hits the target without aiming. How is it that a people so given to order, whether in feudal arrangement, factory, painting, or gastronomy, should stress the spontaneous, the unpredictable? Precisely because order must be broken out of. Without order, there can only be randomness, not true spontaneity. So in spiritual matters the disciplines may be vital, whether as precursors of or spin-offs from the spontaneities of enlightenment or conversion. Of course, one must be wise regarding those disciplines. For all his ferocities and lack of empathy with men of other persuasions, Nichiren was right in propounding the view that the readiness of people in a country to receive a particular form of teaching is vital (he thought, by the way, that countries which had not yet received the Mahāyāna were better off with the Hinayana – is this a prophetic hint at the present importance of the Theravada in the preaching of Buddhism in Western Europe?).

But running through creative Japanese religion is a certain pessimism. This is the *mappo* – the age of decline of the Buddha's religion, so that the simpler, more direct forms of faith must be the only hope of salvation for men. This strong sense of the decline of religion goes with the whole Buddhist theory of history. True knowledge and right conduct keep winding down till restored by a Buddha or a Bodhisattva. Ironically, the Japanese, while their GNP rises and the Hondas multiply, have a presentiment that spiritually matters may be worse. The myth of progress must be taken with a sense of scepticism.

10 THE MEANING OF THE SEARCH

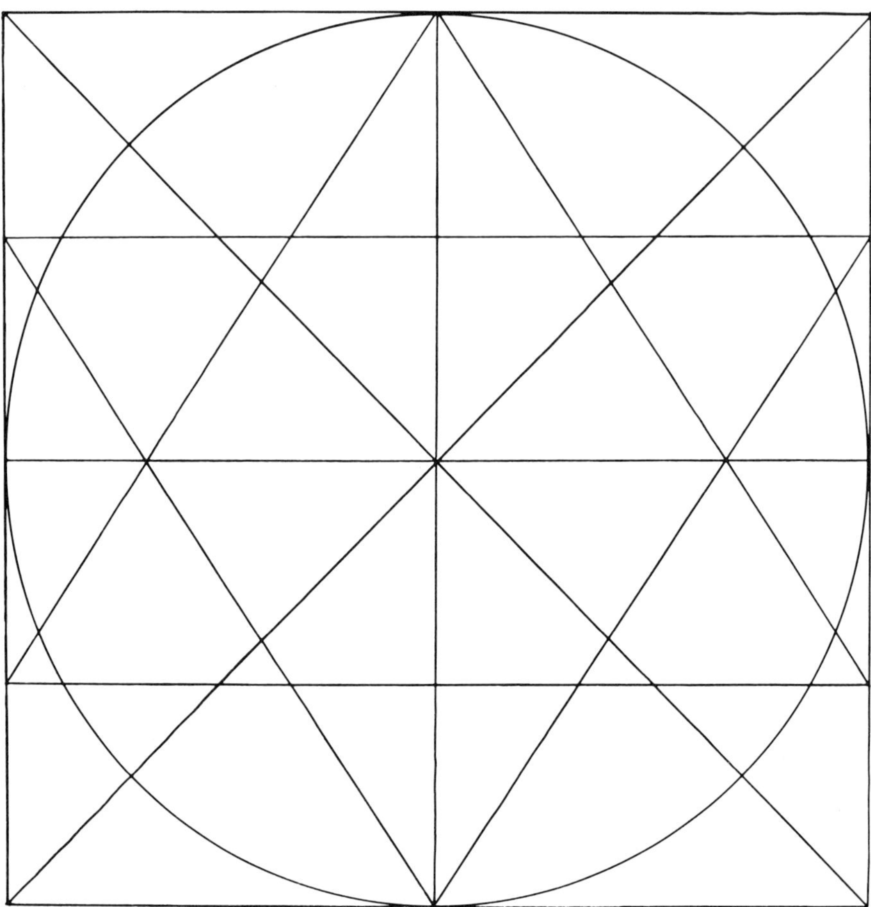

The beliefs and feelings of men operate in a triangle. The apex of that triangle is the universe: what is it really like? Answers about that affect our feeling of being at home or otherwise in the world into which we have been projected. We did not ask to be born, but having been born we try to come to an understanding of the universe, and do a deal with it. If it is ruled by Providence, then certain things follow. If not, then other thoughts arise.

The right-hand corner of the triangle is other people – the societies and cultures of this world. We consciously or unconsciously react to them and are moulded by other people for good or ill. The parent, the friend, the enemy, the language enter symbolically into the fabric of our lives. Our beliefs and feelings tend to place us, give us a centre, from which to deal with our fellow creatures. The left hand of the triangle is 'I'. I write this to 'you'. But when you read you must say 'I'. For religion touches us in our own solitariness.

In this final perspective on the long search I shall move through the three points of the triangle. Since science dictates so much of our perspective on the universe I shall say something of the relation between science and religion (and religion's systematic companion and rival, ideology). Then I shall consider the social and plural role of the spiritual possibilities opened up by the long search which has resulted in the various faiths and unfaiths of men. As for the left point of the triangle I shall express what it means to me. There is no need for any of 'you' to agree. It will be an example of what it all means to a particular person. But inevitably something of me will colour the accounts I give of other points of the triangle.

Science at the apex

Science is awesome. The scientific pundit has an authority far beyond that of the uncertain priest or the slightly defensive *bhikkhu* because science has, as an institution, been so potent in unlocking the mysteries of the universe. A hundred years ago, radioactivity was unknown; biologists were still digesting Darwin, uncertainly; the theory of relativity was some decades away; there was no radio-astronomy and the staggering scale of the universe was unrealised; there were no computers; most of modern logic was undreamt of and much of modern mathematics was only in the making; sub-atomic particles were unexplored; telepathy was not yet a name; psycho-analysis was at best gestating; anthropology was an infant, biased like most children.

One could go on, but we are still doubtless only skimming the surface of the oceans of mystery which constitute the apex of our world. Nevertheless it is vital for us to relate our lives to the new knowledge. And although the content of science may often disturb religion the structure of science causes it to converse with spirituality.

Science shows how the universe keeps hitting back

Very often, as we have seen, the universe has been depicted by religions (and ideologies) in ways which give a certain sense to our existence. Yet infuriatingly the universe hits back. Thus it was important for the medieval church in Western Europe that the earth was at the centre. Had not Aristotle, digested by Aquinas, said so? Did it not conduce to the dignity of man in God's created world? Was it not in accord with the centrality of Christ? Yet Copernicus came to see that the earth might be more movable than we thought. Perhaps this wandering nature of Earth might have strange consequences for the faith. It might portend other moves from the centre.

Later, centrality had more to do with man's uniqueness, over against nature and the animals. But even this division within the world came to dissolve, through Darwin's theory of evolution, indicating the essential kinship between man and other species. In fact, evolution had a double edge, for it sharply called in question the truth of the Biblical narrative, which seemed to state that man was a special creation of God and was implicated in a fall. The newly generated scientific study of history helped to undermine literal interpretations of the scriptures. So the latter part of the nineteenth century saw a traumatic reappraisal of man's place in nature and of the meaning of the Bible.

But at least, people thought, this planet is unique. However, astronomy was waiting to demonstrate the awesome vastness of the cosmos, while biochemistry was waiting to indicate how life emerges from a primeval soup. Consequently, there may be evolutionary processes at work on many a planet scattered through the galaxies.

It is not therefore surprising that the old Christian picture of the universe has faded. Nor is it surprising that modern Christian thinkers see the old cosmology as merely trimming, easily dispensed with, round the faith. Rudolf Bultmann, for instance, could talk of demythologising the Gospel: that is, taking out of the Christian message those miraculous and archaic elements not believable by modern man.

Nevertheless, if scientific knowledge poses serious problems for religion, especially Christianity, another current flows, which brings science towards a new and higher harmony with the traditions of the spirit.

The meaning of life in science

It has been fashionable to see science as essentially based on the material aspect of the universe. Science, we think, analyses things and beings into their material constituents and so explains them. Everything boils down to chemistry and physics. Now no one can or should doubt the fertility of the materialist approach to reality. Whatever you study or explore, the material constituents remain vital to understand. Nevertheless, the reduction of people and things to swarms of atoms and shoals of molecules does not represent the only perspective from which to view the world.

For if it is the case that life is sprouting throughout the cosmos, wherever conditions are suitable, then it is not a sport or an aberration from the norm. Life itself is normal. It is therefore no more suitable to picture the cosmos in terms of its material components alone than it would be to see it in terms of living matter alone. So why not see the world in terms of its thrusts towards life and consciousness? Materialism is just a bias in one direction. That is the first part of my argument.

Science, method and creation

Second, we may ask what, after all, science consists in. Essentially it has to do with method and procedure. Or if you like, it is an attitude of mind. Modern philosophy has spent a lot of time in trying to characterise this frame of mind. What I am about to write is a distillation out of writings of men such as Karl Popper who have contributed centrally to this debate.

Science has to do with procedures, with method, but it depends too on inspiration and for that matter serendipity or meaningful luck. Let me begin with luck. Very often big changes in science accrue upon men's stumbling upon new data which are uncomfortably suggestive. Thus Fleming perceived a new mould which he had the wit to see as significant, and so we have the vast blessing of penicillin. Again, the invention of the telescope allowed Galileo and others to witness the wrinkles and craters on the moon, exploding Aristotle's old distinction between the sublunary world and the rest (the world beneath or this side of the moon, and the rest). These were matters up to a point of luck. They indicate a dialogue between an awkward and surprising world on the one hand and the questing eye on the other.

Much of modern science arises from inspiration, or to put it another way, from conceptual revolutions. Galileo was not just lucky and perceptive; he was also a main figure in the rethink which came to destroy the prevalent Aristotelian picture of the world. Thus he visualised what would happen if two weights of different masses were dropped from the leaning tower of Pisa – which would hit the ground first? Orthodoxy dictated one answer: Galileo said, 'At the same time.' Again, Einstein, by taking thought, arrived in the same sort of way at the theory of relativity which came to revolutionise modern physics.

So the second thing to say about science is that its progress rests upon conceptual inspiration. Like luck it is lucky, that is, it is not something which we can command, though there are conditions which favour it, notably a critical attitude in society at large and within the scientific establishment in particular.

So in a way the method of science is: there is no method, for the scientific spirit bloweth where it listeth. However, the ideas are not random thoughts off the top of the head nor are the lucky discoveries just found and noted. The ideas and the discoveries are tested. This is where method most obviously comes into play. Much has been written about methods of induction, verification and falsification. They have to do with checking out hypotheses. The methods have two sides to them, at least.

In the first place, the methods nowadays involve increasingly sophisticated probes: the electron microscope sees into the little galaxies of which we are composed, while huge radar aerials scan the galaxies in which we have our tiny being. So man's ingenuity has an engineering dimension, through which testing and probing can be generated. At the same time, there is a systematisation of testing by which the scientist can see whether his new ideas actually work. If philosophers have been over-preoccupied by this aspect of science it is not surprising, for it is the easiest both to describe and to prescribe. Likewise scientists often stress routine; like those describing how we ride a bicycle, they describe the banal, and leave the miracles of balance and physiological motion on one side. However, let us not despise the routine, for it is that which assures us of the reality of our surmises. It is also the reason for the resources poured into science, for the methods backed by the gadgetry need many man-hours and many machines. (And if we often pay for men and machines without results, what do we expect? For the inspiration still has to be there.)

Now if all I have said here about science is correct it means that we are taken beyond materialism in a different way from that which I sketched before.

Science and religion

The first thing to conclude from my account of the scientific frame of mind is that that frame must be boundless. There is no way of laying down boundaries of content and saying that on this side lies science and on that unscience. A few years ago acupuncture would have been thought of by most Western doctors as primitive rubbish. Now it has a respected place among medical methods. If one is to be scientific, to be open-minded, any new ideas should be looked at. So science has no fixed bounds. This was one main problem forgotten by the positivists.

Positivism in its modern manifestations is of course a philosophical rather than a strictly scientific doctrine. In its recent form it was best summed up, I suppose, in A. J. Ayer's seminal *Language, Truth and Logic* (1936). There he condemned any statement, for example about God, which could not be verified by sense experience (note the emphasis here on routine method) as being meaningless – without real content. He thought that a descriptive utterance was either in principle 'scientific', i.e. testable, or vacuous, empty. He represented an aggressive scientism of appalling insensitivity, and yet Ayer's thesis expressed a popular mood. Many ordinary folk in Western countries were inclined, and still are, to see in science a new source of authority. The man in the white coat has a kind of priestly function, purveying to us not only the secrets of the universe but also magical ways of manipulating the world. It is thus easy to believe in science as the sole vital source of truth, bypassing old religious and philosophical outlooks.

But since science is boundless and rooted in the critical mind it cannot be dogmatic, either about its own claims or any others. It is unscientific to rule out truths which lie beyond the bounds of science as we know it; and it is absurd not to recognise possibilities of truth accruing from all kinds of insights, religious or otherwise. So positivism itself must fall by the wayside, and suffer death at its own hands, if it truly praises critical science.

Science and the mind

But there is a deeper convergence between scientific and spiritual perspective on the world. This is partly to do with the evolution of consciousness, whereby the universe grows, so to speak, its own mirrors to admire itself in. If we are to understand science we must understand something of mathematics, and the highly complex concepts which we bring to bear to prise open the secrets of nature. So complex are our theories that they cannot be seen simply as matching the world, point by point. They are not photographs of reality, but more like maps. Now if you fly over England or America it is true that the maps will roughly correspond to shapes below; but many conventional signs, directions, elevations, projections and so on will also appear on any map. There is not an absolute point-by-point resemblance between the map and the landscape. Or again, a theory may be a bit like a musical score, formally somewhat similar to the music but having a complex indirect relationship to the parts of the music. Likewise scientific theories bear a sophisticated relationship to the realities they are intended to portray and explain. This being so, one should not be so naïve as to think that everything mentioned in a theory simply exists out there in the outer world. Thus one has to steer a mid path between realism and idealism, that is between the theory that the world exists out there just as we describe it and the theory that on the contrary it is a product of our mental processes. The world revealed by science (or anything else) is a dialectical world – it is brought into being by a dialogue between human consciousness and material stuff. It is between the real and the ideal; and it is both.

Some of these thoughts were brought home to me nearly a decade ago when I was giving a lecture in Santa Barbara, California, about Buddhism. Afterwards a young man came up and asked for the date of my birth. I gave it to him and he looked at me as a write-off. It turned out that Tauruses were not propitious in his eyes. He was, as it happens, the first Westerner I had met who took astrology seriously. He was a harbinger of the counter-culture. What was in his mind? Something as follows, I surmise.

First, he was seeing the apex of the cosmos in what was (then) a new and unfashionable way. He was reacting, perhaps rather blindly, against official science and an 'official' view of the cosmos. Astrology was poised over against legitimate astronomy. He was deeply wrong, and yet he also had a point. For even the astrologer had a place, fleetingly, among those who scan the heavens scientifically. Any theory may be true. He was wrong in that he failed to perceive – what so many others fail to see – that science is essentially revisionary and creative and open. He was no doubt not to be blamed, for the true and shifting shape of sciences is ill-depicted in the world at large and in our schools.

The young man was also part of a wider movement which has come to be known as the counterculture. It was of course no accident that I was in California. Consider the psychology of that delightful region. It can be seen in terms of its spiritual and literal geography.

For long, American consciousness faced two ways. In one direction lay the Old World, with its fascinations and failures. The bold new constitution of the fledgling United States was a gesture itself towards Europe. In the other direction lay the wilderness and the frontier. The nineteenth century saw that frontier rolled back and the vast hinterlands slowly but surely conquered, settled and incorporated. The intrepid went ahead for gold, and this above all lured men to California. And yet, when there, Americans came to realise something. There were no more frontiers, just the amazing ocean. Folk talked about people 'back East'. Unconsciously they were now facing in a different cultural direction.

In the period after World War II that new direction became a lodestar of the counterculture. During the conflict, America had fought a major, brilliant, slow war across the islands of the Pacific. After it was over, hundreds of thousands of Americans were exposed to the unexpectedly delicious and profound culture of conquered Japan. And already Chinese and Japanese immigrants were harbingers of a new Oriental dimension to West Coast culture. If we multiply the Pacific feel by the great new scientific resources poured into California and by the restlessness of those who wanted a new place in the sun, we discover a new and heady equation. California becomes the last frontier of the mind. And since the human mind is brilliant, confused and naughty, California is all these things; and so within it is the counterculture.

The young astrologer showed something. Any new idea, any new cult, rapidly becomes, in California, normal.

California as the wave of the future, if that is what it is

If I tell friends in Europe that California is the wave of the future, they often take it amiss. Surely we in England do things better, long tradition, not many divorces, structures, they mutter. In Italy they enquire about the food, and occasionally mention Firenze and Leonardo. They, of course, miss the point. The past is vital, but I was talking about the future.

Of course, there is an ambiguity about the future. As travel becomes easier, more frontiers are closed, as though totalitarians wish to substitute mental fatigue and danger for the old physical hardships of the voyager. Experience seems to show that the closed society can take a long, sustained grip, despite the heroic extravagances of the rebellious human spirit. Yet one way and another cultural contacts, especially in the Western nations, multiply; and as they do so we get a syncretistic situation – a new world a bit like the old world of the Roman Empire in its heyday.

Then the Mediterranean was a focus of many overlapping and competing religions – the old religions of Greece and Rome, religious philosophies such as Neoplatonism and Stoicism, mystery cults such as those of Isis and Demeter, Eastern-tinged faiths such as Mithraism and Manichaeanism, Judaism and Christianity. Often a citizen of Rome might patronise more than one of these cults – he could adhere to the old gods, be initiated at Eleusis and dabble in Neoplatonism.

Today in the Western democracies particularly, and in California more intensely, men likewise shop around for faiths, and are liable to make experiments in living undreamed of thirty years back. Taoists, Pure Land Buddhists, Zen masters, Hindu swamis, meditation exponents, Benedictine monks, Christian evangelists, Jewish Kabbalists, new forms of Islam, astrology, acupuncture, fringe sects – these form a great smorgasbord of cults and fancies, some serious, others profound, others fashionable, others cliché-ridden, others again explorative. One needs to sift wheat from chaff. But the fact is that we here have a great new meeting of cultures and of forms of spirituality.

Side by side with such experiments in living are the laboratories, observatories, think-tanks and universities. The Californian spirit is also one of intellectual search, at the fringes of science. In a way, the predicament of modern man is summed up. On the one hand, there are the achievements of the intellect; on the other, the offerings of faith for the soul and the feelings. Can they be brought together? The soul quest is so plural, and science so unified, that some disparity between mind and heart is bound to persist. This is something we need to live with; the pluralism of religion is all part of the open society in a plural world. It no doubt is something irreversible, and in this sense there is something in California ineluctably of the future. More staid societies may be sceptical of this, but they can scarcely stay immune. Even in Sweden or Italy, the vogues of the Western world, symbolising and underlying unease, show themselves.

How we all need to take account of all of us

Part of what the counter-culture symbolises, and part of what California says, part indeed of what dancing Hare Krishna devotees say in their own strange way, is that no culture, now, is an island. Every culture tends to impinge on every other. Walk down Oxford Street, London, and whom do you see? Arabs, Cypriots, Americans, Ugandan Indians, Italians, Belgians, Germans, Chinese, Africans, British blacks, Englishmen, Pakistanis, Latin Americans. Many cities in the world experience this plurality. It is a symbol of the fact that every culture and every religion needs in principle to take account of the others. Christianity cannot assume that the problem is atheism: the problem is also Buddhism. The Hindu is aware of the challenge of modern humanism. The Muslim is beginning to worry about the 'idolatrous' religions, despite the old self-assurance. In Africa old cults and thoughts are in interplay with all sorts of new forces, as we have seen. Marxism is acutely aware, even within its own frontiers, of the forces of the spirit, from Solzhenitsyn to the turbulent folk of Central Asia, and from the Orthodoxy of Romania to the Catholicism of modern Poland.

So the long search has two levels. There is the seeking for the right path for the individual or society; and then there is the mapping of the territory seen from that path, so that we can place ourselves in relation to those climbing different slopes or exploring other valleys.

How I place myself

Each person in modern society is in theory prized; and we often in the West value the way in which we accept the burden of making our own individual choices. This applies to the Spirit as much as to anything else. Having been involved in exploring religions and ideologies in this book, and having seen the shifting moods of faith as portrayed through the television series out of which this book grew, I should doubtless place myself. Of course, any decision is provisional; what I think now may easily evaporate in the days to come – but for what it is worth here is a small testament to my experience and reflection, and one which I feel will persist through my life, adapted later I hope, if adaptation be needed.

First, I place myself in my own tradition, which is Christian and (in particular) Scottish Episcopalian. Very often the search occurs within one's own religion; and very often one branches out into the insights and customs of other men when one's own tradition seems to be, in some way, lacking. Therefore, somewhat briefly, I wish to point to the ideas and feelings which are, in my experience, important and which can be incorporated into a new religion based upon my own. I am not saying that everyone should follow my example or ideas. Others will of necessity make different choices and have different perspectives on the search.

Sin, ignorance and meditation

One of the vital and central features of some European religions is a different perspective on the troubles afflicting mankind. Of course, the Christian emphasis upon sin affirms something important about the alienation of man from God. But too often it makes it look as if our troubles have, essentially, to do with a defect of will. But our troubles also stem substantially from a lack of vision – or as Buddhists and Hindus frequently put it, from ignorance. It is largely for this reason that meditation plays so vital a part in Buddhism – for it is a means of clarifying our perception of the true nature of the world. It is a means for overcoming ignorance. This is an element which needs much stronger expression in the Christian outlook. So often our troubles stem from obtuseness, and strength of will can then make matters worse. Consider the heroism of so many who suffer and die in war, and consider how often wars arise from stupid issues.

Further, the Indian tradition has been a counterpoise to the outward-looking energetic Western spirit. The achievements of European and Christian civilisation have been astonishing, but, till recently, gained at the expense of the inner contemplative life. The East may stimulate Christianity to rediscover its old heritage of meditation, once flourishing in the monastic orders and in the late medieval flowering of mysticism.

The personal and the impersonal

The doctrine of the Great Ultimate has another important lesson for the West. Although belief in God brings with it the concept of God as a person, there is a recurrent threat of trivialising God – making him into a sort of superman. Consider those evangelists who talk as though God was at the end of a telephone, and all you need to know is the secret of his number. The Christian heritage, because Jesus is a man as well as God, is perhaps especially prone to a kind of cheap anthropomorphism. Hence we need constant reminding of the 'other side' of God; the impersonal model provided by the Great Ultimate and also by Shankara's concept of *Brahman* is thus salutary.

Let us put it another way. I have argued that the mental aspect of the Universe indicates that matter transcends itself. Old-fashioned materialism fails to take biology seriously. The cosmos is, as it were, two-faced – one face exhibits the material, the other the mental side. It would be highly fitting if – in another realm – the divine Being were to have two faces, the one inscrutable, non-human, darkly mysterious, and the other showing affinity to the creative personhood of men.

A further value which the Western Christian can derive from the Chinese tradition is a sense of stronger solidarity between man and the natural world. An unfortunate consequence of the Christian heritage, as it penetrated into modern philosophy, was a deep gulf perceived between man and matter, between soul and non-soul. This dualism did, it is true, pave the way for the independent investigation of matter, unhindered by theological or old philosophical views about the world, but the price was a reinforcement of an unrealistically arrogant conception of man's place in (or rather *over*) nature. That arrogance has proved dangerous most obviously in technological insensitiveness. Modern materialism which engendered that technology itself springs from this dualism. When the mind is differentiated sharply from matter and the material sciences flourish, they become ambitious to explain the mind, by abolishing it and seeing it as itself a form of matter. Thus behaviouristic psychologists can explore the mind by ignoring consciousness, feelings and so forth. An infection of the spirit of the Tao may moderate the fatal dualism, and restore a greater sense of harmony between men and other living and non-living beings.

Islam, as we have seen, is both close to and distant from the Christian heritage which formed part of its background. One feature it has maintained is a strong sense of solidarity between religious values and social and political practice. This has led it towards theocracy, an ideal embodied in some contemporary Islamic countries such as Libya, Pakistan and Saudi Arabia. I think the ideal of such solidarity is good, but if within the framework of Christian values in the modern world we were to apply this ideal the result would be superficially at variance with the theocratic model. Let me explain.

The progress of creativity in the arts and sciences depends in good measure upon the open, critical mind, likewise the respect for the individual is embodied best in an open society. These achievements of modern social democracy must be protected. Given such a commitment to freedom, and given too the interactive character of the contemporary globe, a theocracy of the old sort becomes impossible – for the commitment necessarily implies an acceptance of pluralism and toleration. In brief the application of the ideal of solidarity between religious and social values leads to a new appreciation of the Christian doctrine of the Spirit, which bloweth where it listeth. The doctrine would look, in brief, something like this.

First, man is made in the image of God because, among other reasons, he participates in creativity. In exploring nature with depth and brilliance scientists echo divine creation. But if a condition of this is letting imagination and criticism act freely, then this indicates an important aspect of the freedom which God grants to men. It also means that the human spirit cannot be rightly shackled by a unified dogma. Christianity itself has to learn freedom and toleration. Thus the Christian must also see alternative religions and points of view as symptomatic in principle of the work of the Holy Spirit. No longer can Christian faith be interpreted with narrow evangelical exclusiveness (though Christians have to learn to tolerate the narrow-minded brethren too).

So we end in a paradox: that we can learn a solidarity from Islam which expresses itself pluralistically.

Images and the limits of speech

Both Islam and Judaism dramatise the war on anthropomorphism by banning images of God. The marvellous geometric designs and arabesques of Islamic art result from this restrictive channelling of artistic energy. But maybe the war on anthropomorphism is better conducted by stressing the Great Ultimate, the impersonal Being behind the more human face of God. At any rate, the Judaic and Islamic distaste for images places the problem of symbolism squarely before us. It is here that my Indian preferences show, at least in the context of our modern world. For the use of images itself connects with the acceptance of pluralism. And yet at the same time we must always remain alert to the limits of symbolism. Let me digress by considering the faces of Christ in and beyond the New Testament.

The faces of Christ

It is hard to read the Gospels without being moved and baffled. The figure of Jesus seems mysteriously elusive. For Jesus is presented in so many ways, and yet somehow none of the categories seem quite to catch him. Part of the time he is the miraculous healer; part he is the convivial party-goer; part he is rabbi and preacher; part he is Messiah; his acts are sometimes political; yet he can also ride into Jerusalem on an ass. He is Son of Man, beloved of his Father; and he is also the suffering servant. How can the central figure of the Christian faith manage to be so ambiguous? There are at least three explanations, the third of which is the most relevant to my present argument. First, Jesus as a creative figure was in various ways unexpected – not fitting into roles laid down by existing conventional or even unconventional thought. Second, he is a numinous figure, expressing the divine mystery, and characteristically the numinous crosses, or falls between, categories. Third, Jesus had a universal message, in the sense that many differing kinds of men were summoned to be his followers, and also in the sense that by the time the Gospels were written the faith was branching out into the Hellenistic and Roman world beyond the confines of Israel and Judaism. And a universal faith has to appeal to different facets of human experience, character and concern. Men are concerned with health, death, power and so on, and Jesus' acts say something to each of these anxieties; his character appeals by turn to the fun-lover, the ascetic, the idle, the hardworking and so on. In art, the various faces of Christ are multiplied – from the Pantocrator in the Eastern icon to the frail figure of the Renaissance crucifixions. This is relevant to a feature of Hindu thinking about gods and images.

The one and the many

As we have seen, it is a commonplace of Hindu thought to look upon the many gods as so many images of the one Divine Being. But, the critic may say, why have the many then: why not just keep the One? Some in the Indian tradition, notably the forerunners and founders of the Sikh religion, have indeed said this very thing. The characteristic reply to this criticism is as follows:

> We keep the many because the gods signify different things – Ganesh reminds us of fortune and wealth; Kali shows us destruction; Sarasvati tells us of learning; Shiva reminds us of yoga and austerity; Krishna speaks of divine and human love – and so it goes on. The symbols are multiple because life is complex, and men have differing needs, locations, loyalties. So the many gods help to give us a richer picture of divine consensus than a single One could. We have therefore a method in our manifoldness. Consider – you can't have God as both male and female in one statue, except as an unsatisfactory third thing, namely a hermaphrodite. It is better to have a male and a consort, as we do in India. That symbolises the different aspects of God better.

Of course, it may not be necessary to concretise the images and the gods, for the same effect could be achieved through a host of symbols depicting different, sometimes even apparently conflicting, facets of the divine. In a way this is what happens in relation to the faces of Christ in both Gospels and art. Thus religion can perhaps be hospitable to a variety of symbols; and Christianity itself can learn again to appreciate the ways in which the symbols speak to differing personal and collective concerns.

Yet always there is a limit of speech. This partly ties up with the impersonal Ultimate lying beyond the faces which God presents to mankind. That limit of speech at one level can be experienced within the world – a major lesson to be learned from Zen. For Zen by breaking our categories can cause us to see the world fresh – as it is, uncontaminated with human concerns and lying beyond conceptual understanding. Likewise, the breaking up of concepts and symbols is one phase of faith, in which we try to see into the ineffable non-personal divine essence. For this reason even that great map-maker of divine territory, Aquinas, could come to see his monumental work as so much chaff: he was both right and wrong.

Incidentally, Zen's breaking of concepts can have relevance to the creative enterprises like science. Very often the problem is constituted by the way the world is perceived – we may be baffled because the concepts we use cannot cope with the data. It is at this point useful to undergo something of the Zen discipline, for out of the destruction of old concepts new visions may arise.

Pluralism and cultural riches

If a richness of symbols is important, so we should not strive dogmatically for a homogeneous human society. It is true that each society needs some measure of agreement and so some set of common patterns of behaviour. But it surely does not follow that such agreement entails cultural conformity. A sad feature of the world today is that men in power so often wish to impose such conformity, with the result that minority groups lose customs and rights. There can be a kind of cultural genocide, as in Tibet (it is not that the Tibetans are killed off but their traditions are increasingly under pressure and their religious institutions tamed and eliminated). Nowhere is this tendency more apparent than among the peoples of small-scale societies. Hence the 'primal' and smaller religions themselves now stand as a symbol for something important, the dignity of individual cultures. Clearly such societies will change and adapt to large outside forces. But cultural diversity remains an important value. Does this then mean that the Christian should no longer send forth missionaries? Where is the old spirit of evangelism and the desire to save men's souls?

Here some vital points have to be made. First, the only satisfactory motive for trying to convert another person or group is that you are sure you have something excellent to confer upon him or them. It is a gift, not an imposition, and moreover it should not be a dangerous gift. Now part of the question springs from that small word 'sure'. For one of the very effects of the long search is that we see different approaches to the truth. Can we be again so absolutely certain that only ours is right or best? Moreover, if the attempt to convert must depend on the excellence of the gift, first we have to see what already is excellent in the receiving culture (if the Christian pearl replaces a Buddhist diamond, it is no real gift). But this exploration of the excellence of others itself implies much caution about the gift. Perhaps those recent missionaries who have stressed the policy of Christian *presence* are right. If Christianity shines through a life then that person exhibits the faith and should not need to preach, since the goodness of the gift will attract a genuine interest.

It is already apparent that my approach is to assimilate what I can use from others. Some would criticise this as syncretism. But it is an approach which can be generalised. It is not for me to lay down how others should conduct their search. If I begin from a variety of Scottish religion, others will doubtless begin from many different places, including no place at all. Some will not feel able to use some of the main Christian ideas, for instance. But even the agnostic has something to learn from Christianity, Buddhism and the other religions. In brief there are virtues in being eclectic.

In effect, there are only two choices. One is to close the mind, and that in turn could be done either by external or internal censorship (in other words police or the subconscious). The other is to remain open to social and world influences. The first choice looks like a rejection of syncretism. It is in a way, but rejection itself makes a major concession – it takes seriously what it rejects. The closed mind is itself in a funny way open, but not in the way which it intends.

Moral values

I have said little about the effect of all this on our personal moral values. Yet a search which does not bear some ethical fruit is not worth conducting. Part of the importance of the search lies in the fact that religions are vitally relevant to human happiness and welfare.

Toleration of other practices and points of view of course follows from the approach here presented. But this in turn presupposes a sense of security. So often our cruelties and stupidity in dealing with others spring from fear and a sense of insecurity and inferiority.

The central insight of the Christian Eucharist is that in it the person of faith is identified with Christ – he participates in Christ's essence. In so doing he participates in both the joy and sorrow of God. He can have nothing greater to gain or lose. So the Christian gains security – or peace as it is otherwise called. It is so to say an exalted humbleness, in accordance with the pattern of Jesus' own life. That this attitude is somewhat rare among Christians symbolises the tragedy of the faith.

Buddhist serenity and the banishing of the very idea of the self represent another approach to the goal of security; and much of devotional Hinduism stresses the way in which love flows into the worshipper from the God worshipped, and such love calms the worries of the world.

Of course the pursuit of inner peace can proceed outside the framework of religious commitment, and in modern times the development of psychoanalysis and psychotherapy have provided, generally speaking, non-religious tools towards spiritual poise.

The other side of security is the ability to provide it in some measure to others. If hell is other people it is because hatred and contempt shown to one tend to shatter feelings of security. One of the main successes of Islam has been the creation of a sense of brotherhood and equal dignity, among men at least – one factor in the continuing spread of Islam in black Africa, too used to the permeation of Christian teaching with racist values.

However, ultimately the test of ethics is general happiness. How is that perceived? Often religion shoots our joys into another world – a heaven, a Pure Land, a happy hunting ground. Such projection can seem to be merely an escape from sadness down here. Yet a main cause of continued interest in religions lies in their capacity to reorder our world and give security and a sense of insight into the relationships around the triangle. This is the primary magnetism of religion and no doubt we become dissatisfied with kinds of Christianity that centre everything on ethical conduct.

The further quest

I hope this passage among the world's religions has helped to show something of their spiritual values. As the globe changes its configurations, so the religious ideologies will change too. And as the configurations of our own lives change we shall doubtless search for different things. There are many paths through the landscape.

GLOSSARY

An asterisk indicates a reference to the relevant entry elsewhere in the glossary. Where necessary a guide to pronunciation in English is given: for example 'Shī'a (she-ah)'.

ADVAITA (ud-vie-ta): the non-dualistic version of *Vedanta, associated above all with the name of the Indian philosopher and theologian Śankara. It is non-dualistic because it affirms the idea that the eternal soul in man is identical with *Brahman, the Divine Reality. Your soul and mine are also thus identical, for we both are in essence the Divine Being.

AHIṀSĀ (uh-ing-saa): non-injury (towards living beings). A concept prominent in Jainism and Buddhism, and later in the thought and life of Gandhi. Basically it involves respect for life, but Gandhi gave it a political dimension in his advocacy of non-violence as a method of gaining freedom for India.

ALBIGENSIANS (alby-jents-ians): a medieval sect who attracted official repression, the so-called Albigensian Crusade. They were mainly found in south-west France, and had views not unlike those of the Manichaeans, but within a definitely Christian framework.

ALLAH (ull-aah): the one God, literally. The name was used by Muhammad for the Divine Being who revealed himself through the Koran.

AMIDA (um-idah): the Japanese name for *Amitābha.

AMITĀBHA (um-it-aab-ha): the celestial Buddha of immeasurable light, who created the Pure Land, the paradise in the West to which the faithful Buddhist who calls upon Amitābha with faith will be translated, according to the *Pure Land School of *Mahāyāna Buddhism. His Japanese name is *Amida.

ANGLICAN: adjective for those people and institutions who are in communion with and are historically related to the Church of England. Very often such churches are referred to as episcopalian, such as the Protestant Episcopal Church in the USA. Anglicans are held together by acknowledgment of a common heritage rather than by much in the way of a formal central organisation.

ARHANT/ARHAT (ar-hunt,ar-hut): literally 'worthy one' – the title given to those in the Buddhist tradition who have already in this life attained to *nirvāna or liberation. The status of the arhant, though high, is less than that of one who has attained to full Buddhahood or Enlightenment (but being a Buddha entails being an arhant, since a Buddha has attained to living liberation).

ĀTMAN (aat-mun): Sanskrit term for the self. In much of Indian philosophy and religion it refers to the eternal soul, lying within a person and not to be identified with the ego as we ordinarily experience it, which undergoes changes, for the ātman is beyond change. It is sometimes identified with the Divine Being, as in *Advaita Vedanta. In English it is usually translated self, sometimes spelt with a capital, i.e. Self.

AVALOKITESHVARA/AVALOKITEŚVARA (uv-a-lawk-it-esh-vara): the *Bodhisattva who as his name implies looks down on the living beings in the world with compassion. He is associated with *Amitābha. In his Chinese version he acquired female characteristics as Kwanyin.

AVATAR: an incarnation of Vishnu, in the Hindu tradition. The most important were Krishna and Rama.

BHAGAVADGITA (b-hugger-vud-ghee-taa): the Song of the Lord, and the most influential holy book in India.

BHAKTI (b-huck-ti): loving devotion to God, as described in the Indian tradition.

BODHISATTVA (bawd-he-sutt-va): a Buddha-to-be, or one destined to become a Buddha. In Mahāyāna Buddhism there arose the idea of the Buddha-to-be who puts off his liberation (*nirvāna) in order to help other living beings on the road to escape from suffering. The most famous of Bodhisattvas is *Avalokiteshvara.

BRAHMAN (brummun): originally a word for the power which operates in the ancient Indian sacrificial and priestly system. Through this power changes were wrought in the world (it was believed). But in the *Upanishads there arose the speculation that the same power is operative throughout the universe. Hence Brahman came to be the word for God, sometimes seen as a personal being, sometimes seen as a non-personal force sustaining the universe.

BRAHMIN: the priestly class in India from ancient times. They have the top status amid the four classes which constitute the main framework of the *caste system. The term is connected with *Brahman.

BUDDHA (bood-ha): Enlightened One, i.e. one who has gained bodhi (bawd-hi). In our age of the universe *Gautama (also *Gotama) the Buddha lived from roughly 563 to 483 BC. His teaching was designed to restore men's knowledge of the truth or *dharma. Later on in the development of Buddhism there arose the notion of heavenly Buddhas who are like gods and attract devotion. The chief of these is *Amitābha.

CARGO CULT: a type of religious movement found in the south Pacific, notably in Papua and New Guinea, in which there is expectation of a divine delivery of cargo – good things such as the Westerner has and which the faithful deserve to have.

CASTE: the social stratification in India (and to some extent elsewhere, as in Ceylon). It consists in a structure involving endogamy and commensality. That is, people of a given caste normally only marry others of that caste (endogamy) and normally likewise only eat together with other caste members (commensality). Caste arose in India partly from the old class system of the Aryans (see *Brahmins), partly from religious differences of practice, partly from craft guilds, partly from the assimilation of tribal groups into the main Hindu social structure. Beneath the regular castes there are the *Harijans or untouchables, who are 'unclean' either by descent or by occupation (because they are, say, sweepers or fishermen).

CATHOLICISM: the usual name for the Roman Catholic Church, defined as catholic or universal, and owing allegiance to the Pope in Rome. Other branches of Christianity also claim to be Catholic, such as the Orthodox and the Anglicans.

CH'ĀN (chaan): literally meditation, and used as the title of a type of Buddhism supposedly introduced into China from India by Bodhdharma in 520 BC. Ch'ān is the Chinese equivalent of **dhyāna* in Sanskrit. The Japanese rendering of the term is *Zen. Ch'ān Buddhism was somewhat influenced by *Taoism.

CHARISMA (car-is-ma): a term used for the charm, radiance and leadership qualities of holy religious people.

CHINVAT BRIDGE: an idea originating in *Zoroastrianism but absorbed by Islam – namely a bridge across which the dead have to pass. The just survive it, the unjust topple into the abyss.

CONFUCIANISM: the religion stemming from the tradition of ancient China reformulated by *Confucius. In later times it was sanctioned by the State, and its general teachings also included the reverence for ancestors (misleadingly called ancestor-worship in the West). The cult of Confucius himself increased in importance, while the study of the Confucian classics became the norm for the education of the Chinese élite, until the modern period.

CONFUCIUS: this is the Latinised name of Master K'ung, who lived from 551 to 479 BC and whose work in reformulating the tradition, as expressed in the classics which he edited, gave rise to a systematic ethic for the Chinese élite. His own teachings are to be found in the brief Analects, consisting for the most part of aphorisms.

DEVANAGARI (day-va-nuggery): the script in which Sanskrit and modern Hindu are written. It is often considered to have a divine origin, and the term literally means 'belonging to the city of the gods'.

DHARMA (d-her-ma): the law, truth or teaching – a term used to express the central transcendent teachings of Hinduism and of Buddhism. It implies that the truth about the universe is also a norm to which men should conform their behaviour.

DHARMAKAYA (d-herma-kaaya): the Truth Aspect or Truth Body of the Buddha – a Mahāyāna conception referring to the Absolute nature of Buddhahood, which is the same as the *Void.

DHYĀNA (dhyaana): the Sanskrit term for meditation, following certain methods of mind control. Different forms of meditation are used in different schools, e.g. the *Yoga School, Buddhism and so on.

DIAMOND VEHICLE: the title sometimes accorded to Tibetan-style Buddhism, as distinguished both from *Mahāyāna and the *Theravāda. The type of Buddhism in question has strong elements of *Tantrism.

ESCHATOLOGY (eskatology): the doctrine of the last things (in Greek, *eschata*), at the end of human history, with the coming of the Messiah, etc. Such doctrines are prominent in Judaism, Christianity and Islam, partly under the influence of *Zoroastrianism.

GAUTAMA (gow-tum-ah): name of the Buddha as spelt in Sanskrit, the *Pali version being *Gotama.

GOTAMA (gaw-tum-ah): see GAUTAMA.

GNOSTICISM: a web of ideas and religious movements quite common in the ancient world around the time of the early development of Christianity. The word derives from the Greek term *gnosis* meaning knowledge, and in particular experience of God as a kind of inner way of knowing. Gnostic elements are to be found in Christianity, notably in St John's Gospel. Sometimes, however, Gnosticism moved in the direction of despising the world, a view unacceptable to mainstream Christianity.

HARIJAN (hurry-jun): the name given by Gandhi to the untouchables. Literally it means sons of Hari or sons of God.

HASIDISM/CHASSIDISM: a form of Jewish piety and mysticism deriving principally from the teachings of Baal Shem Tov, an eighteenth-century East European teacher and visionary.

HESYCHASM (hezzy-kasm): a mystical movement in medieval Eastern Orthodoxy, involving techniques of meditation and the use of the so-called Jesus Prayer, the repetition of which leads to vital spiritual effects ('Jesus Christ, have mercy on me a sinner'). The term hesychasm derives from a Greek word meaning 'peace'.

HIJRA (hidge-ra): Muhammad's migration from Mecca to Medina in AD 622, taken as the base year for calculating the calendar according to *Islam.

HĪNAYĀNA (heen-ah-yaana): the Lesser Vehicle as distinguished from the Greater Vehicle or *Mahāyāna. It was originally a term of abuse and not much favoured by those who belong to its chief modern manifestation, namely the *Theravāda.

HINDUISM: a federation of cults held together chiefly by the fact that they occur within Indian society. Caste, belief in reincarnation and Indianness are the main characteristics of Hinduism. But many Hindus subscribe in one way or another to belief in God, perceived under varying forms as Vishnu, Shiva or other lesser divinities.

HUMANISM: the modern doctrine that the ultimate values in the world are human. Most humanists are atheists, though they respect the Christian precept to love one's neighbour.

IMAM (im-aam): one who leads the congregation in the mosque, and who is typically elected to do so by the local community. The title is also used for the leaders of the whole people under God according to the *Shī'as, who await the coming of the 'hidden Imam', as a kind of *Messiah.

ĪSHVARA/ĪŚVARA (eesh-vara): the Lord, a term used to refer to God in his personal manifestation in the Hindu context.

ISLAM (is-laam): literally submission to God or *Allah, and commonly used as the title of the faith preached by Muhammad (the term Mohammedanism is incidentally somewhat offensive to Muslims, i.e. adherents of Islam, because it suggests a parallel with Christianity: Muhammad though greatly revered is not divine, a blasphemy according to his teaching).

ISMAĪLĪ (is-ma-eely): an esoteric type of *Shī'a Muslim; one of the main branches of the sect being ruled over by the Aga Khan.

JAPJI (jupjee): the Sikh confession of faith and daily prayer, beginning with the words 'This Being is one: he is eternal'.

JĀTI (jaati): the Sanskrit word commonly translated as *caste.

JHĀNA (jhaana): the *Pali term for meditation. See also DHYĀNA.

JIHAD (ji-hud): the duty to engage in holy war if called upon to do so, in the Islamic tradition. It is one of the so-called pillars of Islam, which summarise the chief duties of the faithful.

JINA (jinna): 'victor', a title accorded to the great heroes of Jainism. The term *Jaina* means one who follows a *jina*.

JĪVANMUKTI (jeevan-mook-tea): living release in the Indian tradition, that is the state of a person who in this life has gained *mukti and merely lives out the rest of his life awaiting a final liberation from the round of rebirth.

KABBALAH (cub-allah): the main Jewish mystical tradition, developing from out of Babylon in the first place, from about the sixth century, and later out of Western Europe and especially Spain. It stressed esoteric ways of interpreting scripture, and the correspondence between universal rhythms and the actions and consciousness of men.

KAMI (come-ee): the *Shinto term for a god or spirit.

KARMA (cur-ma): the law determining one's status in the next life, according to the Indian and other traditions. If I commit a bad deed (karma literally means deed), then I shall be likely to be reborn in inferior circumstances. Conversely, virtue conduces to greater spiritual opportunities in the life to come.

K'UNG (coong): see CONFUCIUS.

LOTUS SUTRA: the most famous of *Mahāyāna scriptures, which promises the faithful rebirth in the *Pure Land.

MAHĀBHĀRATA (muh-ah-baar-utter): one of the great Indian epics, the other being the Rāmāyana. It includes, as one section, the famous Bhagavadgita.

MAHĀTMA (muh-aatma): a title accorded to some famous spiritual leaders in India, notably Gandhi.

MAHĀYĀNA (ma-haa-yaana): The Great Vehicle or Greater Vehicle, namely that wing of Buddhism prevalent in East Asian countries historically, deriving from transformations of Buddhism in a direction away from the more austere *Theravāda-type religion. It is so called because it offers a wider way to salvation – to *nirvāna, which is available both to lay folk and monks (whereas the Theravāda has tended to make monasticism a condition of liberation).

MANICHAEANISM (manny-key-an-ism): the religion of Mani (third century AD), a Persian noble. He brought together elements from *Zoroastrianism, Buddhism and Christianity. The faith involved a sharp contrast between good and evil forces at work in the world. A notable convert was Augustine, later to become a Christian. Manichaeanism had a late offshoot in the *Albigensian movement.

MANTRA (muntra): holy verse in Hindu and Buddhist contexts.

MESSIAH: the anointed one, and future deliverer and judge (but in Christianity the Messiah is Jesus Christ, who is past, but also due to return again).

METEMPSYCHOSIS (met-emp-sigh-cozy-ss): a Greek term sometimes used in lieu of reincarnation or rebirth.

MOKṢA/MOKSHA (mawk-sha): ultimate liberation in the Hindu tradition, usually conceived as being liberation from the round of reincarnation.

MORMONS: the generally used nickname for those who belong to the Church of Jesus Christ and the Latter Day Saints, founded in the nineteenth century by Joseph Smith II, and with headquarters in Salt Lake City, Utah.

MUEZZIN: the person who from the minaret calls the faithful to prayer at dawn, in Islam.

MUHARRAM (moo-hurrum): the name refers to the first month of the Muslim year, which is based on the phases of the moon. The tenth of Muharram is sacred to the *Shī'as, for the festival commemorates the death of Husain, son of Ali, at Karbala in Iraq, now a place of pilgrimage.

MUKTI (mook-ti): an alternative Sanskrit term for *mokṣa.

NICENE CREED: the creed as formulated at the Council of Nicaea, convened to deal with the so-called Arian heresy, in AD 325, under the presidency of the emperor Constantine.

NIRVĀṆA (near-vaana): literally the cooling-off or going out as of a flame – the main word used in Buddhism for final release from the round of rebirth (*samsara). One who gains nirvāna in this life is usually referred to as an *arhat.

NUMINOUS: a term invented by Rudolf Otto, in his book *The Idea of the Holy*, to refer to what is awesome and mysterious. He thought of it as the central manifestation of the divine in human experience.

ORPHISM (or-fism): an ancient Greek religious movement focused on the mythic figure of Orpheus.

ORTHODOXY: in the Christian context this refers to the Eastern Orthodox churches which maintain 'right worship', which is what the word literally means.

PĀLI (paali): the language of the scriptures of the so-called *Theravādin countries (Sri Lanka, Burma, Thailand, etc.). It derives from a North Indian dialect and stands to *Sanskrit much as Italian does to Latin.

PARSEES: see ZOROASTRIANISM.

PURE LAND SCHOOL: a movement within Mahāyāna Buddhism stressing devotion to *Amitabha and the *Bodhisattva *Avalokiteshvara. It promises heaven to those who have faith.

SAṀSĀRA (sung-sara): a term used in the Indian tradition for the process of change in the universe, and in particular for the round of reincarnation to which living beings are subject.

SANSKRIT: the language of the Hindu scriptures and of other classical writings in the Indian tradition. It is related to Latin and Greek, and is written in the script known as *Devanagari.

SHAIKH (shy-ch): a prestigious person in general, but more particularly in Islam a religious leader or head of a community (e.g. among the Sufis).

SHAMAN: a spiritually endowed individual of somewhat visionary temperament, found in various societies such as Siberian tribes, North American Indians and so on.

SHARĪ'A (shar-ee-ah): Islamic law.

SHĪ'A (she-ah): the more easterly branch of Islam, prevalent from Iraq through to Pakistan and beyond. They trace their spiritual pedigree back to Ali, son-in-law of the Prophet himself.

SHINTO (shin-taw): the way of the gods, and the traditional religion of Japan, antedating the introduction of Buddhism.

SHIRK (sheerk): the Islamic term for idolatry, that is having some God beside the one God – this being the supreme blasphemy from a Muslim point of view.

STŪPA (stooper): a mound containing relics of some Buddhist holy person, which became formalised into the bell-shaped white structure of many Buddhist temples, and which also in another variant developed into the Chinese pagoda.

SUNNA (soonna): the more traditional branch of Islam, prevalent in most Arab countries and in West Africa.

ŚŪNYA (shoonya): the *Void or Emptiness, which is, according to some teachings in Mahāyāna Buddhism, both the inner nature of things and also the focus of inner meditational experience.

T'AI CHI (tie-jee): Chinese for the Great Ultimate, that is to say the Absolute from which the rest of reality derives according to the teachings of later Confucianism.

TAIPINGS (tie-pings): followers of the Chinese prophet Hung in the mid-part of the nineteenth century, who preached a kingdom of heavenly peace (which is partly what the name means) and led a rebellion which suceeded in capturing the southern capital of Nanking. His teaching had Christian elements.

TANTRISM: a form of Hindu or Buddhist religion, prevalent in North India and Tibet in medieval times, emphasising sacramental means of enlightenment, and sometimes too the breaking of sexual, caste and other taboos as a means of spiritual advancement.

TAO (dow): the Way, considered by Taoists both to be a path of conduct and the principle governing the whole universe. The aim is to

live in harmony with nature: since nature acts spontaneously without effort, so the wise man peacefully 'acts without acting'.

TAOISM (Dow-ism): the western term for the religion which sees as the central principle the Way or *Tao. Supposedly it was founded by Lao-tzu in the sixth century, but he was almost certainly a merely legendary figure to whom was ascribed the famous book of Tao, the *Tao Te-ching* (Dow de jing).

TAPAS (tup-us): literally heat, but used to mean austerity as practised in the Indian context.

THERAVĀDIN (tay-ra-vaadin): the adjective from Theravāda, literally the doctrine of the elders and the name usually given to the kind of Buddhism found in Ceylon and much of South-East Asia. It is the surviving school from the Hīnayāna or Lesser Vehicle tradition of Buddhism. Its scriptures are written in *Pāli.

T'IEN (tyen): Chinese for heaven and also God.

TOMMAH (tom-ah): a Torajan priest, in Celebes (Sulawesi) in Indonesia.

TORAH (taw-rah): Jewish law as revealed by God and recorded in the first five books of the Hebrew Bible (Old Testament).

TRIPITAKA (trip-it-aka): the Buddhist scriptures. The term literally means three baskets, because the scriptures are divided into three main sections, dealing with the Buddha's discourses, the rules of the Order, and metaphysical analysis.

UPANISHADS/UPANIṢADS (oop-un-ish-ads): ancient Indian scriptures, part of the so-called *Veda. They consist in discussions and mythological explanations of various aspects of the ancient Vedic rituals. They also convey a powerful set of philosophical ideas.

VEDĀNTA (vay-daan-ta): Hindu theology based upon the Vedic scriptures; the term means literally the end (or point) of the Veda.

VOID: the unspeakable essence of the world in Māhayāna Buddism – the *Śūnya.

YOGA (yaw-ga): the general name for a body of practices in the Indian tradition involving both mental and spiritual discipline. It is also used for a specific school of thought within Hinduism, the Yoga school. The ultimate aim of yogis' methods is to purify consciousness and gain liberation (*mokṣa) from the round of *saṁsāra.

ZEN: A type of Buddhism influential in Japan. It has two branches, Rinzai and Soto, the former emphasising the sudden nature of the enlightenment experience known as *satori* and using special methods, including the posing of problems or *koans* which by their paradoxical nature break down preconceptions about the nature of reality.

ZOROASTER/ZARATHUSTRA (Zarathoostra): Zoroaster is the Greek form of the Persian name Zarathustra. Zoroaster was the founder of *Zoroastrianism, and lived some think in the early sixth century BC. His teachings are found in the ancient poems known as the Gathas. His religious message seems mainly to have been preached by him in eastern Persia. But there is much uncertainty about his biography.

ZOROASTRIANISM: the religion stemming from the teaching of *Zoroaster. It became the official faith of the Persian Empire, but was extensively weakened by the coming of *Islam. Its modern adherents are referred to often as Parsees, a term literally meaning 'Persians', though their main centre is in Western India.

Further Reading

This list is very selective, but the books themselves include ideas about further reading. The last book on the list supplements the glossary.

NINIAN SMART *The Religious Experience of Mankind* (Scribner, 1969; Fontana, 1971).

TREVOR LING *A History of Religion East and West* (Macmillan, 1969).

R. C. ZAEHNER, ed. *The Concise Encyclopedia of Living Faiths* (Hutchinson, new ed. 1971).

R. C. ZAEHNER *Hinduism* (Oxford University Press, 1966).

RICHARD ROBINSON *The Buddhist Religion: An Historical Introduction* (Dickenson Publications, 1970).

EDWYN BEVAN *Christianity* (Thornton Butterworth, 1932).

JOHN TAYLOR *The Primal Vision* (SCM Press, 1969).

EUGENE BOROWITZ and others *The Bar Mitzvah Book* (Praeger, 1975).

ALFRED GUILLAUME *Islam* (Penguin Books, 1969).

NINIAN SMART *Mao* (Fontana, 1974).

HOWARD SMITH *Confucius* (Paladin, new ed. 1974).

H. G. CREEL *Chinese Thought from Confucius to Mao Tse Tung* (University of Chicago Press, 1963).

RAYMOND HAMMER *Japan's Religious Ferment: Christian Presence amid Faiths Old and New* (SCM Press, 1961).

GEOFFREY PARRINDER *Dictionary of Non-Christian Religions* (Hulton, 1971).

UNITED KINGDOM
PORTUGAL
SPAIN
FRANCE
GERMANY
SWITZ.
DENMARK
SWEDEN
LITHUANIA
CZECHOSLOVAKIA
ITALY
ROMANIA
U.S.S.R.
The Maghreb
ALGERIA
TUNISIA
GREECE
Mt Olympus
TURKEY
SYRIA
LEBANON
IRAQ
ISRAEL
IRAN
AFGHANISTAN
PAKISTAN
R. Indus
R. Nile
EGYPT
R. Euphrates
Sumer
SAUDI ARABIA
SUDAN
ETHIOPIA
1
2
3
4
5
6
7
8
9
10
11
12
13
14
15
16
17
18
19
20
21
22
23
24
25
26
27
28
29
30
31
32
33
34
35
36
37
38
39
40
41
42
43
44
45
46
47
48
68

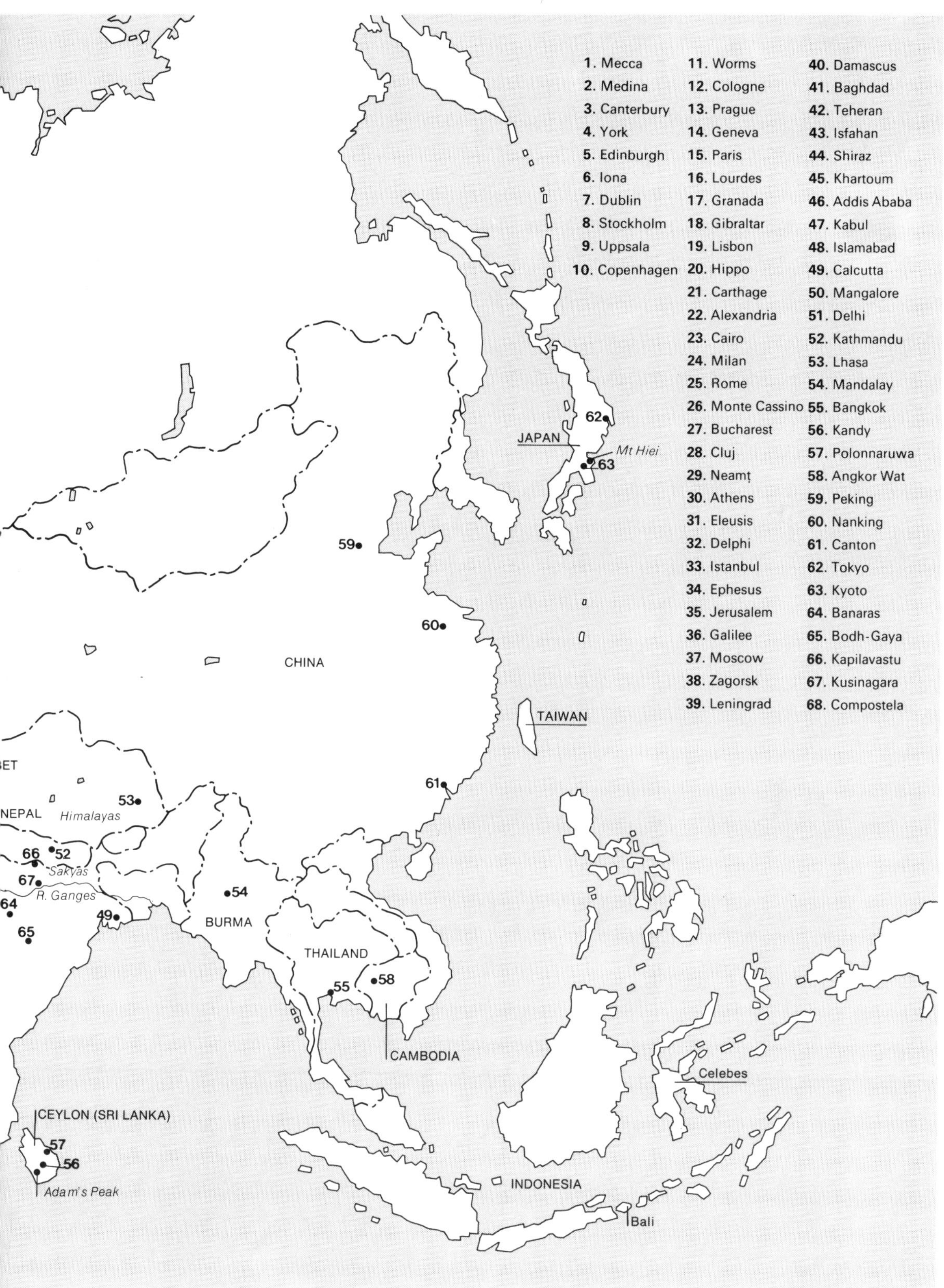
1. Mecca
2. Medina
3. Canterbury
4. York
5. Edinburgh
6. Iona
7. Dublin
8. Stockholm
9. Uppsala
10. Copenhagen
11. Worms
12. Cologne
13. Prague
14. Geneva
15. Paris
16. Lourdes
17. Granada
18. Gibraltar
19. Lisbon
20. Hippo
21. Carthage
22. Alexandria
23. Cairo
24. Milan
25. Rome
26. Monte Cassino
27. Bucharest
28. Cluj
29. Neamț
30. Athens
31. Eleusis
32. Delphi
33. Istanbul
34. Ephesus
35. Jerusalem
36. Galilee
37. Moscow
38. Zagorsk
39. Leningrad
40. Damascus
41. Baghdad
42. Teheran
43. Isfahan
44. Shiraz
45. Khartoum
46. Addis Ababa
47. Kabul
48. Islamabad
49. Calcutta
50. Mangalore
51. Delhi
52. Kathmandu
53. Lhasa
54. Mandalay
55. Bangkok
56. Kandy
57. Polonnaruwa
58. Angkor Wat
59. Peking
60. Nanking
61. Canton
62. Tokyo
63. Kyoto
64. Banaras
65. Bodh-Gaya
66. Kapilavastu
67. Kusinagara
68. Compostela
JAPAN
Mt Hiei
CHINA
TAIWAN
ET
NEPAL
Himalayas
Sakyas
R. Ganges
BURMA
THAILAND
CAMBODIA
Celebes
CEYLON (SRI LANKA)
Adam's Peak
INDONESIA
Bali

INDEX

Bold figures indicate illustrations

Picture Credits

Holy Places

31 Brian Brake. John Hillelson Agency; 32 Josephine Powell. Camera Press; 33 Henri Cartier-Bresson. John Hillelson Agency; 34 Abu Hander. Daily Telegraph Colour Library; 35 Abu Hander. Daily Telegraph Colour Library; 36 Bury Peerless; 37 Ian Berry. John Hillelson Agency.

Temples

51 Georg Gerster. John Hillelson Agency; 52 Edwin Smith; 53 Reflejo. Susan Griggs Agency; 54 Paolo Koch, Rapho; 55 William Macquitty; 56 Bruno Barbey. John Hillelson Agency; 57 Tony Ray-Jones. John Hillelson Agency; 58 Peter Montagnon. BBC.

Priests

65 Mischa Scorer. BBC; 66 Elliott Erwitt. John Hillelson Agency; 67 Colin Davey. Camera Press; 68 Sonia Halliday; 69 Jean Laffes/Gamma. John Hillelson Agency; 70 Werner Bischof. John Hillelson Agency.

Holy Times

77 Sonia Halliday; 78 Bury Peerless; 79 Jaroslav Poncar. Bruce Coleman Agency; 80 Ted Spiegel. John Hillelson Agency; 81 Baldev/Sygma. John Hillelson Agency; 82 Albert Moldway. Susan Griggs Agency; 83 Bruno Barbey. John Hillelson Agency; 84 Jehangir Gazdar. Susan Griggs Agency; 85 Radio Times Hulton Picture Library; 86 Radio Times Hulton Picture Library; 87 Micha Bar-Am. John Hillelson Agency.

Means

93 Bury Peerless; 94 Geoff Howard; 95 Cornell Capa. John Hillelson Agency; 96 Robert McFarlane. Susan Griggs Agency; 97 Homer Sykes. BBC; 98 Leonard Freed. John Hillelson Agency; 99 René Burri. John Hillelson Agency; 100 Radio Times Hulton Picture Library.

Rites of Passage

119 Geoff Howard; 120 Peter Montagnon. BBC; 121 Bury Peerless; 122 Phillippa Berlyn. Camera Press; 123 Geoff Howard; 124 Henri Cartier-Bresson. John Hillelson Agency; 125 Geoff Howard; 126 Geoff Howard.

The Face of Heaven

141 Peter Montagnon. BBC; 142 Toni Schneiders. Bruce Coleman Ltd; 143 Adam Woolfitt. Susan Griggs Agency; 144 Bury Peerless; 145 Constance Cathedral, Germany. Toni Schneiders. Bruce Coleman Ltd; 146 William Macquitty.

Scriptures

161 British Museum; 162 Victoria and Albert Museum; 163 Bury Peerless; 164 British Museum; 165 India Office Library; 166 Paul Popper; 167 Cornell Capa. John Hillelson Agency; 168 British Museum.

Symbols

197 Werner Forman Archive; 198 Vauthey. Almasy Archives; 199 Burrell Collection, Glasgow; 200 Bury Peerless; 201 Erich Lessing. John Hillelson Agency; 202 National Gallery, Prague. Werner Forman Archive; 203 British Museum. BBC; 204 William Rockhill Nelson Gallery, Kansas City.

Stories

237 Scala; 238 British Museum. BBC; 239 British Museum. BBC; 240 British Museum. BBC; 241 Mansell Collection; 242 Prado Museum, Madrid. Bruce Coleman Ltd; 243 Bury Peerless; 244 British Museum. BBC. 245 Victoria and Albert Museum.

Prophets and Teachers

279 Radio Times Hulton Picture Library; 280 Ramakrishna Mission, London; 281 Erich Lessing. John Hillelson Agency; 282 Radio Times Hulton Picture Library.